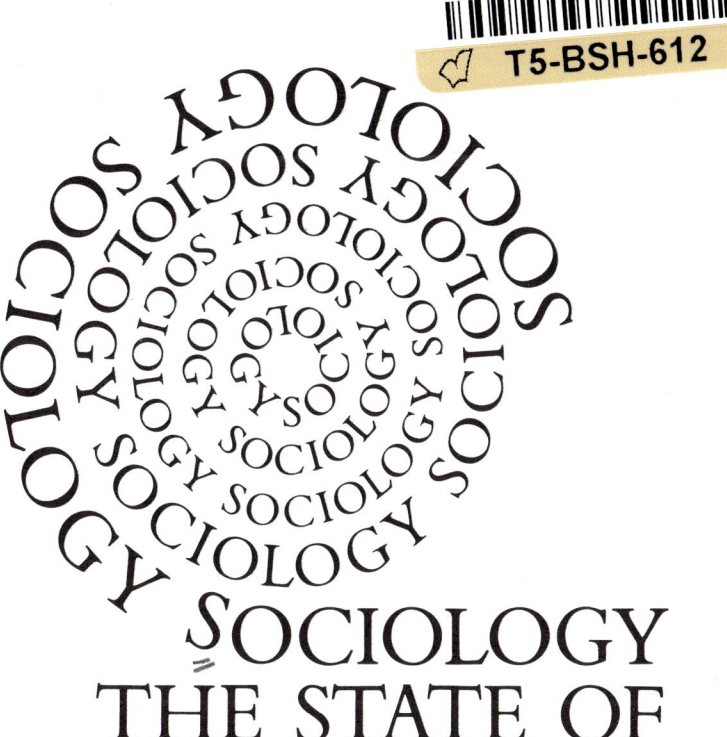

SOCIOLOGY
THE STATE OF
THE ART

EDITED BY

Tom Bottomore

Stefan Nowak

Magdalena Sokolowska

Sponsored by the International Sociological Association/ISA

 SAGE Publications · London and Beverly Hills

Copyright © 1982 by
International Sociological Association/ISA

All rights reserved.
No part of this book may be reproduced
or utilized in any form, or by any means
electronic or mechanical, including
photocopying, recording, or by any
information storage and retrieval system
without the permission in writing
from the publisher.

For information address
SAGE Publications Ltd
28 Banner Street, London EC1Y 8QE

SAGE Publications Inc
275 South Beverly Drive
Beverly Hills, California 90212

British Library Cataloguing in Publication Data

Sociology.
   1. Sociology—Congresses
   I. Bottomore, Tom
   II. Sokolowska, Magdalena
   III. Nowak, Stefan
   301   HM13   81-52748
ISBN 0-8039-9790-6
ISBN 0-8039-9791-4 pbk

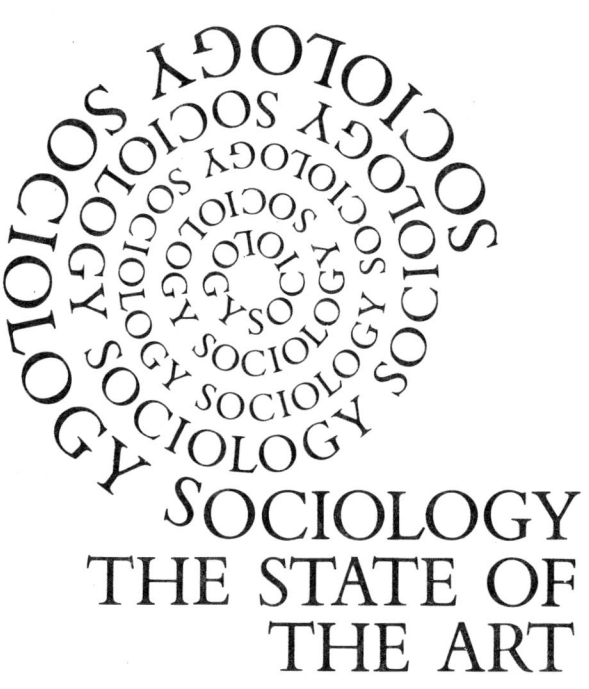

SOCIOLOGY
THE STATE OF THE ART

Contents

Preface Magdalena Sokolowska

Introduction Stefan Nowak 1
  Tom Bottomore 27

1 Innovative Processes in Social Change:
  Theory, Method and Social Practice
  Ulf Himmelstrand 37

2 Contemporary Alienation Theory and Research
  David Schweitzer 67

3 The Sociology of Religion:
  A Critical Survey
  Richard K. Fenn 101

4 The Sociology of Military Institutions Today
  Gwyn Harries-Jenkins 129

5 Recent Trends in Theory and Methodology
  in the Study of Economy and Society
  Harry Makler, Arnaud Sales and Neil J. Smelser 147

6 Convergences in the Sociology of Race Relations
  and Minority Groups
  John Rex 173

7 International and Internal Migration:
  Towards a New Paradigm
  Daniel Kubat and Hans-Joachim Hoffmann-Nowotny 201

8 The Sociology of Educational Systems
  Margaret S. Archer 233

9 Trends in the Development of
  the Sociology of Work:
  In Search of Identity
  Jolanta Kulpinska and Marc Maurice 263

10	Economic Crisis and Urban Austerity: Issues of Research and Policy in the 1980s *John Walton*	277
11	Current Problems and Perspectives in the Sociology of Leisure *Anna Olszewska and Gilles Pronovost*	299
12	From Medical Sociology to the Sociology of Health: Some Changing Concerns in the Sociological Study of Sickness and Treatment *Andrew C. Twaddle*	323
13	The History of Sociology and Substantive Sociological Theories *Jerzy Szacki*	359
Notes on Contributors		375

Preface

Magdalena Sokolowska
Polish Academy of Sciences
Chairperson, ISA Research Council

During the first twenty years of its existence the International Sociological Association (ISA) was a federation of national sociological associations and other institutional members. In 1970, under the presidency of Jan Szczepanski, the ISA statutes were amended to make individual membership available to interested colleagues. At the same time the position of the various research committees was consolidated and a Research Council created. Each committee sends a delegate to the Council, which then elects an executive body, the Research Coordinating Committee. A new structure was thus established, complementary to the supreme governing body of the ISA, the Council, which is composed of national delegates and takes care of the overall policies of the ISA.

The research committees constitute one core of the ISA, and their activities between congresses can be equated with its statutory role and function. Beginning in the early 1950s, the various research committees were among the first organizations to develop comparative research, and they remain a stimulus to the advancement of sociology in various parts of the world. The need for their spokesman within the ISA (the Research Council) is becoming increasingly evident as they grow and diversify. However, the Council is still only in its third term and its methods and forms of work are not as yet well established. Experience shows that the majority of the research committees would welcome continuous mutual contact via the Research Coordinating Committee and the chairman of the Research Council. What is needed is exchange of information about ongoing activities within particular research committees and also a 'feeling of unity' within individual reference groups. However, this makes sense only if centred around a topical matter that can interest and unite the individual research committees in pursuit of well defined common goals.

This is the general background of the project initiated by the present Research Council and resulting in this book. The idea was to launch a series edited by successive chairpersons of the Research Council (producing one book every four years) so that the Research Council can come to the ISA congress with a book ready for sale there. Each book should reflect the efforts of the Research Council throughout the previous four years. Thus the present book will be ready for the tenth ISA congress in Mexico City, having been produced under the general editorial direction of the chairperson of the Research Council. Several ideas and proposals were considered and it was only after lengthy discussions that the project resulting in this book was initiated. Tom Bottomore, Stefan Nowak and Alex Inkeles agreed to act as editors; Alex had later to withdraw for reasons of health but remained an interested supporter of the whole undertaking.

Each research committee was asked to submit one or more papers covering the main theoretical and methodological developments in their given area. Alternatively, they could adopt a narrower approach covering developments in several countries, groups of countries or continents. The field of interest was broadly defined to enable contributors to select those approaches to theory and/or methodology most deserving of analysis and discussion. Their choice should be governed by two alternative criteria: either to concentrate on those theories and/or methodologies most often used in their given subarea of sociology and thereby having the widest application in the given field, or to concentrate on the most controversial theories and/or methodologies. These general guidelines were produced at the request of a number of research committees but contributors remained free to cover anything perceived as relevant within the framework of the project as defined by its title.

The initial enthusiasm with which the project was greeted by the various research committees has been confirmed by the numbers of papers actually produced: only five out of the 36 committees chose not to participate. The papers were prepared in time for the Research Council meeting in Jablonna, Poland, 26-29 August 1980. One should add that the meeting was unique considering its time and place and if only for this reason will probably be long remembered by the 55 participants. Twenty-one of the 29 papers received were presented by their authors in Jablonna, preceded by Stefan Nowak's paper and a short introductory statement by Tom Bottomore. Each paper was followed by questions and discussion and it was these which dominated the meeting.

Returning to the main aim of our undertaking, this was to start a tradition of closely defined activity by the Research Council, and to that end a variety of topics were put forward in Jablonna as a possible theme for the next joint project. These ranged from comprehensive analysis of the foundation of the various research committees (or of them all)[1] to such problems as 'the aged', 'juvenile delinquency' and 'the divorcee', each to be approached by a particular research committee.

In conclusion, I would like to express my thanks to all my colleagues for their participation in the project: I very much enjoyed our collaboration and have gained much therefrom.

NOTE

1. Very little is known of the history of the various research committees, the social characteristics of their members, their geographical distribution and areas of influence, the details of the way they function, their interests, difficulties and other elements of the sociological analysis of any institution.

Introduction

Stefan Nowak
University of Warsaw

One way of writing this introduction would be to summarize the reports of the research committees of the International Sociological Association (ISA) and formulate in a strictly inductive manner certain generalizations about contemporary sociological theory, or at least about that part of it which is being developed under the auspices of the ISA. But it seems more reasonable to treat these reports rather as a nonrepresentative sample of various patterns of theorizing in diverse subareas of contemporary sociology. Such a sample cannot be used — as we know — for warranted generalizations, but if it is sufficiently diversified it can serve as a basis for a typology of situations which do occur in the given area. This paper will therefore try to pose and discuss certain problems related to the construction and use of theories in various subdisciplines of sociological inquiry. I will try to discuss these problems in close relation with our papers, taking freely from them both typical examples of theorizing and more general methodological formulations, but at the same time I will go beyond the problem area covered by our reports if it is necessary for the problem discussed.

The research committees were supposed to deliver a trend report on theory and methodology in their fields, but most of the papers concentrate either on theory or on semitheoretical problems like the definition of the field of study, changes in conceptualization, etc. and very seldom deal with technical aspects of research methodology. For these reasons I will limit my discussion to the problems of theory; its meaning, its types and their uses in particular subareas of sociological studies.

The meaning — or better — the meanings of the term 'theory' to be found either explicitly or implicitly in the papers cover most of the uses of this term in contemporary sociology, and cluster around two basic senses of the term. According to the first, theory is a set — or if possible an internally consistent system — of general propositions describing the relationships between variables, which denote phenomena dealt with by it. These propositions describe what event will occur under conditions specified by the laws of theory or which value the dependent variable will have under given values of independent variables; consequently, they are useful both for prediction and as a guide in practical social action.

According to the second meaning (or better, the second use) 'theory' is understood as a specific 'approach' to the social reality. Taken literally, an approach constitutes a set or system of questions with which a scientist 'approaches' the phenomena of his interest; but here we might say that an approach is rather a given way of asking questions about society, a more or less consistent pattern of asking these questions. If this were the case one could hardly understand how 'approaches' can be mixed up with 'theories' which, whatever their nature, constitute rather the answer to some questions than the questions themselves. But many such approaches are rooted in certain notions about society or various social phenomena, which seem to say, or at least postulate, something about this reality; others are closely related to some 'visions' or images of phenomena so that it is almost impossible to ask the kind of questions constituting the given approach without being aware of the image or the notion of the phenomena in which these questions are rooted. These visions or notions belong to approaches in the broader sense of the term.

Moreover, these images, visions or more or less clear notions of the studied phenomena seem to play a similar role to the role of theories: they make the studied reality somehow 'understandable', even when this kind of understanding does not lead either to the prediction of future events or to efficient manipulation or control of them. Particular elements or aspects of the given 'image' of reality are usually additionally loaded with the scientist's value assumptions about it. Such broader approaches usually include conceptualizations of the field of study, and imply more specific research problems and research strategies, but they do not necessarily have to include strictly propositional generalizations about the relationships between the phenomena which are denoted by the concepts of the approach. If they do not, they cannot be used for prediction.

We find in the papers of this volume many examples of theories (either presented or mentioned) of a strictly propositional kind. Ulf Himmelstrand mentions several such theories for the study of innovation, to mention only one example.

We also find in our papers many examples of theoretical thinking which takes the form of an approach or presentation of changes in the given field which constitute a change of the approaches used, changes of conceptualizations or sometimes even a change of research problems and shifts from one research strategy to another. Since such approaches are focussed more upon the nature of the research problem, upon proper understanding, conceptualization, not to say visualization of the field of study, than upon the formulation of propositional generalizations as hypotheses for empirical testing, and since they almost always start with clear value assumptions about what and why one should study or not study, the conflict between various approaches usually takes the form of conflict about proper conceptualization and strategy of research. Disputes about 'proper' conceptualization seem to be the most frequent form of expression of a value conflict in contemporary sociology, when more or less gradual change in the general normative climate of the scientific community, which leads to gradual change of research interests in it, is often expressed in the change of some basic concepts, defining the area of the study. Let me give a few examples. Ulf Himmelstrand presents the change of interests in the area known primarily as modernization studies. The initial approach started with the assumption that 'the diffusion of innovation in the form of Western ideas, forms of organization and technology was supposed to bring about social change in less developed areas, to make them modern, that is more Westernized'.[1]

The opponents of this approach

> ...did not on the whole question the scientific validity of empirical findings assembled with this approach. Nor did they doubt the actual existence of 'innovations' or their actual 'diffusion'...What was questioned by the opponents of DIA were the meanings of concepts such as 'modernizing social change' and 'resistance to change'. I think that it is fair to say that the term modernization while being an honorific term for DIA-proponents at the time of Varna Congress, was a politically distasteful term for DIA-opponents.[2]

Himmelstrand then presents the reasons for the conflict between these two approaches to modernization, demonstrating that the same process of diffusion of Western technology to developing countries when viewed from two different social perspectives, i.e. from the point of view of developed and developing countries, looks quite different. The two conflicting approaches are rooted in conflicting value assumptions.

A similar theoretical and at the same ideological controversy expressed in the form of a fight for the 'proper concepts' of sociological analysis is described in the paper by John Rex. In applying some assumptions of a Marxist approach to the study of African workers in South Africa, he stresses that:

> ...the African workers in South Africa could only be understood as a political community organized around the class of migrant workers and that what one had in South Africa was a class struggle.
> In interpreting the position of the Bantu people in South Africa as a class position, however, I found myself in conflict with South African Marxists of the time. Their problem was to explain the role of the South African White working class in relation to the Bantu workers. Whereas I was prepared to say that migrant workers migrating to work for nine months of the year unaccompanied by their families, living in compounds, without the protection of the trade unions, had a different relationship to the means of production than White workers and therefore were a distinct class, the orthodox Marxist view of the time was that the differences between Black and White workers were status differences only.[3]

Here again the conflict between two explanatory perspectives was expressed as a conflict about the 'proper' meaning of a certain concept, that of 'social class'. What was nevertheless different in this controversy as compared with the case of 'diffusion of innovation' presented by Himmelstrand, was the fact that the two sides in this conflict were people who applied the same general theoretical — Marxist — approach to the same case.

In other cases the changing concepts reveal the change of focus of attention of the given area of sociological study, even when the ideological differences are much less dramatic than in the cases quoted above. Andrew Twaddle's paper shows this in its title: 'From Medical Sociology to the Sociology of Health'. What all these, and many other examples not quoted here, have in common is that the differences in conceptualization are the most visible expressions of different theoretical interests, i.e. in the nature of the questions one would like to ask when looking at a certain society from this perspective, and of some value differences underlying these theoretical or social interests.

Most of what was presented in the papers for our conference may be classified as being some kind of approach rather than a theory in the propositional sense. This probably represents the state of theory in contemporary sociology in general. To quote Jonathan Turner:

Much of what is labelled sociological theory is only a loose cluster of implicit assumptions, inadequately defined concepts, and a few vague and logically disconnected propositions. Sometimes assumptions are stated explicitly and serve to inspire abstract theoretical statements originated into a logically coherent format. Thus a great deal of so-called theory is really a general 'perspective' or 'orientation' for looking at various features of the social world, which if all goes well, can be eventually translated into true scientific theory.[4]

If we agree with Turner (as I am inclined to do) that this state is far from satisfactory, the question arises what can be done about it? In other words, to what degree and in what way can approaches be transformed or developed into propositional theories? This is for me a crucial problem for the development of future sociological theories. The main aim of this paper will therefore be to analyze the nature of these approaches, the relationships between theories and approaches and to draw certain conclusions for the theoretical thinking in various subdisciplines of sociology.

Before doing that, let me mention some problems connected with the idea of propositional theory, as characterized above. Some sociologists are rather doubtful whether we will ever be able to formulate in sociology universal laws of science stating certain general relationships of constant character between phenomena or variables under specific conditions. There is no doubt that we find many generalizations describing the regularities of social phenomena both in our research reports and in sociological works having the term 'theory' on their cover. When these regularities have been formulated, they constitute generalizations of social science and, if we can do that, they can eventually be systematized into propositional theories which can be used for the prediction or explanation of the phenomena which are denoted by the concepts of these theories. For any level of social reality — from individual human beings through small groups, larger social systems or national societies — we find a number of statements that are definitely propositional generalizations and have by no means poor empirical evidence supporting their validity.

But then the question arises, how general they are? Can it be relied on that they describe 'universal constants' as the laws of physics do? First, let me say that even some physicists suspect that the constants they have established may be valid only for certain areas of space and of the history of the universe, and so admit that they also may deal in their theories only with 'historical generalizations'. Nevertheless, the range of validity of the laws of physics is too broad to constitute a proper methodological reference and comparison for social sciences. Biology might constitute a better example for us. Biologists know that certain regularities of the functioning of mechanisms are valid for extremely large areas of the history of life, i.e. biological evolution, while others are much more limited in their scope. We have much more in common (in terms of biological mechanisms) with other people than with other primates, but more with the totality of primates than with all vertebrates, etc. It is not unlikely that all university professors have a greater number of regularities of social behaviour in common with each other than they have in common with the rest of contemporary mankind, and these are again probably less numerous than those they might have in common with their cousins from Neanderthal, etc. The question of how general our generalizations are is an open empirical question and the only sensible way to approach it is by cross-cultural and cross-historical comparative studies and verifications. They can either prove that our generalizations are at least as broad as the extent of our comparisons, or demonstrate that their validity should be limited and specified within certain historical or cultural limits.[5] Once we discover the historical limits of validity of our theories we should state clearly where they can be applied and where they cannot.

But whatever their tested or hypothesized validity, for this area where they are valid they can be used for the purposes of explanation and prediction as in all sciences. And these generalizations can of course be connected into internally consistent theories which are usually more powerful for that purpose than singular laws.

Now let us return to the so-called 'approaches'. What is the nature of an approach and its functions for theory? More specifically, what are the nature and functions of the visions or images of social reality belonging to various approaches? For a traditional, fact-oriented 'positivist' they were nothing but speculative, nebulous, marginal areas of real science, and science had no use for them. Real science consists first of hypotheses formulated by the scientists, and then tested theories, i.e. logically consistent systems of verified hypotheses. When a traditional positivist applied his criteria of testability to such 'nebulous' visions of social and psychological reality as are involved in Marxism or psychoanalysis, he could formulate only one conclusion; being untestable in their large areas and additionally loaded with value assumptions they have little in common with scientific thinking. They constitute spurious knowledge, belonging rather to the areas of *Weltanschauung* or ideology than to science. The best thing a real science can do is therefore to get rid of them and to start formulating real — i.e. testable, falsifiable — theories, free of evaluations and therefore unrelated to anything but empirical facts.

But are things so simple? And can we really get rid of these visions or other less nebulous notions of the phenomena being studied? Every scientific study begins with certain questions, whether it aims to analyze and interpret one particular case, to formulate certain generalizations, or to test theoretical hypotheses. Every question requires for its validity certain assumptions, both empirical and normative. Let us first look more closely at these empirical assumptions of scientific questions.

Starting with a most banal example: if I want to study the attitudes of a Turkish minority towards the majority in a country, I have to assume, first, that a Turkish minority exists in that country. This assumption is valid in the Federal Republic of Germany, or in Sweden, but not e.g. in Poland. If I want to study class conflict in a society, I have to assume, first, that in this society the classes (as defined by my concept of class in my own problem formulation) do exist and at least that there may exist a conflict between them, etc. This is true for any question, however banal and simple.

These assumptions play a double role in the formulation of the research problem. Psychologically, they play, or at least may play, a heuristic role in suggesting the questions and hypotheses to study. But even when they do not play this strictly heuristic role, i.e. when we formulate our questions without taking their assumptions consciously into account, the assumptions implicitly exist behind any question as the necessary premises that make this question logically valid. Anyone who decides to study something from the point of view of a set of questions implicitly postulates the empirical validity of all assumptions that make his questions logically valid.

Whether his research will be a success depends additionally on the real empirical validity of these assumptions, at least for the case or cases studied. Confirmation of the validity of such assumptions does not necessarily mean the confirmation of the hypotheses formulated on the basis of such assumptions as we would like to test in our study; the rejection of the hypotheses is also a valid scientific answer. For the situations in which my assumptions were not valid I cannot receive any answer other than stating that for this particular case my question is meaningless. Whether we want to test the validity of the 'circular model of a city' — formulated at one time by the Chicago school — in a Polish village, or to evaluate the role of mass media in medieval Europe, the only answer to such questions would be that they are not valid because the cases proposed do not satisfy the empirical assumptions of the question asked. Such answers are then abolishing, falsifying the assumptions of the research problem itself. I cannot say that the attitudes of the Turkish minority in Poland towards anything are either positive or negative. All I can say is that I did not find any Turkish minority in my country, and hence my attempt to study their attitudes was a wrongly formulated problem.

It is the same with hypotheses about relationships between variables. Suppose I want to test a hypothesis stating that X is the cause of Y. My research answer may be that this is either true or false; and both are sensible answers. But if after long research I discover that the phenomena denoted by the variable X or Y do not exist at all, or that they do not occur in my sample, this means that my research problem — testing the causal nature of the relationship between X and Y — was based upon empirically wrong assumptions.

We do not usually make such silly mistakes as exemplified above because we know enough about Polish villages or medieval Europe. To put it more generally: the existing body of factual knowledge and tested generalizations plays its main role in the further development of science by delivering valid factual and theoretical assumptions for the new and valid questions. By the existing body of knowledge I mean not only what 'everyone knows'. On the basis of commonsense assumptions we may ask questions about attitudes of White people towards those whose skin is Black, but not about their attitude towards those who have three legs.

I gave above very simple examples of very simple questions. But in most cases we have to know quite a lot in advance to ask valid new questions: think only how much knowledge about contemporary industrial organizations was needed to ask whether the vertical organizational structure of factories is more efficient than the more horizontal one. The same can be seen in less scientific social situations: foreigners often ask the 'natives' questions about their political system which are perceived as silly or naive, not because the foreigners are stupid but because they do not possess enough knowledge for the formulation of valid questions.

The existing body of common sense and scientific knowledge is a sufficient source of assumptions for the new questions, but only in those situations which Thomas Kuhn calls 'normal science',[6] i.e. science which at the given stage of development constitutes a direct continuation and cumulation of knowledge within an existing 'paradigm'. The development of normal science is a safe thing because its questions are founded upon well tested assumptions. But suppose that someone would like to ask basically new questions — questions so new that the idea of (and therefore the concepts denoting) the new phenomena did not exist before? Or the idea that certain variables, e.g. economic interests and religious beliefs, might be interrelated, which never occurred to anybody before? Even for such basically new questions the existing knowledge may sometimes be a sufficient source of assumptions. But in other cases, to formulate such new questions one has to go beyond the existing, accumulated knowledge, to postulate the existence of something, the existence of which can be believed but cannot be proven, at least at the beginning of the new field of studies. In some less dramatic situations we have at least to look at the known things from a completely new perspective, i.e. to see in them aspects, features and phenomena which were not seen previously, to name and to define them as new properties, and with these new concepts to formulate our new questions on the basis of assumptions rooted in the basically new perspective of the otherwise known objects and phenomena.

In principle one could try to formulate these assumptions, hypothetical as they are, with the rule of maximum parsimony, i.e. postulating only what is absolutely necessary for the new questions; e.g. postulating the existence of some new entities, assuming the possibility that they might be interrelated in the given way, that they might change or that they might be stable and nothing more. If our research produces sensible answers to the corresponding questions it would then mean additionally that our research, indirectly and partially, confirms (or at least does not falsify) the empirical validity of the assumptions on which these questions were based.

But as we know, the idea of parsimony is not the most typical principle of the way the human mind likes to work at this theoretical, and at the same time most creative, stage of scientific thinking. Nor does it like to limit itself to strictly verbal formulations of such assumptions or to mere strictly logical procedures in their formulation. When thinking about the possibility of the existence of basically new phenomena or relationships, we often use our imagination and our tendency to visualize the things to a much greater extent than our logical, verbal thinking. A neurophysiologist might say that the creative but pre-theoretical stage of a basically new scientific study needs much more of the right (imaginative and spatial) hemisphere of the brain than of the left, which is believed to be responsible for logic and verbalization. That is why new theories and areas of study are so often rooted in 'images' and 'visions' of the studied phenomena and why we have so much of spatial metaphors in these visions: these metaphors usually pass into our theoretical language: groups have 'higher' or 'lower' positions in the social structure even when we know that it does not mean that they differ in spatial location; systems are 'seen' as structures composed of boxes with arrows between them, even when their elements are abstract properties of these systems and the interrelations between them are in no way similar to wires in a television set, etc.

Even when vaguely formulated, and when they are more similar to pictures than to propositional hypotheses, these visions often stimulate some kind of strictly scientific activity, both by suggesting new conceptual apparatus (the visualized elements may then be named and defined and these concepts can be used for the formulation of research questions and more or less general hypotheses for further testing), and also by suggesting the questions and hypotheses themselves. They may determine our 'approach' to the reality studied, here understood narrowly as a set of research questions, and consequently these visions or vague notions may eventually lead to propositional theories. Such theories may be formulated by the author of the approach himself and we then have a mixed propositional and vision-like structure in which some of its parts are accessible to direct or indirect empirical testing while others are not. In other cases certain propositional generalizations may be formulated as a result of empirical research organized by the concepts of the approach as the strategic concepts of inquiry. We may then say that the visions of the reality involved in the given approach eventually became theoretically fruitful. Some of them may stimulate many such propositional theories.

Once formulated and tested these theories seem to be parts of a complex and logically more or less consistent theoretical structure organized around the approach, which seems to be their integrative factor and to integrate them with the images or vague notions underlying the given approach. But this integration may be more or less spurious. To give a most simple example: the functional approach stimulated many 'functional theories' of particular phenomena: from social stratification through religion to ideology, to mention only a few, and behind these theories we find an organic or homeostatic vision of society, and the concepts formulated on its basis to study the 'functional' aspects of social systems. But being stimulated by the same vision and being formulated, partly at least, with the use of the same 'functionalist' concepts, did not necessarily make these partial functional theories parts of one internally consistent theoretical structure called the general functional theory. It only proves that many postulates, assumptions, or even organic images, characteristic of this approach seem to be theoretically fruitful; there must therefore be some truth in them. But to what degree, for which phenomena, or under what conditions these assumptions or images are true, the organic or homeostatic visions do not say; they therefore do not constitute a general fundamental theory. To construct such a general functional theory from which we could deduce particular functional theories of various phenomena would require a special effort, and to my knowledge such a theory has not been constructed yet.

It may also happen that an approach stimulates research but does not lead to a propositional theory. The main function of the approach, from the point of view of the development of theoretical science as understood in this paper, is then to deliver the concepts to descriptive and diagnostic studies. Since these concepts are taken from a more comprehensive structure, i.e. from the approach, we may have the feeling that such descriptions have an explanatory character, that we better understand the phenomena studied. But this is a special kind of understanding. If we identify our phenomena as being referents of more general concepts taken from an approach, we can see in them all this, to which the approach intends to turn our attention. We see some of their aspects we would not otherwise see, we turn our attention to their contextual involvement if that is what has been 'prescribed' by the approach. To give a most simple example: suppose someone wants to identify the obligations in a given culture of the father towards his family, and before he collects his data we teach him 'the role approach'. He will then probably say 'aha, I see it now' and he will really see much more than he would otherwise do. But he will not be able to predict very much because there are not many propositions in so-called 'role theory'.

Finally, an approach may neither stimulate propositional theories nor guide conceptually empirical studies but it may nevertheless claim to explain the world. We then come to the borderline of religions which also claim to explain the world, without trying to demonstrate the descriptive or predictive value of their explanations.

Let us return to these images of social phenomena (usually loaded with evaluation) which are involved in many particular approaches. These visions usually include the component parts of the visualized 'wholes'. These composing elements are either denoted by the concepts of the particular approach, if it has been properly conceptualized, or at least by some theoretical terms, the meaning of which is more or less vague. These concepts constitute the verbalizations of the structuralization of these aspects of social reality, which are in the focus of interest of the particular approach; they constitute a classificatory network or frame of reference, in which the phenomena studied are located and from which they receive their more or less theoretical meanings as prescribed by the given approach.

Both the 'visions' and their eventual verbalizations may also include, explicitly or implicitly, some relationships between the phenomena thus denoted. These seem to be the proposition-like elements of the approaches, but they can seldom be classified as general propositions; even if they sound general it is because their generality has been overstated. In reality they are usually what is called 'eliptical propositions', which require for their testability additional qualifiers stating to what degree, where and under what conditions they are true. The proper form for the propositions involved in such approaches should usually be 'X is sometimes related to Y', or 'X may be related to Y', etc. Thus, e.g. the psychoanalytic theory of personality includes many examples of such eliptical pseudo-laws, which in fact are only existential propositions stating that certain relations are possible. The same is true for many other approaches; classes sometimes and somehow determine the views of people who belong to them, but when, how strongly and in what particular way, is up to our research to establish. Roles control people's behaviour, but to what degree, and who will be completely obedient to his role obligations and who will try to modify or change them, may again be a strictly empirical problem, etc.

But these existential propositions assuming the existence, or even possibility of existence of certain phenomena and possible relations may play the role of assumptions which permit us to formulate the research questions, which determine the study of phenomena from that particular angle, and the hypotheses which are then empirically testable (to the degree that we can test any general proposition at all), as was discussed above.

If the 'images' of the phenomena studied that are involved in the given approach are detailed enough it may happen that from a strictly logical point of view only certain elements of these 'images' are necessary to the assumptions of the new questions leading eventually to research on hypotheses, while others may not be necessary for that purpose. But being unnecessary for direct stimulation of science itself they may be necessary for the other elements which are direct assumptions of our question or at least they may be psychologically necessary as elements of a new *Gestalt* which lets us see the old things in a basically new way. Such complex content-rich images postulated by many approaches are therefore important both heuristically (psychologically) and logically for the formulation of new questions and hypotheses of sciences. But it must be clearly understood that large areas of them do not necessarily belong to the body of verified human knowledge. If so, then what is their nature?

I think that they simply belong to philosophy. For at least 25 centuries in the European intellectual tradition (and probably longer in some other areas of our world) philosophy played the role of a reconnaissance of science, trying to say something about the nature, origin, functioning and development of our world, or of such of its components as were important enough to attract the attention of philosophers even when science had little to say about them. Being usually rather speculative, imprecise, sometimes nebulous, etc. effects of human curiosity and imagination, the products of philosophical thinking not only gave mankind some knowledge (true or not true) about the world, thus satisfying human curiosity, people's need to know; but they also played an essential role in stimulating scientific research and theories. Some of the philosophers' guesses about the world then became verified scientific theories, while others became obviously false. The history of science over the last 25 centuries gives enough evidence for such a process; almost all scientific disciplines evolved from philosophical speculation (I say almost because some of them evolved from practical skills) showing that the philosophical assumptions from which they started were in principle at least partly right, while disproving the validity of many other assumptions.

The same is also true for the area of social philosophy and the social science evolving from it. In the past philosophies determined — at least partly — the scientist's approach to the study of social phenomena, and delivered the assumptions for the questions to which answers were sought in empirical studies. We know that the history of sociology as it is taught in our universities goes back to Plato and Aristotle. Jerzy Szacki proposes in his paper[7] to distinguish two patterns of analysis of social thought, especially in the history of sociology: one way consists in testing various products of past or contemporary social thought as more or less loose collections of propositions which may be classified, according to our contemporary knowledge, as either true or false. If we find them to be true we include them in contemporary science, if they are false they are not interesting. In this approach we apply only theoretical criteria of evaluation of these propositions. In another approach we treat them as elements of more or less consistent philosophical systems, ideologies, images of the world, or *Weltanschauungen*, which have their intellectual and social source, their structure and their intellectual and social functions, and should therefore be studied taking into account their origin, structure, their internal dynamism, and functions. I agree with these two perspectives completely, but I would like to add a third one: analysis of social thought of past and present with respect to the social research and theory it stimulates or did stimulate, and with main emphasis upon those elements of particular social philosophies, ideologies, images, or approaches which stimulated essential research questions, constituted their assumptions, and led to empirically verified propositional theories. This is, I think, another perspective than the two distinguished by Szacki, both historical and theoretical, at the same time, because it tries to discover the intellectual sources of the historical process of development of modern social research and theory. An element of a certain approach in social philosophy does not have to satisfy our contemporary theoretical criteria to be treated as an important stimulant of the process of shaping modern social sciences, or as a source of assumptions for the questions to which modern science delivers the answers.

To say that the images of social reality postulated by various approaches, or at least some more speculative elements of these images, belong to the area of philosophy, is not enough. The tradition of philosophical thought usually distinguished several branches of philosophy, namely gnoseology, ontology and axiology. I think that the approaches we discuss here include in a more or less disguised form all these three elements of a philosophical system or orientation. First, they often say something about the nature of the process of cognition of the social world, and therefore include strictly gnoseological assumptions, usually leading the given approach to its specific methodology (which I shall not discuss here). Second, the images of the phenomena which also include or imply the concepts of this approach, and guide (at least conceptually) the formulation of research problems and the formulation of more or less general hypotheses, often belong to the area which might be called the ontology of the social world. Finally, these approaches either explicitly or implicitly involve certain normative, axiological assumptions which give to the various elements or aspects of the postulated 'visions' their positive or negative values.

Let us first say a few words about these axiologies. It is well known that the formulation of any research problem in any science involves certain value assumptions, which make the knowledge expected in the result of the study either a value for itself, or important because of its expected consequences in the area of practical application. On the other hand it is well known that certain elements of the social reality as described or visualized in its given image may be loaded with some positive or negative evaluation, or at least according to the 'theory' underlying the given approach they may lead to positive or negative consequences. These evaluations then play an essential role in the final shaping of the research questions or of research hypotheses born from this approach.

These value assumptions are sometimes so closely connected with certain more descriptive (ontological) elements of the approach that it is hardly thinkable to separate them. The Marxist approach seems to include both certain assumptions about social structure and certain (negative) evaluations of social inequality. It is logically thinkable to separate them but psychologically it is difficult to imagine a scientist who would use the Marxist model of social structure to recommend increasing the amount of inequality or to stop the coming social revolution, i.e. for values opposite to those of Karl Marx himself. And even if we can imagine such a scientist we would probably not call him a Marxist because certain value assumption seems to belong unavoidably to the Marxist approach.

If we deal with an approach which in its original formulation is loaded with specific evaluations, then problems may be explicitly stated. It may then happen that just these normative elements of the approach decide that people who accept these values have the inclination to apply the given approach with its concepts, assumptions, etc., while those who do not accept them look for another approach to the same phenomena and processes.

Let us now return to those images of social phenomena characteristic for particular approaches which were characterized as either theoretical-scientific or ontological elements of these approaches. When one hears the term 'ontology' one thinks about a set of concepts which are in a way all-inclusive, which embrace the totality of social reality and have extremely broad areas of applicability. But if we think that these ontological models are just supplements to our necessarily partial knowledge, that they are added by our insight and imagination to what we know about various aspects or fragments of reality, or that they stimulate these fragmentary pictures of scientific knowledge, we understand that these ontological models are not all-inclusive. They are just a partial picture of social reality seen from one particular perspective. Robert Merton, faced by the 'grand theories' of his time, each of which was claiming its all-inclusiveness and by the same right its monopoly, invented the notion of 'middle range theory' which did not claim to explain everything, but only those phenomena which are explicitly or implicitly covered by its concepts and propositions. He should have said additionally that all theories are from this point of view 'middle range theories', because none of them — however general — is able to explain more than is covered by its conceptual propositions. Each of them therefore leaves enough space for other complementary theories which deal with different phenomena, answer different questions and therefore have to be formulated with the use of other concepts denoting these phenomena. In no natural science do we find any single theory which would be able to explain 'everything', and there is no reason to believe that sociology is different in that respect. This is obvious for any propositional theory, as we have seen above. We find in the background of many of these theories certain ontological models of reality. We also know that such ontologies may exist even when they do not produce propositional theories of their own. Can we say that these ontologies are all-inclusive? I don't think so.

Some of these approaches to the social world are well aware of their partial character. They are then usually called 'models'. Let us think about an author who presents a 'model' as a starting point for his empirical research. He may start with certain commonsense assumptions about the existence of certain objects or about certain characteristics of such objects, or he may also include some assumptions based upon previous research. He then usually makes some conceptual restructuring of the phenomena studied by defining some new concepts, enumerates variables which seem to be relevant for the study of his problem area, and denotes them by certain 'boxes'. He then draws arrows between the boxes denoting these variables, which constitute possible hypothetical connections between them, and leaves to further research the answer to questions about the values of particular variables and how strongly they may be interrelated in each particular case. His approach, his 'model', thus defines his research strategy. Our scientist would not be unhappy if the research revealed certain generalizable, constant relationships between the variables, because it would give a nice propositional theory. But one thing is sure; he does not claim than his model constitutes a universal approach which could explain everything from the class struggle to the formation of unconscious defence mechanisms. The partiality of every such model is obvious. This is not always so with other, more philosophical approaches we find in sociological literature.

There is another thing which, besides the functions mentioned above, some contemporary sociological approaches have in common with traditional philosophies, or at least had until recently; namely, their claim to ultimate and universal validity, to total truth. At least this is the way some of the proponents of these approaches are inclined to see them. Psychoanalysis is the whole of psychology for a 'genuine, believing psychoanalyst', and for him Freud has said everything essential about the human mind. Even an attempt to supplement Freud constitutes the danger of revisionism. For someone who 'believes' in ethnomethodology, multivariate analysis of standardized questionnaire answers is a pseudo-science, and vice versa. On the other hand it is obvious that the Freudian ontology which postulates the existence and the given structure of personality and the functioning of unconscious motivation and processes in the human mind is as partial as the ontology which postulates the conscious purposive nature of human action and thinking. Ontological models visualizing societies as torn by internal conflicts are as partial as those which see primarily their integrative forces. If we could by analogy extend Merton's term, we could introduce the notion of 'middle range ontologies', i.e. partial, perspectivistic, mutually complementary philosophical models of social phenomena. I think that this is what science really needs. Fifty years of the tradition of methodological studies associated rightly with the neopositivistic school has firmly established the concept of philosophy of science. I now suggest that we introduce another notion; namely, that of 'philosophy for science', which would formulate alternative, complementary ontological models of the human mind or of social phenomena which would really guide our future theoretical studies.

Needless to say also that all propositional theories which may eventually be formulated with the use of concepts and problem formulations of particular approaches are also partial and complementary. Their validity is only as broad (provided that they are true) as the area of reality covered by the concepts with which they are formulated. Now suppose we are dealing with something which is called 'a theory of society' (or more often, 'the theory of society') and we additionally know that the propositions of this theory are empirically valid. Is then such theory not the most general one could think about? It seems so as long as we only read the title of such a theory. But when we look at the meanings of the concepts with the use of which it has been formulated, and at the content of its propositions, it turns out that it covers only some aspects of 'the society', specifying certain relationships between its parameters or its component parts, and leaving other parameters to other possible theories. If we are interested in a greater number of aspects or phenomena than is covered by the concepts and propositions of one theory we have to apply as many theories as is needed for our purpose. The same applies to the approaches, and the concepts or problem suggestions implied by them.

This may seem a rather banal and obvious conclusion. Nevertheless, many sociologists who deal with complex, multisided phenomena, and approach them with complex systems of research questions, when asked what kind of theory or approach they are working with, often say apologetically that they are 'eclectic'. Some of our papers clearly mention the 'eclectic' character of their subdisciplines. I think that the notion of 'eclecticism' simply does not make sense in science at all, because science, especially when it is dealing with real practical and therefore complex problems, must use as many theories as are needed for a particular problem. Processes governed by one single mechanism and therefore explainable by one single law or by one theory usually exist only in research laboratories, and they exist there only because we have made these processes or events monocausal, 'monotheoretical', etc., excluding other, alternative mechanisms or other causes of the phenomena, by experimental manipulation or by efficient randomization.

Real life is usually many-sided and it needs various approaches and various theories applied together. The more complex the object or process studied, the greater the number of its aspects in which we are interested, the more approaches must be used in our theoretical thinking or our research design. We have to accept the fact that as we now try to apply interdisciplinary studies in some areas of social reality, we will have to use inter-approach studies too. There is no need to be ashamed of it, and to excuse one's 'eclecticism'.

I think that we can distinguish two kinds of 'ontological models' of various aspects or various components of the reality studied. The first category is those whose images are strictly related to some substantive aspects of reality (e.g. social classes, human minds, roles, religions, etc.). Most of the examples given above and most of the approaches we find in the papers belong to this category of substantive ontological models, the concepts of which denote more or less clearly defined specific (even if very general) phenomena. But we can also find another kind of ontological model which is strictly formal, i.e. content-free. By the nature of their concepts such models do not denote any particular phenomena understood in substantive terms, because they denote any phenomena in any field of study, or even in any science, which satisfy their formal assumptions. They are formulated with the use only of logical, formal tools. Everyone knows the typology of elaborations of statistical relations as proposed by Lazarsfeld, but it constitutes only a strictly formal model of a multivariate causal process which could be valid anywhere when we are dealing with a cluster of variables denoting a loose population of individual elements and when these variables may be either additive or interactive, parallel or ordered in a causal chain, etc. These who oppose the application of this approach to their field of study are entitled to do so if they can prove that the assumptions of this ontological partial model of reality are not satisfied in their field. The model of reduction of one relationship or one theory to another may work in any field of study and in any science, but before we prove its applicability to a particular field it is nothing but a content-free, abstract ontological model of any thinkable reality which conforms to it. Some more abstract formulations of 'functionalism' (e.g. as they were formulated by Ernest Nagel) are again typical examples of a formal approach. Some analyses of the dynamic structure of certain processes belong to this category too.

Actually in contemporary science there are some specialized sciences which construct such general abstract models (which I call ontological models of possible phenomena). This is done especially by cybernetics and general system theory to the degree that they are strictly formal, i.e. free from any reference to any substantive empirical science. In other cases we suspect that content-involvement of the author of the given type of 'mathematical models of social phenomenma' or of a cybernetic system is only a pretext which permits him to pretend that he is doing empirical science, when in fact he is much more interested in the construction of a formal model of a fragment of a thinkable, i.e. logically or mathematically possible, world. Needless to say, such strictly formal models are as partial and complementary as the previous substantive ones.

The distinction I proposed above is rather analytic in its nature, because in the real approaches to social phenomena we find in our discipline that the substantive and the formal 'structural' assumptions usually occur together. We cannot imagine any, even the simplest 'vision' of the phenomena studied, without involving in it certain formal, structural characteristics too; even the simplest one assumes e.g. that the variables postulated by our model constitute a loose cluster of causes of the effect in question, etc. If we take some typical examples of such approaches e.g. Homans' formulation of his theory of behaviour, both its strictly formal (reductionist) and substantive (behaviourist) assumptions are equally visible.

I stressed above that complex, naturally existing social phenomena and complex (especially socially relevant) research problems usually require several approaches and theories to be applied together for the explanation of the phenomena or for the guidance of human activity. But what does it mean in practice to apply several approaches or theories at the same time, and how can we know that the application of a particular approach is valid for a particular case? Or for a particular subdiscipline of sociological studies? There seem to be several steps involved in these procedures.

To make things more clear: suppose that we are representing a sociological subdiscipline dealing with a special category of objects (hospitals, armies, urban agglomerations) or of phenomena or processes (social deviance, alienation, modernization, etc.), and we begin to think how far these objects of study can be interpreted in terms of several approaches applied together. This seems to involve several steps.

First, the conceptual step. If we can identify the properties of the social objects, the characteristics of certain processes, or elements of a more complex higher level, as being the referents (or being potentially identifiable as the referents) of concepts belonging to a certain approach or theory, it means that we can at least apply this approach to our objects for strictly descriptive and comparative purposes. Different aspects of similar objects are usually denoted by different sets of concepts belonging to different approaches. The application of several sets of different concepts is enough for what might be called multidimensional description, and consequently multidimensional comparison, of the objects of our study, when each of these dimensions refers to properties dealt with by its corresponding approach. A better term here would probably be 'a multiperspectivistic description' or 'multiperspectivistic diagnosis' of the object or process studied. Such multiperspectivistic description is not only much richer than any one-sided analysis, limited to one approach only, but it also involves many comparative perspectives; it permits us to compare any object with all other objects which are covered by the concepts belonging to all the approaches we have applied. We then become aware to what degree a hospital is similar to other 'formal organizations' but also to other 'total institutions', if we also include Goffman's approach in our study, etc. Needless to say, the richer the comparative context of our description the more clearly we see which features are characteristic for our object only, and what it has in common with other kinds of objects when regarded from various theoretical perspectives.

The second step is the problem of theoretical explanation of our object or process with the use of several theories at the same time. We then have the problem as to which of these theories and to what degree applies to the case in question. This is often an open empirical question so that we have to study each particular case separately in order to say, how much from the totality of functioning of the object studied or which of its particular aspects (dimensions, variables, elements, etc.) can be explained by reference to each particular law of the given theory, and to what extent we have also to apply to it some laws taken from other theories. To give an example: every society is both somehow integrated and is also characterized by some conflicts between its groups, classes, ethnic categories, etc. But in a particular society much more can often be explained from the point of view of conflict theory (as in the case of French society in the time of the Revolution); while in another society the other, integrative perspective explains more; we can explain more in the behaviour of a neurotic person with the use of hypotheses based upon the assumption of 'psychoanalytic defense mechanism', than by the theory of rational decision making. But when we are dealing with a stockbroker trying to decide how to invest, the ratio of applicability of the two theories mentioned above may be the complete reverse.

Let me here make another analogy; we know from path analysis the idea that in different societies different variables are able to explain different rates of variance of the same dependent variable (e.g. the rate of upward mobility, the respondents' income, etc.). This idea is quite clear to everybody who is familiar with this research approach. But one should be aware that the same idea may be applied (even if not in such a strict mathematical sense) to different partial mechanisms, described by different partial and complementary theories necessary for the explanation of a complex, multisided social object or process. The applicability of each theory for explanation and prediction may differ from case to case, from process to process, even when we are studying the same category of objects or processes with the use of the same set of approaches or theories. In medical practice we are aware that for certain deviations of functioning of the human organism we need toxicology, for others psychiatric theory, and finally, in some other cases, both these theoretical perspectives applied together. Society is no different from this point of view.

The problem is to establish the proportion of total 'variance' of the entire object studied that can be attributed to each of these mechanisms or, in other terms, is explainable by each of the particular theories. This is a very complex theoretical and methodolgical question which cannot be discussed here. Anyhow, just as we have people who are more Freudian while others are less Freudian and more 'cognitive', so we have interactions which are more, while others are less, 'symbolic'. We have some more, and some less, 'exchange-oriented societies', to mention only a few simple examples of the situations when the same theory explains more in some and less in other cases of the same general category. We also have some societies which are more Marxist in their structure and 'behaviour' while others seem to be more Parsonian or Weberian, when we regard certain aspects of their structure, functioning, and/or change. To put it in a more general way, different societies, or other different complex social phenomena (belonging to the same more general category) usually satisfy to different degrees the assumptions on which any social theory is based. They therefore obey 'the same' theory to different degrees. One of these assumptions e.g. is that of theoretical isolation, i.e. the assumption that the mechanisms describable by other theories do not act in a given case, or act to a relatively small degree.

Now suppose that we have analyzed a large number of objects of the same class with the use of the same set of approaches and their laws and theories, and we are able to classify these objects with respect to the 'rate applicability' of each particular approach for each of them. If we additionally discover some general conditions (some general qualifiers) which determine the amount of usefulness of the given approach for the cases of the given class, we may say that we have formulated a new theory of these phenomena. But it would be a special kind of theory which might be called 'a metatheory'. In a 'normal' theory we usually deal with various variables which sometimes interact or constitute additional faces for the given variables. In such a 'meta-theory' the role of particular variables mentioned above would be played by whole, more or less complex theoretical mechanisms, each of them being describable by one or more laws of an 'elementary theory' (which we know from our contemporary handbooks of theories). Additional propositions necessary in such meta-theory should state the conditions and limits of applicability of each of these partial theoretical mechanisms, the degree of impact of each of them upon the complex whole system, and the conditions on which it depends, the amount of possible variance of the whole system which may be generally attributed to each of its composite partial mechanisms, etc. In a way our metatheory would be a complex, 'multicomponential' vector of mechanisms, each component of which would constitute what we are now used to call a propositional social theory.

The same process of integration of particular partial theories into more complex, meta-theoretical 'vector-like' models of the reality studied could also be started from each of particular partial theories. It would simply mean trying to evaluate each of our theories, trying to determine under what conditions it is valid at all, and which generally defined conditions or factors (i.e. which qualifiers) increase or decrease its applicability for the explanation or prediction of the given set of aspects of a complex social phenomenon in process. This is the question which the authors of particular theories rarely ask themselves, especially since they have a tendency to overestimate the applicability of their own theory, even if they do not claim a monopoly for it.

One could therefore foresee two different kinds of systematization of future sociological theories which start from different particular approaches. One of them might be called a vertical one. This means the transformation of the assumptions which we may derive from the images or 'visions' of the given phenomena of the approaches from which these theories start into systems of possibly general and empirically testable theoretical propositions, to increase the internal logical consistency of each of the structures, approach 'image + questions', and theories generated by it, i.e. to transform the philosophical components of the approaches into theoretical, testable ones.

The other pattern of integration of social theories could be called horizontal (we again see a spatial analogy here). It would mean the integration of various approaches and theories into meta-theories described above which seem necessary for the explanation of various aspects and processes of complex social objects. Needless to say, this 'horizontal integration' of theories is mostly needed for specialized subdisciplines of sociological study, including the various research committees of the ISA, because most of them deal with very complex and more or less naturally defined social objects, phenomena or processes. In order to visualize it, it is enough to read the titles of the papers in this volume. That is why I presented and discussed it in this paper.

But we should now turn to one problem which has already been mentioned. If, in many of these approaches or theoretical problem formulations, some value assumptions are involved, what does it mean from this point of view to formulate our meta-approach and meta-theories? Are they then value-free? I distinguished above the ontological and axiological components of the partial philosophies of social reality which may guide our research and theorizing. The factual, historical connection between certain models of social reality and certain axiologies are well known. But one should be aware that in many cases the specific value assumptions are not in a logically necessary way related to the ontological model of social reality and certain ontological assumptions. The fact that in the history of our discipline certain values just happened to occur together does not change this fact. The vision of social integration, especially its Parsonian version, was perceived, primarily by Parsons' critics, as loaded with conservative values, while 'conflict approaches' were usually perceived in a 'progressive' normative context. But it is conceivable that someone may visualize an integrated 'functionalist' society with the intention of changing it towards quite another kind of social system, so that functionalist hypotheses are used for social change. Someone else may be interested in focussing primarily upon social conflicts, but seen as disrupting the existing pattern of social integration, and studying the conflicts with the intention to suppress them in advance. One does not have to accept egalitarian Marxist values to be interested in the problems and theories of the class struggle and revolutionary change of societies. The well known 'Camelot' project, involving studies of Latin American revolutionary movements sponsored by the Pentagon, is a good example of this thesis. The same also applies to eventual proportional theories which can then be used for the realization of quite opposite value systems. Both ontological models and empirical propositions can be used for quite different purposes and in quite different normative contexts. On the other hand there seem to exist certain probabilistic (psychological and logical) relationships between certain ontological assumptions and theories on the one hand and certain values connected with them on the other. This seems to be an interesting problem for the sociology and psychology of social sciences but there is no time to discuss it here.

If, therefore, we regard the reality studied from the point of view of many ontological or theoretical models at the same time, it does not mean that we have to abandon our own social values and to accept altogether different contradictory value assumptions involved in the critically complementary approaches we would like to apply together. When we are aware of a conflict between various social groups and various ideological orientations, our sympathy is clearly on one side of this conflict. But there may be another solution to this value dilemma; by articulation of various approaches in the study of the given complex process or object we may at the same time also articulate the conflicting value assumptions involved in them. Once we reveal this conflict, we may ask an additional question; how this specific value conflict can be resolved and to what degree it seems reasonable to postulate the solution of this value conflict in the way we usually apply in the theory of conflict relations, e.g. by a compromise between these values if we think that there may be some validity in more than one of them. Elimination or decrease of the existing value-conflicts may also constitute a value for some people (sociologists included). Karl Mannheim once dreamed that intellectuals might stand at least sometimes above simple clashes of value systems and intergroup conflicts, and that they might try to find solutions to them because they may be looking at them from a higher or broader perspective. Maybe it was not such a stupid idea, even when the contemporary world does not seem the best place for its realization. At least some of us might try; and the particular branches of sociological enquiry, the various sociological subdisciplines, may constitute a good place for such action, provided that we do not go so far as to accept any value system only because it exists. This was definitely not my intention in the last section of this paper.

NOTES

1. See below, p. 38.
2. See below, p. 39.
3. See below, p. 181.
4. Jonathan H. Turner, *The Structure of Sociological Theory*. Homewood, Ill.: Dorsey Press, 1978, p. 13.
5. See Stefan Nowak, *Understanding and Prediction. Essays in Methodology of Social and Behavioral Theories*, Chapter 4 ('Comparative Social Research and Methodological Problems of Sociological Induction'). North Holland: Reidel, 1976.
6. See Thomas Kuhn, 'The Structure of Scientific Revolutions', in the *International Encyclopedia of Unified Science*, 2, 2, p. 10.
7. See below, pp. 359-74.

Introduction

Tom Bottomore
University of Sussex

It was an excellent idea to arrange a meeting of the ISA Research Council at which representatives of the constituent research committees would communicate their reflections upon the development of international research in relation to the major issues discussed in present day sociological theory. All the papers contributed to the meeting dealt in some way with this central theme, but those which we, as editors, have selected for publication here, are particularly successful in connecting research in a specific field with broader questions of theory, by showing either the influence which theoretical debates have had upon research programmes or, on the other hand, the contributions which research itself has made to the content of these debates.

In the first place, it is quite evident from these papers that sociological research as a whole has been profoundly affected, over the past decade or so, by the increasingly pronounced multi-paradigmatic character of the discipline. Rival theoretical schemes and methodological orientations not only abound but seem to multiply. One consequence of this situation is that many sociologists have become increasingly preoccupied with meta-theoretical questions — with problems of epistemology and philosophy of science — and debates in this field are today just as prominent as they were in the period of the *Methodenstreit* in Germany at the turn of the century. There is, in a sense, a *second* 'revolt against positivism', but also, as on the first occasion, a tenacious defence of positions which are at least close to positivist, neo-Kantian, or 'natural science' views. The paper by Szacki brings out some of these features, in its reference to the fact that 'controversy over the attitude towards the history of sociology is always in a sense a controversy over sociology itself', and in the author's later observation that 'sociology as a scientific discipline has never formed an organic whole', and that its development 'has been strongly multi-linear', so that a question always remains about how far there is 'a real cumulation of knowledge'.

More immediately germane to most of the papers in this volume, however, is the fact that recent debates have diffused a much greater awareness of, and sensitivity to, theoretical issues and the diversity of possible approaches to the subject matter of research, whatever it may be. There can no longer be any question of adopting a crudely empiricist stance in any field of research; rather, it is a matter of formulating and justifying particular research strategies in terms of specific theoretical schemes, whether these are functionalist, structuralist, Marxist, phenomenological, interactionist, or other. All the contributors emphasize very strongly the central importance of deciding upon the concepts and models which are to guide research.

The papers, admittedly, vary considerably in their approach to this question. Some authors draw attention mainly to the diversity of theoretical models, and to the controversies which arise from a confrontation between them. Thus Himmelstrand contrasts two different approaches to the study of innovative processes: that which treats them in terms of 'diffusion' from 'advanced' to 'less developed' countries, within the general framework of 'modernization theory', and that which has emerged more recently, according to which the problem is conceived in terms of 'innovation from below', which may actually involve resistance to the kinds of social change that are diffused from outside or from above. Himmelstrand also raises another issue, which will be considered later, when he argues that these different approaches have emerged largely from ideological and political orientations, though this does not prevent them from being scientifically fruitful as well. Fenn, in his paper on the sociology of religion, similarly asserts that an earlier paradigm (the 'functional synthesis') has broken down and been replaced by various theoretical/methodological orientations, two of which — characterized as the 'systemic' and the 'critical' — he examines from the standpoint of their treatment of the relation of myth to reality in modern societies. Again, like Himmelstrand, he indicates that the different orientations coexist, without any one of them becoming clearly pre-eminent; and he concludes that in the sociology of religion, as in social science as a whole, there is an 'epistemological crisis', 'to the extent that sociology lacks a paradigm for knowing what is central as opposed to peripheral, what is superficial as opposed to what is latent, what is material as opposed to a matter of appearance alone.' To take one further example, Makler, Sales and Smelser, in their paper on the study of economy and society, clearly distinguish a number of different perspectives, beginning with 'modernization theory' and going on to consider the criticisms of it which have led to the emergence of alternative frameworks, deriving mainly from Marxist and neo-Marxist views. They also report, from an impressionistic survey of the members of their Research Committee and other interested persons, that there seem to be four main categories of theoretical orientation which are now seen to be important — Marxist, Marxist-Weberian/Marxist-functionalist, World system and dependency, and Modernization — and that, although Marxist theory has become increasingly prominent over the past two decades, all four perspectives are likely to remain influential in guiding research in the immediate future.

Almost all the papers, in one way or another, recognize this diversity of theoretical frameworks, but some of them place more emphasis upon the 'convergence' of different perspectives, or upon the possibility that a particular theoretical orientation will come to be seen as especially promising. Archer, for example, while recognizing the existence of incompatible and conflicting approaches in the sociology of education, argues that one central, neglected question is that of the educational *system*, and after critically examining some attempts at systemic or structural analysis, she goes on to suggest that the advancement of research in this field can best be achieved by combining structural and historical investigations. From a different standpoint, Rex is also primarily concerned with the problems posed for a particular theory — Marxism — by the phenomena of racial discrimination and racial oppression, and following a discussion of the controversies over the relation between 'race' and 'class', he considers the prospects for constructing a revised Marxist theory — 'a systematic theory of colonial societies' — which would provide adequate explanations of situations and processes in the field of race relations. And to give another example, Kubat and Hoffmann-Nowotny, after reviewing a number of theories of migration, propose a metaparadigm — which posits 'a dynamism inherent in individuals but curbed by constraints of the relevant social system' — and then suggest some reformulations of existing theories that would allow them to be brought within this new framework.

All the contributors, therefore, recognize in one way or another the profusion of paradigms in current sociology, and the influence this has upon the kinds of research undertaken. They differ, to some extent, in their evaluation of this situation; and as I have indicated, while some consider it possible to elaborate a single particularly useful model or approach, or to bring about some convergence or synthesis of diverse approaches, others seem to accept that at least in the short term future alternative approaches will continue to flourish even to the extent of creating a problem about the 'identity' of a particular field of research. Whichever view is taken, however, there is clearly an underlying agreement upon the need for theoretical debate, closely related to substantive research; and several contributors suggest, in a fairly explicit way, that it is along these lines rather than by more abstract kinds of theoretical reflection, that progress is most likely to be made.

The general impression conveyed by these papers, then, is one of intensive theoretical discussion, which has produced not only a greater sophistication and a useful clarification of some major concepts and theoretical views, but also significant shifts in the relative importance of different paradigms. Several contributors point to what is probably the greatest change over the past two decades; namely, the growing influence of Marxist theory, which is most evident in development studies — especially through the revival of Marxist political economy (itself a form of sociology, in my judgment) — but is also apparent in many other fields. This particular reorientation of sociological thought, however, itself shows some features of the general situation in sociology, for there are now clearly alternative and competing versions of Marxism, ranging from the phenomenological to the structuralist. It is in this sense, too, that Marxist theory has now entered into the mainstream of sociological thought and controversy, and has to confront the same general questions about the foundations of a science of society as do all other sociological theories.

One of the principal issues which now divides Marxists, like other sociologists, into two camps[1] concerns the relation between 'human agency' and 'objective structures'. This is, of course, a long standing theoretical problem which has been treated in many different ways; for example, in terms of the individual and society, or of history and social structure. Simmel formulated the problem with great clarity when he wrote:

> The individual is contained in sociation and, at the same time, finds himself confronted by it. He is both a link in the organism of sociation and an autonomous organic whole; he exists both for society and for himself. ...His existence, if we analyze its contents, is not only partly social and partly individual, but also belongs

to the fundamental, decisive and irreducible category of a unity which we cannot designate other than as the synthesis or simultaneity of two logically contradictory characterizations of man — the characterization which is based on his function as a member, as a product and content of society; and the opposing characterization which is based on his functions as an autonomous being, and which views his life from its own centre and for its own sake.[2]

In recent theoretical debates it is not so much the case that more satisfactory conceptualizations, or more convincing solutions, of the problem have been formulated,[3] as that opposing views have been more sharply and intransigently expressed, in the controversies between those who want to emphasize the importance of the individual, the human agent, as the 'creator' of society,[4] and those who, on the contrary, aim to eliminate the idea of individual subjects as the source of social action and to regard them only as 'the "bearers" of objective instances'.[5] No doubt many sociologists adopt, more or less reflectively, an intermediate position, but it is evident that an awareness of the opposition between these extremes suffuses a great deal of sociological research at the present time, and it is discernible (along with various other theoretical problems) in a number of the papers collected in this volume, as well as being explicitly mentioned in some of them.[6]

The diverse theoretical viewpoints of the present time cannot be regarded simply as the outcome of purely theoretical disagreements and controversies in the course of which new scientific paradigms and research strategies have emerged. They are also the product of the changing context of politics and policy making, as is plainly recognized in many of the following papers.[7] For example, it is evident that the substantial revival of interest in Marxist theory, in the Western societies, owes a great deal to the radical movements of the 1960s, which themselves were responses to new political conditions and expressed new social and cultural aspirations. More broadly, I think it can be claimed that the expansion of sociology, and its constitution, at least embryonically, as a truly international discipline, has introduced more prominently into theoretical debate not only new problems — most obviously those of Third World development, of economic dependency (and more particularly, of the nature of post-colonial societies) — but also new points of view, involving different conceptual schemes, which arise from quite distinct cultural traditions and historical experiences. If sociological theory, more than ever before, now has to conceive every particular society in the context of a world system of relationships, then it is also clear that this world system will actually manifest itself in diverse forms (or that different aspects of it will be seen as significant) from different locations within it.

This is not to argue, however, that the various political and cultural perspectives have an ultimately determining influence upon theoretical orientations in sociology. There is clearly a theoretical and meta-theoretical debate *within* sociology — involving arguments about the nature of theory, the formation of adequate concepts, the commensurability or incommensurability of rival theories, the possibility of empirical confirmation or refutation — and the themes which arise from conflicts and changes in practical social life take on a different character when they are subjected to scientific scrutiny on the terrain of a scholarly discipline which sets for itself goals of universality and objectivity. Hence, a sociological analysis of practical issues may itself have a practical effect, by clarifying or redefining the issues and so changing the public perception of them, or even on occasion demonstrating that a particular widely held conception of social relations and interaction is erroneous and misleading.[8]

On the other side it has been claimed that every sociological theory rests ultimately upon a 'philosophical anthropology'; that is to say, upon a nonempirical, metaphysical rather than scientific, conception of man and society.[9] From this standpoint all theories have to be seen as 'value-impregnated'; and although such a view can be adopted with regard to theories in every field of inquiry,[10] there are well-known grounds for asserting that the influence of underlying value orientations is particularly strong in the case of the social sciences. Even so, it is possible, I think, to assert a 'relative autonomy' of theory construction in sociology. One way of doing so would be to follow Max Weber in conceiving science as a separate and distinctive 'realm of value' which, however, is not completely closed to the influence of other value realms, and may be decisively affected, in particular historical circumstances, by general changes in cultural values. In this vein Weber observed, at the end of his essay on 'objectivity', that:

All research in the cultural sciences in an age of specialization, once it is oriented towards a given subject matter through particular formulations of problems, and has established its methodological principles, will regard the analysis of this subject matter as an end in itself. ... it will cease to be aware of its rootedness in ultimate value ideas. And it is good that this is so. But a time comes when the atmosphere changes. The significance of the unreflectively used points of view becomes uncertain... The light of the great cultural problems has moved on. Then science too prepares to change its standpoint and its conceptual apparatus. ...[11]

The two contrasting perspectives that I have outlined may also be brought together, in a way which has some similarities with Weber's view, by arguing, as Roy Bhaskar has done recently,[12] that the social sciences are both 'value-impregnated' and 'value-impregnating'; that sociological theory construction is therefore necessarily influenced by extra-scientific values, but has at the same time a capacity to examine such values critically and to reject or reformulate them. Much of the variety and uncertainty that characterizes sociological theory at the present time seems to me to have its source precisely in a change in the 'atmosphere' and in the new forms assumed by the 'great cultural problems'. In part this change is due, as I suggested earlier, to the introduction into sociology of new values by scholars from hitherto unrepresented and unrecognized areas of the world. Still more, however, it is a response to a very general cultural reorientation in the face of entirely new problems which have emerged in the late 20th century: the long term consequences of industrialism for the relation of human beings to the natural environment, the enormous concentration of economic, political and military power in present day states, and the existence of previously unimagined capacities, in the shape of nuclear weapons, for human self-destruction.

The reassertion, in recent sociological thought, of the active, creative role of the human agent, in critical opposition to conceptions of a 'reified' social system and 'objective forces' is in part at least an expression, in theoretical form, of these public concerns. So too are some more specific sociological preoccupations at the present time; for example, the widespread and growing interest — indicated in Schweitzer's paper — in the concept of alienation, set in the context of a broader reconsideration of human nature and its potentialities. But just as the public — cultural and political — responses to the new problems are varied and uncertain, so also the representation of them in sociological thought is diverse and confused. Whether or not this situation can be the starting point for the development of a new sociological paradigm or, more broadly, of a new social theory which would establish definite norms of inquiry in sociology (and in other social sciences) — and would thus overcome the crucial difficulty mentioned by Fenn, of not knowing 'what is central as opposed to what is peripheral' — remains to be seen. If such a change — a movement towards a more integrated and systematic theory — should take place it would be the outcome, in my view, of two separate developments: one, a clearer articulation of the new problems in practical political life, which would be expressed in the growth of new social movements (of which there is already some evidence); the other, within sociology, an elaboration of new concepts and theoretical formulations which responded to and interpreted the new movements in political life.

NOTES

1. I have characterized these two groups elsewhere as the 'humanists' and the 'scientists'; see Bottomore (1981), Introduction.
2. Georg Simmel, 'How Is Society Possible?' (1908), pp. 350-1 in Wolff (1959).
3. For example, Berger and Luckmann (1966) express these contradictory aspects in their own terminology as follows: 'Society is a human product. Society is an objective reality. Man is a social product.' (p. 79)
4. See especially the vigorous assertion of this view by Alan Dawe, 'Theories of Social Action', in Bottomore and Nisbet (1978). In quite a different context Sartre criticized certain forms of Marxism for having 'entirely lost the sense of what it is to be a man.' (1958: 58).
5. Nicos Poulantzas, 'The Problem of the Capitalist State', p. 242 in Blackburn (1972). The opposition between 'structuralists' and 'humanists' appears in one form in Lévi Strauss' criticism of Sartre in the last chapter of *The Savage Mind* (1966), and it is especially prominent in the separation between the two principal currents of present-day Marxist thought, represented on one side by structuralists such as Althusser and Godelier, on the other side by 'critical theorists' such as Habermas or 'humanists' such as Petrović.
6. Notably in Himmelstrand's paper.
7. See especially the papers by Rex, Himmelstrand and Walton.
8. This might be expressed in Marxist terminology by saying that sociology can sometimes, or does generally, 'expose' ideological thought.
9. As Löwith (1932) suggested in his well-known study of Weber and Marx.
10. Kuhn's idea of a paradigm and paradigm changes introduces the influence of values extraneous to science into the process of development of scientific theory. For further discussion of this question see Mulkay (1979).
11. Max Weber, ' "Objectivity" in Social Science and Social Policy', in *The Methodology of the Social Sciences*. Translation revised.
12. Bhaskar (1980).

REFERENCES

Berger, Peter and Luckmann, Thomas (1966) *The Social Construction of Reality*. New York: Doubleday.
Bhaskar, Roy (1980) 'Scientific Explanation and Human Emancipation', *Radical Philosophy*, 26, Autumn.

Blackburn, Robin (ed.) (1972) *Ideology in Social Science*. London: Fontana/Collins.
Bottomore, Tom (ed.) (1981) *Modern Interpretations of Marx*. Oxford: Basil Blackwell.
Bottomore, Tom and Nisbet, Robert (eds) (1978) *A History of Sociological Analysis*. New York: Basic Books.
Lévi-Strauss, Claude (1966) *The Savage Mind*. London: Weidenfeld & Nicolson.
Löwith, Karl (1982) *Max Weber and Karl Marx* (1932). English translation forthcoming, London: Allen & Unwin.
Mulkay, Michael (1979) *Science and the Sociology of Knowledge*. London: Allen & Unwin.
Sartre, Jean-Paul (1960) *Critique de la raison dialectique*. Paris: Gallimard.
Weber, Max (1949) *The Methodology of the Social Sciences*. Translated and edited by Edward A. Shils and Henry A. Finch. New York: Free Press.
Wolff, Kurt H. (ed.) (1959) *Georg Simmel, 1858-1918*. Columbus, Ohio: Ohio State University Press.

1
Innovative Processes in Social Change: Theory, Method and Social Practice

Ulf Himmelstrand
University of Uppsala

The ISA Research Committee on Innovative Processes in Social Change is a child of controversy, and this controversy is still with us. So far we have not experienced any significant movement of secession, exit or expulsion. The multi-paradigmatic character of the research committee offers opportunities for communication across paradigms which, however, have not so far been fully utilized. This paper is an attempt to define the controversy and to suggest ways to make it more fruitful sociologically. In attempting this I will try to give a reasonably representative account of some of the most important contributions stemming from the two main factions of the research committee.[1]

The Working Group on Modernization and Diffusion of Innovations which held three meetings at the 7th World Congress of Sociology in Varna in 1970 served as the springboard from which our research committee was catapulted into existence a few years later.[2] Yet the catapult did not look like a catapult at all. It was a theoretical framework, conceptually well-structured, extensively tested empirically, generally accepted by sociologists for more than a decade as the most fruitful scheme for the study of the various stages involved in mass-communication processes, ever since Elihu Katz and Paul Lazarsfeld published their pioneering work, *Personal Influence* (1955). This framework which had originally been formulated to account for the two-stage flow of opinions in mass-communication processes had been extended by students of the diffusion of innovations to include not only the communication of new ideas, but also the spread of technical innovations such as fertilizers, machines and wireless sets, and social innovations like formal education in less developed areas and strata where such innovations had not yet penetrated. In Daniel Lerner's once path-breaking study on *The Passing of Traditional Society* (1958) this approach was combined with the notion of 'modernization'. The diffusion of innovations in the form of Western ideas, forms of organization and technology was supposed to bring about social change in less developed areas, to make them more modern, that is more westernized.

A CONTROVERSY

This was indeed an impressive structure of concepts, hypotheses and confirmed empirical findings. Of course it could be improved by further research, but still it looked unshakably sound in its foundation. Further empirical research did in fact show that the 'trickle-down effect' of ideas and innovations in the modernization process was slower and less complete than expected in some cases, and that this process even met with resistance at times. But such qualifying or even negative evidence only helped to strengthen this framework by opening up new and researchable questions and hypotheses on the conditions generating such 'resistance to change'. Research on questions like these, carried out by highly qualified scholars in the sociological and social-psychological community, could also further extend our knowledge about 'overcoming resistance to change'.

But there were sociologists at the Varna Congress who were dissatisfied with this powerful framework for the study of modernizing social change through the study of diffusion of innovations. Their dissatisfaction did not seem to have so much a scientific foundation as an ideological origin. The ideological overtones of the ensuing controversy were difficult to accept for sociologists brought up with the idea of a value-free social science. But this was a period of politicization of sociology, introduced in particular by scholars from developing countries; and over the next few years this new wave swept away a lot of the remaining 'resistance to change' much more effectively than many attempts to spread the use of fertilizers through 'progressive farmers' to more 'backward' rural sectors. But what may have seemed entirely ideological or political to begin with turned out to be scientifically fruitful as well. The ethnocentrism of Western social science, in its application of the concept of modernization to developments in Asia, Africa and Latin America, was scientifically constraining, and its elimination, even when ideologically motivated, opened up new vistas of sociological research.

Those who opposed the diffusion-of-innovation approach (henceforth called DIA) did not on the whole question the scientific validity of empirical findings assembled within this approach. Nor did they doubt the actual existence of 'innovations', or their actual 'diffusion'. In fact, whatever doubts emerged about the actual diffusion of innovations were a result mainly of research carried out by DIA-proponents themselves, such as Everett Rogers and his many collaborators.[3] What was questioned by the opponents of DIA were the meanings of concepts such as 'modernizing social change' and 'resistance to change'. I think that it is fair to say that the term 'modernization', while being an honorific term for DIA-proponents at the time of the Varna Congress, was a politically distasteful term for DIA-opponents. But political taste or distaste is not necessarily only an emotional reaction unrelated to reality. The reality of 'modernization' as seen by sociologists from less developed countries was a reality of increasing neo-colonial dependency, an accumulation of wealth and power among westernized, 'progressive' or 'dynamic' indigenous elites, increasing class and ethnic cleavages, a destruction of traditional patterns of social morality and their replacement with a highly competitive rush for scarce wealth which could only leave the masses even more deprived than before — often without the supportive social networks which made it easier to survive even rather poor pre-colonial feudal or subsistence conditions. With this frogs-eye view of 'modernization', so different from the naively elevated and unidimensional Western view of successive and successful improvements, even 'resistance to change' could seem rational rather than an allegedly 'backward' kind of attitudinal resistance.

These two diametrically opposed perspectives, neither of which were value-free or strictly scientific but rather ideological, constituted the original controversy which led to the creation of our research committee. The lead was taken by Orlando Fals Borda, chairman at one of the sessions in Varna. The call for 25 signatures from at least five countries needed for an application to form the research committee within the ISA made the opposition to DIA quite explicit without in any way trying to scare away DIA-proponents. The research committee even today contains board members as well as regular members representing both views, even though the DIA-view has undergone significant revisions since Varna, as I will indicate later on. The cement which holds us together is our common interest in 'innovations' and their impact on society in the form of 'social change' or 'societal transformation', as some members would like to have it. But while an innovation, in the DIA-perspective, is conceived as a given problem-solution of a technological, organizational or ideational character introduced into society from 'outside', or from the 'top' or the 'centre', and channelled through its networks, the DIA-opponents tended to think in terms of an 'innovative process' in which the innovation is not necessarily given. The innovative process is conceived and defined as including not only the work needed to spread an 'innovation', but also the identification and awareness of the underlying problem to be solved, as seen in the perspective of the periphery, and furthermore the organization of people who suffer from the problem in order to do something innovative about it. Here the innovation is the end rather than the beginning of the process. The 'innovative process' is thus seen as involving both an increasing consciousness of grass-roots problems, and innovative action to solve these problems from below.

The differences between the perspective from above and from below also bring into focus the fact that some problem-solutions introduced as innovations from above, are seen from below as addressing other problems than those of common people in the periphery. The problem-solution coming from above does not always fit the problem as seen from below. A crucial theoretical, methodological and praxiological issue on this point is therefore how to define, to operationalize and to deal with the degree of fit between problems and problem-solutions in innovative processes of change or transformation. Obviously the controversy between the two approaches which are represented in our research committee has made it easier to discover and pin-point this important theoretical and methodological issue.

A theoretical difficulty common to both sides in our controversy is the fact that both sides tend to be idealistic or subjectivistic in their approaches (to use a rather common Marxist terminology). The DIA-perspective focusses a great deal on values and attitudes as they affect diffusion or resistance. DIA-opponents with their concern for subjective problem-awareness and consequent action, in spite of their different perspective, could also be labelled subjectivist. But social processes of change are to a very large extent independent of individual human will and want — a fact which is acknowledged by Marxists and non-Marxists alike. Even if subjective factors are crucial in determining individual action, within given structural options and constraints, the aggregation of a large number of individual actions often results in outcomes which are not wanted by anyone individually, or at least not by all or the majority. Aggregation effects and structural effects, even if not completely disregarded, tend to be overlooked in our work when we focus most of our attention on innovations or innovative processes — which by definition are wanted.

CHANGES IN THE DIFFUSION-OF-INNOVATION APPROACH

My first observation is that the term 'modernization' has all but disappeared from the contributions of DIA-proponents to our research committee meetings — with some significant exceptions. And when you think of it, this term is expendable without any great cost to the DIA, since all the other conceptual elements of this approach can still be retained. You certainly sacrifice the positive value once attached to the term 'modernization'; but at the same time you avoid the negative affective load increasingly attached to that term. You can still go on studying and talking about the underlying effects of diffusion in a more matter-of-fact manner without implying anything in particular about related broad-ranging social changes. This would seem to be a rather typical situation in the social sciences: when we give up one of our grand notions — and give it up for very good reasons — we also narrow our focus. We now have nothing particular to say about the broader context of change to which our deserted grand notion was referring. We are better guarded against critical attacks, but also more limited.

Within these limits excellent contributions establishing new and significant knowledge have been made to the DIA within our research committee. An example of this was the paper by J. Hage and J. R. Hollingsworth on 'Centralization and the Diffusion Process of Medical Innovation' presented at one of our sessions at the 9th World Congress of Sociology in Uppsala in 1978. The innovation treated in this paper was vaccine inoculation. The empirical study reported in this interesting paper dealt with the first adoptions and the spread of certain types of inoculation in a broad comparative and historical perspective. Some of the main explanatory variables were the degree of centralization or nationalization of the health delivery system, and the historical juncture at which centralization took effect. The paper reports that the more centralized the system in a particular country, the later the first adoption, but the more rapid the spread of vaccination, once adopted. In more decentralized systems the first adoptions occurred much earlier, but the spread of the innovation was significantly slower.

But as I indicated earlier there have been some significant exceptions to the dropping of the term 'modernization'. It may be significant that this term has survived longer in contributions from our East European colleagues. A good example of such a contribution was a paper by a Hungarian social psychologist, Károly Varga, presented at the 8th World Congress of Sociology in Toronto in 1974, which used the modernization paradigm without any reservations or misgivings.[4] At the Symposium on Action Research and Scientific Analysis organized by our research committee in Cartagena, Colombia, in April 1977, Varga followed up his previous paper by critically attacking a paper by myself and Anders Rudqvist presented in Toronto. To this latter paper I will return later on. My conjecture is that the modernization approach with its emphasis on impacts coming from outside or from the centre rather than from within the periphery, is more congenial to more centralized political and economic systems in which the responsibility for improvements of human life rests with the state and the administrative apparatus branching out from the centre toward the periphery, as is the case in most socialist countries.

But the consonance between modernization theories and highly centralized political systems would seem to be only one aspect of the acceptability of such theories in socialist countries. Another aspect relates not to the centralized sources of modernization processes but to their outcomes. Whatever reservations may exist about politically repressive traits of East European state-socialism, its accomplishments in terms of social-welfare outcomes must also be taken into account. In welfare terms modernization in socialist countries has led to much more widely acceptable outcomes than modernization in developing countries, or even in some capitalist countries.[5] This acceptability of outcomes of modernization would seem to be reflected in the acceptability of modernization theory in socialist countries.

Superficially my conjecture regarding the consonance between modernization theory and centralized political systems may seem to be refuted by the fact that originally modernization theory was developed mainly by US sociologists on the basis of a sociological tradition stretching back to the classical distinction between *Gemeinschaft* and *Gesellschaft*. However, centralization is also a most distinctive feature of welfare-capitalist developments towards *Gesellschaft*-forms of society, even if political centralization is far less pronounced in the capitalist West. Furthermore, modernization theory in the West received a particularly strong impetus from the Western concern for aid to developing countries; and aid is certainly introduced from outside, from the centre to the periphery. My conjecture is therefore not refuted by the growth of modernization theory in the West; it is only qualified. It does not hold for political centralization alone. However, my main point is rather a different one. The criticism of modernization theory, and the dropping of the term itself, has originated not in socialist countries, it would seem, but in the capitalist world, and particularly in its underdeveloped periphery.

One further theoretical point should be made here before I proceed to look at theoretical, methodological and empirical aspects of work done by DIA-opponents since Varna. The emergence of articulate opposition to the DIA in the capitalist part of the world, and particularly in its periphery, could be interpreted as a reflection of the more 'dialectical' development of capitalism as compared to contemporary state-socialism. The contradictions of capitalism, particularly where it is combined with pluralist democracy, or at least with some scope for opposition, provides more issues and more scope for critical sociology, and thus for opposition to an approach as dominant as the DIA used to be.

ACTION-RESEARCH — A FRAMEWORK FOR RESEARCH OR ACTION?

It has already been emphasized that the conjunction of 'conscientization' and action constitutes the theoretical focus of those research committee members who have been in opposition to the DIA. Combined with this focus is a methodological bias for participatory action-research. Action-research is not conceived in the manner of Kurt Lewin (1948, ch. 13) as an application of existing theory to some practical problem in a field setting with an instrumental, quasi-experimental design resulting in distinctly separate practical results on the one hand, and research reports on the other. Participatory action-research is rather an inseparable combination of theory, research and practice characterized by a dialogue between actors and researchers enlightening the actors as well as researchers about the meaning of the action intended, and eventually resulting in an increasing autonomy of actors in relationship to researchers, and to an emancipation from questionable and restraining beliefs in the inevitability of the given order of things. This is in sharp contrast even to the group-decision-making so typical of Lewinian action-research, where the intentions of decision-making are given in advance by the researcher or his sponsors, and the decision-making process is experimentally manipulated according to given social-psychological theory to render predetermined results which then can be reported in respectable scientific journals.

The participatory action-research favoured by some members of our research committee could also be called discourse-oriented action-research in contrast to the instrumental action-research outlined and practised by Kurt Lewin and his followers. In participatory discourse-oriented action-research the intentions of action are not given in advance by researchers or outside sponsors, but by the actors themselves. But the intentions voiced by some actors may be reflections of hegemonic sociopolitical relationships rather than reflections of their 'own voice'. The role of the researcher is to liberate this voice by helping to clarify the intentions of actors, in the context of relevant structural conditions, options and constraints, in a kind of maieutic dialogue, that is through discourse. And as to research reports, if they materialize at all, they usually take on the character of analytic descriptive accounts of the discursive process, the action, its constraints and consequences, mistakes made and discovered in the process, and fed back to improve understanding of the situation and leading to further action. Statistical estimates of 'dependent variables' never appear in such accounts. The aim of discourse-oriented action-research is to provide people with their own voice, as suggested by Paulo Freire, rather than to estimate and report the success of experimental manipulation in a field setting.

From a research point of view one dilemma of discourse-oriented action-research is that its motivation often implies less priority to reporting research than to providing people 'with their own voice', and with a broader understanding of their own action. Consequently there would seem to be a much larger number of such action-research projects than there are research reports on such projects. A contributory factor on this point could be the political circumstances in some countries where discourse-oriented action-research has been attempted. In some countries people who have come into possession of 'their own voices' are seen as politically troublesome, if not dangerous. Research reports on action-research may expose such actors to repression. Therefore they are not published.

In our research committee the philosophy of participatory discourse-oriented action-research has been presented in papers by Orlando Fals Borda (1977) and Heinz Moser (1977). I will here briefly summarize Moser's account of the structure of discourse-oriented action-research rather than Fals Borda's more penetrating philosophical and meta-theoretical contribution since Moser himself has been helpful in summarizing some of his thoughts in a compact and illuminating figure.

FIGURE 1
Steps in Discourse-Oriented Action-Research

(1) information-gathering on context of action
(2) discussion of information between actors, and between actors and researchers, to clarify problems and intentions, and for working out guidelines of social action
(3) social action

Note: Even though this figure is adopted from Moser (1977, p. 14) it has been slightly revised to incorporate some of Moser's comments.

The information-gathering indicated at the top of the Figure is intended to set the stage for the whole process, that is to provide a context of discourse and argumentation between actors and researchers. Relevant information refers to the stock of local and everyday knowledge — knowledge of local history, of local institutions and rules, of current events — possessed by local actors, or obtainable by 'digging where you stand'.[6] But knowledge about the wider structural contexts of province, nation and international dependencies may also be crucial for understanding the nature of the predicaments which conscientization and action is all about.

Methodologically speaking this initial information-gathering may and must in some respects rely on ordinary 'positivistic' gathering of facts and even statistical data. You cannot enter into meaningful dialogue or discourse with a dominant mode of production, with national power-structures, with patterns of land tenure, or with cartels, and with the trends of change that such objects of information undergo. It is also difficult to engage in discourse with your antagonists in action. Such antagonists are important objects of information in the first attempts to establish the context of conscientization and action. Information-gathering about your antagonists by the method of dialogue does not make sense. Apart from problems of access, the basic conditions of a true dialogue cannot be fulfilled in a relationship to an antagonistic foe. A discourse can be pursued with a non-antagonistic opponent: but information on an antagonist can be collected only by recourse to his public record or through publicly accessible reports on his kind. You can spy on him too, if your ethics allows. In a methodological paper presented at the Cartagena meeting in April 1977 I emphasized some of these points on the role of 'positivistic' fact-gathering in the initial phase of discourse-oriented action-research projects (Himmelstrand, 1977). At that stage the researcher with his probably superior knowledge of the broader context usually has a greater role to play than local actors — even though it is also important to get the actors involved in the search for broader contextual information. But time usually does not allow original research on this broader context. Already available reports and perhaps secondary analysis of available data is the most one can hope for at that stage. However, with regard to the local context more original research can and usually must be done. Local actors with their local knowledge can actively participate in this research. In this manner the process of conscientization is initiated already in the first stage.

In the second stage, as indicated in Moser's Figure, the contextual information obtained in the first stage is used as a context for discussion, argumentation and clarification of predicaments and intentions in a dialogue between actors, and between actors and researchers. The aim is to arrive at an enlightened consensus among actors about the nature of the situation and on what to do. Moser emphasizes that this process should be recorded and described simultaneously with ongoing activities in the project — an awesome and delicate task in settings where premature disclosures of this process can trigger persecution and repression, but less problematic in reasonably democratic societies.

Then follows the stage of social action. This often involves mistakes, ruptures and unexpected consequences, good or bad, on which information must again be assembled for the sake of further action and research, and fed back to a revised assessment of the context and the meaning of action (see the feedback loop in Moser's Figure). While this is the general outline followed in participatory discourse-oriented action-research it is not always that simple. I am not thinking here of the dangers of external persecution and repression imminent in some political settings — even though they also complicate the matter. There are two other problems of an internal nature which concern the role of the researcher, and his or her relations with the actors in the project.

I have already indicated that the requirements of local action may take precedence over the universalistic requirements of research and its publication due to the significant role of actors and action in projects like these. But this problem is not unique to discourse-oriented action-research. Even in ordinary applied research the sponsor may not always be interested in making scientific evaluations of such applications publicly available in research reports. This may create difficulties for the researcher in fulfilling his particular role in the production and dissemination of new knowledge even in ordinary applied research. But these difficulties are of a different nature in discourse-oriented action-research due to the identification of the researcher with the actors involved.

Alain Touraine in a recent book, *La Voix et le Regard* (1979) has warned against the kind of participatory action-research proposed, for instance, by Orlando Fals Borda in which the researcher becomes strongly committed with the actors. The researcher must avoid becoming so identified and involved with the actors that he relinquishes his autonomy as a researcher. Touraine seems to think that Fals Borda's position implies too much of an identification with the actors, and too little emphasis on research as such. But this is not true if one takes note of Fals Borda's recent published and unpublished papers. The resolution of this dilemma may perhaps be found in terms of a distinction made by Ralph Turner (1956) between taking the role of another and taking the standpoint of the other. The researcher in discourse-oriented action-research, immersing himself in the context of action, should take the role of the actor in the ensuing discourse by imaginatively placing himself in the role of the actor, but refuse to identify with the standpoint of the actor. This requires a great deal of personal discipline, and also some didactic skills in explaining the role of the researcher to the actors, so that they can accept the rules of the game which the researcher must follow.

A second even more serious internal problem in discourse-oriented action-research can be identified on the actor level. Such action-research presupposes the absence of antagonistic interests among actors within the project. Their predicaments must be shared, and their intentions roughly similar. Otherwise the basic preconditions of true dialogue among actors, and between actors and researchers, are disrupted. For instance, in a Swedish action-research project among narcotic addicts and social workers claiming to work closely with the addicts in their interest, it soon turned out that there were disruptive conflicts not only between local public health agencies and social workers, but also between social workers and addicts. Under such conditions there was no one single role for researchers to take. Some of the actors-researchers were perceived as taking the standpoint of antagonists. Discourse broke down. The researchers were thus forced to make a choice between doing a more conventional non-action research project, or to take the role of one restricted group of actors, and proceed from there (Björling and Johansson, 1980).

Another example: an action-research project working closely with local groups of small scale peasants and landless rural workers, once its initial success became known, attracted a group of extreme leftist students who wanted to 'serve the people'. But in fact they entered the project with a completely disruptive diffusion-of-innovation approach clearly indicating that they already knew what was best for the peasants. Needless to say this completely undermined the logic of the ongoing project, and made it impossible to pursue it further. Consensus among actors was replaced by disunity.

There are cases where disruption has been less severe — for instance in projects involving the conscientization and action of women textile workers in Sweden — where the different perspectives of local workers and regional or national trade-union leaders made it difficult to pursue a fully-fledged discourse-oriented action-research. But on the other hand, in a case like this, where conflicts of interest among actors can be assumed to be non-antagonistic, the most reasonable approach for researchers in that situation might have been to reassess and broaden the context of discourse by involving actors on local, regional and national levels to clarify common constraints and intentions in this broader context. Differential motivation between local and higher levels with regard to participation in the project could still be a stumbling block. Action may have been initiated locally with a high degree of motivation not represented at higher levels of union organization.

On the other hand it is also possible to conceive of cases where conflicts between actors are assumed to exist, but where in fact there is a much wider consensus among them than expected. For instance, one may find that political parties fighting each other bitterly over various ideological or class issues at the national level, are much more alike in their definitions of problems and potential solutions on the regional or local levels due to the more concrete character of local predicaments, the smaller distance between politicians and regular voters, and the cross-cutting of ideological alignments by local and regional issues. Under such conditions, where they exist, it may be possible to pursue a rather broad-based discourse-oriented action-research project with actors affiliated with rather different parties.[7]

A lesson to be learned from these various examples is that a preliminary analysis of antagonistic and non-antagonistic conflicts of interest in the arena of action must precede the initiation of a participatory discourse-oriented action-research project in order to assure that the preconditions for such a project are met among the actors involved. But such analysis of antagonistic relationships should also be pursued at later stages of a discourse-oriented action-research project. For instance, an action-research project carried out in the context of land reform or non-resisted land occupations may at an intermediate stage involve the allocations of individual family plots to landless rural workers. But this may destroy the collective spirit involved in the project and, in the not so long run, may also place the new landowners at the mercy of money-lenders who thus can recapture the land in the interest of large scale absentee landlords. A continuous analysis of antagonistic relationships could have clarified the need for collective rather than private landholding, resulting in a redirection of action at an earlier point (cf. Himmelstrand and Rudqvist, 1975, p. 21).

But it would seem that the development and use of methods for the analysis of antagonistic relationships among actors has been rather neglected among participatory action-researchers. Marxist class analysis in its more contemporary versions (see for instance E. O. Wright, 1976) more frequently addresses itself to advanced industrialized societies rather than to the rural contexts in which a great deal of radical action-research is taking place. Here is another example of the need for a reorientation among action-researchers to learn more about the hard objective facts of social structure without thereby sacrificing the study of more subjective aspects of conscientization and action.

In this paper I have had more to say about the philosophy and methodology of discourse-oriented action-research than about actual reports on findings and experiences gained in action-research projects. Several of the examples mentioned above stem from projects which I happen to know but which have not yet been systematically covered in available publications. Among the several reports presented at our research committee meetings and describing in some detail the findings and experiences of action-research fulfilling, or at least approximating the participatory model here described, I could mention papers by Gerrit Huizer, Harald Swedner, and by myself and Anders Rudqvist; and others yet unpublished by Alexander Mamak, Peter Park, Cristina Cordero and Christina Sennett.[8] Heinz Moser (1977) has reported on an action-research project in a Swiss educational setting in one of his papers, and Anders Rudqvist is working on a thesis based on his experiences in a semi-action-research project in Colombia initiated by Orlando Fals Borda. I call this a semi-action-research project since it concentrated on the first two stages — information-gathering and conscientization — while social action was relatively minor due to special Colombian circumstances.

Outside our research committee, Alain Touraine (1968, 1974, 1979) has reported on three action-research projects involving movements of students, women and ecologists, respectively. Alfred Willener's book on *The Action Image of Society* (1970), relating to the student and workers' revolt of 1968 in France, covers at least some aspects of what I have called discourse-oriented action-research. In Sweden there are a number of ongoing action-research projects — for instance one led by Åke Sandberg[9] at the Centre for the Study of Working Life in Stockholm — on which we hope to have reports at the next World Congress of Sociology in Mexico.[10]

THE END OF CONTROVERSY?

To provide a reasonably balanced picture of the two theoretical and methodological approaches represented in our research committee is not easy, particularly since I have been collaborating more closely with those representing one side of the controversy. The fact that I have analyzed the work of DIA-opponents more extensively than that of the DIA is not necessarily an expression of my own bias, however. Discourse-oriented action-research is more problematic and much less well developed scientifically than the DIA, and therefore requires more space for discussion. Never having personally carried out such an action-research project of my own, I am both attracted by this kind of research, and troubled by some of its complications and shortcomings. On the other hand our controversy should not be exaggerated. I can envisage a certain rapprochement between the two approaches. The partial dropping of the modernization perspective is one indicator of that rapprochement. A more concrete expression can be found in a paper by Niels Röling, Joseph Ashcroft and Fred Wa Chege, 'Innovation and Equity in Rural Development', presented already at the 1974 Toronto World Congress. Niels Röling in the past had worked closely with Everett Rogers, one of the leading proponents of the DIA.[11] In their Toronto paper, however, these authors were turning the traditional DIA-perspective upside down. The fieldwork reported in that paper did not rely on the traditional trickle-down effect through the transmission-belt of so-called 'progressive farmers', but approached the less developed and more 'backward' strata of the rural African population directly. It turned out that the adoption rates with regard to the innovations introduced were much higher for these 'backward' peasants compared with earlier findings for 'progressive' farmers. Secondly, the 'resistance to change' came from above rather than from below. 'Progressive' farmers would seem to have found the initial adoption of innovations by 'backward' peasants against the nature of things, particularly since it tended to disrupt the prevailing system of stratification. Progress from below was therefore resisted by better-suited 'progressive' farmers. Even though the methodology used in this study was far from discourse-oriented action-research, but instead involved the use of quite traditional research techniques, the perspective from below applied came very close to the perspective defined by Orlando Fals Borda and others on that side of our controversy.

Another interesting paper by Mark van de Valle et al. on 'Policy Research as an Agent of Planned Change in Advanced Social Systems', presented in our research committee at the Uppsala World Congress, points to other possibilities for a rapprochement.

With academically well established research techniques of quantification and multivariate analysis van de Valle has demonstrated that such quantitative academic research which sharply separates the search for knowledge, and its practical application, is less likely to influence practice than more qualitative research based on 'grounded theory' and carried out within contexts of practice. Even though most of the practice studied by van de Valle seems to be rather far from the critical and radical action favoured by most discourse-oriented action-researchers, his findings lend support to one of the basic notions of such action-research: research and action should be closely linked, to make research applicable in action. Another aid to a rapprochement between our factions has been papers which concentrate on structural constraints on innovative processes, thereby filling some of the gaps left by the seemingly subjectivist philosophy of DIA as well as discourse-oriented action-research. An example is Sylvia Hale's paper at the 1974 Toronto World Congress, 'Barriers to Free Choice in Development', which empirically documented structural constraints on development from below in India.

In my own work on societal change in Sweden, on which a first report was presented at a meeting organized by Ellen Hill in Zürich 1976, my collaborators and I have concentrated attention largely on (1) describing and diagnosing the problems, that is the structural contradictions and constraints of mature welfare capitalism in Sweden, (2) empirically assessing the numerical, organizational, consciousness and systemic strength of actors struggling to resolve these problems, actors representing the two sides of capitalist contradictions, namely labour and capital, and (3) analyzing the degree of fit between problems and problem-solutions in Swedish societal change, with particular reference to some recent proposals on wage-earners' funds and economic democracy (Meidner, 1978) for which the Swedish labour movement is struggling. Even though some discourse-oriented meetings were held with employees in our project, this was not done in action contexts. The empirical methods used were quite conventional — even if some of the variables were unconventional — and they focussed attention on economic and environmental indicators, occupational structures and class-distinctions, on survey data concerning social consciousness, historical data on organizational growth and unity, state expenditures on welfare and industrial subventions, etc. (Himmelstrand, Ahrne, Lundberg and Lundberg, 1981). I still maintain that this research project has been strongly influenced by what I have learnt at our research committee meetings about discourse-oriented action-research, in the sense that we have collected data which would seem relevant to action-oriented discourse from the standpoint of the Swedish labour movement. This corresponds to the first stage in Moser's account of discourse-oriented action-research — except that our information-gathering has been done on a much more extensive scale than in most action-research projects of this kind. It took nearly five years to complete the project. But this does not make our research less relevant for action. The labour history of the past, and the future, in countries like Sweden is not paroxysmic, but slow even where it is dialectical. In that kind of situation even rather slow and elaborate research like ours can provide a context of argument and discourse relevant for action.

But even if I see a certain rapprochement and a fruitful division of labour between the various factions within our research committee, I can also see a different possibility: a tolerant but lax polyparadigmatic pluralism where everybody does their own thing without caring much for what others do in the fields of DIA, innovative or not so innovative social processes. I hope that the present paper can help to counteract such a tendency by hinting at the linkages which exist between studies of incremental changes and the growth of structural contradictions of society on the one hand, and action-oriented discourse and discourse-oriented action on the other. Such linkages can be found also in studying diffusion of innovation from above or below, and in the innovative processes where innovations are not simply adopted but made in the light of discourse on the structural contexts of action. Only if we focus attention on these linkages can our respective approaches become more scientifically fertile, and hopefully, contribute to adequate conscientization and action. Only then can the work done in the European regional meetings organized for our research committee by Ellen Hill, and the meetings organized by Orlando Fals Borda, be seen as part of a common project of understanding innovative processes of social change or social transformation. Such a common project need not imply complete harmony; a dialectical community of scholars would seem to be more conducive to understanding the innovative processes which our research committee is all about. In the concluding part of this paper I will therefore outline a tentative model for studying the linkages between the various theoretical, methodological and practical preoccupations manifested in the work of our research committee, a model which should make it possible to foster such a 'dialectical community of scholars'.

LINKAGES BETWEEN THREE OBJECTS OF KNOWLEDGE

In this paper I have pointed out that the members of our committee have focussed most of their attention on three separate objects of knowledge:
1. Ready-made innovations and their diffusion.
2. Innovative problem-solving processes, involving the making of innovations, primarily social innovations, within the framework of participatory action-research.
3. Problem-generating, and solution-constraining socio-economic structures and processes, which set the stage for innovative processes, or set the options and constraints for the spread of innovations.

In Figure 2 I have indicated some important linkages between these three different objects of knowledge. The Figure can be read from below or from above, or from left to right at level 3 as indicated in the Figure. Reading it from below and upwards would be more natural for DIA-opponents in general. Reading it from above and downwards would be closer to DIA, and reading it from left to right at level 3 would seem to represent most faithfully the more limited 'subjectivist' versions of participatory action-research. The differences between these three approaches would seem to be that the DIA (reading from above and downwards in the Figure) considers the objects of knowledge in the lower part of the Figure as restrictions on the diffusion of innovations, while those reading the Figure from below and upwards look at objects of knowledge in the upper part as restrictions. To discourse-oriented participatory action-researchers who read the Figure from left to right, the notion of 'restrictions' is less relevant then the notion of the 'content' of action-oriented discourse. To them the objects of knowledge in the upper and lower parts of the Figure provide the content of the discourse which precedes action. 'Restrictions' will of course be anticipated in such discourse, but their existence and nature in the real world of action will be established in the context of action itself. In addition it is possible to read the Figure from right toward the left as I will indicate later on.

If we read the Figure from below, we start from the box representing structures and processes generating (1) problems or

FIGURE 2
The Interlocking of Cultural Factors, Domains of Action and Basic Structures and Processes

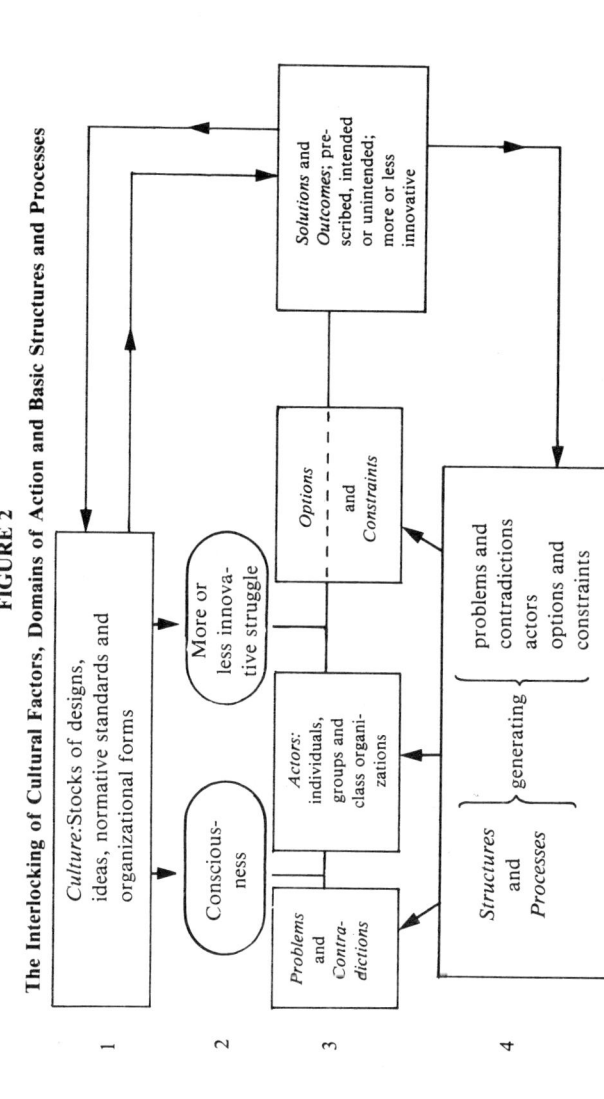

Note: The encircled processes (consciousness, etc.) are blown-up representations of relationships between problems and actors, and between actors and constraints or options. The arrow-line moving directly from *Culture* to *Solutions* and *Outcomes* indicates that a lot of the 'outcomes' are reproductions of already given cultural patterns through processes of socialization without the interference of innovation and struggle. Bu: outcomes which have come about through such interference can certainly influence culture, as indicated by the feed-back arrow.

'contradictions', (2) problem-solving actors and (3) constraints or, as the case may be, options for more or less innovative problem-solving action. Actors are here seen not as given but as generated. People are given, but they become actors only through structures and processes which place them in situations of more or less shared predicaments where they can be mobilized to become actors. Intervening between problems and actors is the process of 'conscientization' which to some extent may be restricted from above by ideological elements of the given culture. Similarly, the more or less innovative attempts by actors to apply their consciousness in tackling the structural constraints, or using the structural options generated from below in the Figure, are restricted, more or less, by cultural factors from above. Constraints or restrictions are thus of two kinds — structural (for instance class relations and dominant classes) and cultural (for instance given ideological or organizational patterns in the cultural sphere).

The same kind of logic applies when reading the Figure from above and downwards. However, it is also possible to read the Figure both from above and from below in a synthetic attempt at systems analysis, and in so doing the feedback loops in the Figure become important. They indicate the extent to which the results of action contribute to the reproduction of 'morphogenetic' transformation of the cultural and structural conditions represented at the top and the base of the Figure, respectively.

But it also seems possible to read the Figure from the right to the left, and not only from left to right. Ready-made solutions or innovations are often handed down to us from political leaders or administrators of the superstructure, and justified with reference to ideological aims specified at the superstructural level in terms such as 'more democracy', 'more freedom', 'more equality', or 'more law and order'. But instead of evaluating such innovations or solutions by using the evaluative standards of the superstructure, we could rather explore the extent to which such solutions fit the problems generated by the base, and fit the capability, incentives and strength of relevant problem-solving actors. This has been done, for instance, in Himmelstrand, Ahrne, Lundberg and Lundberg, (1981, pp. 301ff).

In its present form the Figure has been drawn and the contents of its various boxes indicated in a manner designed to be neutral with regard to Marxist and non-Marxist approaches to the analysis of society. Both Marxist and non-Marxist interpretations of the Figure would seem possible. A Marxist, for instance, would look upon the box at the bottom of the Figure as the economic base, the mode of production. In the case of a capitalist society this base generates the structural contradictions of capitalism and mobilizes actors from the working and bourgeois classes in more or less innovative class struggle to tackle, remove or to maintain the constraints of capitalist social relations of production. The superstructure (the cultural conditions) created as a result of previous bourgeois class action, operates as a restriction limiting the scope of class struggle in such a manner that the mode of production in the economic base can be reproduced and maintained. The superstructure is thus not seen simply as an epiphenomenon or reflection of the base, as in vulgar Marxism, but as a result of class struggle. This implies that the limited working-class victories which are possible as a result of such struggle even within the framework of capitalism, can be incorporated into this superstructure which thus may become more than just a simple reflection of bourgeois class interests alone, even when bourgeois hegemony prevails. Welfare-capitalism is a case in point.

Obviously a synthetic approach to all the various levels and sections of Figure 2 requires contributions from the sociology of culture, education and mass-communications, from social psychology and the sociology of mobilization and social movements as well as from economic sociology, Marxist historical materialism, participatory action-research and political theory. The Figure provides ample scope for a discourse between sociologists in many fields, and between sociologists and actors outside the academic field. But it also provides a conceptual frame of reference for research undertaken in particular perspectives, from below or from above, representing specific class or group positions seen within a larger contextual whole. To anyone who remains unconvinced by my attempt to suggest the possibility of linking together such very different approaches, an example will be given with reference to historical materialism and a symbolic structuralist interpretation of culture. Symbolic-structuralists such as Claude Lévi-Strauss (1967) assume the existence of 'hidden structures' which exhibit their own inherent dynamics, and which thus are independent of any influences from external economic conditions. But if the 'laws' of this dynamic cannot be reduced to conditions given in the prevailing mode of production, how is it then possible at all to combine symbolic-structuralism 'from above' in a synthesis with Marxist historical materialism 'from below'?

One answer takes off from the assumption that alternative 'hidden structures' are often available. This assumption is a crucial one in various structural theories of cognitive balance (Cartwright and Harary, 1959). Such theories assume that different cognitive solutions are possible to a given imbalanced cognitive structure. Among the alternative options which may be part of the 'hidden structures' of cognitive dynamics, the one option which best fits both this dynamic and the action originating from the mode of production, will be chosen. Once 'chosen' such a cognitive solution will continue to display its own inherent dynamic. In such a manner the 'culturalist' and the historical materialist approaches can appear as interlocking rather than as competing approaches.

Another possibility is to look at the mode of production as a producer of at least some of the issues and cognitive elements incorporated in the 'hidden structure', even where no alternative structures are available. The 'hidden structures' may have their own dynamic laws but the material or the elements of these structures would still be produced by the experiences of everyday life within a given mode of production.

But what about the highly different methodological approaches also present in our research committee — ranging all the way from causal inquiries based on multivariate statistical analysis of data to methods of phenomenology, finalistic *Verstehen* and action-oriented discourse? Again, it seems that one methodological approach deals with problems which another method cannot resolve due to its limitations. The dilemma involved thus boils down to the question of whether a particular research project requires more than one approach, and how the division of labour and combination of these approaches shall be arranged, where several methodological approaches would seem to be needed.

When is more than one approach needed? Let us consider a study of 'consciousness-production' based on multivariate causal inquiries made by sociologists of mass communication and opinion formation. For the purpose of my argument I will consider the findings of such a study as a base line, or as premises for further changes in beliefs and attitudes, or of 'consciousness'. Such findings can be used in two different ways depending on the action context.

1. If the action is intended to 'persuade' people to change their minds, whether for political reasons, or as part of a laboratory experiment, there is no need to go beyond the methodological approach already used in previous studies of consciousness-production. These studies have established both the base lines or

premises for further change, and how such change is brought about. An application of these findings would 'only' require a manipulation of variables which have turned out to have, for instance, sizable multiple-regression coefficients in the multivariate studies already reported.

Similarly, a Marxist attempt to relate the content and structure of consciousness statistically to types and levels of class struggle (if such empirical Marxist studies of consciousness-production were available), would not call for any new approach in attempts to change consciousness, but 'only' require the appropriate change in style of class struggle in order to achieve the change of consciousness desired. The feasibility of such applications of statistical causal inquiry will not be discussed here: the point is rather that the methodological approaches mentioned in these two examples are seen as self-contained and complete, in the sense that they do not seem to call for any supplementary approach of a different, say phenomenological or discourse-oriented type. But there is a second use to which one can put the kind of research results indicated above.

2. Assume that a manipulation of beliefs on the basis of sociopsychological findings, or a fomenting of specified types of class struggle on the basis of more or less empirically based Marxist theory, is rejected by researchers and actors, simply because the relevant project is based on the active participation of actors as creative and innovative subjects rather than as objects of manipulation or class agitation. In such a case, which is the typical one in participatory discourse-oriented action-research, the results of statistical causal inquiries on consciousness-production are not necessarily irrelevant or uninteresting. They could be part of what Moser has called the information-gathering stage in discourse-oriented action-research. Such studies tell us what base lines and premises have been produced in consciousness, and how, just as we have indicated above. But whereas these base lines were taken as points of departure for persuasive manipulations of people considered as passive objects in action contexts of type 1, they are seen as premises for discourse among people seen as active subjects in action contexts of type 2. Raising the consciousness of people in contexts of type 2 may require some element of knowledge about modes of manipulation of human consciousness, or of the process by which various types of class struggle shape class consciousness. But in addition a transcendence of such manipulative or processual

consciousness-production is required in action contexts of type 2, and such transcendence involves discourse.

Our argument can now be summed up as follows. Since manipulative and processual consciousness-production is a fact of life it must be studied as such with research methods relevant for the discovery of the causal relationships involved. But the consciousness produced and studied in such a manner could be seen not as base lines for further manipulative or processual consciousness-production among those previously submitted to such manipulations or processes, but as premises for inquiry and discourse among actors becoming involved in projects of emancipation and self-managed change. Such action projects require a different research methodology which supplements the other methods mentioned above. These different methods are not less scientific in character than methods geared to causal manipulation, unless you assume that only impersonal causal relations and not human discourse is the rightful domain of scientific analysis and application.

The fact that social sciences were for a long time preoccupied with tackling problems of causal explanation, and therefore left the domain of human discourse unexplored, explains the scientifically rather undeveloped stage of methods relevant for studies within this latter domain, but does not make such study less significant from a scientific point of view. We are all produced by society — but we are also producers of society. Social science paradigms still prevailing have a lot to contribute to the understanding of how we are produced by society — but have little if anything to say on how we produce or could produce society. Both domains are legitimate areas of scientific analysis, but the area most neglected obviously needs more attention at present.

Rejected long ago were the ideas of Rousseau and Hobbes on the construction of society through a 'social contract' emerging out of some original 'natural condition'. These ideas were replaced not by a more scientific analysis of modes of construction of society by conscious and innovative human beings, but rather by theories viewing the development of society and the societal moulding of man as a result of impersonal and irresistible laws similar to those established in the natural sciences. As I have already indicated such theories are needed and quite legitimate, but also insufficient. Insufficient also are the various phenomenological theories on the construction of individual social reality, since they leave the problem of the conscious construction of society unattended.

Today theories on modes of construction of society by man must take off not from a reconstruction of a mythical 'natural condition' but from an understanding of contemporary society as a given point of departure for the construction of the future. Such construction involves a struggle, with an uncertain outcome, among actors with diverse and even contradictory interests, contradictions produced by the given social structure and resolvable by structural transformations, that is by rational rearrangements of structural elements. The true successors of long-since outdated ideas of social contract are therefore theories of structural contradictions, and structural rearrangements or transformations addressing themselves to such structural contradictions in a realistic, rational and innovative fashion, with due regard to the relative strengths and possible strategies of various groups of actors struggling to promote or prevent such structural change. A crucial element in the building of such theories is the explication of concepts of structural rationality. Existing theories of actor rationality cannot resolve the problems here involved since the aggregation of rational decisions by individual actors cannot be used as a method to arrive at conclusions regarding overall societal rationality.

In the Marxist tradition we can find the beginnings of a discussion of structural rationality based on concepts of structural compatibility and contradiction. But many Marxist intellectuals so far seem to have been interested mainly in applying their theories in a natural-science-like fashion to 'explain the world' better than other intellectuals. The task of 'changing the world', subject as it is to all kinds of constraints ranging from military and police repression to the limitations of more or less effective reformist struggle, has usually not been enlightened in concrete detail by careful and realistic Marxist analysis. This is a neglect which our research committee might wish to remedy, remembering that the main difference between an idealistic or utopian construction of the future, and a scientific and innovative mode of construction, is the care and attention given to an understanding of the present societal problems and contradictions to be resolved. For the idealist utopian the point of departure for the construction of the future is not a scientific account and understanding of the present, but ethically-based observations on discrepancies between ethical norms and social realities.

In attempting to remedy this neglect, we will certainly become involved in new controversies. The notions of structural rationality and structural innovation lend themselves to explications both in terms of top-heavy, centralized social engineering and in terms of local conscientization in a grass-roots struggle for a change from below. As long as no one of us claim, or are believed to possess, the whole truth, these further controversies will probably contribute a great deal to a fruitful discussion of innovative processes in societal change within our research committee.

NOTES

1. Through the devoted efforts of the Secretary of the Research Committee on Innovative Processes in Social Change, Ellen Hill, quite a number of the papers presented at the 7th and 8th World Congresses of Sociology in Varna 1970 and Toronto 1974, and also some papers presented at a regional meeting of the research committee in Zürich, September 1976, have been published in three volumes of the *International Review of Community Development* (Winter 1972 and 1975 and Summer 1977). Ellen Hill and Orlando Fals Borda have supplied these three volumes with useful introductions which elucidate the birth and part of the history of the research committee. See also a shorter notice by Ellen Hill (1974) published in *Current Sociology*. Papers from an International Symposium on Action Research, organized by Orlando Fals Borda and held in Cartagena, Colombia, in April 1977, have been published in two volumes: *Crítica y Política en Ciencias Sociales. El Debate Sobre Teoría y Practica* (Bogota: Punta de Lanza, 1978). Heinz Moser and Helmut Ornauer (1978) have published German translations of a selection of the Cartagena papers. An interesting meta-theoretical and methodological paper presented by Paul Oquist at the Cartagena Symposium has been published separately in a Scandinavian journal, *Acta Sociologica* (1978). Fals Borda's paper at the same Symposium, 'For Praxis: How to Investigate Reality in Order to Transform It' has been published in *Dialectical Anthropology* (Spring 1979). Y. M. Bodeman (1979) has further developed his Cartagena contribution in 'The Fulfillment of Fieldwork in Marxist Praxis' in the same journal.
2. The three sessions of the Working Group on Modernization and Diffusion of Innovations held at the World Congress of Sociology in Varna in 1970 were chaired by Orlando Fals Borda, Everett M. Rogers and Alex Inkeles, respectively, and contained papers, for instance, by Lalit Sen ('Modernization as Synthesis'), Luis A. Costa Pinto ('Social Change, Modernization and Crisis'), Everett M. Rogers et al. ('Cross-Cultural Generalizations about the Diffusion of Innovations Research in Brazil, Nigeria and India'), Astrid Nypan ('Diffusion of Innovation and Community Leadership in East Africa'), M. Chernea et al. ('Socioeconomic Structure and Diffusion of Innovation in the Cooperative Village'), William H. Form et al. ('The Accommodation of Rural and Urban Workers to Industrial Discipline and Urban Living: A Four-Nation Study') and Olatunde Oloko ('Management Rationality and Employee Commitment to Industrial Employment in Nigeria').
3. See Everett Rogers et al. at the Varna Congress (see note 2) and the paper by Niels Röling et al. mentioned later in this paper.

4. Varga's paper, 'Modernization: A Hungarian View', was distributed in the form of reprints. Unfortunately I have lost the reprint, and cannot now indicate the source of publication.

5. For an empirical comparison of distributional and welfare aspects of one socialist and one non-socialist country, Bulgaria and Greece, which were at about the same level of economic development immediately after the Second World War, see a paper by Hans Apel published in Jens Qvortrup (1978). In the book by Raymond A. Bauer, Alex Inkeles and Clyde Kluckhohn (1956) *How the Soviet System Works*, based on extensive interviews with emigrés and refugees from the Soviet Union, the authors point out that those interviewed, in spite of their negative attitude toward the political system of Stalin's USSR, were virtually unanimous in their appreciation of the Soviet welfare system — particularly in comparison with the systems of welfare in the European and North American countries where they were interviewed.

6. The expression 'dig where you stand' derives from the title of a book by a Swedish author, Sven Lindqvist (*Gräv där du står*, 1978). The book is a manual for the layman about how to carry out research on the local history of enterprises, communities, etc., with illustrations from research carried out by the author himself on the basis of material found in generally-available archives, documentation centres and public libraries, or derived from interviews with old-timers who spent most of their lifetime at the enterprise chosen as object of research.

7. The two last examples, illustrating some of the problems involved in delimiting actors in action-research, I came to know in a series of seminars on action-research held at the Centre for the Study of Working-Life, Stockholm, in the Spring of 1980, and organized by Åke Sandberg, a well-known Swedish action-researcher.

8. The papers by Huizer, Swedner and Rudqvist were presented at our Symposium in Cartagena, April 1977, and have been published in the two volumes in Spanish mentioned in note 1. A paper by U. Himmelstrand and A. Rudqvist, based on the research carried out by Rudqvist in a project initiated and planned by Orlando Fals Borda, was published in *International Review of Community Development*, Winter 1975. The papers by Mamak, Park, Cordero and Sennett (presented at the 9th World Congress in our committee) refer to projects in New Guinea, South Korea, Chile and Australia respectively. A world meeting on participatory research held in Ljubljana (Yugoslavia) in April 1979 under the sponsorship of UNESCO and the International Council for Adult Education produced a significant advancement in identifying projects and circulating pertinent literature.

9. The DEMOS project (Democratic Planning and Control in Working Life) has published most of its reports in Swedish. However, a presentation of the project in English can be found in Åke Sandberg (ed.), *Computers Dividing Man and Work* (Stockholm: Arbetslivscentrum, 1979).

10. Any readers involved in or knowing about other such projects are invited to get in touch with the president or vice-president of our research committee: Orlando Fals Borda, Apartado Aéreo 52508, Bogota DE, Colombia; Ulf Himmelstrand, Institute of Sociology, PO Box 513, S-751 20 Uppsala, Sweden.

11. See the paper by Everett M. Rogers et al. mentioned in note 2.

REFERENCES

Bauer, R. A., Inkeles, A. and Kluckhohn, C. (1956) *How the Soviet System Works.* Cambridge, Mass.: Harvard University Press.

Björling, Bam and Johansson, Stina (1980) 'Behandlingsforskning — problemlösande eller konfliktskapande?' (Research on Care and Treatment — Problem-solving or Conflict-generating?). Uppsala: unpublished paper.

Bodeman, Y. M. (1979) 'The Fulfillment of Fieldwork in Marxist Praxis', *Dialectical Anthropology*, 4: 155-61.

Cartwright, D. and Harary, F. (1959) 'Structural Balance: A Generalization of Heider's Theory', *Psychological Review*, 63: 277-93.

Fals Borda, Orlando (1977) 'Por la Praxis: el Problema de Cómo Investigar la Realidad para Transformarla', ch. 9 in Volume I of Collection 3 (see below); also in English, in *Dialectical Anthropology* (Spring 1979).

Fals Borda, Orlando (1980) 'Science and the Common People'. Unpublished paper.

Hage, J. and Hollingsworth, J. R. (1978) 'Centralization and the Diffusion Process of Medical Innovation'. Paper presented to the Research Committee on Innovative Processes in Social Change at the 9th World Congress of Sociology, Uppsala, August.

Hale, S. M. (1974) 'Barriers to Free Choice in Development'. Paper presented to the Research Committee on Innovative Processes in Social Change at the 8th World Congress of Sociology, Toronto, 1974, published in Collection 2 (see below).

Hill, Ellen B. (1974) 'Innovative Processes in Social Change', *Current Sociology*, XXII, 1-3.

Himmelstrand, U. (1977) 'Action Research and Applied Social Science: Scientific Value, Practical Benefits and Abuses', published in Spanish and German in Collections 4 and 5 (see below).

Himmelstrand, U. and Rudqvist, A. (1975) 'Structural Contradictions, Predicaments and Social Change. Some Theoretical and Empirical Observations'. Paper presented to the Research Committee on Innovative Processes in Social Change at the 8th World Congress of Sociology, Toronto, 1974, published in Collection 2 (see below).

Himmelstrand, U., Ahrne, G., Lundberg, L. and Lundberg, L. (1981) *Beyond Welfare Capitalism. Issues, Actors and Forces in Societal Change.* London: Heinemann.

Huizer, Gerrit (1977) 'Investigación Activa y Resistencia Campesina. Algunas Experiencias en el Tercer Mundo', published in Collection 4 (see below).

Katz, Elihu and Lazarsfeld, Paul (1955) *Personal Influence: The Part Played by People in the Flow of Masscommunications.* Glencoe, Ill.: Free Press.

Lerner, Daniel (1958) *The Passing of Traditional Society. Modernizing the Middle East.* Glencoe, Ill.: Free Press.

Lévi-Strauss, Claude (1967) *Structural Anthropology.* New York: Doubleday Anchor Books.

Lewin, Kurt (1948) *Resolving Social Conflicts.* New York: Harper & Brothers.

Lindqvist, Sven (1978) *Gräv där du står* (Dig Where You Stand). Stockholm: Bonniers.

Meidner, Rudolf (1978) *Employee Investment Funds. An Approach to Collective Capital Formation.* London: Allen & Unwin.
Moser, Heinz (1977) 'Action-research as a New Research Paradigm in the Social Sciences', published in Spanish as ch. 5 in Volume I of Collection 4 (see below); also in 5 (below).
Oquist, Paul (1977) 'The Epistemological Basis of Action-research', *Acta Sociologica*, 1, 1978: 143-63 (also published in Collections 4 and 5; see below).
Qvortrup, Jens (ed.) (1978) *Social struktur og levestandard i Osteuropa.* Esbjerg: Sydjysk Universitetsforlag.
Rogers, E. M., Ashcroft, J. and Röling, N. (1970) 'Cross-cultural Generalizations about the Diffusion of Innovations Research in Brazil, Nigeria and India'. Paper presented at the 7th World Congress of Sociology, Varna.
Röling, N., Ashcroft, J. and Chege, F. W. (1974) 'Innovation and Equity in Rural Development'. Paper presented to the Research Committee on Innovative Processes in Social Change at the 8th World Congress of Sociology, Toronto.
Rudqvist, Anders (1977) 'Reflexión Crítica sobre una Experiencia de Investigación-Acción en Colombia', published as ch. 4 in Volume II of Collection 4 (see below).
Sandberg, Åke (ed.) (1979) *Computers Dividing Man and Work.* Stockholm: Arbetslivscentrum.
Swedner, Harald (1977) 'Deficiencias en la Investigación-Acción y en el Trabajo de Communidad', published as ch. 5 in Volume II of Collection 4 (see below).
Touraine, Alain (1968) *Le Mouvement de Mai ou le communisme utopique.* Paris: Le Seuil.
Touraine, Alain (1974) *Pour la sociologie. Lettre à une etudiante.* Paris: Le Seuil.
Touraine, Alain (1979) *La voix et le regard.* Paris: Edition Seuil.
Turner, Ralph (1956) 'Role-Taking, Role Standpoint, and Reference-Group Behavior', *American Journal of Sociology*: 316-28.
van de Vall, Mark et al. (1978) 'Policy-research as an Agent of Planned Change in Advanced Social Systems'. Paper presented to the Research Committee on Innovative Processes in Social Change at the 9th World Congress of Sociology, Uppsala.
Varga, Károly (1974) 'Modernization: A Hungarian View'. Paper presented to the Research Committee on Innovative Processes in Social Change at the 8th World Congress of Sociology, Toronto.
Willener, Alfred (1970) *The Action-Image of Society.* London: Tavistock.
Wright, Erik Olin (1976) 'Class Boundaries in Advanced Capitalist Societies', *New Left Review*, 98.

COLLECTIONS OF PAPERS PRESENTED TO THE RESEARCH COMMITTEE ON INNOVATIVE PROCESSES IN SOCIAL CHANGE

1 *International Review of Community Development*, Winter 1972. Rome: Centro di Educazione Professionale per Assistenti Sociali. This and the following two collections were international issues of *Centro Sociale*.
2 *International Review of Community Development*, Winter 1975. Rome: Centro di Educazione Professionale per Assistenti Sociali.

3 *International Review of Community Development*, Summer 1977. Rome: Centro di Educazione Professionale per Assistenti Sociali.
4 *Crítica y Política en Ciencias Sociales. El Debate Teoría y Práctica*, Vol. I and II. Bogota: Punta de Lanza, 1978.
5 Moser, Heinz and Ornauer, Helmut (eds) (1978) *Internationale Aspekte der Aktions-Forschung*. München: Kösel-Verlag.

2
Contemporary Alienation Theory and Research

David Schweitzer
University of British Columbia

INTRODUCTION

Despite some scepticism which has arisen over the meaning and viability of alienation, either as a tool of social inquiry or as an instrument for social criticism, scholarly interest in the idea of alienation has persisted as never before in the contemporary career of the concept. The large and rapidly increasing body of literature in philosophy and the social sciences, and the growing international multidisciplinary group of scholars and researchers presently engaged in alienation theory and research, suggest that the study of alienation has emerged today as a firm and legitimate field in its own right.[1]

Considerable controversy over important problems and issues which divide alienation theorists nevertheless remains. The debate over a wide range of intellectual and ideological issues can be traced largely to fundamental epistemic problems concerning the way questions and answers about alienation are formulated, researched, and ultimately acted upon. Several of these issues have arisen in the course of the evolution and secularization of the concept, from its early intellectual roots which go as far back as ancient philosophy and the Gnostic-mystic tradition in medieval theology, to contemporary theoretical and empirical research applications in the social

---

I am indebted to Dr. R. Felix Geyer of the Netherlands Universities' Joint Social Research Centre for his invaluable support during almost a decade of collaboration on numerous scholarly and organizational projects associated with the ISA Research Committee on Alienation Theory and Research, including the joint delivery of an earlier version of this essay at the ISA Research Council meetings in Warsaw, August 1980.

sciences. Another set of issues are centred more specifically around a fundamental debate within contemporary Marxism concerning the meaning, usefulness, and relevancy of the alienation concept.

Many of the current trends and issues outlined below are closely interconnected. They have been separated only for purposes of the present discussion in an attempt to bring some critical clarity to several of the debates and controversies which divide students of alienation today.

ALIENATION: AN OBJECTIVE SOCIETAL CONDITION OR A SUBJECTIVE STATE OF INDIVIDUAL CONSCIOUSNESS?

The uncompromising emphasis on alienation as a strictly objective or materialist structural phenomenon has been a long-standing one in most Marxist approaches. Yet one striking development within contemporary Marxist theory is the increasing recognition that subjective elements of individually perceived and felt alienation are worthy of theoretical and empirical examination in their own right.

At the same time, non-Marxist scholars and researchers, often disenchanted with standard survey research techniques and individualistic psychological approaches, are rediscovering Marx's classical idea of alienation as an objective condition pertaining to the structural relations of domination and subordination, appropriation and exploitation, and power or control in society. Several survey researchers are focussing specifically on structural forms or manifestations of alienation arising from the substantive complexity of work, or the extent to which workers have immediate control over the work process.

Most scholars today, Marxist and non-Marxist alike, recognize and often address themselves to both the subjective and objective dimensions of alienation. A major controversy has arisen in the last two decades, however, concerning the legitimate point of departure for conceptualizing, analyzing, and then responding to alienation. To emphasize one dimension over another in one's conceptual approach implies a more fundamental epistemic choice with ideological and practical implications.

The controversy has evolved in two distinct, yet related, directions: (1) the humanist-materialist debate within Marxism, which not only revives the long-standing controversy over 'two Marxisms or one', but also pits the new wave of Althusserian structuralism against the growing thrust of Marxist humanism on both sides of the Atlantic; (2) the response, especially among the European theorists and Marxist critics, to the psychological reduction and neutralization of the alienation concept which prevails in the mainstream American tradition of empirical survey research. Controversies over these fundamental issues within the alienation field have been conducted with near-religious fervour.

What is at stake here is a choice not so much between objective and subjective definitions of alienation, but between competing epistemologies and departure points explicitly associated with these distinct conceptualizations of alienation. The choice between objective and subjective concepts, with their concomitant points of departure, determines not only the way questions and answers about alienation are formulated, but also the methodologies, strategies, and remedies for change, action, and de-alienation. At this level, the stakes among intellectuals and practitioners alike seem to be very high.

Most theorists and empirical researchers working within a Marxist frame of reference today tend to take a dual stance on the objective-subjective issue. Polish philosopher Adam Schaff (1980), for one, recognizes and expands upon both objective and subjective conceptions of alienation in Marx's works. In the first instance, alienation is treated as an objective relation pertaining to the products of man which become, in a metaphoric sense, alienated, regardless of how he thinks or feels about it. Schaff distinguishes this from self-alienation, a subjective social relation in the sense that it is man who alienates himself from a world that he has socially created, from other people, and from his own 'ego'. Subjective self-alienation for Schaff then rests in the feelings, experiences, and attitudes of man.

The Chasm between Classic Theory and Empirical Research

While Marxist analysis and survey techniques may appear as odd bedfellows, especially given the long-standing association between structural-functional analysis and the mainstream tradition of survey research, a few recent empirical efforts have indicated that survey techniques can be applied in certain qualified ways toward an empirical investigation into Marx's theory of alienation.

Canadian sociologist Peter Archibald (1976), for example, provides a few useful leads with his conceptual reformulation of

Marx's four dimensions of alienated labour and the application of corresponding behavioural indicators and measures of work alienation (e.g. overtime work without extra pay), in addition to the usual attitudinal job-satisfaction items. This operational procedure at the same time adheres to a reasonably firm Marxian analytic framework.

A few other empirical efforts in this vein are worth noting (e.g. Kohn, 1977, 1976; Tudor, 1972; Meissner, 1970; Blauner, 1964) where emphasis is placed on some of the objective conditions of work in addition to the standard survey items on the subjective alienations. The objective dimensions in these studies include measures of the technical constraints and substantive complexities of work, the degree of individual responsibility on the job, the variety of tasks to be performed, the conditions of occupational self-direction, the extent of routinization and supervision, and the extent to which workers have immediate control over the process of work and production. Manifestations of labour unrest, tardiness, absenteeism, labour turnover, insubordination, industrial accidents, and product sabotage might be singled out as possible behavioural indicators of alienated or degraded labour amenable to empirical measurement (cf. Braverman, 1974, pp. 31-39; Rinehart, 1975, pp. 68-81; Afonja, 1978).

Empirical efforts in the Soviet Union and a few East European countries have also included survey items in their research designs concerning the extent of influence that structural factors such as the division of labour, specialization, technology, and automation have on work dissatisfaction (cf. Ludz, 1975, p. 37; Fischer, 1967, p. 15; for a unique alternative to all of these approaches from a prominent Marxist philosopher of the German Democratic Republic, see Klaus, 1962, and the review by Ludz, 1975, pp. 32-33).

These empirical efforts among Marxists and non-Marxists alike point to some of the theoretical directions and empirical possibilities for further work which attempts to bridge the chasm between the classic Marxian notion of alienation and contemporary empirical research applications (also see the criteria for a bridging solution outlined in Fischer, 1976).

This clearly remains as one of the priority concerns in the alienation field today. Apart from these efforts, there is little systematic empirical research that provides for an adequately grounded investigation into Marx's theory of alienation. Although Marx's analytical differentiations of alienated labour are cited repeatedly by social scientists, they are seldom developed to the point where they can be usefully applied in empirical research.

The Debate within Marxism

Not all alienation theorists or researchers, however, are in agreement with these current trends. Joachim Israel (1976), a Danish sociologist, among others, takes exception to the emphasis on subjective alienation in Marxist analysis. He has argued for a shift in the point of departure: from Marx's philosophical anthropology to historico-structural and empirical analysis; from alienated labour to commodity fetishism; from a theory of alienation to a theory of reification. His emphasis is on objective structural forms of alienation and the process of reification. Implicit in his rationale for a new departure point is the suggestion that Marx abandoned his theory of alienation — with its essentialist preconditions — in his later, more mature works.

Another current element in the debate within Marxism is taken up by two American Marxist sociologists in the Althusserian vein, John Horton and Manuel Moreno (1981). Rather than abandoning the concept of alienation, they argue for a careful Marxist rethinking and reformulation of the concept from the point of view of historical materialism. Their charge is that the concept has been coopted by 'petty bourgeois idealists' and some socialists. The 'philosophical reductionism' of Lukaćs and the Budapest School, the humanist concerns of Marković and others of the Yugoslav Praxis group, and the essentialist readings of Marx by Marcuse, Adorno, Horkheimer and others of the Frankfurt School are especially singled out for vehement attack.

As Horton and Moreno see it, these different approaches to alienation have distorted or subverted the main object of Marxist analysis: class analysis and class struggle. Moreover, cooptation of the concept by humanists, economistic bureaucrats, revisionists, and reformers alike has obscured and perpetuated class differences in both capitalist and state-socialist societies. While Horton and Moreno recognize that the Marxist conception of alienation may point to real, often new, forms of class contradiction and struggle, they argue that it is too often formulated from what they consider to be a theoretically and politically regressive class standpoint. Or as Althusser (1976, p. 63) puts it, the revival of alienation in the last couple of decades signals a 'regression from the theoretical gains of historical materialism and a revision of proletarian politics.'

The call here is for a purge which exorcises the concept of its philosophical humanism, essentialist underpinnings, and ontological connotations inherited from Hegel by the young, presumably 'immature' Marx. It must be reappropriated, restored, and returned to its rightful place: to a proletarian standpoint within the theoretical framework of historical materialism and class analysis.

Harry Braverman's (1974) study of the conditions of labour in contemporary American society, considered by many Marxists a landmark of critical analysis, provides what Horton and Moreno see as the model for future Marxist studies of alienation. Braverman's analysis of the degradation of labour places the concept of alienation squarely in the framework of class analysis and in the hands of the proletariat by extending Marx's analysis of the division of labour to the conditions of monopoly capital. His approach toward a rehabilitated treatment of alienation narrows on the specific conditions of the working class and the very specific history of the producer's loss of control over the process of production. This has generated lively sectarian debate over both major and trivial points among American Marxists concerning the political implications and theoretical adequacy of Braverman's work, and more specifically concerning the concepts of alienation and class, the process of class formation, and the nature of class struggle (see the commentaries by Szymanski et al., 1978).

The humanist-materialist debate over is a long-standing one which continues today in new forms under the impetus of Althusser's works, and in France with the backlash polemics and controversies generated by several of his disenchanted students of the 1960s, *les nouveaux philosophes* (cf. F. Lévy's *Karl Marx, histoire d'un bourgeois allemand*; J.-M. Benoist's *La revolution structurale*; A. Glucksmann's *Les maîtres penseurs*; also see Gouldner, 1980). Despite the new twists and turns that the debate has taken, there nevertheless appears to be a marked consensus today among both Marxists and non-Marxists concerning at least one important point: while Marx may have abandoned the term 'alienation', he did not abandon the idea or the fundamental questions raised by it.

The Mainstream Tradition of Empirical Research and Its Critics

Ironically, the growing acceptance of subjective notions of alienation among some Marxist scholars today is paralleled by a gradual recognition of objective conceptualizations among non-Marxist scholars and empirical researchers. Marvin Olsen (1976), for one, has documented his recent disenchantment with standard attitudinal approaches to psychological conceptualizations of the alienation phenomenon. He suggests, for example, that the term 'political powerlessness' be reserved for those objective situations in which the sociopolitical system prevents individuals from exercising an effective influence on governmental decisions, policies, and actions.

The call here is for social scientists—especially survey researchers—to 'rediscover' Marx's classical idea of alienation which refers to a set of objective social conditions; political powerlessness in this sense is an objective fact, not a subjective view of the world.

Olsen and others are responding to the mainstream social psychological tradition of survey research which has dominated most empirical approaches to alienation in the United States since Melvin Seeman's (1959) influential conceptual work more than two decades ago. The emphasis in this empirico-conceptual approach is on the actor's personal expectations and values, and the psychological varieties of alienation (e.g. individual perceptions of powerlessness, meaninglessness, normlessness, isolation, and self-estrangement) are generally treated as intervening variables which link structural conditions to behavioural outcomes. It is rare, however, that this full macro-triadic relation is treated within a single study. And while most researchers in this empirical tradition tend to recognize this general scheme, it is seldom understood in any substantial theoretical way. This approach has nevertheless led to a staggering proliferation of terms in the social sciences and to a massive outpouring of empirical results.

One recent development in the debate over subjective conceptualizations and empirical measures of alienation is reflected in the charges levelled specifically at survey researchers who claim to have reconciled their empirical applications with Marx's theory of alienation. Archibald et al. (1981), for example, claim that while there is some overlap between some of Seeman's varieties of psychological alienation and certain psychological aspects of Marx's conceptualization, an important gap between theory and research nevertheless remains. In their view, these psychological conceptualizations of alienation gloss over Marx's four analytical dimensions of alienated labour (i.e. alienation from labour, products, others, and self) by relying too exclusively on individual perceptions, feelings, and attitudes as indicators of alienation rather than on behavioural indicators and structural measures of alienation. They are consequently reluctant to accept at face value many of the conclusions generated in previous research concerning the validity of Marx's theory of alienation.

This critique is not very new. But as they aptly point out, researchers who continue to apply these standard attitudinal alienation items in their surveys continue to mislead us in a number of important ways. They especially take issue with the claim by researchers from Blauner (1964) to Kohn (1976) that propertylessness is not an important source of subjective alienation. Archibald and his associates argue the contrary: first by starting from what they view as a more theoretically relevant Marxian conception of class which treats private property, the division of labour, and commodity exchange as interdependent structural components; and second by employing a mixture of alternative and presumably more appropriate attitudinal and behavioural indicators of work-related alienation among comparative samples of the Canadian and American labour forces. Their results contradict previous findings by indicating, among other things, that property ownership does have an important explanatory impact on alienation according to their measures, i.e. owners of the means of production express much less work-related alienation than do the propertyless.

The issues at hand are theoretical, conceptual, and empirical. The call is for theoretical analysis, conceptual refinement, and empirical measures which remain true to Marx's classic theory of alienation in general and to his concept of alienated labour in particular. The work by Archibald represents one effort toward bridging the wide gap which exists between classic theory and empirical research applications in the social sciences.

The vigorous response among the francophone sociologists and critics adds another important dimension to the debate (Thibault, 1981: Touraine,1977; Vidal, 1969; Lefebvre, 1961). As they correctly argue, the subjective emphasis on the actor's state of mind usually takes the problem out of the domain of sociological analysis and understanding. Or, as the Althusserian structuralists argue, any kind of reductionism (philosophical, essentialist, empirico-psychological) takes the problem of alienation out of the proper domain of historical materialism, class analysis and class struggle.

What is at stake here is a strategic epistemic choice between competing paradigms and departure points in the study of alienation — a choice which determines not only the way questions and answers about alienation are formulated and researched, but also the strategies for change, action, and de-alienation. The starting point for the empiricists is usually the isolated individual rather than the organization of social relationships. By relocating the problem of alienation in the individual, solutions to the problem also tend to start with the individual, i.e. solutions which emphasize individual adaptation or conformity to the predominant values and institutions of society rather than organized collective action directed toward substantive or radical structural changes. There is often no other recourse in an approach to alienation which ignores or underplays sociological analysis.

In the realm of work, for example, this usually means accommodating changes within the existing structure and process of the work situation, or adjustive changes in workers' attitudes toward it. As Mandel and Novak (1970), also Braverman (1974) argue, what the 'human relations' experts in industry are attempting to abolish is not the objective reality of alienating labour but the worker's awareness of this reality. Or, as German social psychologist Walter Heinz (1981) observes in a recent study, preoccupational class-influenced socialization processes are operating already at an early age. The family prepares individuals for an adaptive normative acceptance of alienating work conditions and a built-in readiness to absorb inhuman or impersonal conditions associated with the organization of work. In the process, individuals develop coping mechanisms, value orientations, and attitudes which blur or mask fundamental contradictions in the work situation in order to alleviate the stress that they would otherwise experience. It is interesting, in this respect, to compare Heinz's approach with Manderscheid's (1981) unique biopsychosocial perspective on alienation, stress, and coping.

Existential Psychiatric, Phenomenological, and Ontological Perspectives

While the accent has been on sociological and sociopsychological approaches to alienation, social scientists have also begun to draw from the long-standing traditions of psychiatry, phenomenology, existentialism, and ontology. One of the current trends in the interdisciplinary field of alienation is characterized by recent theoretical efforts which draw on these traditions, toward a critical synthesis with Marxist theories of alienation, reification, and false consciousness.

Joseph Gabel's innovative development of a general psychological theory of consciousness, and of the conditions of dialectical thought in particular, appeared in English only recently (1975, orig. edn. 1962), and it is now beginning to have some impact on the anglophone social sciences. Gabel, a Hungaro-French sociologist and student of Lukács, has drawn a few striking parallels and potential lines of cross-fertilization between Marxist social theory, existential psychiatry, and phenomenological sociology. While these perspectives stem from separate intellectual traditions, they are to some extent complementary and convergent. As Gabel observes, Marx's early writings on alienated labour 'anticipated certain mechanisms that psychiatrists discovered only much later in their own research' (p. xxi). For Gabel, the concepts of reification and false consciousness developed in Marx's later works find their parallels in schizophrenia, i.e. false consciousness viewed as a diffused and depersonalized state of mind resulting from a regression in the dialectical quality of experience.[2]

Another ambitious preparatory effort toward merger and synthesis comes from an American social psychiatrist, Frank Johnson (1976). He draws from phenomenology, existential psychiatry, and several analytical leads in Israel's (1971) reformulation of reification theory, toward the development of a therapeutic orientation to alienated or schizoid persons.

And in an entirely different vein, American philosopher John Lachs (1976) has formulated his approach around the concepts of 'psychic distance' and 'mediation'. These terms, he claims, deal more objectively and accurately with all the phenomena embodied in the classic Marxian idea of alienation. The individual and his actions are the point of departure in Lachs' philosophy of action. Mediated action — or action performed on behalf of another person — produces certain dehumanizing consequences: a growing readiness to manipulate human beings and to view them as tools, as means to an end; a growing sense of passivity and impotence; and an increasing sense of psychic distance between men and their actions.

Shlomo Shoham (1976, 1979), an Israeli sociologist and criminologist, departs radically from the mainstream with an illuminating brand of ontological existentialism and the application of rich illustrative metaphors from Greek mythology. Alienation, for Shoham, is an ontologically given condition which propels individual action but which cannot be overcome by action. 'Separation', a vector opposed to 'participation' in this conceptualization, refers to universal influences on the individual which operate independently of social relationships. The pressures of separation which stem from three developmental stages that every individual passes through (birth, the moulding of an 'ego boundary', and socialization into an 'ego identity') produce a corresponding desire for participation; but striving to overcome separation through participation is futile: this gap between ontological separation and ineffective participatory efforts to overcome it cannot be bridged.

The important point here is that ontological separation is the consequence of interaction with the environment. Shoham therefore rejects the Marxist principle of involvement through action. Yet he does not deny that individuals try to reach their goals through social action, even though this is self-defeating insofar as their real goal — regaining a lost participatory bliss — is concerned. The achievement motive, for example, which characterizes the more industrialized 'tool-oriented' societies is viewed as a participation surrogate that leads to either one of two possible final states. Allowing oneself to be propelled by the achievement motive ultimately leads to *anomic ressentiment*, illustrated by the myth of Sisyphus; but when the individual comes to the full realization that the achievement motive does not bring him what he had hoped for and consequently gives it up, the result is *accidie*, represented by the myth of Tantalus.

PSYCHOLOGICAL REDUCTIONISM: A METHODOLOGICAL CHOICE WITH IDEOLOGICAL IMPLICATIONS

One of the continuing trends in the evolution of the alienation theme in the social sciences is the empirico-psychological reduction and value-neutralization of the classic concept according to the specifications and requirements of mainstream survey research methods. Marxist critics in particular have argued that this secularization or 'dehumanization' (Horton, 1964) of the concept has obscured its classic meaning.[3] By reducing alienation to psychological variates and attitudinal measures, the emphasis in meaning has shifted from normative evaluation to descriptive analysis. This, of course, is one of the intended purposes of such reductionism, i.e. to produce a scientific empirico-analytical tool devoid of evaluative pretensions.

One of the underlying issues at stake centres around questions concerning the viability of an empirical research tradition which continues to operate exclusively within a rigid positivist logic of social inquiry, especially when dealing with concepts such as alienation which stem primarily from a dialectical paradigm of critical inquiry. By shifting the source of meaning from an historico-structural conflict frame of reference to an ahistorical socio-psychological frame of scientific analysis, the meaning of alienation has been severed from its roots in the critical philosophies of Hegel and Marx. The concept, in effect, has been stripped of its radical polemical content and normative critical power.[4]

But it is only the appearance of value-neutrality and objectivity that has been achieved by this secular reduction. Built into this 'neutrality' is a masked or unwitting brand of conservatism which tends to emphasize individual adaptation or conformity to existing structural conditions at the expense of substantive or radical structural changes. The neutralization and reduction of alienation then — from a critical normative-evaluative concept to a descriptive analytic tool for scientific inquiry — is a normative process in its own right, with its own predetermined value-judgments and directives for change and action.

These trends have inexorably led to what might be viewed as the over-psychologization of the concept of alienation, reinforced by a limited theoretical understanding of the classic notion of alienation and the virtual absence of macrosociological research methods. With only a few exceptions, it is rare for empirical alienation studies to encompass the structural or environmental determinants of the psychological alienation variates typically selected for investigation. As a result researchers in this tradition are severely restricted in their efforts to make grounded judgments about the determining structural conditions of alienation in the wider society. Basically at issue here are only individual feelings, perceptions, and attitudes at a given moment in time. By focussing on the subjective state of individuals, social structural problems and historico-material conditions which are assumed to lie at the source of the psychological alienations are, by definition, too easily ignored or excluded from the analysis.

What appears to be lacking in this predominantly American-styled tradition of empirical research is a certain critical dialogue and understanding concerning the broader questions of theory, history, and structural analysis — questions raised largely by European sociologists, and by Marxist critics in particular (e.g. Israel, 1971; Kon, 1969; Vidal, 1969; Touraine, 1967; also Horton and Moreno, 1981). What is usually lacking is a larger mental picture, a macrotheoretical grasp, or an historico-structural understanding of the variables, relationships, and processes involved. The call here is for a balancing emphasis on the larger, more interesting and imaginative questions of sociological theory and historical analysis which draw into their purview some understanding of the structural processes and conditioning mechanisms presumed to lie at the source of the psychological alienations typically selected for special investigation in the mainstream empirical studies. The parallel call is for macrosociological research methods which begin to tap in more direct theory-specific ways the material or structural components of alienation and de-alienation, as well as their subjective manifestations.

THE PROBLEM OF UNITY

The proliferation of alienation concepts, terms, and synonyms which has occurred over the last two decades has produced a corresponding interest in finding a core theme, a common denominator, or a unifying multidimensional concept under which all varieties of alienation can be subsumed. The suggestion is that alienation is a 'syndrome' of diverse forms or manifestations which display a certain unity, and that there is a common meaning which extends beyond some general notion of separation.

Whether this suggestion is plausible, or whether it is even worth pursuing, is a matter for debate. It has been argued that alienation in abstracto does not exist, but that there are innumerable concrete alienations, and that any attempt to merge these into a single multidimensional concept should be abandoned as theoretically and conceptually impossible. Even Marx's subtypes of alienated labour share little more than a common origin and the idea of separation. Ludz (1975, p. 39), however, concludes an earlier review of the literature on an optimistic note with the suggestion that the construction of a general theory of alienation which ties together divergent concepts and methodologies is an ultimate possibility.

Perhaps the single most important factor which has led to the proliferation of terms and concepts of alienation in the social sciences today stems from Seeman's (1959) original conceptualization of five (later extended to six) psychological alienation categories: powerlessness, meaninglessness, normlessness, cultural estrangement or value isolation, self-estrangement, and social isolation. He has insisted, however, that there is no inherent unity among his categories (1972, p. 513). Some theorists nevertheless operate on the principle that there is indeed a common denominator, provided they are viewed at a sufficiently high level of abstraction.

David Hays (1976), for example, has attempted to demonstrate this through a unique application of linguistic philosophy by locating a common denominator in the failure of what he calls the 'natural contract': the principle that an organism can act to obtain what is good for it. The varieties of alienation elucidated by Seeman reflect some of the ways in which this natural contract can be broken, through a severance of positive interaction between a person and his or her natural and social environment.

Felix Geyer's (1980, 1976) innovative application of advanced General Systems Theory to the question of unity is similar. Individuals are conceived of as systems operating in more or less open interaction with significant parts of their environment. Viewed from a relatively high level of abstraction, all forms of alienation involve information processing problems of individuals, and Seeman's varieties of alienation are treated as partial breakdowns of 'normal' system functioning. Powerlessness, for example, is linked with information processing problems located primarily in the system's output such that behavioural alternatives for the individual are severely limited. Geyer and Hays, each in their own way, have attempted to demonstrate a certain kind of unity by raising the level of abstraction.

The empirical evidence on the unity question, based on correlational and factor analyses of attitudinal survey data, is contradictory and inconclusive (cf. Neal and Rettig, 1967, 1963; Streuning and Richardson, 1965; Cartwright, 1965; Simmons, 1964-65). The lack of unity according to the empirical evidence may be due to methodological problems throughout the operationalization procedure, from the different conceptualizations and measurements of the psychological alienation variates to differences in the statistical techniques applied in different studies.

The explanation, however, probably lies more in fundamental epistemic differences which separate these varieties of alienation. The social histories of the concepts of alienation and anomie, for example, are rooted in competing ideologies and normative assumptions about the nature of man and society and about the relation between them. Yet an attempt has been made to merge Marx's radical and optimistic perspective on alienation with Durkheim's basically conservative and pessimistic notion of anomie. The empirico-analytical approach has led to a reduction of Marx's structural-relational concept of alienation to measures of individual powerlessness or inefficacy, and Durkheim's purely sociological concept of anomie to measures of personal normlessness, anomia, or anomy. Once reduced to these psychological categories, efforts are then directed toward demonstrating their unity or disunity statistically.

But if we trace these categories and variates back to their presumed roots in the classic theories, we find that alienation and anomie are counter-concepts. They may both describe similar behaviours and discontents, and they may serve as ethically grounded metaphors for a radical assault on the dominant institutions and values of industrial society, but they are also grounded in different ideologies and assumptions with different directives for change and action (cf. Horton, 1964, 1966; also Lukes, 1967).

This suggests, as many alienation theorists and researchers do , that we would do better to find different and more accurate terms for what is too often subsumed under the term 'alienation'.

PRIORITIES

Conceptual and Terminological Clarification

Perhaps the single most important task which continues to face alienation theorists and researchers of all persuasions centres around problems of meaning, conceptualization, and terminology. What has been lacking is a systematic survey and analysis of the different ways in which alienation theorists and researchers have used the term. Systematic work toward conceptual clarification and terminological precision which cross-cuts traditional disciplinary and paradigmatic boundaries remains a priority concern and a prerequisite for the firm advancement of substantive knowledge in the larger field of alienation theory and research. A few scholars have devoted themselves recently to this difficult undertaking, although they differ considerably in their approaches.

One of the more definitive contributions to date is Peter Ludz's (1979) recent effort toward a systematic terminological and conceptual analysis. He has presented a viable design for studying the etymology and *Geistesgeschichte* of the word and for identifying and analyzing the key writers and different uses of the term. While only in its preparatory stages, it nevertheless provides innovative leads for further terminological and conceptual work which covers an extensive range of meanings and uses in the legal, societal, medico-psychological, and philosophico-theological spheres.

In a parallel effort at breaking new etymological and conceptual ground, Ludz (1981), a German social scientist, retraces the evolution of the term and concept of alienation in Occidental thought. Focussing on the often neglected positive value-connotations of the concept, he delineates the lines of conceptual development — from ancient philosophy and Gnostic-mystic thought (i.e. in Mandean and Manichean thinking, in the philosophy of the *Corpus Hermeticum* and the early Christian Gnosis) through the works of Plotinus (205-270), Augustine (354-430), Thomas Aquinas (1225-1274), and Meister Eckhart (1260-1327) to Fichte and Hegel.

Ludz's treatment of the development of the term and concept in the history of ideas reveals a broader, richer spectrum of meanings and uses encompassing positive, neutral, and negative value-connotations. This tradition stops rather abruptly with Feuerbach and Marx. Ludz, however, picks up the thread again by tracing the Gnostic and Hegelian tradition further to a few 20th century German social scientists (Simmel, Adorno, Gehlen) who have revived, in one way or another, both the positive and negative value-connotations of the concept.

Another major effort in tracing and distinguishing the different meanings and uses of alienation in the history of ideas appears in the chronology of works by American philosopher, Richard Schacht. They range from his survey of the diverse literature on alienation (1970) to several conceptual efforts which attempt to untangle the different meanings of, and distinctions between, objective and subjective forms of alienation. What is particularly refreshing is the systematic logic that Schacht applies to the organization of his arguments and conceptual categories.

In a recent conceptual effort, Schacht (1981) focusses on the economic alienations. The notion of economic alienation is narrowed down to specific relations between economic agents and their economic activity, i.e. between a worker and his labour or role-performance at work. Two types of economic alienation are distinguished: one referring to an economic-relational state of affairs which can be rendered useful as a purely descriptive analytical (neutral) concept in the social sciences; the other referring to an interpretative-evaluative (normative) construct, best suited for moral and humanist criticism with regard to the dominant institutions and values of industrial society. Schacht is concerned with the former. Economic alienation, as a purely descriptive analytical category, is carefully distinguished in objective and subjective forms. The objective forms consist of observable socioeconomic relations and behaviours, and alienation is manifest in economic activities which are uncontrollable, impersonally regimented, and basically anonymous. Uncontrollability here involves the relinquishment or loss of autonomy and control in relation to one's labour and products. The subjective forms of economic alienation consist of experiential and attitudinal states of individuals involved in economic activity, i.e. intrinsic work dissatisfaction.

Schacht also recognizes and works with the positive and neutral value-connotations of alienation, as well as the negative ones. Certain forms of alienation are viewed as objectionable only to the extent to which they are grounded in a normative philosophical anthropology. Negative evaluative significance is conferred on those forms of alienation which contain essentialist claims and humanist commitments concerning the nature of man and the character of a genuinely human life. But part of the formidable task that he has set for himself is to develop a notion of alienation which is independent of any essentialist ideas or normative assumptions about the nature of man and society. His aim is to arrive at a rationale for employing certain notions of alienation for purposes of value-neutral description and empirico-theoretical analysis in the social sciences. Schacht, in effect, has attempted a rationale for neutralizing the concept and transforming it into an objective analytical tool, while at the same time maintaining much of its classic meaning.

Another scholarly effort of recent note appears in John Torrance's (1977) conceptual restatement of the distinct alienation and estrangement themes in the classic theories. Torrance, a British sociologist, maintains a sharp distinction between two elements that are often confused in the concept of alienation: between 'alienation' in the sense of loss or relinquishment (*Entaüsserung*) and 'estrangement' in the sense of strangeness or hostility (*Entfremdung*). While few scholars have pursued this distinction very far, Torrance traces the evolution of these two meanings of alienation, illuminating the theoretical significance of each in ways which fundamentally depart from the approaches of most other contemporary writers. One of the guiding concerns here is to counter the usual ambiguities which have plagued alienation theory by separating and contrasting these two elements in rigorous definitional and conceptual terms that are relevant to sociological theory and empirical research.

More recently, Torrance (1981) has extended this work in an ambitious effort to find a use for the concept of alienation which incorporates social-structural components, owes nothing to philosophy or psychology, is potentially scientific, does not duplicate existing sociological concepts, but nevertheless can claim legitimate descent from the classic theories of Hegel, Feuerbach, and Marx. At the same time, Torrance draws from sociological theories of action and group formation in a bridge-building effort at fusing such neglected theoretical elements as social emotions, meanings, and actions into a reformulated theory of alienation.

Much of the literature and dialogue on alienation is still bedevilled with overly-comprehensive conceptualizations, terminological ambiguity, and indiscriminate applications such that serious discussion is often impaired. In fact, the very meaning of alienation is often diluted to the point of virtual meaninglessness. The etymological and terminological work of Ludz and the conceptual work of Schacht and Torrance, among others (Geyer and Schweitzer, 1981; Hays, 1976; Fischer, 1976; Johnson, 1973), represent a determined effort at countering these tendencies.

Toward a Propositional Inventory and General Theory Construction

Alienation theory and research have evolved to the point where we could now draw on the leads of Ludz and others toward establishing an inventory of propositions and empirical findings. This calls for a systematic survey of the literature in the field, especially with regard to empirical statements and hypotheses about alienation in relation to available empirical results. This could be viewed as an early step toward determining the extent of grounded knowledge in the field.

The only effort which begins to touch on these concerns appears in Seeman's (1975) summary review of developments in the empirical literature with respect to his psychological varieties of alienation. While restricted to the mainstream empirical tradition of survey research and ad hoc or middle-range theorizing, it is nevertheless a useful account of the present stock of knowledge within at least one influential tradition.

An inventory need not be restricted to this empirical tradition. As Ludz (1975, p. 31) concludes in another review, an inventory of all manifestations and of all propositions concerning alienation is urgently needed. Such an inventory could incorporate into its larger purview systematic generalizations and theoretical statements which draw on the history of the term and concept in Western thought.

While the problems and obstacles confronted in such a pursuit are enormous, propositional inventories have been attempted with varying success in other fields (see Schermerhorn's 1970 schematic application of both inductive and deductive methods to the literature on comparative ethnic relations). It is primarily to the American theoretical sociologists that we might turn for some of our leads, especially concerning methods and strategies of theory building (e.g. Cohen, 1980; Gibbs, 1972; Mullins, 1971; Blalock, 1969; Stinchcombe, 1968).

The requisite building blocks for the construction of a more comprehensive theory of alienation entail a careful specification of the main concepts, variables (an important type of concept), and theoretical statements; and the development of a format for systematically organizing these statements, i.e. according to the principles of axiomatic reduction, pluralistic parallel deduction, or causal inference (see Turner, 1978, pp. 2-13). The order of priorities for a general theory of alienation seems quite explicit here. Ludz, Schacht, and others, each in their own way, have begun some of the conceptual and terminological work that could begin to clear the way for a more comprehensive theory-building effort.

The next step is to consider some of the possibilities for systematically organizing the main concepts, variables, and statements into a viable format. If one opts for an axiomatic format, for example, it may call for a delineation of abstract axioms, through logical derivations, to specific propositions and hypotheses that predict how events in a concrete situation should occur. These steps in the process of theory building, in turn, could pave the way for the preliminary scaffolding of a general theory of alienation which transcends traditional disciplinary and paradigmatic boundaries.

Theoretical Extensions and Reformulations

There is an increasing readiness to explore alternative theories and paradigms, and a marked trend toward reconciliation or qualified merger between traditionally opposed approaches to the study of alienation. Several recent theoretical extensions and reformulations based on the classic theories of alienation have incorporated elements from a wide variety of other theoretical approaches and intellectual traditions, including sociological theories of social action and group formation (Torrance, 1977, 1981), socialization theory (Heinz, 1981), and existential psychiatry and phenomenology (Johnson, 1976; Gabel, 1975).

Other recent theoretical and schematic efforts in the field have focussed more specifically on attempts at reformulating questions about alienation through a variety of formal models and approaches: Hays' (1976) psycholinguistic construction of cognitive maps and conceptual models; Ludz's (1979) etymological maps and formal design for terminological and conceptual analysis; Geyer's (1980) application of General Systems Theory; Manderscheid's (1981) cybernetic biopsychosocial systems model of stress and coping; Nowakowska's (1981) formal mathematical model construction; Hajda and Travis' (1981) schematic work toward delineating some of the causal paths in the standard triadic relationship among macrosystemic causal variables, the subjective varieties of alienation, and hypothesized behavioural consequences within the sociopsychological tradition of survey research and middle-range theorizing.

These efforts signify a priority study concern among a growing international group of theorists. While grand theoretical efforts and formal model constructions may provide some heuristic insights with respect to alienation, they must nevertheless deal with the usual charges of abstraction which often distorts or mystifies the concrete conditions of alienation. One of the long-standing requirements in the field is that theoretical and schematic work of this kind have more direct potential for empirical research application and verification, and more concrete leads for substantive change, action, and de-alienation relevant to the commonsense experiences and realities of everyday life. (A more comprehensive assessment of recent theoretical advances appears in Schweitzer and Geyer, 1981.)

Continuing Concerns within Marxism

The current, almost staggering profusion of works directly or indirectly related to Marx's theory of alienation is such that a confusing element of satiety has emerged in the Marxist literature with respect to the meaning, purpose, and usefulness of the concept of alienation. This is due in part to the way Marx formulated his theory. Alienation for Marx is a total phenomenon which encompasses the entire human condition. With such an all-encompassing view, it can be argued that Marx has not accomplished very much with his theory; that it still lacks specific meaning despite the analytical distinctions in his early treatment of alienated labour, repeatedly referred to in the literature, but seldom pursued.

There is little agreement within Marxism concerning its meaning, purpose, or usefulness. Uncompromising materialist interpretations are pitted against abstract philosophical and essentialist readings of Marx; charges of revisionism and economism are levelled at any interpretation which is seen as undermining class analysis and struggle; while others argue that Marx actually abandoned the concept of alienation.

The contradictions within contemporary Marxism need to be examined more carefully and the evolution of the concept placed more firmly within a Marxist history of ideas. This could include, among other things, sorting out in a systematic way the different meanings, uses, and connotations imputed to the term and concept according to the different types of Marxism. (For a general survey of Marxist meanings and uses of alienation, see Strmiska, 1974; more thorough treatments of the theory and concept in Marx's works appear in Ollman, 1976, and Mészáros, 1975.)

The question of alienation under socialism remains another priority concern among some Marxists. It has developed in new critical ways since Schaff's (1970, orig. edn. 1965) pronouncement that the abolition of private property does not signify the end of all forms of alienation, not even the economic alienations detailed by Marx. Socialism has not completely overcome any of the known forms of alienation, if only because of the continued existence of a coercive state apparatus. New or modified forms of alienation have emerged, associated with new forms of contradiction and struggle in the changing class structure of socialist societies (cf. Connor, 1979; Wesolowski, 1979; Konrad and Szelenyi, 1979; attempts at restoring the concept of alienation among Soviet scholars appear in Oiserman, 1963; Amnrosov, 1972; Glezerman, 1972; see also the review by Yanowitch, 1967, and the efforts of Dawydow, 1964).

Yugoslav Marxist philosopher, Mihailo Marković (1981) tackles several of these problems from an explicit humanist standpoint. His notion of alienation is grounded in premises and commitments concerning the nature of man and the character of a genuinely human life. Man is viewed as essentially independent, autonomous, creative, and sociable . The ideal human community is seen as free from any external domination, where self-determining individuals can interact in a cooperative climate of mutuality and reciprocity. It is with a vision of an emancipated self-determining society, where individuals and communities take control over the products of their human activity, that Marković's conception of workers' self-management takes on full meaning and historical perspective. Workers' self-management is seen as a necessary, but not sufficient, precondition for reducing certain forms of alienation and for radically improving the quality of working life under socialism. He does not stop with the socialist situation but extends his analysis to some of the comparative examples and possibilities for improving the quality of working life through the development of self-managing enterprises in capitalist and social-democratic societies (cf. Cherns, 1976, 1981; also compare the case of the Israeli Kibbutz in Rosner, 1980).

Perhaps the most useful and penetrating part of Marković's recent contribution concerns his critical schematic emphasis on the inseparable link between micro- and macrolevels of analysis (and change) with respect to alienation, de-alienation, and workers' self-management under socialism. He is quite explicit about the obstacles and limitations that must be dealt with. As the Yugoslav experience indicates, collective experiments with workers' self-management cannot fully survive, and the quality of life cannot be radically or wholly improved, without a corresponding emancipatory restructuring of the larger social system. Such a restructuring necessarily entails firm checks against the fundamental authoritarian structure of state power; against official ideology which glosses over basic systemic contradictions and undermines workers' socialist consciousness; against moves for more power by the technocracy and political bureaucracy; against tendencies toward inequality and hierarchy in the larger structure of society; and against increasing state control in all spheres of human activity in the name of economic rationality.

While Marković focusses on the macrotriadic relation between workers, self-management collectives, and society, his debunking line of analysis could extend to the political economy of the larger world-system. If, as he tries to show us, small collective forms of workers' self-management cannot fully survive under the constraints of an authoritarian power structure in the society at large, then it is likely that for similar reasons a more totally emancipated and restructured society also cannot fully survive within the global framework of the capitalist world-system. We are reminded here of Marx's early world-embracing call for the emancipation not just of the workers alone in a particular society, but of humanity as a whole.

One of the explicit themes among many East European Marxist critics who organize much of their analysis around the concepts of alienation, reification, or fetishism is the charge that socialist states have lost sight of the humanistic concerns which presumably gave original impetus to strategies for socialist development, modernization, and economic growth (cf. Heller, 1978; Kolakowski, 1978; Bahro, 1978; Horvat et al., 1975; Supek, 1970; Stojanovic, 1969; Vranicki, 1965; Almasi, 1965). It is only in recent years that Marxist scholars and researchers have begun to make a few reasonably sober analytic inroads into this neglected area of study, often by applying a Marxist methodology to the critical analysis of official mainstream Marxist theory and practice in socialist societies.

Despite the recent profusion of Marxist literature and the massive outpouring of empirical results on alienation, there is little systematic empirical research, especially of a comparative cross-societal nature, which provides for a firmly grounded investigation into Marx's theory of alienation. The methodological problems involved seem almost insurmountable, especially when attempts are made toward a merger of Marxist critical analysis with empirical survey methods. A few recent empirical efforts, however, have indicated that survey techniques can be applied in certain qualified ways toward an empirical investigation into Marx's theory of alienation both in state-socialist (e.g. Whitehorn, 1979) and capitalist societies (e.g. Archibald et al., 1981).

The call here is for more advanced conceptual and empirical work which adheres firmly to a Marxist analytic framework. The ultimate objective is to develop viable strategies for bridging the chasm which exists between classical theory and contemporary empirical research applications. Among the prerequisites for Marxist-based empirical work are conceptualizations and measures which tap the objective forms of alienation specified by Marx, especially his analytical differentiations of alienated labour. Most mainstream empirical research to date has focussed almost exclusively on the psychological varieties of alienation, so much so that the radical tradition of normative evaluation and critical analysis in Marx's theory has been largely compromised.

International Comparative Research

Most empirical alienation research has been restricted to the problems and contradictions of single societies, with the bulk of this research concentrating largely on the American situation. Those studies which lay claim to some comparability are only quasi-comparative in the sense that an analytic sample survey conducted within one society is simply replicated, often many years later, in another society. The lack of explicit comparative work which extends systematically across different societies and cultures (or between various time spans involving longitudinal data) represents another neglected area. Recent efforts in this vein, however, suggest that comparative cross-societal empirical studies of alienation are now part of a developing research trend in the field (cf. Reimanis, 1978; Shepard and Kim, 1978; Armer and Isaac, 1978; also Seeman, 1977; Schweitzer, 1974; Simpson, 1970).

The rationale for more advanced international comparative research is self-evident to those who formulate their questions about alienation within a positivist paradigm of social inquiry. In this vein, the main objectives of comparative inquiry are to specify or delimit those aspects of a given theory or proposition about alienation which hold for all societies, those which are systematically relevant only to certain types of societies, and those which are unique and valid only for single societies. The aim, in effect, is to universalize theory and continually reassess its propositions in comparative perspective (Marsh, 1967; also Schweitzer, 1979).

Comparative studies of course need not be restricted to empirical surveys. They could also extend to comparative sociohistorical analyses which, for example, reformulate questions and answers about alienation in more encompassing terms, as a phenomenon that is inseparably interconnected with the wider world-economy. The study of alienation from the standpoint of historical materialism and class conflict in single societies could be extrapolated to the international division of labour, unequal exchange, and the relations of domination and exploitation among nations and states. An approach along these lines has a certain affinity to current neo-Marxist theories of Third World dependency and underdevelopment among capitalist formations at the periphery of the modern world-system (e.g. Fröbel et al., 1980; Amin, 1980; Wallerstein, 1979; Frank, 1979).

The problems involved are numerous, yet it appears a legitimate line of pursuit. If the problem of alienation can be formulated according to contradictions between subjects and objects, and then extended to structural contradictions between classes or between the forces and relations of production, then it follows that this can be extended further to the relations of domination and subordination, appropriation and exploitation, and production and resource control on the larger world scale.[5]

NOTES

1. For a sampling of major works that have appeared within the last decade alone, see Schaff (1980), Geyer (1980), Archibald (1978), Torrance (1977), Ollman (1976), Mészáros (1975), Gabel (1975), Marković (1974), Johnson (1973), Walton and Gamble (1972), Israel (1971), and Schacht (1970); also the volume of papers edited by Brenner and Strasser (1977). For a review of the extensive empirical literature, see Seeman (1975); also the trend report and annotated bibliography in Ludz (1975); and the exhaustive bibliographic work containing over 7,000 references in van Reden et al. (1980).

The Research Committee on Alienation Theory and Research was formed in 1972, initially as an Ad Hoc Group of the International Sociological Association. Roughly 100 professional papers were delivered in the sessions on alienation theory and research at the 8th and 9th World Congresses of Sociology in Toronto, Canada (1974) and Uppsala, Sweden (1978), resulting in two edited volumes of original papers (Geyer and Schweitzer, 1976, 1981). The sessions in Toronto and Uppsala were organized around a fundamental concern for further conceptual and terminological clarification, theoretical refinement, and the development of empirical research methods which draw explicitly from the classic theories. The programme of sessional themes for the 1982 World Congress of Sociology in Mexico City has been broadened to include hitherto neglected topics in the field, i.e. theological perspectives; literary, dramatic, and artistic perspectives; international comparative research; the socialist experience; social practice and strategies for change, action, and de-alienation.

Other current activities associated with the research committee include the publication of another volume of papers under the editorship of Shlomo Shoham, based on an international workshop on anomie and alienation held in Messina, Italy, November 1980. It will consist of original contributions from scholars and researchers representing different theoretical-ideological and methodological orientations. Also, in 1983 the research committee will begin the publication of its own quarterly — *Alienation Theory and Research: An International Multidisciplinary Journal*, with Gordon and Breach Science Publishers, London — under the managing editorship of Felix Geyer (SISWO, PO Box 19079, 1000 GB Amsterdam, Netherlands) and the co-editorship of Frank Johnson, Richard Schacht, Adam Schaff, and David Schweitzer.

2. Cf. Lukács (1971), where the underlying notion of alienation encompasses some of these clinical dimensions. Parallels can also be drawn between psychological elements in Marx's early works and certain psychoanalytic concepts, i.e. Horney's (1950) 'neurotic personality', or Erikson's (1968) 'identity crisis'; also in this vein, see Fromm (1965), Marcuse (1964), and Tucker (1961).

3. The 'secularization' referred to throughout the discussion in this section is only one instance of a broader secular trend in the historical evolution of ideas in Western thought. The concept of alienation, prior to Marx, contained a richer spectrum of meanings encompassing positive, neutral, and negative value-connotations (see Ludz, 1981). This tradition stops rather abruptly with Marx. The concept was reduced primarily to its negative value-connotations, largely in response to the intellectual climate of his times and more specifically to Hegel's idealism in accordance with Feuerbach's materialist prescriptions and conception of human self-alienation in religious life as a dehumanizing process. In this sense, Marx was an instrumental figure in the early secularization of the concept and a part of the larger progressive secularization of Occidental thought.

4. The debate began with Melvin Seeman's pioneering conceptual work (1959). With full awareness of many of these problems, Seeman frankly states that his decision to 'secularize' the concept of alienation — i.e. 'to translate what was sentimentally understood into a secular question' (p. 791) — was a calculated risk, a strategic enterprise geared ultimately toward the achievement of greater clarity without necessarily compromising the intellectual scope or the humanistic concerns that lie at the heart of the classic theories. Seeman (1971: p. 508) has responded to a few of the criticisms: 'there is no doubt about the critical power shown by more recent advocates of the normative approach (Marcuse, Goodman, Fromm and others). But what is gained in critical force is often lost in repetition and unanalytical pronouncement — which is why the latter-day improvement on Marx...in this recent critical literature is often hard to catalogue.' Most researchers in this tradition who draw on Seeman's lead also draw implicitly on his rationale: 'The secularization of the concept of alienation is a strategic enterprise that does not restrict our interest in, or our competence to talk about and examine, the full range of problems that are captured in words like justice, evil, trust, ignorance, or personal development' (p. 508; also Seeman et al., 1967).

5. A more comprehensive assessment of trends, issues, and priorities discussed in this essay can be found in Schweitzer (1981).

REFERENCES

Afonja, S. A. (1978) 'An Investigation of the Relationship Between Accidents, Alienation, and Withdrawal from Work', *Labour Society*, 2: 135-57.

Almasi, M. (1965) 'Alienation and Socialism', pp. 125-42 in *Marxism and Alienation*, edited by H. Aptheker. New York: Humanities Press.

Althusser, L. (1976) *Essays in Self-Criticism*. London: New Left Books.

Amin, S. (1980) *Class and Nation, Historically and in the Current Crisis*. New York: Monthly Review Press.

Amnrosov, A. (1972) 'U.S.S.R. Working Class: Position in a Society and Prospects of Development', *Transactions of the Seventh World Congress of Sociology*, 2: 83-89.

Archibald, P. (1976) 'Using Marx's Theory of Alienation Empirically', pp. 59-76 in *Theories of Alienation: Critical Perspectives in Philosophy and the Social Sciences*, edited by R. F. Geyer and D. Schweitzer. Leiden: Martinus Nijhoff.

Archibald, P. (1978) *Social Psychology as Political Economy*. Toronto: McGraw Hill Ryerson.

Archibald, P., Owen, A. and Cartrell, J. (1981) 'Propertylessness and Alienation: Reopening a "Shut" Case', pp. 149-74 in *Alienation: Problems of Meaning, Theory, and Method*, edited by R. F. Geyer and D. Schweitzer. London and Boston: Routledge and Kegan Paul.

Armer, M. and Isaac, L. (1978) 'Behavioural Consequences of Psychological Modernity: Comparative Evidence from Three Societies'. Paper presented in the sessions on alienation theory and research at the 9th World Congress of Sociology, Uppsala, Sweden.

Bahro, R. (1978, orig. German edn. 1977) *The Alternative in Eastern Europe*. London: New Left Books.

Blalock, H. M. (1969) *Theory Construction: From Verbal to Mathematical Formulations*. Englewood Cliffs, NJ: Prentice-Hall.

Blauner, R. (1964) *Alienation and Freedom: The Factory Worker and His Industry*. Chicago: University of Chicago Press.

Braverman, H. (1974) *Labor and Monopoly Capital: The Degradation of Work in the Twentieth Century*. New York: Monthly Review Press.

Brenner, M. and Strasser, H. (eds) (1977) *Die Gesellschaftliche Konstruktion der Entfremdung*. Frankfurt: Campus Verlag.

Cartwright, D. (1965) 'A Misapplication of Factor Analysis', *American Sociological Review*, 30: 249-51.

Cherns, A. (1976) 'Work or Life', pp. 227-44 in *Theories of Alienation: Critical Perspectives in Philosophy and the Social Sciences*, edited by R. F. Geyer and D. Schweitzer. Leiden: Martinus Nijhoff.

Cherns, A. (1981) 'Accounting for Alienation', pp. 248-74 in *Alienation: Problems of Meaning, Theory and Method*, edited by R. F. Geyer and D. Schweitzer. London and Boston: Routledge and Kegan Paul.

Cohen, B. C. (1980) *Developing Sociological Knowledge: Theory and Knowledge*. Englewood Cliffs, NJ: Prentice-Hall.

Connor, W. D. (1979) *Socialism, Politics, and Equity: Hierarchy and Change in Eastern Europe and the USSR*. New York: Columbia University Press.

Dawydow, J. N. (1964, orig. Russian edn. 1962) *Freiheit und Entfremdung*. Berlin: VEB Deutschen Verlag der Wissenschaften.
Erikson, E. (1968) *Identity: Youth and Crisis*. New York: W. W. Norton.
Fischer, C. S. (1976) 'Alienation: Trying to Bridge the Chasm', *British Journal of Sociology*, 27: 35-49.
Fischer, G. (1967) 'Sociology', in *Science and Ideology in Soviet Society*, edited by G. Fischer. New York: Atherton.
Frank, A. G. (1979) *Dependent Accumulation and Underdevelopment*. New York: Monthly Review Press.
Fröbel, J., Heinrichs, J. and Kreye, O. (1980, orig. German edn. 1977) *The New International Division of Labour: Structural Unemployment in Industrialized Countries and Industrialization in Developing Countries*. New York: Cambridge University Press.
Fromm, E. (1965) 'The Application of Humanist Psychoanalysis to Marx's Theory', pp. 228-45 in *Socialist Humanism*, edited by E. Fromm. Garden City, NY: Doubleday.
Gabel, J. (1975, orig. French edn. 1962) *False Consciousness: An Essay on Reification*, translated by M. A. Thompson. Oxford: Basil Blackwell.
Geyer, R. F. (1976) 'Individual Alienation and Information Processing: A Systems Theoretical Conceptualization', pp. 189-226 in *Theories of Alienation: Critical Perspectives in Philosophy and the Social Sciences*, edited by R. F. Geyer and D. Schweitzer. Leiden: Martinus Nijhoff.
Geyer, R. F. (1980) *Alienation Theories: A General Systems Approach*. Oxford: Pergamon Press.
Geyer, R. F. and Schweitzer, D. (eds) (1976) *Theories of Alienation: Critical Perspectives in Philosophy and the Social Sciences*. Leiden: Martinus Nijhoff.
Geyer, R. F. and Schweitzer, D. (eds) (1981) *Alienation: Problems of Meaning, Theory, and Method*. London and Boston: Routledge and Kegan Paul.
Gibbs, J. (1972) *Sociological Theory Construction*. Hillsdale, Ill.: Dryden Press.
Glezerman, G. (1972) 'Contradictions Under Socialism', *World Marxist Review*, 15: 106-15.
Gouldner, A. W. (1980) *The Two Marxisms*. New York: Seabury Press.
Hajda, J. and Travis, R. (1981) 'Causes and Consequences of Powerlessness and Meainglessness', pp. 211-30 in *Alienation: Problems of Meaning, Theory and Method*, edited by R. F. Geyer and D. Schweitzer. London and Boston: Routledge and Kegan Paul.
Hays, D. G. (1976) 'On "Alienation": An Essay in the Psycholinguistics of Science', pp. 169-88 in *Theories of Alienation: Critical Perspectives in Philosophy and the Social Sciences*, edited by R. F. Geyer and D. Schweitzer. Leiden: Martinus Nijhoff.
Heinz, W. (1981) 'Socialization and Work: Notes on the Normative Acceptance of Alienated Work Conditions', pp. 233-47 in *Alienation: Problems of Meaning, Theory, and Method*, edited by R. F. Geyer and D. Schweitzer. London and Boston: Routledge and Kegan Paul.
Heller, A. (1978) 'Alienation and Reification, with Particular Respect to East European Societies'. Paper presented in the sessions on alienation theory and research at the 9th World Congress of Sociology, Uppsala, Sweden.
Horney, K. (1950) *Neurosis and Human Growth*. New York: W. W. Norton.
Horton, J. (1964) 'The Dehumanization of Anomie and Alienation: A Problem in the Ideology of Sociology', *British Journal of Sociology*, 15: 283-300.

Horton, J. (1966) 'Order, and Conflict Theories of Social Problems as Competing Ideologies', *American Sociological Review*, 71: 701-13.

Horton, J. and Moreno, M. (1981) 'Class Determination in Marxist and Empiricist Concepts of Alienation', pp. 99-129 in *Alienation: Problems of Meaning, Theory, and Method*, edited by R. F. Geyer and D. Schweitzer. Boston and London: Routledge and Kegan Paul.

Horvat, B., Marković, M. and Supek, R. (eds) (1975) *Self-Governing Socialism*. White Plains, NY: International Arts and Science Press.

Israel, J. (1971, orig. Swedish edn. 1968) *Alienation: From Marx to Modern Sociology*. Boston: Allyn and Bacon.

Israel, J. (1976) 'Alienation and Reification', pp. 41-57 in *Theories of Alienation: Critical Perspectives in Philosophy and the Social Sciences*, edited by R. F. Geyer and D. Schweitzer. Leiden: Martinus Nijhoff.

Johnson, F. (ed.) (1973) *Alienation: Concept, Term and Meanings*. New York: Seminar Press.

Johnson, F. (1976) 'Some Problems of Reification in Existential Psychiatry: Conceptual and Practical Considerations', pp. 77-102 in *Theories of Alienation: Critical Perspectives in Philosophy and the Social Sciences*, edited by R. F. Geyer and D. Schweitzer. Leiden: Martinus Nijhoff.

Klaus, G. (1962) *Kybernetik in philosophischer Sicht*. 2nd edn. Berlin: Dietz.

Kohn, M. (1976) 'Occupational Structure and Alienation', *American Journal of Sociology*, 82: 111-30.

Kohn, M. (1977) *Class and Class Conformity*. 2nd edn. Chicago: University of Chicago Press.

Kolakowski, L. (1978) *Main Currents of Marxism: Its Rise, Growth and Dissolution*, Vol. 1: *The Founders*; Vol. II: *The Golden Age*; Vol. III: *The Breakdown*, translated by P. S. Falla. New York: Oxford University Press.

Kon, I. (1969) 'The Concept of Alienation in Modern Sociology', pp. 146-67 in *Marxism and Sociology: Views from Eastern Europe*, edited by P. Berger. New York: Appleton-Century-Crofts.

Konrad, G. and Szelenyi, I. (1979, orig. German edn. 1978) *The Intellectuals on the Road to Class Power: A Sociological Study of the Role of the Intelligentsia in Socialism*, translated by A. Arato and R. E. Allen. New York: Harcourt Brace Jovanovich.

Lachs, J. (1976) 'Mediation and Psychic Distance', pp. 151-68 in *Theories of Alienation: Critical Perspectives in Philosophy and the Social Sciences*, edited by R. F. Geyer and D. Schweitzer. Leiden: Martinus Nijhoff.

Lefebvre, H. (1961) *Critique de la vie quotidienne* II, *Fondements d'une sociologie de la quotidienneté*. Paris: L'Arche.

Ludz, P. C. (1975) 'Alienation as a Concept in the Social Sciences', *Current Sociology*, 22, 1; also pp. 3-37 in *Theories of Alienation: Critical Perspectives in Philosophy and the Social Sciences*, edited by R. F. Geyer and D. Schweitzer. Leiden: Martinus Nijhoff, 1976.

Ludz, P. (1979) 'Alienation: Toward a Terminological and Conceptual Analysis', in *Social Science Concepts*, edited by G. Satori. Chicago: University of Chicago Press.

Ludz, P. (1981) 'A Forgotten Intellectual Tradition of the Alienation Concept', pp. 21-35 in *Alienation: Problems of Meaning, Theory, and Method*, edited by R. F. Geyer and D. Schweitzer. London and Boston: Routledge and Kegan Paul.

Lukaćs, G. (1971, orig. German edn. 1923) *History and Class Consciousness: Studies in Marxist Dialectics.* Cambridge, Mass.: MIT Press.

Lukes, S. (1967) 'Alienation and Anomie', pp. 134-56 in *Philosophy, Politics and Society*, edited by P. Laslett and W. Runciman. Oxford: Blackwell.

Mandel, E. and Novak, G. (1970) *The Marxist Theory of Alienation.* New York: Pathfinder.

Manderscheid, R. (1981) 'Stress and Coping: A Biopsychosocial Perspective on Alienation', pp. 177-91 in *Alienation: Problems of Meaning, Theory, and Method*, edited by R. F. Geyer and D. Schweitzer. London and Boston: Routledge and Kegan Paul.

Marcuse, H. (1964) *One-Dimensional Man: Studies in the Ideology of Advanced Industrial Society.* Boston: Beacon Press.

Marković, M. (1974) *From Affluence to Praxis: Philosophy and Social Criticism.* Ann Arbor: University of Michigan Press.

Marković, M. (1981) 'Alienated Labour and Self-Determination', pp. 130-48 in *Alienation: Problems of Meaning, Theory, and Method*, edited by R. F. Geyer and D. Schweitzer. London and Boston: Routledge and Kegan Paul.

Marsh, R. M. (1967) *Comparative Sociology: A Codification of Cross-Societal Analysis.* New York: Harcourt, Brace & World.

Meissner, M. (1970) 'The Long Arm of the Job: Social Participation and the Constraints of Industrial Work', *Industrial Relations*, 10: 239-60.

Mészáros, I. (1975) *Marx's Theory of Alienation*, 4th edn. New York: Harper and Row.

Mullins, N. C. (1971) *The Art of Theory: Construction and Use.* New York: Harper and Row.

Neal, A. and Rettig, S. (1963) 'Dimensions of Alienation Among Manual and Non-Manual Workers', *American Sociological Review*, 28: 599-608.

Neal, A. and Rettig, S. (1967) 'On the Multidimensionality of Alienation', *American Sociological Review*, 32: 54-64.

Nowakowska, M. (1981) 'Alienation: A Formal Theory', pp. 192-210 in *Alienation: Problems of Meaning, Theory, and Method*, edited by R. F. Geyer and D. Schweitzer. London and Boston: Routledge and Kegan Paul.

Oiserman, T. (1963) 'Alienation and the Individual', *Soviet Studies*, 23: 39-43; also pp. 143-51 in *Marxism and Alienation*, edited by H. Aptheker. New York: Humanities Press, 1965.

Ollman, B. (1976) *Alienation: Marx's Conception of Man in a Capitalist Society*, 2nd edn. Cambridge: Cambridge University Press.

Olsen, M. E. (1976) 'Political Powerlessness as Reality', pp. 245-64 in *Theories of Alienation: Critical Perspectives in Philosophy and the Social Sciences*, edited by R. F. Geyer and D. Schweitzer. Leiden: Martinus Nijhoff.

Otto, L. and Featherman, D. (1975) 'Social Structural and Psychological Antecedents of Self-Estrangement and Powerlessness', *American Sociological Review*, 40: 701-19.

Reimanis, G. (1978) 'Alienation and Powerlessness in Four Cultures'. Paper presented in the sessions on alienation theory and research at the 9th World Congress of Sociology, Uppsala, Sweden.

Rinehart, J. W. (1975) *The Tyranny of Work.* Don Mills: Longman Canada.

Rosner, M. (1980) 'The Quality of Working Life and the Kibbutz Community', pp. 132-44 in *Quality of Working Life and the Kibbutz Experience*, edited by A. Cherns. Philadelphia: Norwood Edition.

Schacht, R. (1970) *Alienation*. London: Allen and Unwin.
Schacht, R. (1976) 'Alienation, the "Is-Ought" Gap and Two Sorts of Discord', pp. 133-50 in *Theories of Alienation: Critical Perspectives in Philosophy and the Social Sciences*, edited by R. F. Geyer and D. Schweitzer. Leiden: Martinus Nijhoff.
Schacht, R. (1981) 'Economic Alienation: With and Without Tears', pp. 36-67 in *Alienation: Problems of Meaning, Theory, and Method*, edited by R. F. Geyer and D. Schweitzer. London and Boston: Routledge and Kegan Paul.
Schaff, A. (1970, orig. Polish and German edn. 1965) *Marxism and the Human Individual*. New York: McGraw-Hill.
Schaff, A. (1981, orig. German edn. 1977) *Alienation as a Social Phenomenon*. Oxford: Pergamon Press.
Schermerhorn, R. A. (1970) *Comparative Ethnic Relations: A Framework for Theory and Research*. New York: Random House.
Schweitzer, D. (1974) *Status Frustration and Conservatism in Comparative Perspective*. London and Beverly Hills: Sage Publications.
Schweitzer, D. (1979) 'Comparative Social Mobility: Problems of Theory, Epistemology, and Quantitative Methodology, pp. 57-91 in *Problems of International Comparative Research in the Social Sciences*, edited by J. Berting et al. Oxford and New York: Pergamon Press.
Schweitzer, D. (1981) 'Alienation Theory and Research: Trends, Issues, and Priorities', *International Social Science Journal*, XXXIII, 3 (in press).
Schweitzer, D. and Geyer R. F. (1981) 'Advances and Priorities in Alienation Theory and Research', pp. 1-17 in *Alienation: Problems of Meaning, Theory, and Method*, edited by R. F. Geyer and D. Schweitzer. London and Boston: Routledge and Kegan Paul.
Seeman, M. (1959) 'On the Meaning of Alienation', *American Sociological Review*, 54: 783-91.
Seeman, M. (1972) 'Alienation and Engagement', pp. 467-527 in *The Human Meaning of Social Change*, edited by A. Campbell and P. Converse. New York: Russell Sage.
Seeman, M. (1975) 'Alienation Studies', *Annual Review of Sociology*, 1: 91-123; also 'Empirical Alienation Studies: An Overview', pp. 265-305 in *Theories of Alienation: Critical Perspectives in Philosophy and the Social Sciences*, edited by R. F. Geyer and D. Schweitzer. Leiden: Martinus Nijhoff, 1976.
Seeman, M. (1977) 'Some Real and Imaginary Consequences of Social Mobility: A French-American Comparison', *American Journal of Sociology*, 82: 757-82.
Seeman, M. et al. (1967) 'Débat de l'utilité sociologique de la notion d'aliénation', *Sociologie du Travail*, 2: 180-209.
Shepard, J. and Kim, D. (1978) 'Alienation Among Factory Workers in the U.S. and Korea: A Comparative Study'. Paper presented in the sessions on alienation theory and research at the 9th World Congress of Sociology, Uppsala, Sweden.
Shoham, S. G. (1976) 'The Tantalus Ratio: A Scaffolding for an Ontological Personality Theory', pp. 103-32 in *Theories of Alienation: Critical Perspectives in Philosophy and the Social Sciences*, edited by R. F. Geyer and D. Schweitzer. Leiden: Martinus Nijhoff.
Shoham, S. G. (1979) *The Myth of Tantalus*. St. Lucia, Queensland: University of Queensland Press.
Simmons, J. (1964-65) 'Some Intercorrelations Among Alienation Measures', *Social Forces*, 44: 370-71.

Simpson, M. (1970) 'Social Mobility, Normlessness and Powerlessness in Two Cultural Contexts', *American Sociological Review*, 35: 1002-1013.
Stinchcombe, A. L. (1968) *Constructing Social Theories*. New York: Harcourt, Brace and World.
Stojanovic, S. (1969) 'The Dialectics of Alienation and the Utopia of Dealienation', *Praxis*, 3-4: 387-98.
Streuning, E. and Richardson, A. (1965) 'A Factor Analytic Exploration of the Alienation, Anomie, and Authoritarianism Domain', *American Sociological Review*, 30: 768-76.
Strmiska, Z. (1974) 'Structure de la problématique sociologique marxienne et notion d'aliénation', pp. 43-115 in *L'aliénation aujourd'hui*, edited by J. Gabel, B. Roussett and T. Thao. Paris: Editions Anthropos.
Supek, R. (1970) *Soziologie und Sozialismus: Probleme und Perspektiven*. Freiburg: Rembach.
Szymanski, A. et al. (1978) 'Braverman Symposium', *The Resurgent Sociologist*, 8: 33-50.
Thibault, A. (1981) 'Studying Alienation Without Alienating People: A Challenge for Sociology', pp. 275-83 in *Alienation: Problems of Meaning, Theory, and Method*, edited by R. F. Geyer and D. Schweitzer. London and Boston: Routledge and Kegan Paul.
Torrance, J. (1977) *Estrangement, Alienation, and Exploitation: A Sociological Approach to Historical Materialism*. London and New York: Macmillan Press.
Torrance, J. (1981) 'Alienation and Estrangement as Elements of Social Structure', pp. 68-96 in *Alienation: Problems of Meaning, Theory, and Method*, edited by R. F. Geyer and D. Schweitzer. London and Boston: Routledge and Kegan Paul.
Touraine, A. (1967) 'L'aliénation: de l'idéologie à l'analyse', *Sociologie du Travail*, 9: 192-201.
Touraine, A. (1977, orig. French edn. 1973) *The Self-Production of Society*. Chicago: The University of Chicago Press.
Tucker, R. (1961) *Philosophy and Myth in Karl Marx*. Cambridge: Cambridge University Press.
Tudor, B. (1972) 'A Specification of Relationships Between Job Complexity and Powerlessness', *American Sociological Review*, 37: 596-604.
Turner, J. H. (1978) *The Structure of Sociological Theory*, rev. edn. Homewood, Ill.: Dorsey Press.
van Reden, C., Grondel, A. and Geyer, R. F. (1980) *Bibliography Alienation*. Netherlands Universities' Joint Social Research Centre, PO Box 19079, 1000GB Amsterdam.
Vidal, D. (1967) 'L'aliénation, structure du non sens', *Sociologie du Travail*, 2: 185-90.
Vidal, D. (1969). 'Un cas de faux concept: la notion d'aliénation', *Sociologie du Travail*, 11: 61-82.
Vranicki, P. (1965) 'Socialism and the Problems of Alienation', pp. 299-313 in *Socialist Humanism: An International Symposium*, edited by E. Fromm. Garden City, NY: Doubleday.
Wallerstein, I. (1979) *The Capitalist World-Economy*. New York: Cambridge University Press.
Walton, P. and Gamble, A. (1972) *From Alienation to Surplus Value*. London: Sheed and Ward.

Wesolowski, W. (1979) *Classes, Strata, and Power*. Boston: Routledge and Kegan Paul.

Whitehorn, A. (1979) 'Alienation and Industrial Society: A Study of Workers' Self-Management', *Canadian Review of Sociology and Anthropology*, 16: 206-17.

Yanowitch, M. (1967) 'Alienation and the Young Marx in Soviet Thought', *Slavic Review*, 26: 29-53.

3
The Sociology of Religion: A Critical Survey

Richard K. Fenn
University of Maine

The functionalist synthesis in the sociology of religion has dissolved. In its place are left broad theoretical orientations and general methodological approaches to interpreting and explaining accounts of religious commitment and practice. Two of these broad theoretical orientations will concern us here, and they are far more general, for instance, than 'exchange' or 'symbolic interactionist' theory. One is critical, and focusses on contradictions, while the other is what I shall call systemic. They fail to confront each other with sufficient clarity and force, however, to resolve differences of sociological opinion.

Functionalism provided a privileged methodological stance from which the sociologist could interpret and transcend the accounts of groups and individuals. As a trained interpreter the sociologist could provide a coherent text of a community's beliefs, but as one skilled in delving below surface appearances the sociologist could also identify 'latent' functions and, in the process, call into question a community's account of its own life. These methodological approaches are still adopted, but the sociologist does not enjoy a privileged position from which to put them together. The result is parallel and competing perspectives without a single viewpoint.

Sociologists of religion still employ the critical distinction between myth and reality as their theoretical point of departure. Some wish to call attention to human achievements otherwise disguised in religious myth as the work of the gods or to point to cruel aspects of social life masked by sacred mysteries. Some claim that myth expresses what is true, but pathological, about social reality, while others go further by claiming that myth makes pathology appear to be healthy and sickness virtuous. Sociologists as different in their viewpoints as Durkheim, Marx and Weber, being offspring of the Enlightenment, were therefore positivists to the extent that they shared this common interest in sparing reality the disguises and justifications of religious myth. The use of that distinction requires a privileged methodological position, however, that is no longer available to the sociologist in the light of advances in sociologists' understanding of their influence as well as of their limitations. The distinction also calls for a nearly arbitrary choice between theoretical viewpoints, neither of which is capable of directly challenging the other. In this paper I will illustrate this assertion in some detail and consider one proposal for resolving it.

Some sociologists tend to separate myth from reality for the sake of myth. They may have inherited a religious myth that sees man as the creature and creator of social life and of history, while they do not like what they see of man's historical products. Marx saw a world shaped by an aggressive and effective bourgeoisie, a world productive beyond any historical expectation, but he was disenchanted with a regime in which the primary producers had to pay the costs of production. How could one still entertain a belief in man as responsible in history and masterful over nature when confronted with these human sacrifices? The same myth, of free and responsible individuals active in social structures of their own creation, underlies Weber's studies of ethical prophecy and his pronouncements on science and politics. But Weber, like Marx, deplored the acquisitiveness of an entrepreneurial class that kept its jobs while losing its vocation, and he warned further of a bureaucratic administration that confines individuals in structures of their own creation. Durkheim sought to reconstruct the sacred myths of social life from the fragments and remains still apparent in 'so-called civilized societies': myths that could be reconstructed after patterns more easily discerned in still primitive societies. This sense of responsibility for the founding myths of Western society accounts for the conservative tendency in even the most radical sociological criticism.

The sociology of religion is the activity par excellence in which sociologists continue to sift the fragments of myth from social reality. Some sociologists are interested primarily in saving the national myth from the discrediting aspects of social reality, as in the case of Bellah's (1975) recent work on civil religion in the United States, while others gather observations that call into question national mythology, as in discussions of civil religion in Russia or the 'management of consensus' (cf. Lane, 1979). Those with the former interest are likely to view symbols as 'constitutive' of social reality and not as merely expressive; the symbols are necessary if not sufficient conditions for the societies that they define. Sociologists more interested in rescuing social reality from the obscurities of myth take a more positivistic view and reduce national myths to the interests of certain classes and strata: a strategy most likely to be found in those drawing on the Weberian and Marxist traditions in Western sociology. The two theoretical orientations are often juxtaposed in sociological debates without leading to falsification or verification: an impasse that is unnecessary, however fruitful it has been in generating controversy.

THEORETICAL ORIENTATIONS: THE SYSTEMIC AND THE CRITICAL

Let me begin by illustrating these two theoretical orientations that seem to coexist in the sociology of religion. They are implicit in two quite different appraisals of the relation of myth to reality in modern societies. The first, which I will call systemic, argues that it is possible for secularizing societies to achieve a level of symbolic integration in which most individuals are able to act and to communicate effectively with one another, despite the variety of their situations and regardless of the diversity of their separate intentions. Acquaviva clearly believes that such integration is entirely possible:

...it is possible to embrace the two worlds (sacred and profane) within a single logical discourse and to identify, within a basic logico-cognitive unity, a tight and orderly network of relations at all levels in the society within which these two components, the sacred-hierophanic and the profane, participate in each other (1979, p. 177).

Of course, to specify the conditions under which such understanding is possible is well beyond the scope of this paper. As Acquaviva himself points out, the sacred does not always lead to the conviction that there exists a separate world, ontologically beyond the world of everyday life. Where the sacred is embodied in rituals that emphasize an ontological 'leap', as he calls it, societies may have more difficulty in establishing a single realm of discourse for relating the sacred to the profane. But where the sacred exists outside of such religious structures, such a single, integrated universe of discourse may be developed through mediating institutions like the university and the judiciary. Again, it is the task of sociological theory to develop notions that are capable of testing the existence of a single realm of discourse rather than to exclude such a possibility by definition from the outset. I will return to that point after considering an alternative to the systemic orientation. It is enough for the moment to note that a systemic view assumes and looks for the interaction of myth and reality in the formation of societal rules and institutions.

An alternative orientation (I will call it 'critical') informs Robertson's (1978) recent diagnosis of religion in Western societies. Robertson argues that myth is largely removed from everyday reality, whether it is objectified and abstract or carried as fragments in individual minds. The 'objectification' of culture makes the formation of individual identity more possible at the same time, however, that it makes identity-formation more problematical. The possibilities open to individuals confront them as an obligation to a continual process of self-realization and may lead to successive conversions at several stages of the life-cycle. It is the very separateness of myth from reality that reminds individuals of the variety of their choices for a coherent and legitimate life-style and that makes them morally responsible for the making of such choices. On the other hand, the objectification of culture makes the achievement of personal identity more problematical partly because it is an individual achievement subject to revision and therefore subject also to the possibility of being taken less than seriously by others. The achievement of a serious identity becomes more problematical when the individual encounters social life as objective and constraining (Robertson, 1978, pp. 190-91). One alternative is to abandon the search for a personal identity, while another is to take less seriously the social situations in which the individual seeks to establish his identity as authentic and authoritative.

Paradoxically, Robertson attributes the separation of sacred myths concerning individual identity from social situations to the success of Christian sacramental theology and practice in Western societies (1978, p. 201). On this view, it is not surprising that Wesley translated 18th-century ideas concerning the revolutionary transformation of whole societies into ideas concerning perpetual and decisive 'inner-renewal at the individual level' (Robertson, 1978, p. 197). The myths of total regeneration carried in Western religious cultures have been so separated from the realities of everyday life, on this view, that ideas of total regeneration remain as merely individual options that do not involve, although they may indirectly affect, the society as a whole (Robertson, 1978, p. 201). Of course, in some societies it may be difficult to understand the myths of regeneration without perceiving their implications for both the individual and the entire society. The individual in certain societies may be renewed in the society's rituals of rebirth, while the society is renewed in the individual's initiation-rites at successive points in the life-cycle (Robertson, 1978, p. 200). These are what Robertson (1978, p. 199) calls the 'primitive and traditional situations': situations in which individuals work out their salvation in mythic terms and through ritual practices that engage their decisions with the fate of larger societies. To locate these situations in modern societies is one point of current sociological interest in the ritual aspects of public demonstrations and trials.

One issue in both these perspectives is the grounds of hope. The perspective I have illustrated in Acquaviva's writing, the 'systemic', clearly holds out the hope that individuals will turn their myths into reality through a communicative social process akin to the one in which sacraments are produced and recognized. Ritual activity is human action par excellence: the paradigm of what it means to create a human social system by turning hopes into symbolic actions and actions into new relationships. But this hope for systemic symbols that make it possible to communicate across the boundaries of regional or socioeconomic subsystems requires consideration of systemic factors that appear to operate independently of religions or secular beliefs and values. Economic and educational progress favours the development of religious interest or involvement in the middle classes (Acquaviva, 1979, p. 168), while limiting the direct effect of religious culture on social or economic institutions. The systemic perspective awaits development in a theory of communicative action, of language itself, that spells out the process by which individual action transforms and is constrained by social structures. But that process can only be idealized as a quasi-natural evolution of meaning or as a 'ritual process' by ignoring the hard facts of power, the costs of injustice and inequality, the burden of the past, and the reductions of myths from a source of transcendence to an object of consumption.

Conversely, the picture offered by Robertson is of individuals enmeshed in an everyday reality that finds myths too distant and abstract to serve as a base for individual identity and authority. It is a 'critical' perspective in which myths are objects that elude the grasp of social action although they may be used or consumed like any other social product (cf. Berger and Luckman, 1967). In the meantime, individuals confront the hard facts of economic or bureaucratic limitations on their freedom without owning or creating the symbolic means to interpret and transcend those limits. These two perspectives also differ in their rise of cybernetic metaphors. A critical orientation does not assume on cybernetic grounds that all societies can understand, accept, and act upon the myths which they inherit or import from the outside, but a 'system' orientation assumes practically by definition that a society can process and use the information that comes to it coded in mythic form. A debate between theorists such as Luhmann and Habermas takes precisely this form: the argument concerning whether social systems generally can be assumed to have the capacity to process such information, especially when it comes in such radically coded form as to require a radical transformation of the society itself. The debate does not concern us directly, and in any event its complexities are carefully reviewed elsewhere (cf. Sixel, 1976; 1977). But it is interesting to know how crucial the issue is to understanding current debates on civil religion or the new religious movements, indigenous or imported from the outside, currently attracting adherents in both Eastern and Western societies.

For instance, Bellah (1967) appears to argue initially that as a social system the United States cannot be understood without reference to its guiding national myths, that provide meaning and direction to the society and give it stability amidst crises and an inner dynamic toward justice as well as toward expansion. Bellah (1975) later argues, however, that the same myths must be taken literally but can no longer serve the cybernetic function in a society whose institutional realities negate them in practice regardless of whatever rhetorical service is still paid them. Even the myths themselves appear in a distorted form because of the rigidities and inequalities in the society itself. To process and act upon the information contained in the civil religion would therefore require a radical change in the United States rather than a moving equilibrium or continual cybernetic process.

The same difference of opinion exists in sociological commentary on new religious movements not only in the United States and other Western countries but in the Far East. Wilson (1979) observes that the Eastern-oriented movements will remain tangential to Western societies and supply a set of myths that cannot be 'processed' by such social systems as England and the United States, where they will remain the objects of private and irregular devotion, whereas in Japan, Wilson suggests, new religious movements can serve as 'mediating' structures between otherwise atomic individuals and the central institutions of the state and society. It is a matter of open debate, for instance, whether Eastern religious movements will lose their distinctive quality as they are processed within Western societies or provide the 'seeds of cultural reintegration' (Tiryakian, 1974), but either side of that debate still permits the Eastern movements to be articulated within Western social systems. But the central question is whether or not Eastern religious systems can retain their identity although they may occupy only a marginal place in Western societies: sharing the periphery with magic, the occult, and private preoccupations of one sort or another. It is the systems-theorists who appear to hope that whatever Western societies might find useful in their religious cultural environment can be processed and utilized without radical disruptions occurring in Western institutions, whereas from a critical orientation sociologists despair of such renewal, announce crises in legitimation for societies whose realities are incapable of finding support or direction in sustaining myths of any provenance (Bellah, 1976), or prepare a place for religious myth on the peripheries of modern societies (Wilson, 1975).

METHODOLOGICAL ORIENTATION: THE PRIESTLY AND THE PROPHETIC

Cutting across the distinction that I have made between the critical and the systemic theoretical orientations is the distinction between what I will call the prophetic and the priestly methodological orientations. The distinction is far easier to illustrate than to define. The priest stands for a communicative system in which meanings and intentions are understood and assumed to be in harmony with each other, whereas the prophet stands for a communicative system in which intentions and meanings are problematical and potentially incongruent with each other. The priestly orientation among sociologists takes the meanings and the intentions of speakers as 'understood' because they are presumably congruent with certain established meanings, although these correspondences may be implicit until they are explicated by the sociological inquirer. When

Robert Bellah examines the sermons of John Winthrop and the addresses of Abraham Lincoln, for instance, he assumes that these documents adequately express the meanings of the speakers and that those who heard the addresses inhabited with the speaker a symbolic universe whose existence could be inferred from the documents themselves (Bellah, 1967, 1975). The same methodological orientation underlies Weber's use of Franklin's observations about credit, craftsmen, and Calvinist theology. The observations are reliable evidence of a moral universe linking Protestants' economic and religious roles: a universe into which sociologists could enter precisely because they understood it.

Not all priestly orientations suit a systemic view; indeed some fit a critical perspective in which religious myths do not fit hard economic or political realities. Geertz (1973) notes that speakers at a funeral may mean what they say and share crucially important meanings, although the political structure of the larger society may intrude on the ritual until the ritual fails. Wilson (1979) understands holiness and piety as these sacred values come within the grasp of the laity as a whole (very much as other items of consumption in health, sexuality, and recreation are popularized for a mass market). But he notes that these myths of religious salvation are not congruent with the facts of a bureaucratized society, where power and its justifications elude popular grasp and restrict the possibilities of human community to the peripheral aspects of social life. Reid (1979) notes that certain church leaders in Japan, whose intentions and understandings were not problematical but entirely understood, demanded a Christian rejection of Japanese militarism and a prophetic confrontation with Japanese national goals and identity. A 'priestly' sociological orientation can reconstruct myth and achieve understanding of the way words and actions 'hang together' while still taking a critical view of the relation of myth to reality in the larger society; its defining characteristic is an acceptance of what is usually called the hermeneutic paradigm.

It is possible for the priestly orientation, therefore, to transpose meanings from one context to another: to translate the wording, for instance, of the followers of Meher Baba into the framework of sociological discourse without distortion or loss of meaning (cf. Robbins, 1969). The prophetic-sociological orientation, however, considers the translation-process problematical and the relation of sociological to other modes of discourse entirely contestable (Fabian, 1979). In pointing to the prophetic orientation toward language, it is simplest to refer directly to the work of Habermas, who is perhaps the most consistent theoretical exponent of this orientation. (He is considered 'critical' by his interpreters for reasons that I here consider typical of a 'prophetic' rather than critical orientation: a possible source of confusion unless one keeps it in mind.) The emphasis of the prophetic orientation is on procedures for accounting rather than on understanding. What matters is the degree to which individuals can give adequate accounts of themselves without significant omissions and distortions; otherwise their competence to communicate is in question along with their legitimacy as authoritative or trustworthy speakers (Habermas, 1979). Habermas focusses on a limited range of communicative acts in which the speakers' intentions are to be understood and to be taken seriously. But even within that limited range understanding is problematical, and it is the task of the sociologist adequately to describe the techniques by which individuals give satisfactory accounts of their intentions, statements, and actions. In ideal-typical terms, the prophetic orientation takes all statements as partially distorted and liable to significant omissions, because all actors are subject to the constraints of institutions and of power-relations that limit their freedom to speak and therefore bias their meanings in favour of sustaining their authority.

In Luckmann's (1978, pp. 19ff.) view, however, even this orientation is not sufficient because it examines too narrow a range of communicative actions. Habermas's work is still too hermeneutic to be genuinely prophetic, and no social science can describe or explain human accountability that places a 'hermeneutic' paradigm at its own methodological centre. As Luckmann points out, not all social action is meaningful, not all meaningful acts are communicative in intent, and not all communicative actions can be understood by reference to typical, objectified meanings. The origin of these remarks is not surprising, in view of Luckmann's (1967) earlier work on the 'invisible religion' that escapes typical and objectified meaning-systems and is only partially viable in the activities even of everyday life. But Luckmann is especially useful in establishing some of the central characteristics of the prophetic methodological orientation. In a word, that orientation sees even the accounts that individuals give of their religious behaviour as partial and distorted, partly because of objective constraints on the speaker, partly because the sociologist is too far removed from everyday life and places his informants in the position of speaking for the record, of accounting for themselves.

To put it another way, the sociologist engages others in the activity of producing a text whenever inquiry is conducted. Sociologists then mistakenly apply the techniques of interpretation suitable to texts: 'mistakenly' because the texts are not central, because many religious experiences and actions are noncommunicative or nonsocial, and because understanding is not to be sought in terms of institutional or vernacular meanings. Even when religious action is social and communicative, the intent may be in fact to speak, so that outsiders will hear without understanding the message (Martin, 1980, p. 121). A prophetic orientation rightly suspects the accounts that others give, especially when those accounts are elicited in response to sociological inquiry. Of course, some accounts are constructed to conceal or to leave certain meanings implicit. Not all of everyday life or subjective experience is oriented toward accountability, let alone to the production of data or texts.

The accounts that individuals give may serve to attract social credit in the form of trust, respect, authority, or money. These accounts are likely to employ the same terms and justifications used by institutions to dominate. Thus minority groups couch their protest in the religious symbols of the dominant majority. A system not only teaches a new generation about itself through parents and teachers but is formed by the process in which that new generation talks back to its elders (Giddens, 1979). It is a similarly dynamic process that Beckford (1979) calls to our attention in the phenomenon of modern religious movements. He notes the goodness-of-fit and interplay between the accounts given by sociologists of the dangers inherent in membership in certain cults and the accounts given by jurists and the man-in-the-street. One can learn about a system from the accounts that individuals give concerning their activities, whether that system is a sect like the Jehovah's Witnesses or one as large and complex as a modern nation. These accounts reflect societal beliefs and values, and individuals realize or place themselves in their relation to the system by giving a certain, system-based account of themselves. Since Beckford focusses on the evolutionary aspects of religious change within modern social systems (Shofthaler, 1979, p. 262), I consider him more systemic than critical in his analysis. Beckford holds out hope that the gap between new religious myth and established social reality is not permanent but negotiable.

The distinction between what I have styled as priestly and prophetic methodological orientations to language and communication can also be illustrated by the seriousness (or lack of seriousness) that sociologists attribute to ritual. Prophets have always doubted the seriousness of religious rituals, ever since they first came to despise solemn assemblies. Prophets are populists who find sacred mysteries as suspect as foreign currency and intrigue in high places. But priests assume that one cannot grasp the meaning of the everyday and the ordinary until it is expressed in a liturgical context. It is, therefore, simple enough, from a priestly viewpoint, to draw conclusions about the vitality of a religious tradition from figures on attendance at ecclesiastical rituals, such as the Eucharist, or at rituals that celebrate life or death, coming of age and marriage, within the context of a particular religious institution. These figures, over time, may give one a sense of decline, for instance in the Church of England, a sense of remarkable and continuing vitality in the case of the Roman Catholic Church in Ireland (Phadraig, 1976), or of the resurgence of conservative churches (Kelley, 1972). I cannot begin here to chronicle the trend-data already well established for a wide range of countries in which there are practising sociologists and Christians, not to mention those countries in which the majority are of other traditions entirely and sociologists are few.

Even the categories by which the data are reported tend to reflect priestly concerns with the regularity of lay attendance: some parishioners being marginal and others nuclear or modal (cf. Fichter, 1969). The relative importance given by some sociologists to the central feasts of the Catholic tradition as compared with the celebrations of the life-cycle or, worse yet, the popular celebrations of a somewhat Christianized population at harvest and spring-time, reflect ecclesiastical preoccupations that are only partially altered by respect for the piety, albeit somewhat pagan, of the laity (cf. Isambert, 1977). Indeed, it is difficult for sociological theories not to reflect ecclesiastical concerns and serve ecclesiastical interests (Guizzardi, 1977). At issue is not only the weight one attaches to the festivals most enjoyed by the laity, whether they are baptisms or harvest celebrations, but whether one attaches weight to the national or recreational festivals of the laity and finds religious significance in rituals of sport and politics. The prophet (whether theological or sociological) tends to prefer the rituals of the people to those of the priest, because of their location in everyday life and the home. It is no wonder, as Guizzardi (1977) has pointed out, that sociologists most intimately connected with the Catholic Church have not openly embraced Luckmann's distinction between ecclesiastical religion and the religion that expresses individual transcendence in everyday life. Luckmann (1978) has himself recently chided sociologists for being too concerned with the interpretation of formal and authoritative texts rather than with understanding those human expressions that form the basis of everyday life and seldom reach the level of seriousness and codification of the text: another prophetic riposte at priestly tendencies within the sociological community, couched at the level of appropriate methodologies rather than of a broad theory of secularization. Prophets tend to see ritual in the acts that make sense of the actions of everyday life and preserve the authority of the ordinary individual over and against the weight of traditions and the power of sociological or religious priesthoods. However, as Dobbelaere (1979, p. 41) acutely points out, Luckmann therefore must explain away signs of continued ritual vitality in the churches as disguising an 'internal secularization', i.e. a radical accommodation to popular assumptions, needs, and beliefs.

The difference between the two approaches concerns the trust that they place in language itself. A prophetic view of language that regards metaphors as slippery and regards words as a screen filtering out reality is likely to look for omissions and distortions in any testimony, especially testimony that demands to be taken as seriously as formal religious utterances. A prophetic view of language that looks for real meaning in terms of everyday life will distrust the formal and prescribed meanings of liturgical language as too constrained by the institutional context to be the vehicles for authentic communication. In the prophetic approach, speech is taken more readily as expressive of individual feelings or useful for individual strategies rather than taken seriously unless, of course, it is marked by visible signs of personal commitment and even sacrifice. The sacrifices offered on behalf of the people by a liturgical elite will not guarantee that the words of the people are serious in intent and meaning. From a more priestly approach to language, however, communication is serious when it in effect creates a text on the basis of which consensus can be developed precisely because the text makes intentions explicit and leaves no doubt about the meaning of the words. The question is indeed where to locate the linguistic grounds of authority.

The prophetic orientation therefore makes three assumptions: that any statements about social action will be partially distorted and leave much unsaid; that accounting as such is a form of serious, communicative action that does not by any means encompass everyday life and the possible range of subjective meanings; and that the accounts given to sociological inquirers will be dependent on various institutionalized sources of meaning including the sociological frame of reference itself. In speaking for a sociological as well as for a psychiatric or judicial record, individuals will attempt to follow the norms of rationality in giving their reasons, as these norms are institutionalized in the law, in therapeutic systems, in the religious community itself, and not only, of course, in the sociological interview. The methodological choice is therefore not simply between an attempt to understand or an attempt to explain, but between either of these and a method that focusses on the significant distortions and omissions that result especially from a demand for account-giving. The method is particularly necessary in the study of religious groups or movements whose beliefs and values are not readily understood within the taken-for-granted values and beliefs of the larger society (on these dilemmas, cf. Barker, 1979a).

To summarize: in the presence of two different theoretical orientations that neutralize each other without putting an end to speculative debate, it is necessary to choose a strategy with an eye to the possibility of falsifying the one theory or the other. But more than logical considerations enter into the choice of a methodological orientation to offset one's theoretical predispositions. To know whether to take speakers seriously is difficult in a society that blurs the boundary between serious and strategic communication. When are promises or statements of intent, for instance, merely the casual talk of everyday life or strategic manoeuvres in compromising situations rather than acts of serious communication? Even where societies have rituals that make it quite clear when a person is to be taken seriously, not all speech is thus readily solemnized. The boundary between discussion and pronouncement is not entirely clear in seminars or board rooms, although ethnomethodologists may look for the linguistic signs that mark the shift from one to the other. Where the ritual process of a society leaves the boundary between strategic or expressive and serious speech in doubt, the choice of a methodological orientation must remain problematic. For that reason I will propose that sociologists pair one theoretical orientation with the most contradictory approach to speech: e.g. the systemic with the prophetic and the critical with the priestly. In this crossing of theories and methods, two opposing statements and discussions can be developed that are not reducible one to the other, nor can they be simultaneously maintained as equally true on different 'levels' of analysis or abstraction.

An additional advantage to this approach is the distinction it maintains between statements about language and statements about social systems. Statements about social action are not the same as theories about how societies work. But to say on the one hand that social action is communicative, and on the other hand to say that societies are cybernetic systems for processing messages and information, is to narrow the gap between sociological inquiries into human action and into the working of social systems. The gap virtually closes when a theorist can resolve the two sets of statements into a semiotic theory about language (including nonverbal signs and codes). Like language, societies provide meanings and rules for interpreting messages. The rules provide coherence and structure: the very prerequisites for any social action and for the continuity of social systems. Like language, however, societies interpret and communicate meanings between individuals or corporate actors in a fluid and shifting process that leads to the discovery and renegotiation of what particular actors intended or of what particular acts and messages actually mean. It is therefore possible to argue that social structures are both as stable and as dynamic as language. But if the equation between language and society is true by definition and therefore tautological, sociologists have succeeded only in reconceptualizing without resolving their inconclusive debates on such topics as modernization and secularization. In the next section, however, I will illustrate these alternative combinations of theory and method from current sociological discussions on the role of religion in the process of modernization.

MODERNIZATION: STATIC AND DYNAMIC COMBINATIONS OF THEORY AND METHOD

It would be difficult to find a more decisive example of the simplistic combination of critical orientation and prophetic method than Weber's thesis on the Protestant ethic. For Weber, the reality of modern states and bureaucracies represents the paradoxical effect of a myth, once explicitly religious and alive in a Calvinist culture, that assigns to the individual a heroic but disciplined responsibility for practical conduct and the creation of social organization. The everyday reality is the opposite of the one envisaged by the myth that gave it birth, so to speak: a reality of acquisitiveness in a capitalist society that began by subduing the impulse to consume, and a reality of confinement that began by an impulse to be free from any laws other than those based on one type of rationality or another. For Weber the hope of a free and rational society, once carried by Protestantism, was so diminished that no Christian should delude himself that he could practise his faith in politics, and no student generation should hope to find spiritual excitement in solving the 'hard tasks of the day'. The Protestant dream of a consistency between works and faith may have led to a rational and disciplined ordering of economic and political organizations and even to a 'congruence' between the Protestant ethic and the spirit of Calvinism, but the actual organization of social life eventually depended on a notion of consistency that was far more 'formal' than filled with any spiritual context.

Consistency called for accountability based on legal precedent and on uniform treatment of different cases before the law: a form of rationality that substitutes account-keeping for genuine, personal accountability. The prophetic examination of this form of accounting is a conspicuous element in the critical tradition of sociology. Berger et al. (1974) find in the bureaucratic organization of work and politics the source of alienation: a radical separation between social organization and everyday life. Rubenstein (1975) attributes the capacity and willingness of the Germans to exterminate the Jews to these secularized forms of religious culture. The indictment is clear enough.

The logical (but also simplistic) combination of the systemic theoretical orientation and the priestly methodological approach is found in Parsons's search for congruence through understanding. Secular norms, like bread and wine, are never just what they seem, but carry within and outside, above and beneath them another, latent reality. The relation between myth and reality is organic and subtle rather than discontinuous and contradictory. The myth of human freedom and responsibility carried within the Western religious tradition is for Parsons (1963) the symbolic foundation that constitutes the serious element in social life and makes possible the degree of freedom normally accorded the average citizen as well as the high levels of responsibility and accountability required of politicians, celebrities, bureaucrats, and scientists. On the level of 'civilizational analysis', there is little change in social systems over time, and regardless of the high levels of differentiation in any Western society, there is a consistency in moral standards that can only be accounted for by the pervasive and persisting effects of the

Western religious myth. Even in scientific occupations that self-consciously dispense with that myth, the standards for truth and for professional responsibility can only be understood in their seriousness as constituted by the original myth itself (Greeley, 1973). The carriers of cultural change, especially university faculties themselves, should therefore be the first to understand the extent to which little has changed in the fundamental norms and values of Western societies and of the academic world itself (Nisbet, 1969).

It is fruitful, however, to point up what can be gained from crossing a systemic orientation in theory with a prophetic methodological approach to modernization studies. The two are combined in a phrase from one of Berger's recent titles, referring to the commitments and costs of the process of modernization: 'pyramids of sacrifice'. The loyalties given by children to their fathers are transferred in this process to civic authorities; hence the development of legitimate authorities that can demand from the citizenry the commitments once absorbed by a household economy and by patriarchal local regimes (Slater and Bennis, 1968). The loyalties once conferred on family and co-religionists alone are extended to one's fellow citizens in an occidental city, thus making a form of social organization essential, in the West, to the development of urbanization and capitalism (Weber, 1966; Nash, 1979). The vocational commitments once contained within monastic walls or worked out among religious virtuosos are mobilized by a bourgeoisie that takes disciplined risks and postpones premature satisfactions and judgments in the economic sphere until a long sequence of investment and development warrants a faithful accounting. The self-discipline and commitment given by local nonconformists to congregations and their communities bursts through religious ghettoes and shapes a liberalism and a morality in national politics: a disciplined investment of national resources and the mobilization of moral commitments from the periphery to the national centre (Martin, 1978). It is a process of mobilization that requires the services of religious or secular intellectuals who are autonomous and yet open as much to the political centre as they are to the future (Eisenstadt, 1968): a prophetic community of intellectuals that may be in certain modern Western countries Catholic rather than Protestant (Martin, 1978) or a secular intelligentsia who have been likened to 'clergy without a church' (Shils, 1972). They succeed in taking the loyalties and symbols of 'valued associations' in local communities, friendship, the family, and placing them symbolically at the disposal of the larger society.

From a purely systemic viewpoint, rituals are the ceremonies of a mediating institution that shape the future of a society. They are in effect the vehicles of hope for both individuals and the social order, but sociologists with a prophetic methodological interest, however, are likely to stress the tension between the ritual and the social order and to insist on the distance between rituals and everyday life: the 'otherworldliness' of the social order galvanized and acted out in symbolic form in the liturgies of the sacred community. Liturgies that are too much like the discourse of the market or the garden lose their prophetic tension with the world, just as clergy who ignore their flocks and hanker after the recognition of secular intelligentsia are likely to 'soften the frames of discourse' by translating the hope for a divine kingdom into the expectations for a socialist collective order (Martin, 1979). The prophet therefore holds the mediating institutions and their functionaries responsible for taking the commitments and sacrifices of the people and laying them at the disposal of the nation and its major political or economic organizations; and the prophet also asks for an accounting.

The prophetic approach in sociological analysis inevitably focusses, therefore, on the ways in which particular status groups or classes use social institutions for their own benefit. There is no lack of sociological analysis of the clergy and the middle class who use religious organizations in order to dramatize and legitimate their social roles and to foreclose discussions on alternative social arrangements. Certainly, religious institutions and bureaucracies are alike in reinforcing a 'reality principle' that serves the needs of some strata or professional groups more than others, and the prophetic orientation locates this principle in the accounts given by religious intellectuals or bureaucrats and examines those accounts for significant omissions and distortions. Within religious organizations, it is the more highly educated clergy in positions of the middle or upper ecclesiastical bureaucracies that have advocated social policies far more radical than those favoured by the majority of the laity. Among those changes are internal reforms that provide for new liturgies and new informal relationships between the clergy and the laity. Whether or not there is an actual devolution of power to the laity remains an open question. But the bureaucratic demand that policies be effectively implemented is a partial result of the institutionalization of what Weber identified as a sectarian Protestant commitment to consistency between faith and life and to the consonance of religious words in secular deeds (cf. Robertson, 1979). This norm of consistency may legitimate what Beckford (1979) has noted as the internal prophetic demand of both secular and religious organizations.

When the sociologist chooses a methodological and a theoretical orientation for looking, not at ritual processes, but at larger units, whole societies, or changes over a relatively long time-span, there are primarily three alternatives. The first is simply to relate the methodological approach to the theoretical orientation with which it has the greater affinity; and conversely, to move on to the basis of affinity from theory to method. For instance, a prophetic approach that looks for the gaps and distortions in the accounts given by individuals of their own standards and beliefs has a natural affinity with a critical orientation that focusses on the contradictions between myths and certain objectifiable social facts. The compromises that individuals make between their religious values and the practices of a particular institution or subsystem in everyday life can easily be interpreted or explained in terms of the contradictions in the larger society between religious myths and the norms of bureaucratic or capitalistic institutions. If, however, one adopts a *Verstehen* approach to interpreting the sometimes latent affinities between religious values and goals in work or politics, a systemic orientation enables one to discover at the macrosocial level, a degree of congruence between these various forms of rationality. The relationship between priestly observation and systemic theory is similarly simple and static. Neither theory, however, can confront the other with more than an alternative viewpoint; falsification is out of the question.

A second strategy, however, is to pair one's theoretical choice with the more unlikely methodological approach. Robertson (1978, p. 239) notes that theories in the Weberian tradition tend to ignore 'the modes and categories of the thought of the "ordinary" individual in modern societies' in the interests, presumably, of a *Verstehen* approach that emphasizes the capacity of the observer to perceive the ways in which various aspects of social life hang together regardless of the accounts of the sociological laity. But Robertson is quite right in insisting that the connections be drawn between everyday life and civilizational themes, between large-scale processes and the strategic accounts of individuals in concrete situations. Otherwise the sociologist fails to determine what connection, if any, may exist between folk religion and the religious symbols of the nation. It is interesting, but clearly not sufficient, to note that various shamans, for instance, were the intermediaries between local cults and national shrines (cf. Susumu, 1979), just as it is interesting that a middle level of religious leaders has preached the cross on the periphery of Britain both in the Crusades and in the 19th century. But without ascertaining the accounts of everyday life as given by individuals in local contexts, and without sifting those accounts for distortions and omissions, there is no inner check on the systemic description of a dynamic process linking centre to periphery, abstract religious symbol to individual commitment, national shrine to local cult. It may indeed be, as Robertson (1978, p. 236) suggests, that an adequate account of religion in everyday life would fail to yield 'a set of cultural premises about the working of social life'. The check on systemic orientations is not in the eye of the sociological beholder but in the more or less spontaneous and complete accounts of individuals in the contexts of everyday life.

The same argument can now be made with much greater brevity about the pairing of critical theory and a priestly methodological orientation. The stock-in-trade of critical theory, that Western *gemeinschaftliche* or religious values dash themselves on the hard rocks of industrial and urban societies simply may not fit the practical experience of individuals from the viewpoint of an observer trained to perceive the way life-styles, political beliefs, and religious orientations hang together. It may require the virtuoso interpretations of sociologists trained in the dramaturgical arts to perceive, for instance, dress and conversational styles as a condensed code for political ideologies and religious values (but it can indeed be done — cf. Barker, 1979b). That is the project of sociologists examining 'implicit' religious commitments: implicit because these commitments find inadequate articulation in the social myths of the larger society and inadequate institutionalization. Nonetheless, social anthropologists and sociologists (Douglas, 1975) rightfully chide themselves for missing these correspondences, although they are not elaborated or codified in symbolic systems or explicit civilizational themes. Robertson (1978, p. 130) is getting at just such a possibility, I suspect, in his suggestion that individuals are able to synthesize asceticism and mysticism in the pursuit of individual perfectability, although the larger society lacks any explicit or coherent symbolic synthesis. Ascetic mysticism in fact may be one version of Luckmann's invisible religion: invisible precisely because it is not coherently typified in a particular cultural system.

The choice of a dynamic combination of theory and method makes possible a dialetical opposition between one combination and another. Although it may be premature to grasp for falsification, a critical-priestly theory of religious change in modern societies appears on the face of it to contradict a systemic-prophetic one. The former holds that individuals may be integrating in their own minds and behaviour those values and commitments that the larger society places in opposition to each other, whereas the latter theory suggests that whatever religious and secular values the larger society may succeed in synthesizing may well be held in abeyance or radically separated by individuals in the concrete situations of everyday life, regardless of their efforts to be accountable in terms of the larger society's value-systems. The two theories can of course be specified to different groups, communities, or time-spans within a single society, but they seem clearly to contradict one another when applied simultaneously to the same social unit. The improvement over the relatively simple combinations of critical-prophetic and systemic-priestly orientations should be clearer when illustrated in their application to recent studies of the ritual aspect of modernization in societies as different as Soviet Russia and Belgium. Undertaken by two different authors for separate purposes, the two studies are not comparable in scope or design. But they illustrate the potential fruitfulness of juxtaposing antagonistic theoretical orientations and methodological approaches to language in the interest of reaching a critical test of hypotheses concerning religion and the process of secularization.

In examining the resurgence of ritual in Soviet society, Lane (1979, p. 264) points to the contradiction between a Marxist myth, which erodes the distinction between manual and intellectual labour in a classless society, and the reality into which rituals of induction into the working class introduce their participants. It is ironically a reality in which ritual specialists are freed from manual labour to provide rituals which will raise manual labour in public esteem and help to lower the aspirations of working-class youths for more privileged occupations. Up to this point, the critical orientation prevails in Lane's analysis as she contrasts Soviet myths with the hard fact of persistent class distinctions and the postponement of hopes for a more egalitarian society.

Lane's analysis of rituals in Soviet society is thus far within the usual limits of the critical intelligentsia who characteristically reduce the meaning and significance of ideology and myth and fits an analysis of Russia as being a fundamentally secular society governed by such objective goals as a five-year plan or by the use of force rather than by symbolic acts (cf. Moore, 1965). But Lane takes a more systemic view in arguing that the new rituals in Soviet society are widespread, generally accepted, and growing in their influence as a means of normative control highly valued by a political leadership bent on cultural integration in Soviet society (Lane, 1979, pp. 268-70). To put it simply, the rituals are fast shaping the reality with which sociologists must cope in analyzing Russia. These rituals shape the society to come, as Harre (1976) puts it, by changing certain action into acts. Lighting candles, marching, giving, and receiving promises are actions which in the context of ritual become acts intended to create a proud and conscious working class or to place the death of a citizen in a continuous and promising historical context. The test of this critical orientation, therefore, is the significance that the rituals in fact have for the individual on the working class. Lane (1979) suggests that at first the participants may not be entirely serious in their participation, but that meanings and intentions may require seriousness in time.

One can also study rituals, however, from a more systemic point of departure. In discussing the secularization of Belgium, Dobbelaere (1979) has noted that, on the macrolevel, Catholic and Protestant churches enjoy the status of 'pillars' that serve their constituents as national organizations in such areas as work and education, health and welfare: the column of the Church reaching from the local community to the central organization of the state (cf. Dobbelaere, 1979). But within Catholic hospitals and schools, he notes an internal secularization that is the result of professionalization. Dobbelaere (1979, pp. 46ff.) argues that Catholic rituals have been reduced to a marginal role in the everyday life of these institutions, and the sacramental aspects of medical care have been reduced to purely personal transactions between patients and a specifically 'religious' nursing staff specializing in kindness. Dobbelaere challenges systemic hypothesis by examining the actual transactions of hospital routines, where 'medical' standards dominate hospital policy and practice. Institutional accounts that are biased toward a Catholic hegemony tend to distort the 'inner secularization' of everyday life. The accounts of the Church, therefore, disguise the domination of a medical profession that tolerates faith and religious practices only in the interstices of the institution and at the level of personal relationship.

Sociologists do not, of course, assume that rituals link the larger society's values to everyday life. Some sociologists have criticized

Church officials who have emptied even the liturgy of its magical significance and deprived lay devotion of its communal and ethnic vitality (cf. Douglas, 1972). In the name of laicizing the liturgy, according to this critique the hierarchy have deprived the laity of their most valued symbols and practices and given them in turn a formal and empty rite justified by archaism and specialized liturgical scholarship. Among such modernized rituals one finds

> ...insufficient provision with purpose-built accommodation for the life-cycle rituals, hasty and amateurish work in their execution, undue formalism and weak utilization of artistic means and symbolism due to insufficient participation by the creative intelligentsia (Lane, 1979, p. 270).

This criticism is directed at the new Soviet rituals, but the same words might well have been written by Douglas in her attack on the new Catholic rites, or by Martin (1979) in his appraisal of the Church of England's efforts at liturgical reform. A critical orientation toward the separation between religious myth and social reality may test itself in the light of the common sense that individuals make of their beliefs and actions. Critical intelligentsia will then more easily understand the survival of religious transcendence despite the apparently hopeless contradictions between religious culture and secular societies. Conversely, sociologists who perceive interlocking religious and secular institutions in the larger society may correct their systemic vision by examining the strategies, limitations, and compromises of individuals within those institutions in the decisions of everyday life.

CONCLUSION

It is unlikely that sociologists of religion will abandon the distinction between myth and reality, intractable and problematical as it inevitably is. To abandon the distinction would eliminate the capacity of the sociologist to demonstrate how the practices of everyday life and the institutional rules in a wide range of social contexts are rooted in myths or justified by them. Without such a distinction the critical sociologist would lack a standpoint from which to correct the distortions in the accounts of social life provided by commentators with limited perspectives or covert ideological interests. But to employ the distinction between myth and reality is to claim a privileged standpoint for the sociologist of religion: a claim that has been increasingly undermined by the self-consciousness and reflexivity of the sociological community during the past decade.

Functionalism has provided a privileged standpoint for the sociological inquirer in the past, but it no longer guarantees the sociologist's own immunity to debunking and correction. Functionalists have been able to complete what was missing in the personal accounts of religious commitment and behaviour by introducing variables from the social system. Thus the sectarian is portrayed as unwittingly engaged in draining tension from the system or in recruiting new adherents to traditional values associated with work and the family. Functionalists have also been able to correct for distortions in lay accounts of religiosity by inferring the existence of needs left unsatisfied by the larger society, whether needs for basic satisfaction, for a stable and respected identity, or for a predictable and understandable social environment. Functionalists have therefore been not only exponents of the values embedded in particular societies, but they have also interpreted religious myths as opposed to the disappointing facts of social life. Not restricted simply to understanding what individuals mean when they express their religious commitments and motivations, functionalists have also completed and corrected individuals' accounts by examining data from everyday life and from official statements of a society's or organization's religious identity and purpose (Glock and Stark, 1965). The very attractiveness of functionalism has been its openness to the two methodological approaches that I have termed 'priestly' and 'prophetic' in this discussion. Despite its detractors, furthermore, functionalism is capable of social criticism as well as of a benign viewpoint that perceives order where others see only conflict or chaos (Hadden, 1973). To abandon functionalism is therefore to abandon a privileged methodological stance and a synthetic theoretical viewpoint. Some might therefore argue that sociologists of religion have exchanged their functionalist birthright for a mess of ethnomethodological or philosophical pottage.

It is unlikely that sociologists of religion will abandon the search for a privileged standpoint from which to improve on the accounts that others, lay or professional, give of their religious activities. The claim that a sociologist's account of a given religious group or practice is an improved and not merely adequate translation of that group's own experience and understanding rests on the sociologist's more direct and complete access to common sources of knowledge. Sociologists who regard religion as a universal and perennial aspect of social life will infer the existence of deep structures, e.g. of an unconscious that is a mixture of libido and internalized cultural images, access to which enables the sociologist to decode and translate the meaning of others' religious experience. It is this methodological stance that I have been terming the 'priestly'. Sociologists who regard religious knowledge as 'produced' within the interests of social classes and the limits of social contexts will supply missing data from a variety of other sources, e.g. from the accounts of others and from actual behaviour: a prophetic orientation, as I have already noted.

Both methodological stances, however, will increasingly need to take into account the interaction between sociological and lay versions of social reality. Functionalist accounts are used by judges and ecclesiastical lobbyists to justify social policies. The notion of alienation has for some time entered into journalistic and popular culture as not only interpreting but justifying deviant religious behaviour and religious withdrawal from the larger society. Sociologists, as Friedrichs (1970) notes, have projected the alienation of the free-floating intelligentsia on to the societies in which they live, and in so doing they have provided a rhetoric for social protest. Politicians draw upon popularized sociological criticisms of modern societies, and the leadership of racial and student protest in the 1960s was largely informed by sociological perspectives. In the sociology of religion, Robert Bellah's notion of a civil religion has entered into politicians' and ecclesiastics' definitions of their own situation in the United States. In England David Martin has directly intervened in the process of liturgical change. It is no longer possible for sociologists of religion to take a privileged standpoint, since they are in fact continuing to produce the effects that they observe and to influence the official and unofficial accounts given of social life by a wide range of groups and individuals.

An epistemological crisis is therefore an apparent fact of the contemporary situation of the sociology of religion. The crisis is shared with the social sciences as a whole, to the extent that sociology lacks a paradigm for knowing what is central as opposed to peripheral, what is superficial as opposed to what is latent, what is material as opposed to a matter of appearance alone (Luckmann, 1979). Practice, whether defined as fieldwork or secondary analysis, is still the only criterion of the validity of ideas, as indeed Marx and Mannheim once insisted (Giddens, 1979, pp. 183-84). But practice, however defined, is still subject to the limitations imposed by social context and by the distribution and use of power. Although sociologists may wish impartially to interpret the new religious movements to those concerned about the latter's goals and techniques, it is not likely that sociologists of religion will successfully disclaim contextual limitations and bias.

The more effective interpreters, moreover, will have uttered prophesies that are either 'self-defeating' (Friedrichs, 1970) or self-fulfilling, according to their content and the outcome of public discussion. Sociologists of religion have credited various myths with constituting social reality: myths of national identity and purpose, myths of human nature and destiny. Conversely, the mythology of sociological thought has in turn passed into popular and official versions of the progress of secularization from traditional to modern societies, of the passage from alienation to transcendence, and of continuity and change in religious institutions and movements. In this transition the world begins to look to itself the way it has looked to sociologists for several generations. It may be necessary for sociologists to detach themselves from their own mythology in the future in order more clearly to assess the realities of the world around them.

REFERENCES

Acquaviva, Sabino S. (1979) *The Decline of the Sacred in Industrial Society.* Oxford: Basil Blackwell.
Barker, Eileen (1979a) Mimeographed essay on Methodological Issues in the Study of the Unification Church.
Barker, Eileen (1979b) 'Implicit Religion' (mimeo).
Beckford, James (1979) 'Politics and the Anti-Cult Movement', *The Annual Review of the Social Sciences of Religion*, 3.
Bellah, Robert (1967) 'Civil Religion in America', *Daedalus,* Winter.
Bellah, Robert (1975) *The Broken Covenant.* New York: Seabury Press.
Bellah, Robert (1976) 'The New Religious Consciousness and the Crisis of Modernity', pp. 333-52 in *The New Religious Consciousness*, edited by C. Glock and R. Bellah. Berkeley, Calif.: University of California Press.
Berger, Peter L. and Luckmann, Thomas (1967) *The Sacred Canopy.* New York: Doubleday.
Berger, Peter et al. (1974) *The Homeless Mind. Modernization and Consciousness.* Harmondsworth: Penguin.

Dobbelaere, Karel (1979) 'Professionalization and Secularization in the Belgian Catholic Pillar', *Japanese Journal of Religious Studies*, 6, 1-2 (March-June): 39-64.
Douglas, Mary (1972) *Natural Symbols: Explorations in Cosmology*. New York: Random House.
Douglas, Mary (1975) *Implicit Meanings: Essays in Anthropology*. London: Routledge and Kegan Paul.
Eisenstadt, S. N. (1968) *The Protestant Ethic and Modernization: A Comparative View*. New York: Basic Books.
Fabian, Johannes (1979) 'The Anthropology of Religious Movements: From Explanation to Interpretation', *Social Research*, 46, 1 (Spring): 4-35.
Fichter, J. H. (1969) 'Sociological Measurements of Religiosity', *Review of Religious Research*, 10, 3: 169-77.
Friedrichs, Robert W. (1970) *A Sociology of Sociology*. New York: Free Press.
Geertz, Clifford (1973) *Interpretation of Cultures*. New York: Basic Books.
Giddens, Anthony (1979) *Central Problems in Social Theory. Action, Structure, and Contradiction in Social Analysis*. London: Macmillan.
Glock, Charles and Stark, Rodney (1965) *Religion and Society in Tension*. Chicago: Rand McNally.
Greeley, Andrew (1973) *The Persistence of Religion*. London: SCM Press.
Guizzardi, G. (1977) 'Structuration et transformations d'un pouvoir symbologue', *Acts of the 14th International Conference on the Sociology of Religion*. Strasbourg: CISR.
Habermas, Jürgen (1979) *Communication and the Evolution of Social Order*. Boston: Beacon Press.
Hadden, Jeffrey K. (1973) *Religion in Radical Transition*. New York: Transaction Books.
Harre, Rom (1976) *Life Sentences: Aspects of the Social Role of Language*. New York: Wiley.
Isambert, F. (1977) 'Structuration et transformations d'un pouvoir symbologue', *Acts of the 14th International Conference on the Sociology of Religion*. Strasbourg: CISR.
Kelley, Dean M. (1972) *Why Conservative Churches are Growing*. New York: Harper and Row.
Lane, Christel (1979) 'Ritual and Ceremony in Contemporary Soviet Society', *The Sociological Review*, 27, 2 (May): 253-78.
Luckmann, Thomas (1967) *The Invisible Religion*. New York: Macmillan.
Luckmann, Thomas (1979) 'Hermeneutics as a Paradigm for Social Science?', in *Social Method and Social Life*, edited by Michael Bremer. Oxford: Academic Press.
Martin, David (1978) *A General Theory of Secularization*. London: Blackwell.
Martin, David (1979) 'The Cultural Politics of Established Churches', *Japanese Journal of Religious Studies*, 6, 1-2 (March-June): 287-302.
Martin, David (1980) *The Breaking of the Image*. London: Blackwell.
Moore, Barrington (1965) *Soviet Politics*. New York: Harper and Row.
Nash, Gary (1979) *The Urban Crucible: Social Change, Political Consciousness and the Origins of the American Revolution*. Cambridge, Mass.: Harvard University Press.
Nisbet, Robert A. (1969) *Social Change and History: Aspects of the Western Theory of Development*. Oxford: Oxford University Press.

Parsons, Talcott (1963) 'Christianity in Western Industrial Society', pp. 33-70 in *Social Values, Tradition and Change*, edited by Odiv A. Tiryakian. New York: Harper and Row.
Phadraig, Maire Nic Ghiolla (1976) 'Religion in Ireland: Preliminary Analysis', *Social Studies — Irish Journal of Sociology*, 5, 2 (Summer): 113-80.
Reid, David (1979) 'Secularization Theory and Japanese Christianity: The Case of the Nihon Kirisuto Kyodan', *Japanese Journal of Religious Studies*, 6, 1-2 (March-June): 347-78.
Robbins, Thomas (1969) 'Eastern Mysticism and the Resocialization of Drug Users: The Meher Baba Cult', *Journal for the Scientific Study of Religion*, 8, 2 (Fall): 308-17.
Robertson, Roland (1978) *Meaning and Change. Explorations in the Cultural Sociology of Modern Societies*. New York: New York University Press.
Robertson, Roland (1979) 'The Sociology of Religious Movements: Shifts in the Analytical and Empirical Face'. Paper read at the American Sociological Association session on Contemporary Religious Movements, Boston.
Rubenstein, Richard (1975) *The Conning of History*. New York: Harper and Row.
Schofthaler, Traugott (1979) 'On the Concept of Systems Theory in the German Sociology of Religion', pp. 261-2 in *Acts of the 15th International Conference on the Sociology of Religion*. Venice: CISR.
Shils, Edward (1972) *The Intellectuals and the Powers, and Other Essays*. Chicago: University of Chicago Press.
Sixel, Friedrich W. (1976/7) 'The Problem of Sense: Habermas v. Luhmann', in *On Critical Theory*, edited by John O'Neill. New York: Seabury Press, 1976; London: Heinemann, 1977.
Slater, Philip and Bennis, Warren (1968) *The Temporary Society*. New York: Harper and Row.
Susumu, Shimazono (1979) 'The Living Kanir Idea', *Japanese Journal of Religious Studies*, 6, 3 (September): 389-412.
Tiryakian, Edward (1974) *On the Margin of the Visible: Sociology, the Esoteric and the Occult*. New York: Wiley.
Weber, Max (1966) *The City*, translated and edited by D. Martindale and G. Neuwirth. New York: Free Press.
Wilson, Bryan (1979) 'Contemporary Transformations of Religion', *Japanese Journal of Religious Studies*, 6, 1-2 (March-June): 193-216.

4
The Sociology of Military Institutions Today

Gwyn Harries-Jenkins
University of Hull

Since its inception in 1962, the Research Committee on Armed Forces and Society of the International Sociological Association has sought to promote the study of sociology of the armed forces. As the field of interest develops and particularly as new persons become interested in the subject matter, the committee, under the guidance of Morris Janowitz, its founding chairman, has been concerned with the need to maintain an integrated development of the subject and, at the same time, to relate it to other social science disciplines. This brief essay is a review of the development and relationship of the sociology of military institutions to other themes and perspectives. As such, it is an outline of a fuller review which is to be published by the International Sociological Association as a Trend Report.

Because of the diffuse nature of this area of study, a common starting point in overviews of the sociology of military institutions is the establishment of some system of classification which reflects the main links of contemporary interest and emerging tasks.

A CLASSIFICATION OF MILITARY SOCIOLOGY

One way in which the study of armed forces and society can be categorized is to relate the extant literature to discrete topical constructs. These, for example, can be initially presented in terms of the power-elite soldier, the professional soldier, the common soldier, the citizen soldier and the Third World soldier. This is a heuristic division which sets out to counteract the diffuseness of studies in this area. It is also a division which can be rationalized on cenceptual grounds. Each of the five noted topic areas has an ongoing research tradition which is not necessarily present in or related to analysis in a second area. Thus the study of the *common* soldier may necessitate the evaluation of a cultural pattern which is not readily identified with the concept of the *citizen* soldier. For the former, a major research hypothesis can be identified with the documentation of a pervasive resentment among enlisted men towards the privileged status of the officer. For the latter, on the other hand, a more critical question is the extent to which the citizen soldier can be identified with an ideal-type. This suggests that the defining characteristics ideally stress a willingness to take up arms at the behest of the parent society, a wish to retain civilian values while serving as a member of the armed forces, the ability to bring ingenuity into the military structure and the readiness to resume easily civilian pursuits on completion of a tour of duty.

Underlying these distinctions, however, is a pattern of a convergence of interests which links the otherwise disparate topic areas subsumed under the generic heading of 'armed forces and society'. Initially this convergence can be identified in terms of the intraorganizational effects of the changing functions of armed forces and in terms of the extent to which the military exerts an influence on the parent civilian society. Looked at in more detail, this communality of interests can be equated with a system of classification which is essentially tripartite. In brief, this schema reflects a simple division of labour which has been seen to be the most productive both to maintain an integrated development of the field, and at the same time to relate the subject to other social science disciplines.

This classification organizes the sociological study of the military under three headings: first, the military professional and the military organization; second, civil-military relations; and third, the sociology of war and armed group conflict. Although boundaries between their interests can be carefully delineated, we find in practice that there is considerable blurring of interests along any dividing line. Thus the study of civil-military relations, to take one example, may involve a consideration of the problems of military professionalism. This is particularly so if in these studies we create a conceptual framework which begins from the thesis that 'the existence of the officer corps as a professional body gives a unique cast to the modern problems of civil-military relations' (Huntington, 1957, p. 7).

This tripartite division, moreover, reflects previously postulated concepts, for each division corresponds directly to an important earlier contribution to sociological theory. This link thus stresses the continuity of interest and concerns, while concomitantly recognizing a persistent use of research development. In turn, the established background to this conceptual framework rationalizes the adoption of the interdisciplinary approach to the study of armed forces and society. This is most marked in the manner in which three contributions which were prepared in the 1930s set out to encompass history, political sciences, and psychology and thus provide a broad background to the hypotheses which were formulated. Indeed it is the width of this approach which has been one of the major strengths of the teaching and research on the sociology of military institutions.

The first of these major works was Karl Demeter's pioneer study, *Das deutsche Heer und seine Offiziere* (1935). This constituted the first extensive and major historical-sociological research on a specific group of military personnel. It drew heavily on both historical and sociological methodology even though its sociological stance was more implicit than explicitly formulated. Nevertheless, the sociological theory which is used is an important contribution to study in this field, for it is a development of Max Weber's brilliant and penetrating analysis of military institutions. In the same way that this theory has had a continuing impact on the social scientific community, the work of Demeter is also a valuable commentary on Alfred Vagts' *The History of Militarism* which appeared in 1937 and offered a clear and noteworthy distinction between 'militarism' and the 'military way'.

In Demeter's study the framework of much subsequent research into the social origins, education and career development of an elite group was meticulously laid down. This later research owed a very considerable debt to the earlier work and it is no exaggeration to conclude that the study by Demeter was the prototype for a whole generation of more elaborate and more explicitly sociological analysis of military professionals, professionalism and professionalization. The emphasis which is now placed on the more systematic application of organizational theory to this field thus reflects the evolution of this study of the military profession and the military organization as one of the most developed aspects of the sociology of the military.

In the second area — that of civil-military relations — the genesis of much subsequent study was the publication in 1941 of Harold D.

Lasswell's classic essay, 'The Garrison State' (1941). Drawing on his earlier conceptual statements, Lasswell refined the analysis of the dangers of militarism in an advanced industrialized society which was subject to a sustained threat of war. His basic hypothesis completely rejected earlier notions of military dictatorship, for he argued that militarization and militarism in these advanced societies could not be — and would not be — characterized by direct rule by military elites. Rather it would be identified by expansion of the military into those political roles which are traditionally held by civilian elites. This interpenetration of the military and civilian elites would then be characterized by coalitions of an authoritative type.

The flow of research which has stemmed from this conceptual antecedent has been very considerable. The controversy generated by the publication of the original article in 1941 anticipated the subsequent debate about the power elite and about the military-industrial complex. Some of the debate rested on highly polemical statements which stemmed from the manner in which Lasswell offered his formulations not as rigid prediction but as the very basis of social and political policy. What the volume of research also suggests is that the analysis of the relationship between armed forces and society in this specific area raises fundamental issues which require continuing assessment. Questions about the balance of civil-military influence within a given society thus continue to be central to the study of the sociology of the military.

In the third area of research, the social scientific analysis of the courses, processes and consequences of armed conflict and warfare, the boundaries of the area of concern were succinctly documented by Quincy Wright in his perceptive work *The Study of War* (1939). Wright tried to go beyond the descriptive historical case study which had hitherto characterized much of the research in this field, and set out to provide a text which would serve as a stimulating analytical and statistical research summary. Such a text, in time, it was hoped, would act as a powerful stimulus in promoting analysis in an area which, hitherto, had largely resisted the introduction of systematic research.

What remains a matter of some controversy is the extent to which Wright was successful. In general, it cannot be said that the results and the intellectual outcome were all successful and beneficial. There can be no doubt that he was very much aware of the methodological and conceptual imperfections of his approach. But, irrespective of the criticisms which may emerge, the main import of Wright's work is that he was a pioneer in the establishment of a novel approach to the study of a particular area. It was, in short, an approach which in this part of the postulated classification — as in other sectors — served to promote further and more specific research into that generic area which may be subsumed under the heading of military sociology.

In these preliminary comments, we have sought to outline briefly the boundaries of the subject under consideration. To effect this, we have adopted an approach which is based on a specific conceptual framework that utilizes a three-fold division of interests. Such a division is derived from major theoretical antecedents which characterized the emergence of the sociology of military institutions. This division, however, is not only a reflection of what occurs in Western industrialized democracies. There is neither a need nor a rationale for ethnocentricity. Although the study of military sociology as a subject is firmly located in Western intellectual traditions and initiatives, we nevertheless retain a world-wide perspective. This is not to deny that it may be necessary to modify categories and concepts in order to accommodate traditional, cultural and regional differences. In the study of armed forces and society, as in other fields, no simple-minded theories of institutional convergence will negate these differences. The patterns of similarities, however, are most striking and we can accept that the subject matter of military sociology is of global interest, thereby encouraging both national and international research and scholarship.

THE MILITARY PROFESSIONAL AND THE MILITARY ORGANIZATION

As we have suggested in the Introduction, this field of interest is one of the most developed and diligently researched aspects of the sociology of the military. The basic referents for discussion are the two major studies of Huntington (1957) and Janowitz (1960). These share a common overall perspective, for they stress that the career military officer is a member of a profession that possesses certain characteristics which could contribute to effectiveness and responsiveness. However, as Larson (1974) notes in a perceptive essay it is the difference between these two theorists which highlights the conceptual and problematic questions of modern military professionalism.

Huntington thus argues that military officership is a fully developed profession because it manifests to a significant degree three principal characteristics of the ideal-type professional model: expertise, corporateness and responsibility. The military, however, carries out its purpose within a political environment without regard to political, moral or other nonmilitary considerations, so that its professionalism can be summarized as its expertise over lethal violence, a corporate self-identity and ultimate responsibility to the larger polity.

According to Huntington, only officers involved in and dedicated to the central expertise of the management of violence are members of the military profession. This implies that neither commissioned specialists such as lawyers and doctors nor enlisted men can be typed as military professionals. Furthermore, the characteristics of the latter are derived from, and are shaped by the content and function of the military task. Thus the professional officer is, above all, obedient and loyal to the authority of the state, competent in military expertise, dedicated to using his skill to provide for the security of the state, and politically and morally neutral. His sense of professional commitment is shaped by a military ethic which reflects a carefully inculcated set of values and attitudes. These are seen to constitute a unique professional outlook or military mind which may be characterized as 'pessimistic, collectivist, historically inclined, power-oriented, nationalistic, militaristic, pacifist and instrumentalist...in brief, realistic and conservative' (Huntington, 1957, p. 79).

Janowitz, in contrast, treats the military as a social system in which the professional characteristics of the officer corps change over time and are variable in that they encompass norms and skills including, but also going beyond, the direct management of violence. While he specifies the characteristics which make officership a profession — expertise, lengthy education, group identity, ethics, standards of performance — he identifies the profession not as a static model but as a dynamic bureaucratic organization which changes over time in response to changing conditions. This recognizes the extent to which the form of existing military organizations and professionalized officer corps has been shaped by the impact of broad social transformations since the turn of the century. More specifically, this implies that armed forces are experiencing a long-term transformation toward convergence with civilian structures and norms. It can thus be hypothesized that as a result of broad social changes, the basis of authority and discipline in the armed forces has shifted to manipulation and consensus; military skills have become more socially representative; membership of the elite has become more open and the ideology of the profession has become more political. As a result of this, the traditional heroic warrior role has given way to an ascendant managerial-technical role. In short, the military profession as a whole has become similar to large, bureaucratic, nonmilitary institutions. It has, in effect, become civilianized.

The comparisons and contrasts between these two studies of the significant theoretical aspects of military professionalism have served to encourage a considerable body of further research. Much of this analysis is stimulated initially by a wish to evaluate critically the way in which control is exercised by society over an occupational group. Here, the basic premise is that the controls by which effectiveness and responsiveness are achieved in any public bureaucracy may be divided into those which are 'external' to it and those which are 'internal'. The former are imposed and enforced by the state, often as an element of coercive control. The latter in contrast can be defined as 'self-regulation' for this is a form of social control based on the values and standards of individuals within the bureaucracy.

THE MILITARY ORGANIZATION

The study of the military as a profession has been consistently paralleled by the study of the military as an organization. This pattern of research reflects the argument that in modern society profession and formal organization are the most important institutional variables controlling occupational and administrative decisions and actions. Research in this field has also shown that these variables contain many common elements. Such characteristics as universal standards, expertise and affective neutrality therefore invite further analysis as do such major issues as the extent to which authority in both cases is derived from special knowledge and skill rather than rank, and how far professional and organizational status are derivatives of achieved, not ascribed, positions.

There are, however, significant differences between these two institutional patterns, and the study of the military as an organization tends to concentrate on these. In this context, the basic conceptual framework is derived from the Weberian model of the ideal-type bureaucracy, so that the field of research focusses on the concept of the military as a bureaucratic organization. Concomitantly, the boundaries of this research are set by the overriding reality that military formations are organized on a national basis and that many features of armed forces as bureaucracies are equally to be found in civilian organizations.

Theories of military organization are thus more closely related to general theories of sociology and to a specific theory of military sociology than many other subject areas in this field. A review of the literature reveals three major problems of general sociological interest which, though not entirely unique to the military, are nevertheless encountered there in aggravated fashion. The basic issues are: (1) how to bring the traditional military authority structure into line with the new technology; (2) how to cultivate and promote innovation; and (3) how to maintain organizational effectiveness under severe strain.

In recent years, however, the bulk of research in this area has tended to focus on cross-comparative analysis. One hitherto unexplored area is the sociological analysis of nonconventional military forces such as liberation armies or guerrilla forces. Studies of more conventional military organizations, as we have hitherto stressed, have begun from the premise that the military can be regarded as the prototype of bureaucratic organization with an emphasis on stratification and centralization of authority. This premise has been criticized as part of a call for further investigation of the relationship between Weberian bureaucracy and the military model. The link between 'bureaucracy' and 'military' which was so admirably summed up by Friedrich continues, however, to dominate the trend of research in this field.

CIVIL-MILITARY RELATIONS

It is fair to say that before the Second World War, civil-military relations received very little attention from social scientists. This is not to suggest that contemporary issues have no historical precedent for, as a number of studies have shown us, these issues have been of longstanding concern in industrialized societies. More recently, however, the genesis of increased interest can be traced back to the publication in 1956 of Mills' *The Power Elite*. This posited a small and unified ruling elite within American society who controlled the means of resource allocation and power. In contrast with the stress placed on economic determinism in the classical

Marxist concept of 'ruling class', Mills drew attention to the military and political determinism of this power elite. He thus argued that senior military officers — the war lords — were integral members of the power elite in common with other individuals coming from the apex of the corporate and political bureaucracies.

This theme of a dominant military elite was to become a leitmotiv in much of the later literature that appeared in the 1960s on the subject of the military-industrial complex. It was reflected, for example, in the terms which were used to describe this complex or to portray the subsidiary effects of its operations: 'warfare state'; 'armed society'; 'weapons culture'; 'military socialism'; and 'military-industrial bureaucracy'. The theme was essentially characterized by a belief that the military was an organization which could impose its will on society, would receive a disproportionate share of scarce resources, and could shape the pattern of economic distribution within the nation state.

This attribution of a primary if not dominant role to the armed forces in the industrial-military complex is, however, questioned by some studies in this field. On the one hand, the autonomous bureaucracy of civilian administrators is held to be paramount; on the other, Marxist writers have consistently pointed to the predominance of corporate wealth over military aggrandisement. In general terms, however, the significance of these questions is not that they produce a precise and accurate evaluation of the distribution of power within a society, but that they reflect an attempt to move research into armed forces and society away from too exclusive a concern with intramilitary variables. In this attempt, studies of civil-military relations have traditionally had two major foci. Firstly, analysis concentrates on the normal participation of the military in that part of the policy process by which missions and levels of support are determined. Secondly, studies consider intervention by the military in civilian politics. Most of the work on these two topics has been by political scientists. In this they have produced an abundance of case studies. These look critically at the reorganization of the defence machinery, and at those specific situations where the military have coercively intervened to bring about the fall of civil governments.

Although a large number of case materials have been produced, the study of civil-military relations has not led to the rigorous formulation of those variables which are significant for comparative study. All suggestions that the various inquiries be placed on a firmer theoretical footing have seemingly gone unheeded. Comparative study, it can be concluded, needs to go much further in seeking systematic relationships between such factors as the internal characteristics of the military, the nature of the contacts and exchanges between them and civilians on various levels in and out of government, and general social and political conditions. In addition, comparative study must look for a specific pattern of political relations between soldiers and their governments.

MILITARY MODERNIZATION

An important group of case studies are those which look critically at the issue of military modernization. Put simply, the military modernizers school begins from the premise that society — and more particularly the Third World — embarked on an upward developmental curve. This leads to representative politics as well as to socioeconomic growth. Ideally, it refers to a developmental system in which, within the constraints of the Westminster model of political structures, newly independent countries are able to exercise national sovereignty or pursue a national policy free from the dictates of Western imperial control.

In the ensuing analysis of the role of the military in this developmental system, a basic assumption hinges on the observation that all new nations desire to become modern. This apparent universal goal creates a number of problems. Firstly, the meaning of modernization is either undefined or is variously defined. The general statement implies that military modernization is concerned with the social, political and economic scenery of the developing societies. Yet there is a tendency for analysts to focus on the potential for economic development, since many definitions emphasize the economic dimension as one of the few basic variables to the exclusion of other considerations.

A wider analysis of the multidimensional definition of modernization stresses four significant areas of concern: (1) structural change involving institutional differentiation; (2) sociodemographic changes; (3) changes in the value-system and (4) the capacity for sustained growth. From this, we are presented with various indices of modernization such as economic differentiation, communication, urbanization and political development. It is, however, in this later area that the role of armed forces as agents of modernization is seen to have particular relevance. This reflects the conclusion that the critical question is that of the role of armed forces in such components of political development as national integration and the institutionalization of political organization. Consequently, the role of the military in the political development of new nations has become a matter of considerable academic interest and debate.

Here, the heritage of Turkey under Ataturk serves as a focal point for intellectual formulation. The policy issues of military assistance and basic questions of the political strategies of social and economic development have produced numerous academic studies. Two stages of intellectual development characterize such studies. In the early phase of interest in the modernizing role of armed forces, research produced a series of speculative essays which were also exercises in comparative analysis. The lasting contribution of these efforts, however, was the emphasis that was placed on the restrictions and difficulties which military regimes would encounter in their attempts to achieve economic development and political stability. Additionally, these early studies tended to stress that the emergence of different configurations of political and social structure in the process of modernization was the result of the diverse circumstances of revolutions and coups d'etat.

In looking critically at such a system, a primary issue of concern is the qualitative and quantitative contribution which the military makes to the creation and perpetuation of innovation. In short, this is seen as the modernizing role of armed forces. It has attracted considerable interest. Much of this is concerned with the critical analysis of national case-studies. An alternative approach looks more critically at the theoretical constructs which validate or rationalize the thesis of military modernization. In this later perspective, the arguments of the military modernizers, as we have noted elsewhere, are essentially fourfold: (1) the armed forces are seen to be the most modernized institution in the Third World and therefore readily able to implement economic development (2) military leaders are considered to be less prone to personal corruption than civilian counterparts (3) military socialization is accepted as the means whereby tradition-bound recruits are acculturated into modern belief systems and (4) the armies of Third World societies are seen to be instruments of a new middle class, serving as the vanguard of nationalism and social reform.

These arguments have been related to a number of specific studies. The Middle East, Africa and South East Asia have all attracted considerable attention. A particular subset of regional studies that constitutes a dominant theme in the literature of civil-military relations, concerns itself with the study of military governments and modernization in Latin America. Here, the initial premise of discussion is the thesis that the role of the military as governors is inseparable from their role as military officers. From this, it is possible to identify a conception of modernization which emphasizes the significance of social, economic and political change. A concern with internal security is then reflected in the military's attempts to improve the distribution of increments in national economic resources and to institutionalize an apparatus of political participation over which the military can exercise predominant control. A common theme in all these studies is the issue of the ability of the military to establish new structures of political participation. This theme is reflective of other instances in which societal factors are seen to provide a basis for potential modernization. Studies of military modernization in Latin America are thus legion, but a particularly provocative analysis of such modernization is to be seen in the contention that the armed forces, especially in Latin America, have become the representative of an ascendant and progressive middle class. The major rebuttal to this view, although agreeing that the middle class was indeed the driving force behind many new military regimes, argues that the same middle class was committed to a foreclosure of reforms beneficial to the mass of the population. In a related but more general statement, Huntington defines the military as radical in the world of oligarchy, participants in a middle-class order, and reactionary when the mass society looms.

The ensuing debate has engendered a controversy which looks at the relationship between social class and modernization in a worldwide context. This argument is, however, indicative of a wider critical awareness of the significance of military modernization. It is a topic which encourages emotive reactions, for discussion necessarily involves, as we shall see, a further consideration of the legitimacy of armed forces. A more balanced evaluation of the role of the military in modernization, however, emphasizes a more logically constructed analytical framework. This stresses that analysis is concerned with an evaluation of those qualities which supposedly enable armed forces to deal with social change and modernization more effectively than other organizations. The contrast here is between two opposing interpretations of such qualities. On the one hand, it is argued that the military is a pioneer in the technological, logistic and administrative fields. Concomitantly, advanced education and training produces officers who are essentially agents of order, efficiency and social change. On the other hand, it is concluded that armies are not necessarily efficient. Their small size, limited resources, primitive organizational structures and lack of operational experience inhibit their ability to handle complicated administrative problems.

ARMED CONFLICT AND WARFARE

Research in this field is, in general, concerned with what Quincy Wright termed *The Study of War*. Some studies are essentially descriptions of a specific occurrence. Since they are related to a particular time context, the sociological content in what are primarily historical analyses is more implied than actual. Alternatively, research is based on a theoretical framework which seeks to subsume the issues under consideration within general propositions which originate in the field of organizational theory.

A primary interest in this field is reflected in numerous studies which are concerned with the evaluation of combat effectiveness. These studies originated during the course of the Second World War. As Moskos (1976) points out: 'How with all the malcontent among the rank and file documented in the World War II surveys, could the American soldier give a good account of himself in combat?'. A potential answer to this question was to be found in the works of Stouffer and his colleagues. These stressed that a key explanation of combat motivation was to be attributed to the solidarity and social cohesion of military personnel at small group level. Subsequently, on the basis of participant observation in Korea, it was suggested, inter alia, that the critical variable — although it continued to be located in the primary group framework — differed from previously assumed conclusions in that it described the basic unit of social cohesion as the two man or 'buddy' relationship rather than as following squad or platoon boundaries.

It was, however, a generally expressed dissatisfaction within the United States at the time of the Vietnam War which served as the major impetus for the stimulation of further research in this field. This is not to deny that extensive 'in-house' reports have been a consistent feature of research into combat effectiveness. Nor does this reawakening of scholarly interest in this area overlook the persistence of other themes as varied as the philosophy of war, military organization during war, or studies of the impact of war on the social development of a nation state.

One aspect of this dissatisfaction is reflected in studies which consider military cohesion and disintegration. The former is identified as the assurance that a military unit will attempt to perform its assigned orders irrespective of the situation. Disintegration of a military organization is defined as 'the emergence of conditions which make effective operations impossible. These conditions are desertion, mutiny, assassination of leaders and other phenomena at odds with discipline, such as drug usage' (Savage and Gabriel, 1976). Subsequent research, however, particularly that which adopted a phenomenological perspective, has questioned such a definition. More importantly, research has focussed on these important subthemes: the continuing importance or otherwise of the primary group; the potential disarticulation of this group from the military and society; and the internal organizational dynamics of contemporary armed forces.

In evaluating the importance of the primary group to this issue of cohesion and disintegration, it has been argued that from observations in Vietnam it would seem that the concept of primary groups has limitations in explaining combat behaviour even beyond those suggested by Little in Korea. From this, it is concluded that three contrasting interpretations of the network of social relations in combat units can be identified: the primary group of the Second World War, the two-person relationship of the Korean War, and the essentially individualist soldier of Vietnam. An alternative explanation, however, questions the primacy of an individualistic ethos, notwithstanding the argument that it was already to be found among American soldiers in the Second World War. What has to be questioned, nevertheless, is whether these perceived differences represent conceptual differences on the part of the researchers or whether they are indeed indicative of substantive differences in the social cohesion of the American soldiers being described.

An ancillary question is how far any potential isolation of this primary group is indicative of the more general isolation of armed forces from society. The initial debate is reflected in that argument which states baldly that 'there appears no causal relationship between the quality of an army and the quality of its society', and the more generally accepted conclusion that armies reflect 'the societies they serve'.

The critical issue which follows from this is whether the postulated failure of the American Army in Vietnam can be essentially attributed to social processes in the host society, whether it was a function of collective and psychological shortcomings among personnel, whether it was fundamentally a structural problem of inadequate organizational and institutional arrangements given a set of definable objectives, or whether the perceived failure stemmed from a complex mix of these potential explanations.

CONCLUSION

We have briefly traced the development of military sociology and have attempted to evaluate new trends in teaching and research. In general, notwithstanding remarkable advances which have been made in this field during the last decade, we still believe that the field is underdeveloped and that the full potential of using sociological concepts in the study of armed forces has yet to be realized. One reason for this can be attributed to a failure to ensure the widespread acceptance within the broad academic community of this subject as a legitimate area of study and research. In this context, any increasing stress on the perceived advantages of applied research creates an even more unbalanced presentation of the depth and importance of the subject field.

A second reason for this lack of development is to be seen in the apparent reluctance — or inability — of theorists, irrespective of their acceptance or rejection of the Marxist paradigm, to examine adequately the political and power dimensions of the military both in the national and international environment. What this implies is that although the military may be in theory a nonpartisan institution, the manner in which it is conventionally associated with a conservative ideology has inhibited studies in depth of the relationship between armed forces, conflict and the parent society. Instead we find a large number of studies associated with an eclectic model of civil-military relationships. These quite naturally then tend to consider critically such referents as the modernization thesis, the social psychological hypothesis and the professional/organizational continuum. Alternatively, we find a smaller number of more recent studies which concentrate on the cultural/historical, social structural and ideological dimensions of this relationship between armed forces and society within a political framework.

A final but no less important constraint is derived from the interdisciplinary character of the study of the military. This has made it difficult and problematic to determine the boundaries of the research field. An ever-expanding area of study in which the scope and material of interest crosses traditional disciplinary boundaries has been both a strength and weakness of the subject. The weakness has been the development of fragmented forms of research which are an alternative to the growth of studies which build upon each other. The strength of the interdisciplinary approach, however, has been the generation of highly sophisticated conceptual theory which combines a high level of abstraction with the use of qualitative data.

The future trend of research, therefore, would appear to be the further development of this wider approach. This will facilitate the use of sociological data, methods and analyses as important methodological tools. At the same time, such an approach escapes from the possible sterility of analyses which concentrate on a structuralist perspective that stresses the stability, continuity and homogeneity of military values while disregarding conflict or viewing it as dysfunctional. In short, the development of research, we would argue, will reflect a wish to look at the influence of the environment and of social and historical factors on the military organization. The sense of this broadened scope is thus epitomized in the use of the term 'armed forces and society' with its more inclusive connotation rather than the more restricted term 'military sociology'. In this wider approach, future research will concentrate on an in-depth explanation of military phenomena in its search for an analysis which includes both the internal dynamics of the military and the processes of change between armed forces and society.

REFERENCES

Demeter, Karl (1935) *Das deutsche Heer und seine Offiziere* (The German Army and its Officers). Berlin: Verlag von Reimar Hobbing.

Huntington, Samuel P. (1957) *The Soldier and the State: The Theory and Politics of Civil-Military Relations*. Cambridge, Mass.: Harvard University Press.

Janowitz, Morris (1960) *The Professional Soldier*. New York: Free Press of Glencoe.

Larson, Arthur D. (1974) 'Military Professionalism and Civil Control: A Comparative Analysis of Two Interpretations', *Journal of Political Military Sociology*, 2(1): 57-72.

Lasswell, Harold D. (1941) 'The Garrison State', *American Journal of Sociology*, 46: 455-68.

Mills, C. Wright (1956) *The Power Elite*. New York: Oxford University Press.

Moskos, Charles C. (1976) 'The Military', *Annual Review of Sociology*, Vol. 2: 55-77 at 61.
Savage, Paul L. and Gabriel, Richard A. (1976) 'Cohesion and Disintegration in the American Army: An Alternative Perspective', *Armed Forces and Society*, 2: 340-76.
Wright, Quincy (1939) *The Study of War*. Chicago: University of Chicago Press.

5
Recent Trends in Theory and Methodology in the Study of Economy and Society

Harry Makler
University of Toronto
Arnaud Sales
Université de Montréal
Neil J. Smelser
University of California, Berkeley

In the compass of a few pages it is impossible to carry out the charge implied by the title of this essay in an exhaustive or even an adequate manner. For one thing, the literature that falls under the heading of 'Economy and Society' is so vast that it could not be listed, much less systematically surveyed, in the number of pages at our disposal. And second, any effort to identify 'trends' in a fully objective way is difficult, since observers with different theoretical preoccupations and bents will select and highlight different families of trends. Given these difficulties, we present the reader with two different kinds of impressionistic accounts. The first half of the essay is based on the pooled reflections of various members of the Executive Board of the Research Committee on Economy and Society; it is meant to be illustrative and to identify the most general trends. The second is a description of the responses of more than 100 scholars who responded to a questionnaire survey circulated by the Research Committee on Economy and Society in 1979 to its members and other interested persons; the questionnaire contained some queries relating to trends in theory and method, and we reproduce the results here, recognizing, however, that the respondents do not represent anything like a systematic, representative sample of scholars throughout the world. Both impressionistic accounts are therefore imperfect; we take some solace, however, in noting that the overall results of our own reflections and those of the survey point generally in the same direction.

The area of 'economy and society' is a curious intellectual jurisdiction in two senses: first, it is inherently interdisciplinary (more so than some other areas in the social sciences) and, second, the 'economy' side of the area has traditionally been the preserve of perhaps the most advanced and sophisticated of the social sciences, economics. It is our impression, moreover, that for many years sociologists and others have taken the economy as a kind of major, unexamined 'independent variable', which was not to be studied or explained as such, but, rather, whose social and psychological consequences were to be assessed. This is true, for example, of the long-term preoccupations with topics such as the impact of urban-industrial development on the community (in the traditions of Toennies, Wirth, and others), the impact of urban-industrial development on the family (in the tradition of the Chicago School of the 1920s and 1930s), and others. Yet in the past several decades that kind of inquiry has given way to a concern with the impact of noneconomic structures and processes on economic structures and processes (including development); the sociological interest in enterpreneurship, the concern with cultural and institutional obstacles to growth are but two examples. At the same time, sociologists and others have shown an increasing interest in the application of economic models to subjects as diverse as marriage rates, crime deterrence, race discrimination and social interaction generally. Moreover, social scientists other than economists are looking more and more closely at economic processes themselves (for example the labour process, the concentration or the internationalization of capital, or the mutual interplay between economy and polity or culture). All these developments have made for a greater interpenetration among the concerned social science disciplines, and a greater blurring of the boundaries among them.

THE 'MODERNIZATION' PERSPECTIVE

Perhaps the most convenient starting-point for identifying broad trends is the dramatic crystallization of the perspectives that went under the heading of modernization in the two decades following the Second World War. The main impulse for the development of this perspective lay, it seems, in the emergence of dozens of colonies into independent nations and their apparent aspirations to join the ranks of the prosperous and powerful nations of the world.

Modernization theorists picked up this impulse and built it into their theoretical formulations. It focussed on the 'new nations' or the 'developing nations', mainly in the Third World. It also included the theme that these countries were aspiring to dismantle their fettering traditions (kinship, community, religion), and develop institutions that would bring them economic growth and entry into the modern world. The particular theoretical form that this took was that the journey of the emerging nations into the modern world would have notable similarities to the kind of journey that the West itself had already experienced. Perhaps the most conspicuous expression of the modernization formulation is found in the world of Daniel Lerner (1958). The assumption that informed this work was that there were certain changes that characterized the move from tradition to modernity, and that these changes would unfold, with varying degrees of regularity, in the developing nations. (Incidentally, this perspective borrows much from the classical sociological tradition, which characterized modern change in the West as transition from *gemeinschaft* to *gesellschaft*.) It was, in short, a resuscitation and refinement of various theoretical models of change that had existed in the past in the social sciences, and the application of these models, in appropriately modified form, to the developing nations of the present. Among the changes noted in the comprehensive processes of modernization were the adoption of scientific technology, the commercialization of agriculture, the industrialization of manufacture, the urbanization of population, the secularization of religion, the opening of the stratification system, the rise of systems of formal education, the decline of the extended family, the decay of informal customs and the rise of systems of formal law, the development of new forms of political mobilization (for example, political parties) and the development of more complex systems of political administration.

One of the characteristics of modernization theory was that it tended to focus on specific internal societal determinants of economic and social change. These were frequently related to the dichotomy between traditional and modern values, and the psychosociological process of their integration by the individuals as a condition and a consequence of change. Less attention was given to historical conditions, social forces, power struggles, and of course to the structure and operation of the international economy. With respect to the impetus, we might mention the psychological school of entrepreneurship including the work of David McClelland (1961) and Everett E. Hagen (1962). At the same time, attention was given to the question of availability of resources for entrepreneurs and states (especially capital), and the question of resistances to entrepreneurial efforts, mainly from traditional customs and institutions. In treating these obstacles to development, modernization theorists continued to focus mainly on internal societal determinants, stressing especially communal, familial, religious, tribal, and stratification systems that conspired to undermine entrepreneurial efforts themselves, and to encourage motivations on the part of labourers not to respond to wage incentives or to wage labour itself.

While to some degree displaced by other perspectives — which will be reviewed presently — the modernization perspective has continued into the contemporary period, and many empirical investigations have been informed by it. The most pronounced development in the modernization tradition has been the preoccupation with cross-national studies of functional relationships, particularly among political scientists but also by others as well. The character of much of this work is to correlate various kinds of technological features of society with changes in political governance, as well as various other kinds of political phenomena, such as violence, social movements, and the like. The effort to establish such connections between economic change, literacy, the development of mass communication systems, and the like, also continues. One of the methodological features of this development of cross-national studies is the increasing preoccupation with the development of measures and indicators of the phenomena involved (see, for example, the methodological preoccupations in Ted Robert Gurr, *Why Men Rebel*) (1970), and an effort to use the most sophisticated techniques of association and causality, including the use of time-series. The modernization tradition has thus tended to become more self-consciously positivistic in orientation.

One of the corollary features of modernization theory was the notion that nations, as they develop irregularly and by different paths, will come to resemble one another more and more. The name given this assumption was the 'convergence thesis'. The thesis took a variety of forms, and covered a variety of institutions. Examples of the enunciation and attempted demonstration of the phenomena of convergence are Clark Kerr et al., *Industrialism and Industrial Man* (1960) (systems of industrial relations), William J. Goode, *World Revolution in Family Patterns* (1963) (family), and, more recently, Alex Inkeles and David Smith, *Becoming Modern* (1974) (the social psychology of work-people and others).

CRITICISMS OF THE MODERNIZATION PERSPECTIVE AND THE RISE OF ALTERNATIVE FRAMEWORKS

One way of regarding the range of intellectual developments of the late 1960s and the 1970s is as a progressive criticism, dismantling and reformulation of modernization theory with reference to each of the various noted components of that theory. Moreover, just as the formulation of modernization perspectives was rooted in the dominant historical fact of the anti-colonial revolution and the proliferation of nations, so the alternative theoretical formulations that have displaced the modernization perspective to a degree are rooted not only in the perception of evident difficulties of 'modernizing' societies to develop through efforts to dismantle some and build other institutions (such as mass education systems, meritocratic civil service systems, ...), but also on the analysis of what has been called the neo-colonialist process; the increased internationalization of capital and the establishment of a new international system articulating hegemonous and dependent societies. Speaking most broadly, many scholars have concluded that modernization theory is not well-equipped to diagnose and explain these phenomena and that other perspectives must be sought. The main source of these alternative perspectives, moreover, has been the Marxist and neo-Marxist literature, in particular those facets of that literature that stress the *international* character of capitalism. Accompanying those developments is a corresponding ideological debate that casts the 'modernization' theorists into a more conservative role, as ignoring or endorsing a certain mode of capitalist world domination, with the 'revisionist' theorists adopting a more radical political stance.

The first range of critical attacks and reformulations in the research relative to modernization concerned the convergence thesis, with the contributions of Joseph Gusfield (1967), Alexander Gerschenkron (1962) and Reinhard Bendix (1964) pointing out that the causal significance of different kinds of impetus and obstacles is varied, and that the erasure of traditional forms is not necessarily a concomitant of the adoption of modern ones. These lines of criticism made the claim that modernization theory was not adequate as a comparative diagnosis and explanation of historical and contemporary processes of economic and social change. On a more positive note, Bendix and others (for example, W.W. Rostow, 1956) argued that the international dimension of leadership and followership is very important, and that, historically, the political competition between established industrial powers and latecomers is a factor that must be taken into account in explaining different national histories with respect to economic development. Indeed, the research of some (e.g., Ronald Dore, 1973) attempts to account for contemporary international differences by pointing to the use and consolidation of *different* institutional forms at different points in economic development.

Among the more radical attacks came a major one from the underdeveloped regions themselves in the form of dependency theory. It is important to recall that during the 1950s and 1960s, modernization theory at times had profoundly influenced reflections on the process of development in Latin America. During the same period, however, a more critical analysis of this process appeared among the members of the United Nations Economic Commission for Latin America (ECLA). This led to the formulation of a theory of development which had considerable influence in Latin America, especially amongst policy makers. The writings of Raúl Prebish (1980), of Celso Furtado (1970), of Osvaldo Sunkel and of Pedro Paz (1977), are among the better known. Included was a fundamental criticism of the international division of labour and the need, according to them, to restructure this division in a more egalitarian perspective. They also opened the way to the recognition of structural differences between the developed and underdeveloped nations. These writings, on the other hand, placed little attention on the analysis of social processes, namely on relations between social classes and on imperialist relations between nations.

The criticism of this target led to a counter theory integrating more closely historical, economic and sociological perspectives and data. Dependency theory, as it was called, emphasized the historical and structural nature of the situation of underdevelopment and attempted to relate the production of this situation, as well as its reproduction, to the dynamics of the development of capitalism on a world scale. The works of Fernando Enrique Cardoso (1969) and André Gunder Frank (1969), are among the most representative of this approach but many others like those of Dos Santos, Quijano and Marini may also be mentioned. What was specific to the dependency approach was not the stress placed upon 'external dependency' but rather the analysis of the structural patterns which, asymmetrically and regularly, link central and peripheral economies. Thus the notion of domination was introduced, but domination was not seen as merely between nations; there was an attempt to show how the latter presupposes domination between classes. In that sense the relations between internal and external social forces constitute an integrated complex. These relations are not based on simple external forms of exploitation and coercion but have their roots in the convergence of interests between the dominant classes of a specific country and the international dominant classes.

Stimulated partly by these works, partly by a new reading of the classical Marxists, and also by the question posed by the extension of the multinational corporation, the notion of internationalization characterized most evident developments in the late 1960s and 1970s. Several authors such as Samir Amin (1974), Christian Palloix (1971), Immanuel Wallerstein (1974), and Charles Albert Michalet (1976), carried the theme of internationalization even further if not to its extreme by regarding the world economy as one system. These works mark the most radical rejection of the modernization theorists' stress on internal determinants, obstacles, and stages of development. National differences are accounted for in terms of their place of the international relations among core, semi-periphery, and periphery economies.

Also on the internationalist note, a diverse array of social scientists have become focussed on the profound impact of the multinational corporations and multinational financial institutions on the world economy and its component nations. The hallmark of the multinational corporation is the internationalization of *production*, not merely capital (see Robert Gilpin, 1975, or Charles Albert Michalet, 1976). Scholars have made efforts to trace dozens of ramifications of multinational production and financial penetration — for the changing hegemonic patterns of world domination, for the increasing impotence of national states, for international political instability, for the international pattern of wages, for local economic control, for internal class relations, and the like. Theoretical perspectives on multinational institutions are highly varied — as they are in each of the other lines of reformulation and re-emphasis mentioned — but much of the analysis of these phenomena has been informed by neo-Marxist and other conflict perspectives.

Up to this point the tracing of trends has been focussed at the most macroscopic processes of economic and social change, and several themes — namely the rising salience of neo-Marxist and conflict perspectives and the stress on internationalization — have been noted. But it can also be pointed out — illustratively, at any rate — that the sort of intellectual change noted is probably more pervasive than indicated, and that similar drifts of emphasis can be noted in a variety of different other areas:

(1) In the study of mobility in the stratification system, the rise of the study of status-attainment (especially in Peter Blau and Otis Dudley Duncan, 1967, Christopher Jencks, 1972, and Raymond Boudon, 1974), marked an important substantive and methodological advance over traditional studies of social mobility. Yet the major intellectual focus of the status-attainment studies is on the individual, and on the degree to which various background characteristics (education, father's education, father's occupation, race) could account for his or her career vicissitudes. This kind of research has been criticized from a neo-Marxist point of view (for example, in the work of Christian Baudelot and Robert Establet, 1971, Samuel Bowles and Herbert Gintis, 1976, or Daniel Bertaux, 1977), stressing in particular the constraints of class inequalities and market structure (e.g., the dual market structure) in determining — from a systemic point of view — educational, occupational, and income inequalities.

(2) In industrial sociology, the preoccupations of the field with worker interaction, restriction of production, status systems and worker satisfaction (alienation) have shifted in some degree to an interest in the labour process, as characterized in the neo-Marxian tradition, with the themes of deskilling, increasing control through specialization, other developments associated with capitalist organization of work (see Harry Braverman, 1974).

(3) Regarding the relations between economy and polity considerable developments have taken place from the end of the 1960s until today. These strongly influenced our field of study not only with respect to general methodological approach but also content. The debate was started and developed by Nicos Poulantzas (1973, 1976, 1980) and deals with the nature of the state in capitalist social formations. One of the merits of these writings was to pose first of all the general question of the relations between economic and political spheres, more particularly of their autonomy, thus open-

ing the way to the study of the relations between social classes, political power and its exercise through the state apparatus. Obviously one of the basic objects of this theoretical current is the economic intervention of the state. This intervention is seen as a fundamental element in the social reproduction of capital, particularly in the monopoly stage because it is at the very essence or core of this process, while at the same time spreading to a multitude of other fields. The economic functions of the state become preponderant filling at the same time two contradictory functions — accumulation and legitimation even if fiscal limits of state activity are becoming more and more apparent, as argued by James O'Connor (1973).

The growth of the economic functions of the state is a cause for concern to the theoreticians of this current, who stress the resulting decline of democracy. State intervention which has become more and more direct in the process of accumulation, it is argued, leads to a definite rise in bureaucratic and executive power to the detriment of legislative power, and perhaps points toward an authoritarian state.

From a methodological point of view, the resurgence of a variety of conflict perspectives — particularly those emphasizing class conflict — has meant a methodological shift, too, downgrading research methods such as field observation and stressing the dialectical diagnosis of historical and comparative situations. At the same time many scholars who have embraced and utilized one or another neo-Marxist perspective (for example, Jeffrey Paige, 1975 and Erik Olin Wright, 1979) have, at the same time, displayed a strong interest in methodological issues of measurement, sampling, multivariate analysis, and other techniques associated with the tradition of positive social science, which some Marxist scholars have criticized as trappings of bourgeois social science. Developments such as these further complicate the kaleidoscope of intellectual styles in the study of economy and society, and make the application of traditional distinctions among those styles more difficult.

One final qualification is in order. Though our remarks have referred to dominant perspectives and methods as well as shifts and drifts in perspectives and methods, the reader should be cautioned to assess these assertions in the context of the more general observation that, at any given moment in the recent history of the study of economy and society, the main story is always one of a continuing multiplicity and a diversity of perspectives, methods, and styles, and that the shifts and drifts are to be regarded as occurring on the surface of this bed of diversity. Any given shift toward a new, temporarily dominant perspective, moreover, sets the stage for criticism of that perspective, and the rise of new ones, which process continually adds to the diversity of traditions of theory and ongoing empirical research.

THE INTERNATIONAL SURVEY OF SCHOLARS

During the Fall of 1979 and early Spring of 1980, the Research Committee on Economy and Society conducted a small survey among those who attended our sessions at the Ninth World Congress of Sociology (Uppsala, Sweden, August 1978) and among other scholars whose names were derived from recognized scholarly journals on the economy and society during the past five years.

We derived a list of 300 names, most of which were scholars from the United States, Canada, Western Europe, and Latin America. Most of these (70 percent) had attended the World Congress at Uppsala. While we do not claim a representative sample, we believe that our report will provide some idea of what research is being done, who is doing it (e.g., which disciplines, which nationalities), and whether it is a singular or collaborative effort. Also we will provide some idea of the theoretical and methodological approaches that are being used to study the economy and society as well as those approaches which are seen by our respondents as most promising for study of the economy and society in the future.

WHAT RESEARCH IS BEING DONE? AN OVERVIEW

The reply to the first question on our questionnaire, 'Kindly indicate your current and planned research on the economy and society plus the names and nationality of any collaborators, their disciplines, and sources of funding?' revealed a variety of promising studies, encompassing economic, political, or social processes (e.g., power and the state, the legitimation of violence), economic-historical studies (e.g., the development of the sugar industry in Kenya), institutions (e.g., state-owned enterprises, international banking), stratification and social class (e.g., worker ownership and control of industry), and studies of national economies (e.g., the Caribbean countries' political economy).

Most of the 100 replies we received were from North Americans (50 percent), Europeans (25 percent), and Asians (15 percent); few questionnaires were returned from Latin Americans (less than 10 percent), although almost as many were mailed to them as to North Americans and Europeans. We received replies from scholars residing in nearly every European nation, the Middle East from Israel, Egypt, and Turkey, and in Asia from Japan, Sri Lanka, and Thailand. From Latin America most replies came from Brazilian scholars (most likely explained by the Brazilian representation on our Executive Committee), while from Africa we heard from Kenyans, Senegalese, and South Africans.

As might be expected the majority (80 percent) of the respondents indicated that they were sociologists, and most of these were North Americans. About 10 percent were political scientists and these were mainly Latin Americans. The remainder were either economists or were of combined disciplines, e.g., economist and sociologist, political economist. Most respondents, as also expected, were affiliated with universities, but once again these were North Americans and Europeans. The Latin Americans and Africans (except South Africans) tended to list a research institution affiliation or at least gave such institutions priority over a university affiliation which we suspect they held. Only one scholar, a Hungarian, had no affiliation. He simply stated 'I am alone'.

Affiliations with research institutions tended to correlate positively with collaboration, and when there was collaboration it tended to be cross-disciplinary, as for example, a sociologist with an economist. Despite the pattern of university affiliation among North Americans, about 50 percent indicated that they were collaborating with others. But like themselves these collaborators tended to be sociologists, giving the impression that North American sociology is much more incapsulated perhaps owing to its greater emphasis on professionalism. There is little doubt that this affects both choice of specialization, topic, and methodology in research. After completing his questionnaire, one of our Latin American members described the virtues of collaborating with someone from another discipline (in this case an economist). He said:

Needless to say, an economist's approach to the topic of industrial policy-making would stress different variables and problem areas. In fact, we have had a good experience at our Institute in this respect, contrasting the opinions of economists and our group in a discussion group that regularly meets to discuss issues related to economic policy-making.

But we wondered whether cross-fertilization affected choice of research topics. Of course without an in-depth study, there is really no way of knowing which comes first. Perhaps, however, a review of research topics will provide some clues.

Current and Planned Research

A brief review of the responses shows that most scholars of the economy and society are studying institutions and processes within their own country, or these topics in historical perspective. Very few are engaged in studying a topic cross-nationally. We found that the respondents are conducting research in four main areas: (1) the relation of social classes or groups to the economy; (2) institutions, the state and the economy; (3) the world system; or (4) socio-economic process or indicators. We will list some of this research.

(1) Social class. Among the studies of social class and the structure of the economy there is one in Canada on class and mining and another on entrepreneurial activity and underdevelopment in the country's eastern region. Another scholar is studying internal stratification of the American and French working classes, and along similar lines there is a study of working ownership and control of industry in America where one of the collaborators reported that their team is interested in '...the growing phenomenon of worker cooperatives, worker collectives, and worker purchases of plants that would otherwise be shut down...' (and how this) '...is related to changes in the structure of the U.S. economy'. Similar research is being conducted in Western Europe. In Portugal, for example, where new forms of industrial and agricultural ownership emerged after its 1974 revolution, a doctoral candidate in political science chose to study the politics of worker-managed factories and their relations with the state while an industrial sociologist in Great Britain is analyzing worker participation in business strategy.

The economic plight of certain classes in the world of work is concerning more than one researcher. An American sociologist, with the support of the National Institute of Mental Health (NIMH), is studying economic absorption and cultural integration of immigrant blacks and Chicanos in the United States. The recent wave of Cuban immigration to the United States and the violent reaction of some local minorities testifies to the timeliness of such concerns. Equally timely is the study of black employment in the Western Cape Province of South Africa which is being conducted by a South African sociologist.

Studies of class associations, interest groups, trade unions and their relation to the economy and policy appear to be attracting more attention, particularly among European social scientists or those interested in Europe. For example, a West German sociologist is focussing on rural cooperatives and economic programs in Mexico and Egypt. One political scientist is studying corporatism and another is studying the changing role of business associations in Western Europe. A team of two sociologists is currently studying class coalitions and macro-economic policy in postwar Europe and a West German scholar is concerned with white-collar employees and their trade union.

Research on industrialists and entrepreneurship seems to have waned. Interest seems to have shifted to other units of analysis such as large corporations, state enterprises, groups, and financial institutions. Nevertheless, our survey did reveal some research on the role of businessmen and entrepreneurship. For example, there is a collaborative study of Korean small businessmen in Los Angeles supported by the National Science Foundation (NSF). In Latin America a Brazilian political scientist reported a collaborative nationwide study of industrial entrepreneurs and the economy, and in the Brazilian North East an American sociologist reported his study of the role of the local economic oligarchy in the development of that large and important region in Latin America. To the north, an Anglo-Canadian sociologist is also conducting a study of regional underdevelopment and entrepreneurship in Eastern Canada and a French-Canadian sociologist reported that he had completed a study of the Quebec industrial bourgeoisie and its national and ethnic differentiation.

One cross-national study with an historical perspective concerning the proliferation of scientific management is underway in France, Germany, and Italy in the inter-war period. And there seems to be some attempt to summarize many of the existing studies of businessmen and industrialists. One scholar, for example, told us that he was developing a '...Synthetic Theory of Entrepreneurship'.

In all, we judge that approximately 25 percent of our respondents are dealing with questions of the role of social class or the role of groups in the economy and society.

(2) Institutions, the state, and the economy. About a third of our respondents are studying economic institutions and among this group most are focussing on public and private economic institutions.

Given the increasing role of the state in the economies of the non-Communist nations, particularly the economies of developing Third World nations, state-owned and controlled enterprises have been the concern of a number of social scientists. One American economist reported that he is studying state-owned enterprises and the international economic system and a team of his countrymen are engaged in a historical, cross-national study of state management of capitalist economies in a number of Western European countries (France, West Germany, Great Britain, Italy, and Sweden). Along similar lines a French-Canadian sociologist reported his study of the economic and political relations between public and private sectors in Canada's Quebec province.

Equally the focus of research are studies of transnational (or multinational) corporations and their social, economic, and political roles. A series of studies in Europe, Latin America, and Africa is now in progress on this topic. For example, an American sociologist is studying the effects of transnationals on employment in several underdeveloped nations, and another is analyzing the relation of large corporations to social class in capitalist countries. An Italian and a Japanese sociologist are studying the political and social implications of transnationals, and an American is concerned with the policy implications of corporate power in American cities. He cautions us against studies which do not specify the economic implications of various social, political, or institutional factors.

Banks and other financial institutions have also been the focus of studies. While these have long been the concern of economists and economic historians, recently a few sociologists and political scientists have recognized the importance of these institutions as social and political actors. Two American sociologists are now studying the social and economic effects of credit allocation, using mainly a case study approach. One is focussing on the history of credit allocation in an important New England commercial city in North America, while the other is studying credit allocation and industrial development in Brazil. A political scientist reported here a study of the impact of international loans on the national economies and policies of some developing nations in Latin America; a French economist is collaborating with other social scientists in the study of transnational banks and their restructuring of the international economic order; and an Egyptian political economist apparently cognizant of the shift in financial centres has indicated that he is studying the impact of Third World financial institutions on Third World economic development. The study of ownership and control of the firm has also continued to develop country by country.

Some respondents are studying recent crises. One, for example, is focussing on the restructuring of the American automobile industry and its consequences on unemployment and investment. A British sociologist is studying local housing policy, building laws and poverty in the United Kingdom.

Unfortunately, very few reported studies of food or agricultural production, at least among our respondents. This important institution and crisis is being neglected among sociologists interested in the economy and society. The few studies which were reported focus on plantation economies in the Third World nations. For example, a political scientist reported a study of the sugar industry in Kenya; a Brazilian sociologist is writing his doctoral dissertation on capitalist expansion in the cocoa region of Brazil; and a South East Asian sociologist is studying the impact of the plantation economy on a local population in a developing region in Sri Lanka. Only one of our respondents, a British economist, reported a study of economic development and food self-sufficiency. A sociologist in Quebec is working on the agro business.

Studies of other social institutions and the economy were even more sparse. Only one American sociologist reported a study of the family. This he described as a study of socioeconomic change in the family and its life course in the 1930s and its short as well as long-term effects. While social scientists interested in the family might be affiliated with other ISA committees, it seems that there are very few studies of this institution and its relation with the economy. Similarly, no studies on religion and the economy were reported to us. Scholars of Latin American society are well aware of the importance of this institution and its relation to the policy and economy. In Brazil, for example, which has the largest Catholic population in the world, the Catholic Church continually addresses the economic policies of the government.

(3) The world system and national economies. Stimulated by the work of Amin, Palloix, Wallerstein, and Michalet, the world

system, as it is commonly referred, was the object of research by about a fifth of our respondents. A Swiss and an American sociologist, for example, are collaborating on a study of international dependence and cycles and trends of the capitalist world economy. A West German sociologist reported his study of the contemporary world economic and social crisis in historical perspective and an Egyptian economist also indicated his research on the world crisis. Wallerstein and his associates at the Fernand Braudel Center in New York State, are continuing to develop the theory of the world system and currently as he informed us their '...most relevant work is on the "Cycles and Trends Project" presently funded by the National Science Foundation'.

A half dozen scholars are conducting research on national economies. A Turkish sociologist reported his study of 'Capitalist Development and the State', and an Italian sociologist specified 'The Welfare State'. But there are studies of specific economies such as a West German's study of structural change in the economy and society of West Germany, an American sociologist's study of the economy of Greece, a Canadian's study of the economy and social structure of Sardinia, and another Canadian's study of the socioeconomic development of Japanese Society since 1600.

One scholar who reported 'no identification with any discipline' is studying the 'Two Visions of Post-Industrial Society'.

(4) Socioeconomic indicators and processes. Finally, there are individuals who are studying processes, or indicators of socioeconomic change. These range from political states of being such as stagnation to quite specific economic indicators such as income distribution. In this regard, a Finnish scholar reported his study of the national income of his country from 1860 to 1914. A Japanese mathematician and sociologist is studying the quality of life and consumption behaviour and an Italian sociologist is concerned with 'moonlighting' work or 'double jobs'.

A few scholars are attempting to develop theories about processes. These include a Danish team interested in developing a model of development strategies for developing countries; a West German who is studying public control of economic processes and the possibilities of extended legal intervention; and an Israeli who is concerned with the legitimation of economic development in a series of presumably developing countries.

To summarize this review, the research of our constituency is varied and certainly colourful. It ranges from micro to macro, is often cross-national and historical in approach, and is multidisciplinary. Half of it is collaborative, most of it is conducted in university settings and most, given the nature of our sampling, is being conducted by North Americans. What is notably lacking are studies which are concerned with the development of public policy or at least have public policy implications: perhaps the studies we have reviewed will conclude with public policy proposals but from the material returned to us we have no indication of this concern. What is also missing are studies of the economic and social crises of the world's most important nations. How do we explain, for example, the loss of American hegemony in Europe, Latin America, and other countries of the Third World?

ATTITUDES AND BELIEFS ABOUT THE STUDY OF THE ECONOMY AND SOCIETY: OVERVIEW

In addition to learning about the research interests of scholars interested in the economy and society we wanted to know what methodological and theoretical approaches these scholars thought were most used in studying the economy and society, what approaches were increasing in popularity, and what positions hold most promise for research.

The questions 'What theoretical position and methodological approaches do you believe are most often used in the study of the economy and society?' and 'Have any theoretical orientations or methodologies come to assume special importance or salience in the past 20 years (1960 to 1980)?' will be briefly considered in this descriptive analysis of our small survey.

Practically all or 90 percent of our respondents indicated that Marxist or neo-Marxist approaches are most often used in the study of the economy and society. Even 'classical' economists who replied to our questionnaire acknowledged this orientation and admitted its growing salience in the past 20 years for the study of the economy and society. For example, one such scholar, commenting on two most often used and most important approaches, said: 'The classical free market approach, accompanied by classical analysis based on economics and a neo-Marxist exploitation approach accompanied by philosophical, historical analysis is most often used.'

We noted that very few differentiated between theory and method. Perhaps our respondents thought that specifying their theoretical position had priority on a questionnaire which admittedly had limited space (in order to encourage a quick return). Or perhaps people felt that their methodological approach could be deduced from their theoretical orientation, or that their methodology would vary with their particular research topic. Whatever the case the replies of the few scholars who did specify methods are worth noting. An American sociologist studying the sociology of credit allocation observed that

> In terms of methodologies plainly the advent of computer techniques has made the 'new' social science possible which (in turn) has forced an empirical infusion into economics. For instance, the massive social/economic experiments (e.g., income maintenance); micro-stimulations (e.g., the Brookings Institute tax model); and massive panel studies (e.g., Morgan on economic behaviour of families) hold serious promise.

Another American sociologist collaborating in a study of foreign investment and transnational corporations in Latin America reported that modernization, structural-functionalism, imperialism/dependency, and world systems approaches are the theories most often used, and historical-structural quantitative, cross-national correlational, and Weberian ideal-type analysis are the most common methods. A Canadian sociologist studying comparative social security policy also thought multivariate, quantitative techniques, and historical case studies were most often used.

The few that did reply to the methods question emphasized cross-national approaches in the study of the economy and society. Only one or two scholars mentioned survey research, an approach more widely used a decade ago. Case studies and the use of census data seem to be appearing more and more. This could be explained by the increasing availability and accessibility of census materials and the types of more 'macro' problems which are being studied. Survey research is also becoming more and more costly and cross-national studies, involving a series of countries and collaborators, take years to complete.

APPROACHES TO THE STUDY OF THE ECONOMY AND SOCIETY IN THE 1980s

In this final section of this paper we wish to provide only a summary of what our respondents think has occurred in theoretical orientations during the past 20 years (1960 to 1980) and what approaches they judge hold most promise for future study of the economy and society.

What Approaches Have Emerged and What Is on the Horizon?

While our respondents were quite consistent in specifying that Marxist and structural-functional approaches had been used, their views on which orientations have emerged in importance were quite diverse. In spite of this diversity it is possible to group the replies into four categories.

(1) Marxist. Considering that the majority of our scholars had indicated that Marxist approaches had been most often used in the study of the economy and society, it was not surprising that a third of our respondents, the biggest group, also thought that a Marxist theoretical and methodological approach held most promise for future studies. Most of these were not 'Third Worlders' as we might expect, but North Americans, or as one respondent remarked, 'gringo' sociologists. The Europeans in this group were much more deliberate as we hope to show. While it is not our intention in this report to do a 'correlational' analysis, nevertheless it is worth noting that the majority of the scholars who subscribed to the Marxist approach are currently studying some form of the state's relation to the economy, e.g., state-owned enterprises and the international economic order.

We also noted that some appear to be solely committed to the Marxist approach. In this regard one scholar remarked:

For me the most relevant approach is the historical one based on a Marxist ontology and epistemology. Marcel Mauss, the French Annales School, some English historians like Hobsbawm, Thompson, Hill, Karl Polanyi's works, George Lukacs' ontology have been of special importance for me.

Another said 'Marxist — because of its analytical richness and the possibility of opening up to political praxis'. Or a Danish sociologist, studying development strategies, remarked that for him the holistic and class struggle with emphasis on the praxis was the approach and it 'can be used as tools in changing society into new modes of production and bringing a better quality of life for the people'. A British sociologist, concerned with the theories of modern capitalism, while not admitting it would provide tools to change society, saw it as '...particularly since Hilferding (as holding) most promise for a realistic analysis of the tendencies of late 20th century capitalism'. And a fellow countryman of his spoke in a similar vein about the utility of the Marxist approach when he said '...it is only unified body of theory and practice which locates economy and society into a coherent world'.

From an economist of an African country there was an expression of singular commitment when he told us that 'conventional economics and political science, which are "very bad", are most often used, but historical materialism still seems to be the most efficient method; also the only one capable of integrating all "aspects" of social life (economics, politics...).'

Others opted for a Marxist approach because they apparently saw it as providing an excellent framework for studying social and economic change and a way of integrating the myriad of empirical studies conducted during the past two or three decades. For instance, an American sociologist, studying worker ownership and control of industry, remarked that:

> Theoretically I believe a Marxist approach holds the most promise because it has clear causal propositions which can be empirically tested and because the dialectical view focusses attention on the sources of change in any social-economic system. Also a class analysis appears critical for understanding the social base of those who support or oppose changes...Methods — here I believe that the generation of theoretical models and propositions from data (i.e. grounded theory) holds the most promise. The creation of original and heuristic theory, grounded in data, implies intensive field observation at the level of the organization and *not* huge, cross-national, quantitative studies which haven't the richness of data necessary to generate new theoretical insights.

Similarly, an African political scientist saw the necessity of 'mastering the tools of analysis of Marxism and its use, not as a dogma, but as a tool of analysis to understand complex social phenomena for what they are'. 'Without a revolutionary theory', he continued, 'there cannot be a revolutionary change'.

The view that only Marxism provides a framework to understand economies and societies as totalities was consistently shared by this group. They also attested to its growing popularity. In this regard a Brazilian sociologist studying capitalist expansion in Brazil's cocoa region noted that

> ...other research and researchers attached to it have grown faster than any other orientation...the main reason, I would argue, is that the frantic development of empiricist traditions in the West during the 1950s and the 1960s has not built any real

alternative epistemology but rather an enormous collection of dispersed studies showing little connection among each other...

A West German sociologist, also studying agricultural ownership in Latin America, believes that the theories and methods of the past two decades 'pretty much accomplished answering those unanswered questions which require different kinds of questions and new perspectives regarding exploitation, contradictions, political movements, etc.' For him the Marxist approach is much more effective in raising and answering questions than the traditional modernization approach.

Finally, among the Marxist group there were a few scholars who believe that certain schools or offshoots of Marxism offer the most promise. One American sociologist studying power and the state sees the Gramscian understanding of hegemony and crisis as the most promising for understanding the capitalist crises. Another American feels that Karl Polanyi '...focussed our attention on the totality, both across time and internationally, as the prerequisite for analyzing any particular relationship between the economy and society...and was the critical forerunner for much of the dependency literature including the later development of world systems thinking by Wallerstein'. And a Brazilian sociologist believes that critical theory developed by the Frankfurt School holds most promise because '...it tries to reconcile a Marxist inheritance with other approaches'. Similarly, an Italian sociologist believes that Jurgen Habermas' work is most promising for understanding the economy and society since he has raised the questions of the 'reproducibility' of the global system. And a French-Canadian sociologist aptly stated that unlike previous theoretical and methodological approaches the Marxist approach will continue to generate numerous studies because it has within it a capacity to change and develop. Again, this scholar hints at the strength and totality of the Marxist approach. Or, as a Latin American sociologist put it, '...This approach opens innovative possibilities in methodology and in the construction of theory and explanatory design'.

(2) Marxist-Weberian/Marxist-functionalist. A few of our scholars thought that a Marxist combined with a Weberian approach had grown in importance during the past 20 years and held great promise for future research. In this regard a Latin American political scientist studying comparative processes of democratization cogently remarked that there has emerged '...a combination

of a sophisticated neo-Marxism and neo-Weberian à la Economy and Society combined with historical analysis.' And for him the most promising approach was '...the detailed study of changing social-economic (and state's...) structures along an explicit historical dimension is by far the best way to look at phenomena which only exist as sets of co-constitutive interrelationships and unfold along time (not as something that is first, say, economic and then afterwards combined with, say, the social)'.

Sharing this perspective were some North Americans. One, for example, who is currently studying state-controlled industries, thought that '...a blend of neo-Marxist and neo-Weberian approaches which combines an appreciation of class relations with a recognition of the relative independence of the state and certain cultural institutions' should be the approach. Another, studying race and ethnic stratification, thought that 'a class analysis approach modified by the insights of Simmel and Weber and the consideration of multiple as opposed to unitary class memberships' held the most promise.

Several scholars held a 'Marxist-functionalist' approach to the study of the economy and society. These were mostly European and Asian sociologists. One Japanese sociologist studying attitudes about planning said 'I think that the most noteworthy trends have been the neo-Marxist ones in both theory building about the world system and inquiries into the problems of the advanced industrial societies'. For him the most promising approach is a synthetic blend of Marxism and functionalism. In a similar vein an Italian sociologist thought that a combination of structural-functional and Marxist theory in order to analyze complex social systems was the best approach. And a German sociologist, analyzing the economy of his country, opts for a mixture of neo-Marxism of the Frankfurt School, structural analysis of economic and societal change, using social demographic and social indicators to provide the necessary empirical data. In sum, this group thinks that a structural-functional and Marxist approach provides the ability to analyze the dynamics and forces at work in the economy and society. However, an American sociologist studying class relations and large corporations claimed that dependency theory, quasi-Marxism, and world system theory are all '...in one way or another variants of functionalism. Genuine class theory continues to be extraordinarily rare in the analysis of the relationship between the economy and society in the United States. We need an empirically sound comparative analysis of the relationship between economy and society from the standpoint of a class theory of political relations and historical development'.

(3) World system and dependency approaches. Amin, Palloix and Wallerstein's works on the world capitalist system have stimulated research on this topic, particularly among North American and European social scientists. For example, a West German economist/sociologist studying the contemporary world economic and social crisis in historical perspective reported that the analysis of capital accumulation holds most promise and a North African political economist indicated that '...we are moving toward a global system in which North-South contradictions are increasingly becoming fundamental and which only can be understood on the basis of historical materialism applied on a global scale'. One American sociologist suggested that through longitudinal multilevel analyses the world system perspective could become a synthetic theory.

A half dozen of our respondents, mostly from Third World countries and Canada, are *dependentistas*. This school emerged in the late 1960s and early 1970s stimulated by the Economic Commission on Latin America (ECLA), Celso Furtado, Fernando H. Cardoso, André Gunder Frank and others. As an American sociologist noted '...it is the fastest rising orientation'. Others view it as 'both an explanation and a methodology of analysis' and still others see it as an integral part of the world system perspective. For example, an American sociologist studying foreign investment said:

I believe the world system and dependency perspectives are highly complementary. They have the advantage of broadening our scope of inquiry from the nation-state considered as a quasi-isolated unit to the nation-state in the context of (and influenced by) global-politico system...

With nation-states and even cities within nations facing tremendous economic and political crises as we enter the 1980s it is likely that there might be a shift of research emphasis from the world system to the weakening advanced capitalist nations. Or as one of our respondents questioned 'Who is dependent on whom now?'

(4) Modernization, social-psychological, and other approaches. There were a few remnants of the modernization and social-psychological approaches among our respondents. One American sociologist felt that 'Symbolic interaction analysis with special reference to language, ideology and perception...which has both a long history of research in many fields including biology and

psychology as well as empirical studies in "mind and thinking" in a comparative and cultural setting' would be an important approach in the 1980s. Another who is studying 'Bitterness in Low Income Countries' stated that 'I believe that the incorporation of current personality theory — theory of personality formation — into sociological models and especially systems analysis in sociology is necessary for the most effective further advance since without it social theory has a large element of non-analyzable "free will" '. And indeed among our respondents there were some North Americans who are engaged in systems analysis, economic models of individual behaviour, deductive formal modelling, public choice theory, game theory, and inductive time series analysis. One, in referring to a general systems approach, said 'This approach appears most amicable to a more systematized (mathematical) modelling approach; it also inherently allows for the existence of complex regulatory networks and non-linear relationships between variances and variables'. And some reported using systems theory in their research on dual labour markets. In this regard, an Italian sociologist studying 'double jobs', noted that 'Dual labour market theory renews our view about social classes (while) systems theory might develop into a logic for model construction of advanced soceities...'

While there were other views of the most promising approaches to the theoretical and methodological study of the economy and society the four we have described will likely be the most conspicuous during the coming decade.

REFERENCES

Amin, Samir (1974) *L'accumulation à l'échelle mondiale* (Accumulation on a World Scale). New York: Monthly Review Press.
Baudelot, Christian and Establet, Robert (1971) *L'école capitaliste en France*. Paris: Maspero.
Bendix, Reinhard (1964) *Nation-Building and Citizenship*. New York: Wiley.
Bertaux, Daniel (1977) *Destins personnels et structure de classe*. Paris: Presses Universitaires de France.
Blau, Peter and Duncan, Otis Dudley (1967) *The American Occupational Structure*. New York: Wiley.
Boudon, Raymond (1974) *Education, Opportunity and Social Inequality*. New York: Wiley.

Bowles, Samuel and Gintis, Herbert (1976) *Schooling in Capitalist America*. New York: Basic Books.
Braverman, Harry (1974) *Labor and Monopoly Capitalism: The Degradation of Work in the Twentieth Century*. New York: Monthly Review Press.
Cardoso, Fernando Enrique (1969) *Dependencia y Desarrollo en America Latina*. Mexico: Siglo Veintiuno Editores.
Dore, Ronald (1973) *British Factory-Japanese Factory*. Berkeley: University of California Press.
Frank, Andre Gunder (1969) *Capitalism and Underdevelopment in Latin America* (revised and enlarged edition). New York: Monthly Review Press.
Furtado, Celso (1970) *Théorie du développement économique*. Paris: Presses Universitaires de France.
Gerschenkron, Alexander (1962) *Economic Backwardness in Historical Perspective*. Cambridge: Belknap Press.
Gilpin, Robert (1975) *U.S. Power and the Multinational Corporation*. New York: Basic Books.
Goode, William J. (1963) *World Revolution in Family Patterns*. New York: Free Press of Glencoe.
Gurr, Ted Robert (1970) *Why Men Rebel*. Princeton: Princeton University Press.
Gusfield, Joseph R. (1967) 'Tradition and Modernity: Misplaced Polarities in the Study of Social Change', *American Journal of Sociology*, 72 (January): 351-62.
Hagen, Everett E. (1962) *On the Theory of Social Change*. Homewood, Ill.: Dorsey Press.
Inkeles, Alex and Smith, David (1974) *Becoming Modern*. Cambridge: Harvard University Press.
Jencks, Christopher (1972) *Inequality*. New York: Basic Books.
Kerr, Clark et al. (1960) *Industrialism and Industrial Man*. Cambridge: Harvard University Press.
Lerner, Daniel (1958) *The Passing of Traditional Society*. Glencoe, Ill.: Free Press.
McClelland, David (1961) *The Achieving Society*. Princeton: Van Nostrand.
Michalet, Charles Albert (1976) *Le capitalisme mondial*. Paris: Presses Universitaires de France.
O'Connor, James (1973) *The Fiscal Crisis of the State*. New York: St. Martin's Press.
Paige, Jeffrey (1975) *Agrarian Revolution*. New York: Free Press.
Palloix, Christian (1971) *L'économie mondiale capitaliste*. Paris: Maspero.
Poulantzas, Nicos (1973) *Political Power and Social Classes*. London: Sheed and Ward.
Poulantzas, Nicos (1976) *Classes in Contemporary Capitalism*. Atlantic Highlands, NJ. Humanities Press.
Poulantzas, Nicos (1980) *State, Power and Socialism*. London: Verso.
Prebish, Raúl (1980) *El Desarrollo Economico de la America Latina y algunos de sus Principales Problemas*. New York: United Nations.
Rostow, Walter W. (1956) 'The Take-off into Sustained Growth', *Economic Journal*, LXVI: 25-48.
Sunkel, Osvaldo and Paz, Pedro (1977) *El Subdesarrollo Latino-Americano y la Teoria del Desarrollo*. Mexico: Siglo Veintiuno Editores.
Wallerstein, Immanuel (1974) *The Modern World System*. New York: Academic Press.
Wright, Erik Olin (1979) *Class Structure and Income Inequality*. New York: Academic Press.

6
Convergences in the Sociology of Race Relations and Minority Groups

John Rex
University of Aston

Sociologists concerned with the topic of ethnic and racial minority groups have perhaps, more than any of their other colleagues, been drawn into a political debate at an international level about the area of their expertise. Racial discrimination, racial oppression, the propagation of racist ideas and genocide have all been topics of international concern and sociologists have been called upon to delineate their field and indicate the major causal factors responsible for these phenomena. Thus the 1967 UNESCO meeting (Montagu, 1972) on the nature of racism and race prejudice included several sociologists, one of whom was later to become President of the International Sociological Association's research committee, and that same research committee has subsequently been called upon to make other studies, as for example that carried out for UNESCO on Apartheid and Social Research in South Africa (Rex, forthcoming). The work of the research committee has therefore been dominated by practical political concerns and the theoretical problem which it has faced is how to define its field in such a way as to contribute to the understanding of those problems.

This practical political concern has inevitably meant the underplaying of certain themes normally thought to be part of the sociology of race relations as it is taught. Emphasis has not been placed upon the phenomenology of microsociological associations (i.e. how racial typing and labelling operates in essentially interpersonal encounters). Nor has it been possible to look at the purely formal aspects of intergroup processes such as assimilation, absorption, integration and so on, without relating these processes to their historical, political and economic structural contexts. The emphasis has inevitably been on cross-national comparative work, looking at the comparative socioeconomic systems and the effect which these have on major forms of group interaction. Such work, moreover, places the detailed empirical studies of desegregation which have preoccupied some of the ablest American sociologists since the Brown vs. the Board of Education decision of 1954 in a larger context.

Prior to 1967 the number of sociologists who were concerned with race and minority group relations on the cross-national comparative level was small. In many European countries, of course, racial distinctions were not thought of as a very significant basis of social differentiation and race relations hardly emerged as a special topic of investigation even on the national, let alone the international, level. But even in the United States and in Great Britain, whose policies and practices did make race salient both at home and overseas, the tendency was for race relations studies to be confined within the general study of domestic social problems. Van den Berghe (1978) and Schermerhorn (1964) in the United States and Banton (1968) and Mason (1970) in Great Britain stood out because they addressed themselves precisely to cross-national comparative problems. The work of these authors laid the basis of a systematic sociology of race relations outside of Marxism and was intertwined with theories of the plural society which developed as a way of explaining the specific nature of social differentiation in certain colonial societies (Furnivall, 1939; Smith, 1965; Smith and Kuper, 1969; Van den Berghe, 1978).

For the mainstream of Marxist thinking even in the West, the focus on race and minority groups seemed to be a diversion drawing attention away from the primary fact of exploitation on a class basis. Nonetheless there was, during the 1960s, an increasing concern with the different types of class relations and perhaps modes of production to be found at the centre and periphery of the world economic system (Brenner, 1977; Banarji, 1977; Alavi, 1975); while at the same time Marxists were forced to respond to the plural society debate and to offer their own explanations within such areas as the comparative study of slave-plantation systems (Genovese and Foner, 1969).

Van den Berghe says that he is concerned with races in the sense of human groups that define themselves or are defined by other groups as different from other groups by virtue of innate and immutable physical characteristics. 'These physical characteristics are in turn believed to be intrinsically related to moral, intellectual and other non-physical attributes or abilities' (Van den Berghe, 1978). The emphasis here is on social (and not necessarily scientifically valid) definitions which purport to refer to physical characteristics. It excludes situations in which, even though there is sharp differentiation and inequality between groups, that differentiation and inequality between groups is thought of as resting on non-physical (e.g. cultural and historical) characteristics.

Van den Berghe (1978) does, however, recognize that physical differences can exist without being thought of as salient: 'In addition to their physical differences... groups also have to be culturally different (at least when they first met) and in a position of institutionalised inequality for the idea of inherent racial differences to take root'.

Cultural differences and institutionalized inequality of this kind are to be found in situations of military conquest of one group by another, gradual frontier expansion, the involuntary migration of labour (e.g. in the slave trade) or in the case of the migration of refugees.

Van den Berghe does not, however, use his account of the kinds of situation in which racial differences may come to have salience as a basis for classifying race relations situations. Rather he makes an empirical distinction between situations which he describes as 'paternalistic' and those which he describes as 'competitive' while at the same time being drawn into the debate about pluralism. The distinction between paternalist and competitive situations is a broad one and seems to coincide with that between pre-capitalist and capitalist societies, though it blurs the distinction between those plantation societies in which plantations were in fact capitalist enterprises producing for the market and those which had more of a manorial character by representing both as 'paternalist'. On the question of pluralism on the other hand he makes a distinction between cultural and social pluralism, seeing race relations situations as one particular case of pluralism in which the social pluralism which follows from the duplication of institutions is independently supported by social differentiation on a racial basis, and which makes plural differentiation far more permanent than in other cases.

All in all it must be said that Van den Berghe's approach is a highly eclectic one, full of interesting insights insufficiently developed. Most strikingly, it does not anywhere refer to the way in which the economy and the mode and social relations of production structure race relations. The same is also true to some extent, though his work is far more systematic, of the work of Richard Schermerhorn.

Schermerhorn first of all sees ethnic relations as involving problems which are general to the study of social systems. These problems have to do with integration. Whether one approaches a society from the point of view of consensus theory or conflict theory, the question of how integrated groups are is important and one of the main variables in ethnic relations is seen as the degree to which they are integrated in a larger society. Inter-ethnic relations will vary in accordance with the power differential between groups, in accordance with their cultural similarity or dissimilarity and in accordance with the degree of compatibility between the attitudes of two or more groups towards being incorporated (i.e. one group might wish to be assimilated, while the other might reject and oppose its desires, or one group might desire secession and the other force integration or assimilation on it and so on). Certain of the situations which result from this matrix of possibilities are the basis on which inter-ethnic conflict and sometimes racism emerge.

Schermerhorn does not, however, simply offer us this formal theory as the basis for classifying inter-ethnic relations. He also suggests that there are certain recurrent historical social sequences which tend to produce intergroup situations with these characteristics. These are (1) the emergence of pariahs, (2) the emergence of indigenous isolates, (3) annexation, (4) migration, and (5) colonization. Under (4) migration, he includes the importation of foreign slaves, forced labour transfers within a country, indentured labour, movement of displaced persons and admission of voluntary migrants.

The formal classification offered in the earlier part of his work is then combined with the repeated historical sequences to see whether the kinds of cases which emerge involve racism or pluralism, which are seen as separate, though not necessarily mutually exclusive, structural outcomes. Finally, these kinds of outcome are seen as having a greater or lesser probability of occurrence within the national societies of the world divided in terms of cultural regions, in terms of whether they have predominantly free or predominantly planned economies and in terms of concrete historical cases.

Schermerhorn's work is undoubtedly a classificatory tour de force and he has shown in his own more recent empirical work how his categories might be applied to a particular empirical instance. It is to be hoped that there will be sociologists who will relate their work to his and fill in the empirical content of some of his theoretical boxes. Nonetheless, it must be said that there are so many variables involved in this system that racism and pluralism seem to crop up in oddly unrelated boxes, while their recurrent appearance under certain specific historical, political and economic conditions seems under-explained. Here, as in the case of Van den Berghe one feels that the formal basis of the typology would be given a better focus if it was combined with something like a Marxist approach which started from some conception of the range of possible economic systems.

The main British contributors to this debate about the cross-national study of race relations in the 1950s and 1960s were Banton and Mason. For Banton race is one possible 'role sign' for ordering the relations of one group and another. These relations may take any one of seven forms at a particular time: (1) peripheral contact, (2) institutionalized contact, (3) acculturation, (4) domination, (5) paternalism, (6) integration and (7) pluralism. The sequence in which these orders follow one another is somewhat reminiscent of Van den Berghe's. The stage of contact may lead either to paternalism or to domination. In the case of domination later development may be towards pluralism, while in the case of paternalism integration might follow. Separate from these is the case in which there is no initial power imbalance between the two parties and acculturation occurs, leading eventually to integration.

Banton's typology seems theoretically weak when compared to Schermerhorn's but, like Van den Berghe's, it classifies some colonial cases as paternalist, while also emphasizing the possibility of a pluralistic outcome. Unfortunately, when Banton turns to dealing with concrete political cases of race relations he seems to forget this typology and to adopt theoretical categories ad hoc to suit the particular material. In this respect his approach shares much with that of Philip Mason, whose *Patterns of Dominance* represents a complex historical and empirical attempt to classify types of political domination of one group by another.

While these theories were offered as general theories for explaining any society at all, the theory of the plural society was developed specifically to explain colonial society. In the case of the founder of the theory, J. S. Furnivall, it was developed as a means of explaining the main structural ways in which tropical colonial societies like Indonesia differed from capitalist societies in Europe. In the case of M.G. Smith it was thought of as providing a more suitable framework for the study of Caribbean societies than was available in conventional sociological theory.

Furnivall accepted what one might call the Durkheimian point about modern market-based societies, namely that, although the key relationships in the society were individualistic market relationships, nonetheless markets themselves existed within a framework of a common will or a shared consensus that force and fraud at least were to be outlawed. In the Indonesian case as he saw it, however, the market existed without any such common will and both structurally and culturally men were united into groups only outside of the market place. On the one hand there was a world in which life was, as Hobbes would have said, poor, nasty, brutish and short, while on the other there was the world of the ethnic group in which men lived out their private non-economic lives in harmony and solidarity. Furnivall's problem then was to see how a common will could be imposed upon the market place transcending the separate common wills which were so strongly developed in domestic and tribal life.

M. G. Smith addressed himself to a different kind of colonial society, based not so much on trade and peasant production, but on the slave plantation and on imported indentured labour. For him the cultural division between groups was even more radical than that suggested by Furnivall. Each of the separate ethnic groups had a nearly complete set of cultural institutions of its own including its own separate economic institutions. In these circumstances Smith does not pose the question of a market place without a common will. The only institution which binds the members of one group with those of another is the political one and that rests upon the domination of all other groups by the dominant colonialist or successor group. If Furnivall's problem is that of a market place without any political will, Smith's is that of a polity without normative consensus.

These, then, were the theories that the present writer encountered in the field of sociological enquiry loosely called race relations when he participated in the UNESCO experts' meeting on Racism and Race Prejudice in 1967. The problem was how to systematize such insights while at the same time concentrating on situations of serious political concern.

The first issue to be faced was the relationship between the terms 'ethnicity' and 'race', or, more precisely, between 'ethnic' and 'racial' situations. Obviously, all of those who had experienced the fraudulent scientific teaching of the Nazis were unwilling to use the term 'race' as an important one in explaining the political differences between men. It was tempting, therefore, to say that there was only one field of study, namely that of ethnic groups. This, however, could also be misleading because ethnic groups were often taken to be groups which were to be distinguished solely in terms of culture. They were often thought of as a benign political phenomenon. But if this was the case how did one distinguish that group of situations of more malign sort in which groups were not merely different but unequal in power and in which one group exploited or oppressed another?

It was this malign feature of the situation which had seemed at the UNESCO meeting to be even more important than whether or not the characteristics in terms of which groups differentiated themselves from each other were physical. I suggested, therefore, that the term 'race relations situation' should be reserved for a situation characterized by three elements, namely (1) severe competition, exploitation or oppression going well beyond that which occurred in normal market situations, (2) the existence of sharp group boundaries which made it impossible for individuals to transfer easily from one group membership to another so that the competition, exploitation or oppression mentioned above was of group by group, and (3) the acceptance by the dominant group of a deterministic belief system of some kind which held that the characteristics which divided one group from another were more or less immutable.

This was in many ways a perverse definition. It avoided limiting the term 'race relations situation' to those situations in which physical characteristics were the primary basis of classification as in Van den Berghe's definition of the field and it did not confine the term to those situations in which biological or genetic theories were used to justify inequality. The reason for this, however, was that the class of situations which were distinctively problematic could not be limited in this way. Mere possession of distinct physical characteristics need not lead to oppression and exploitation, even where such characteristics were recognized, and, on the other hand, precisely because bodies like UNESCO had discredited racist theory of the biological sort, the forms of theory used in justifying group inequality were very often of a non-biological sort. In the Six Counties of Northern Ireland, for example, the differences between Protestants and Catholics were not physical, nor was the justification used for discriminating against Catholics biological, yet it was clear that this particular political situation had much in common with other colonial situations in which a native people were oppressed by settlers from the metropolis. The definition of a race relations situation offered was, therefore, intended to bring together situations which had these essentially political elements in common. Van den Berghe's account of the historical origins of race relations problems and Schermerhorn's repeated historical sequences seemed to be attempts to capture the same empirical and historical reality.

In my own earliest formulations of this problem (Rex, 1970a, 1970b, 1973) I also listed the kinds of situations in which the three conditions of my definition were likely to be fulfilled. My list included:

1. Situations of conquest.
2. Frontier situations.
3. Slave plantations.
4. Other unfree labour systems.
5. Situation of migrant workers from colonies in the metropolis.
6. Situation of refugees.
7. The situation of certain pariah groups who carried out certain essential but despised tasks and were punished for so doing.

I am not sure that I would any longer wish to defend this precise list, but I am interested nonetheless to note that Van den Berghe, Schermerhorn and I, despite our divergent definitions, tend to come together in our list of the actual empirical situations which we wish to classify together.

Much earlier than in this comment on the definition of race relations situations, I had joined in the debate about the plural society (Rex, 1958). It seemed to me at that time that in a sociological debate dominated by the consensualist functionalist theory of Talcott Parsons, the great value of the plural society debate was that it posited a society in which there was no simple community of values, no common will. I sought to reinterpret Furnivall, as well as Malinowski (1961) and Myrdal (1969), so as to claim their support, not so much for a theory of pluralism of a fairly benign political sort, but for conflict theory. The plural elements in the societies which they described I treated as being, like Marx's classes-for-themselves, political societies in conflict with one another.

When M. G. Smith joined in the plural society debate, it seemed obvious that he was missing this class and conflict dimension of the segments which he described. I therefore argued (Rex, 1970b) that that debate must be 'marxized', that is to say that, even though we might agree that the social bonding of the various ethnic segments might derive from culture and kinship, the new raison d'être of these segments in the colonial situation was to be found in the relationship of each ethnic group to the means of production. The nature of these segments could not be understood, I argued, unless it was recognized that they had some of the attributes of Marxian classes.

The Smith theory of pluralism was least of all applicable in those situations in which a highly-developed capitalist economy had come into being. When, therefore, Smith's collaborator, Leo Kuper (1969), and Van den Berghe (1966 and 1978) sought to apply it to South Africa, I reacted sharply, pointing out that the African workers in South Africa could only be understood as a political community organized around the class of migrant workers and that what one had in South Africa was a class struggle (Rex, 1971).

In interpreting the position of the Bantu people in South Africa as a class position, however, I found myself in conflict with the South African Marxists of the time. Their problem was to explain the role of the South African White working class in relation to the Bantu workers. Whereas I was prepared to say that migrant workers migrating to work for nine months of the year unaccompanied by their families, living in compounds, without the protection of trades unions, had a different relationship to the means of production than White workers and therefore were a distinct class, the orthodox Marxist view (Wolpe, 1970) of the time was that the differences between Black and White workers were stratum differences only (Wolpe, 1970).

A new contribution of some importance was made to this debate by Edna Bonacich who had worked with Van den Berghe in the University of Natal (Bonacich, 1966, 1972, n.d.). This was that the South African situation was to be understood as arising from a split labour market. This was a considerable improvement on Van den Berghe's classification of the South African situation as 'competitive' while at the same time providing a non-dogmatic conceptualization of my own dispute with the Marxists. What Bonacich seemed to me to accept was that a sociological analysis needed to be based upon a detailed structural analysis of labour markets, a notion which was more analytical than either a simplistic conception of class or one of plural ethnic segments.

The concept of the split labour market also seemed to fit the American labour market situation between the wars. There Black migrants to the North found themselves in competition with White native Americans and with European migrants who responded to their potentiality for employment at lower rates or in worse conditions with a racist demand for their exclusion. At the same time Bonacich, who had settled in the United States, combined her analysis of split labour markets with one of the role of middlemen minorities like the Koreans to produce a flexible and semi-Marxist analysis of labour problems in the USA.

William Wilson later placed the notion of the split labour market in a longer historical context (Wilson, 1977). According to his view, American race relations had gone through three phases. First, there was the phase of plantation slavery in which racism could be understood simply as a means of justifying a White supremacy system. In the second phase, when Black and White workers competed for the same jobs, one had Bonacich's split labour market situation. In recent years, however, there had been a twofold development. On the one hand the increasingly important tertiary sector of the economy had been compelled to take Black workers in white-collar and professional jobs thus making possible the emergence of a Black middle class. On the other the bulk of the Black population, having been successfully excluded from the more desirable blue-collar jobs, found themselves either unemployed or in unpleasant and unstable employment. This new total situation was one in which there was actually far less racism than there had been in the 1930s. On the one hand the visible new Black middle class took some of the steam out of the situation for the Blacks. On the other the Whites felt more protected because Blacks were not competing for the same blue-collar jobs but were confined in the less desirable part of a dual labour market (Doeringer and Piore, 1971).

Of course, by the 1970s, the specific political situation in America had changed remarkably from that in the immediate postwar situation. The semi-colonial social and political arrangements in the South, collectively known as Jim Crow, had been eliminated, the Brown vs. the Board of Education decision had started a flow of desegregation decisions, there had been urban riots in the North on a scale which possibly justified the use of the term 'Black revolution', and the mainstream of the American political parties seemed committed to desegregation. Much of the most technically excellent American sociology was now devoted to quantifying and measuring the degree to which the government's declared goals were being achieved.

The problems facing the United States were in part at least reproduced in the more successful European countries. All of them, in the period between 1945 and 1970, had recourse to the use of immigrant labour. Nearly everywhere this was what Peach (1968) in Britain called 'replacement labour' and the question arose as to whether the immigrants would form a separate and relatively rightless subproletariat or underclass differentiated from the main body of organized labour and having to defend its own interests not merely against capital but against organized labour. (For a discussion of the development of the 'underclass' concept first used by Gunnar Myrdal, 1969, see Rex and Tomlinson, 1979; for a discussion of the European evidence, see Castles and Kosack, 1973.) In my own work I noted that the relative acceptance of immigrant workers because of a segregated dual labour market situation in industry nonetheless permitted the development of a class struggle over housing (Rex and Moore, 1967; Rex, 1973; Rex and Tomlinson, 1979).

The existence of an immigrant labour problem did not necessarily create a race relations situation. In continental European countries and most notably in West Germany the crucial difference was simply between citizens and non-citizens since the so-called guest workers were more than sufficiently distinguished by their lack of civil and political rights. In Britain and to some extent in France, however, many colonial immigrants had the rights of citizenship and their economic and social exclusion was often justified ideologically on racist grounds. It remains to be seen whether these differences will continue. There is, of course, a certain general drift within the system towards gradual incorporation of immigrant workers as workers into the working class and, given the cultural similarity of Southern Europeans to their hosts, this process there might be accelerated. It could, however, be the case that European capitalism finds it convenient to have a permanently divided working class and also that the contrary pull on former colonial workers to engage in the struggles of their homeland might well keep them divided from the native-born proletariat.

In referring to the South African situation and in referring to the situation in the United States and Europe we have of necessity to raise the question of the interrelationship between race and class or, more exactly, between race and class struggle. It would be useful before we return to this, therefore, to consider the whole question of the relationship between Marxist theorizing and the thinking of predominantly Western non-Marxist scholars whose work we have been discussing.

Surprisingly, there seems to be little to be gained at the moment from colleagues in the Communist countries which would help to illuminate the comparative study of ethnic and race relations. This is not because of any particular insensitivity on the part of Communist sociologists, but because in theory, as well as to some considerable extent in practice, ethnic groups in Communist countries cannot, as they can in the West, be explained away as expressions of class (see Bromley). Insofar as it is the case that classes have been abolished then the persistence of ethnicity must have some other explanation and Soviet scholars in particular have been inclined to pursue this question in a way which appears to their Western colleagues, and perhaps especially to their Western Marxist colleagues, as antiquarian. Some Western critics of the Communist world might, of course, argue that ethnic differences persist because class differences persist under Communism. There is, however, insufficient evidence available to us as yet as to the disappearance or continuance of ethnic differentiation in the Communist world. Evidence from Cuba would be particularly important since it might provide some evidence of the effect of Communism on a formerly colonial and racially stratified society.

Few Western Marxists until recently managed at all seriously to address the question of race relations and racial conflict. Oliver Cromwell Cox, a Black American Marxist, was one of the few who did (Cox, 1970) but, since his solution was to argue that the exploitation and oppression of Blacks was simply capitalism's oppression of the working class, he seemed unable to explain either the nature of the privileged White working class or the variation in labour systems in the capitalist world which employed Blacks. Meanwhile, in the field of comparative slavery, while the principal scholar called himself a Marxist, he went so far in insisting upon the diversity of kinds of capitalism and upon the independence of the superstructure, that it is hard to see that what was being advanced was a specifically Marxist view at all (Genovese, 1971).

The major scandal to which Western Marxism had to address itself was, of course, the behaviour of the White working class in South Africa. The legend that in 1922 White workers unfurled banners saying 'workers of the world unite for a White South Africa' was used as a refutation of Marxism and as the basis for the claim that racism had nothing to do with capitalism and was simply endemic in the working class itself. Such claims about class behaviour were readily extended to other societies and the whole question of the explanation of the relation between capitalism and racism threatened to become Marxism's intellectual Achilles heel.

Frederick Johnstone (1975) sought to deal with the problem in the South African case by arguing that the race relations situation grew out of a wages colour bar imposed by the employers and that it was only within that framework that the workers protected themselves by imposing a job colour bar. This argument came very close to that of Edna Bonacich, except that in Johnstone's case the setting up of the split labour market was attributed to the employers.

Much more radical was the revision of Marxist theory eventually proposed by Harold Wolpe. He had earlier replied to my own assertion that Black and White workers were in a different class position by arguing that since both produced surplus value and had it extracted from them they must be in the same class position. Later, however, building on the sociological theory of Poulantzas and Carshedi, he suggested that while the White workers were part of the 'collective worker' they also performed some of the 'global functions of capitalism' (for the earlier view, see Wolpe, 1970; for the later view, see ibid., 1976). If this was the case it seemed possible to me that one could argue from a Marxist point of view that the position of Black workers under South African capitalism was different as a class position from that of their White co-workers and that, far from being a diversion, their struggle as a nation against White dominance was the central theme of the class struggle.

More far-reaching in its implications in relating Marxism to race relations theory and the theory of colonialism was the development of new theories about the nature of capitalism as a world system. Earlier generations of Marxists had simply approached colonial society with the unilinear theory of social evolution derived from Europe, arguing that such societies were pre-capitalist or feudal (Dobb, 1964; Sweezy et al., 1959). Now Frank (1969) argued that there was one capitalist process and that economic development in Europe and the USA and underdevelopment in the Third World were two sides of the same capitalist coin, while Wallerstein (1974) looked back to the 16th century to argue that at this time the new development of capitalism at the world centre was accompanied by a related development as part of one system of the slave plantations in the Americas and of the second serfdom in Eastern Europe.

Not all Marxists by any means were prepared to accept the new revisionism. Many argued against Frank particularly (Laclau, 1971) that capitalism could not be defined in terms of market exchange and that a Marxist analysis required consideration of the mode of production and the social relations of production. What is notable about this debate, however, is that both sides are agreed that the pattern of relations between employer and employee is different in the periphery and the colonies. Whether this difference is due to the economics of capitalist development or to the accidental fact of conquest and political domination of the colonial world matters little. It could be that herein lies the crucial difference between those situations which assume a racial and racist character and those which do not. It is perhaps surprising that those who have developed the capitalist world system idea have not sought to develop this distinction and to apply their ideas to the explanation of race relations. Probably this is because, in Wallerstein's case at least, the emphasis is so much upon one system, that the whole dynamic of class struggle is seen as taking place at the centre without due consideration being given to the implications of the differences at the periphery which the theory itself posits and which might well have long-term dynamic implications.

Another feature of the Wallerstein theory which deserves notice is the deliberate underplaying of the role of political empire. For him political domination is a costly feature of an early stage in the development of the world system and that this system develops as a world system without the need of continued political coercion. This is questionable. While it is certainly true that empires eventually fade away and that colonialism continues through exploitation by multinational corporations, the actual positions of various ethnic groups, segments and classes within the total imperial system is only explicable in terms of their subjection to power other than that of a simple market sort. Multinational corporations indeed tend to be deliberately anti-racist. Money knows no colour. Yet the world is a world marked by racism and race conflict and this is something which the world system theory should be called upon to explain.

One thing which emerges from our review of the comparative theory of race relations is now clear. If we look at non-Marxist theory we notice that, even if it starts from formal classifications and typologies, it has in the long run to concede that the groups which it describes have some features in common with classes and require explanation not merely of a culturalist sort but in terms of their relation to the means of production and the political order. On the other hand, if we look at Marxist theory, it becomes increasingly clear that intergroup conflict, whether in the metropolis or in the colonies and the periphery, cannot be explained in terms of simple models of class conflict derived from European experience in the 19th century. What seems to be necessary, therefore, is a picture of social stratification and intergroup conflict generated by European political and economic imperialism during the last four hundred years. It must be in the development of a theory of this kind that the further development of the comparative sociology of race relations must lie. What follows is an attempt to indicate the lines along which such a theory might develop.

The starting point of this theory must be found in something like Wallerstein's theory of the world economic system. This suggests, as we have seen, that as a matter of empirical and historical fact that system was marked at its inception by a distinction between the new capitalism of the centre marked by, amongst other things, the use of free labour and two alternative systems of production at the periphery, the second serfdom of Eastern Europe on the one hand and the slave plantation system of the Americas on the other. It is not suggested in this theory that these are separate modes of production interpenetrating each other, but rather that they are parts of a single system.

Why the world system should develop in this way is not made clear. One argument would be that a certain primitive accumulation or plunder was necessary in order to set up capital for its encounter with labour at the centre, a view which is argued and well documented by Eric Williams of Trinidad in his *Capitalism and Slavery* (1944), but not a central part of Marx's own theory. Another would be that the production of certain types of agricultural, horticultural and mining products lent itself to this type of labour organization and that these products were central to the development of capitalism at that stage.

Certain concepts derived from Max Weber (1961) are at least partially helpful here. For him capitalist production of the Western European sort was to be understood as a development of the notion of capitalist enterprise of a more general sort. All that the notion of a capitalist enterprise implies is that one or more entrepreneurs count up assets and after using them to finance a particular enterprise count them up again with a view to achieving a profit. A distinction then has to be made between capitalist enterprises in terms of the kind of activity undertaken. In capitalism of the kind which existed quite widely in the Roman Empire and on the margins of other societies the assets were usually applied to relatively discontinuous high risk and often non-peaceful activities. In the modern Western European type of enterprise, on the other hand, the activity was continuous and peacefully oriented to market opportunities.

It is worth pointing out that, in making this distinction, we do not necessarily have to claim that no element of compulsion is concealed in contracts in the capitalist market. Whether or not such compulsion exists, however, in an empirical system thus established there is no need for recourse to force or violence. This is as true in regard to the acquisition of raw materials and other products within the free capitalist system as it is in relation to obtaining the use of labour power. It is possible, therefore, to talk of the modern Western capitalist system as characteristically employing free labour and thereby distinguishing it from earlier forms of capitalism and that which goes on at the periphery of the modern capitalist world system.

At the centre the characteristic feature of the labour system is first free bargaining, then collective bargaining and finally class struggle. Such developments may in fact involve quite crucial periods of brutal repression and one should not rule out the possibility that in the long run the whole institution of free labour might be abandoned. Nevertheless, for long periods the political order of such societies is determined by the fact of class struggle and in the later periods of the system a certain minimum protection of workers' rights has been achieved in the form of a welfare state.

By way of contrast, Weber suggested, adventurer capitalism or booty capitalism deals in force. Its characteristic enterprises are the financing of risky voyages, the financing of wars, plantation slavery, mining and tax farming. All of these involve, at some point along the chain of exchanges, the direct use of force and it was around such enterprises that the colonial systems of the 16th century were conducted. (In the case of the second serfdom, of course, these new institutions of compulsion did not have to be constructed. Ancient institutions were simply put to a new capitalist use.)

What emerged then in the new capitalist world system were two separate systems of labour exploitation. At the centre there was a system of free labour and developing class struggle. At the periphery there was a variety of forms of more or less compulsory and violent economic exploitation. So it was at least in the period in which colonies were constituted. To say this, however, is not to say that there remain in existence colonial societies of precisely this form. Many of them have undergone change and development in accordance with the needs of the world system as a whole. Others have dropped out of that system and have stagnated. Rarely, however, have the former colonies simply become like the metropolitan societies that brought them into being. What we have to do, in constructing a typology of colonial social forms, is to give due weight both to the structures which were built into them at the outset and to the various processes of change which they have undergone.

The interest of my particular research committee, of course, is in the development of patterns of race and ethnic relations and the position of minority groups. What is being suggested here is that, if we are to avoid a crude culturalist approach to analyzing these relations, we must be able to relate the position of the various ethnic and racial and minority groups to their position in the system of colonial production and exploitation. A systematic theory of colonial societies would provide the basis for doing this.

So far as race and minority relations in the metropolis itself are concerned we have two problems. On the one hand we have those situations in Britain and in France where immigrants are colonial immigrants (one might also add that in the United States one has Black immigration to the North from the 'internal colony' in the South), and which have to be explained in terms of the interaction between colonial and metropolitan societies. On the other we have the case of short distance immigrants from neighbouring countries as in many parts of North West Europe, where what needs to be developed as a basis for analyzing the class position of immigrants is a theory of dependent societies equivalent to that which we shall propose for the colonies.

I have suggested in several recent essays that, although we cannot yet begin to set out a systematic sociological theory of colonial societies, we can indicate what the principal variables are, both at the initial stage in which colonial social systems are being constituted and in the subsequent period when they undergo development. I have therefore suggested that we begin to analyze as constitutive variables the range of types of societies which were subject to colonial incorporation, the range of enterprises which were established within them, and the estate systems which arose around the main economic system and turned it into a society, and as processual variables the forms of economic liberalization and their consequences which resulted from the transition within the world system from mercantilism to laissez faire, the transition to political independence under differing classes, estates and segments, the partial incorporation of the former colonies into the post-imperial world system and the kinds of internal revolutionary change which the colonial systems undergo.

An attempt is made to summarize these variables in Table 1. While it is impossible to review here all the problems which this Table indicates it will now be worthwhile to indicate what some of the major areas of sociological study should be:

CONSTITUTIVE VARIABLES

It is a mistake to suppose that the societies which were conquered and incorporated by European colonialists were simply clay in their hands. In some cases, it is true, social institutions were nearly completely destroyed in the business of initial colonial plunder and individuals therefore made available for individual exploitation, and in others individuals were captured, torn from their social and cultural context to be transported as slaves to wholly new societies being constituted. Yet even in these cases some remnants of the old pre-colonial culture and society remained and were incorporated into a culture of resistance, while in other cases ranging from the small tribal bands encountered by the Hudsons Bay Company in Canada to the mighty Moghul Empire to which the East India Companies first addressed themselves, the cultures and social structures encountered were not completely malleable for capitalist and colonialist purposes.

We may perhaps take as reference points for developing a typology of pre-colonial forms the following:
1. The Moghul Empire in India.
2. The Bronze Age Empires of Central America.
3. The West African Empires whose social institutions were exploited as a basis for the slave trade.
4. The societies of slaves and other transported workers in the newly constructed colonial societies.
5. The small-scale societies of nomads which were marginalized in reservations.

TABLE 1
Variations in Structure and Development of Imperial and Colonial Societies

METROPOLITAN CAPITALISM		COLONIAL CAPITALISM			
		Pre-Colonial Social Form	Mode of Exploitation	Variety of Forms	Overall Stratification of Society
Capitalist enterprise employing free labour leading to class struggle, hypothetical socialist revolution and the welfare state. Subsequent employment of underclass labour	CONSTITUTIVE VARIABLES	Ranging from bands of nomadic hunters through tribal states to complex empires, e.g. Moghul Empire in India	Exploitation through unequal exchange. Tax farming and military exploitation. Exploitation of primary producers through marketing. Manorial systems. *Latifundia* and estate systems. Plantations and mining, with unfree labour	Slave emancipation. Land reform. Free trade. 'American' model, colonial bourgeois rule. 'Asian' model, native bourgeois rule. 'African' model, one party state	Possible classes or estates include 1. Peasants and farmers 2. Slaves 3. Sharecroppers 4. Planters and overseers 5. Freemen, incl. freed slaves, poor Whites and Coloureds 6. Secondary traders 7. Free White workers, capitalists and farmers 8. Administrators 9. Missionaries
		Type of Process			Effect on Class Situation
	PROCESSUAL VARIABLES	Economic liberalization			Move from fixed status to system of mobility and contract. Continuous stratification
		Political independence			Emergence of political elites. Europeanized elites. Racial domination. Independent capitalism
		Incorporation into world economic system			Subordination of local capitalism to multi-national corporations → Neo-colonial elites. *Comprador* bourgeoisie. Emergence of free proletariat
		Processes of revolution			Late struggle for political independence. Struggle against neo-colonialism. Nationalism and socialism → Military coups. Alliances with superpowers. Worker and peasant revolt

Understanding the structure and dynamics of these societies is important for at least three reasons. Firstly, the structure of the colonial society established would differ according to the pre-colonial social type with which it was dealing. Secondly, the capacity of the colonizers to exploit and the capacity of those exploited to resist would depend upon the social and cultural resources available to the people concerned. Thirdly, in the post-colonial period it would seem to be quite possible that the kind of pre-colonial social form involved would affect the capability of the new post-colonial society for independent development.

It is to be noted here that European scholarship in relation to colonial society has gone through two main phases. In the first a kind of intellectual racism led to emphasizing the difference between the societies of the 'heathens' and those of their Christian colonial masters. This stance was criticized from a liberal anti-racist position which maintained that all men were equal and similar. Liberal scholarship, however, was likely to develop its own kind of racism based upon the undervaluing of all cultures other than the Western one which was deemed to be universal. Weber and Marx shared this perspective. For Weber only Western rational capitalism seemed possible as a path to economic development, while for Marx the British occupation of India was the only revolution which Asia ever knew.

The second of the constitutive variables is to be found in the range of types of colonialist enterprise on which the economy of the new colony was to be based. These include simple trade, trade based upon fraud and force, the purchase and marketing of peasant crops, the farming of rents on large-scale estates, plantations and mines using slaves and indentured labour and tax farming. Such operations were carried out in the 16th and 17th centuries and again at the end of the 19th century not only by individual colonial adventurers but by specially chartered capitalist companies which were a distinctive imperialist social form which had existed in the Ancient World, but which now became central to the expansion of Europe overseas.

Initial colonial adventures were, of course, less orderly than those systematically organized by the chartered companies. In the case of the conquest of the Central American empires exploitations consisted in taking the gold away as booty, and in the case of some trade the trader simply took advantage of his knowledge of distant markets to make a profit out of the native hunter or trapper. As time went on, however, the business of colonial exploitation became more systematically organized.

Three useful reference points for the development of a typology of colonial economic enterprises would be:
1. The activities of the East India Company in India in the 18th century, centring on the business of tax farming with various opportunities for trade and the exploitation of peasants occurring as a result.
2. The establishment of plantations with imported labour, consisting in the first place of slaves, but with these being replaced by indentured labour. This type can also be seen as being used in relation to mining.
3. Settlement by farmers exploiting squatters, share croppers and rent-paying tenants on *latifundia*.

It is assumed that the exploitation of peasants is a universal colonial fact. In fact the very term 'peasant' implies an agriculturalist who is not wholly free but is subordinated to some larger system of subordination (Wolf, 1966; Shanin, 1972). A fully independent agriculturalist engaged in pure subsistence farming would by definition be outside the colonial system.

It is also assumed here that although these enterprises are basically to be classified as capitalist, they do have a tendency to relapse into seignorial forms whenever there is no strong market demand for their product. Moreover, it must also be recognized that colonizing powers included some amongst whom capitalism was less strongly developed than amongst others and that in these cases a colonial enterprise varied between booty capitalism and a search for manors.

A colonial society is not fully described merely by referring to its primary economic enterprises. The maintenance of even these assumes that there will be other groups available to perform necessary functions while the developing system also throws up new groups with marginal status who have to be incorporated in special ways. The principal groups emerging are likely to include the following:
1. Marginalized individuals who have become displaced from other available statuses. In plantation societies, these include freed slaves, Coloureds and poor Whites.
2. Secondary traders usually having an ethnicity different from that of either the main colonialists or the main body of workers who take up trading opportunities insufficiently profitable to or beneath the dignity of the main colonialists.

3. 'White settlers', being colonists from the metropolis who are not involved in the main exploitative institutions but who seek and usually find rewarding opportunities as free capitalists, workers or farmers. While having internally conflicting interests they tend to be a privileged group as a whole with shared interests to defend.
4. A cadre of administrators who represent the colonial state whose relationship to the main colonialists is as ambiguous at least as is the relationship of the state to metropolitan capitalism.
5. A cadre of clergy who have a moral task equivalent to the political task of the administrators and who, like them, have a relatively independent role to play.

Such groups as these are distinguished by their differential legal and political rights and are, quite appropriately, called estates. Their distinction one from another, however, is reinforced by cultural, ethnic and racial differences.

PROCESSUAL VARIABLES

A theory of colonial society of the type thus far outlined would not by itself serve as a basis for analyzing intergroup conflicts at the present day. What is not sufficiently realized, however, is that it is equally misleading to imagine that these conflicts can be fully grasped in terms of concepts, including Marxist concepts derived from European experience as though these were simply new instances of metropolitan capitalist society. What we have to do, therefore, is to build models of these societies which start from the constitutive variables but which give recognition of the ways in which the societies thus constituted undergo change and development.

The first of the processual variables is that of economic liberalization. While there may be much argument about why the process occurred, it is clear that at the beginning of the 19th century economic thinking and practice in the metropolitan capitalist countries moved from mercantilism to laissez faire and there was therefore pressure on the colonial social systems to liberalize themselves, replacing institutions based upon force and compulsion with new ones based upon free competition and equality of opportunity. In saying this, however, we should not allow ourselves to lapse into ideology. No ideal world was being created in the colonies. Land reform and slave emancipation occurred, but undercapitalized peasants were unable to benefit from free competition and were forced into dependence of a new type, while the freed slaves who migrated to the cities usually found themselves ghettoized and excluded from the new industrial jobs which were taken by new waves of European settlers. Nowhere is the nature of this transition more evident than in the United States. The Black emigrant from the Jim Crow South might not find Jim Crow in Chicago but he came up against the harsh realities of a competitive quest for jobs and housing.

It should also be noted that the process of liberalization was far from universal or complete. Slaves were not replaced by free labour but by forced immigrants on indentures and an even more oppressive system of short-term indentures became, and remains, the basic social form in mining and in many industrial enterprises in South Africa. The liberalism of laissez faire must therefore be understood as having an incomplete and aborted form in colonial contexts.

The second process is that of political independence. The complex social and political estate systems which we have described become independent of the metropolis for one of two reasons. Either one of the estates becomes sufficiently powerful in relation to the others and in relation to the metropolitan government or that government is itself so weakened by wars and economic crises that it can no longer exercise its authority and looks for a successor.

In North America an alliance of the plantocracy and the settler capitalists was able to take power in a War of Independence and the parties to that alliance in due course fought for control of the system in a civil war. In Latin America the movements headed by Bolivar brought to power a mestizized or straight settler bourgeoisie in most parts of Spanish America. In the Old British Commonwealth again a settler bourgeoisie took power, although in the case of South Africa White settlerdom retained many of the practices of the earlier booty capitalist period.

A new phase, however, came into being in 1945, when Britain, Holland, France and Portugal were all so weakened that they were no longer capable of colonial rule. In the remaining colonies, however, there was no obvious dominant estate to whom power could be handed over and it had to be given to the Europeanized elite who were capable of appealing to the masses and the majority group. This elite organized its own national group through the instrument of the centralized party as a new nation and then very often questioned the special privileges of surviving settler and secondary colonialist minorities. Since, however, these successor governments lacked the economic means to rule they were usually forced into some kind of neo-colonial dependency on the imperial and multinational corporations.

The third process which we list is precisely this incorporation into this neo-colonial system led by the surviving imperial and multinational corporations. No-one would wish to deny the importance of this new system. Clearly there is truth in the notion that the centres of power today are not in the colonial ministries of the great powers but in boardrooms whose directors do not necessarily have a single overriding national loyalty. But it is not true that such an international ruling class can achieve its purposes without the aid of governments and one of the interesting phenomena in metropolitan countries is precisely the development of new agencies such as the European Economic Community to do this. One should also note, moreover, that supranational government on behalf of an international capitalist class is still challenged by national governments and national capitalisms.

But if the transformation from nationalism to a supranational world economic system is as yet incomplete at the capitalist centre, it is still far from having transformed the whole neo-colonial world in its own interests. Many areas it is happy simply to ignore and to allow to stagnate unless and until their labour and resources might come to yield a profit. But there are in any case ancient pre-colonial economic and social forms, some of which survive in reasonably good heart from the constitutive booty capitalist period of colonialism, some of which are still governed by national imperialisms and some of which are subject to new national and even socialist control. One may fear that the power in the long run will be on the side of the multinationals, but for the moment at least one sees a world in which a complex and many sided class struggle goes on between groups and in which at most the multinationals seek to play the system to their own advantage.

Finally, if it is the case that class struggle goes on in post-colonial society the question arises as to how that class struggle may be theorized and how far any such theorization will enable us to predict the outcome.

Obviously, Marxism as an international theory of revolution seeks to mobilize the exploited peoples of colonial and neo-colonial societies in order to overthrow the capitalist system and usher in an international socialist order. But Marxism has the same problems in relation to this complex world system that multinational corporations do. The classes and estates of the colonial world are no more responsive to the dictates of Marxist analyses than the economic enterprises of the colonies are to the needs of multinational capitalism. Not surprisingly, therefore, its analyses, particularly when they have been advanced by Eurocentric groups like the French Communist Party, have been challenged by intellectuals and leaders like Franz Fanon.

Fanonism and like doctrines are, however, capable of serving as ideologies for diverse groups. In principle Fanon was in fact a socialist, urging that, while the national revolution should at all costs be supported against metropolitan capitalism it must also be held in a state of permanence so that it is not sold out by a *comprador* bourgeoisie. It is easy to see, however, how it might be an ideology in the interests of a national bourgeoisie seeking power in the kind of political vacuum to which we have referred in late transitions to independence.

COLONIAL IMMIGRANTS IN THE METROPOLIS

The total model which is being suggested here is not simply a model or a typology for colonial societies. It refers to an imperial system which united colonial and metropolitan societies. The whole of what we have said is designed to suggest that the separate colonies each contain their own complex and many sided class struggles. On the other hand there is the class struggle as it is understood in metropolitan societies, very often leading to the incorporation of the working class within some welfare state system. The problem which now arises is that of how colonial immigrants of varying class origins within the imperial and separate colonial systems are likely to be related and relate themselves to the metropolitan class struggle and system.

A first possibility here is that they will come to form a sub-proletariat or underclass separated from the mainstream working class in a divided labour market and in segregated housing and schools. Such a process is never complete, however, and there is at least a partial absorption of colonial minorities into the mainstream working class. The real problem is that in order to ensure its participation even in working-class struggle it has to organize and fight in its own interests.

It would, however, be wrong to assume that all immigrants will enter colonial society in a simple proletarian position. There is a great deal of evidence to suggest that almost any ethnic minority, if it is well organized, fights against proletarianization and there are many groups of Indian immigrants, for example, who both in their Indian class position and on arrival in the metropolis see opportunities for themselves either in or in parallel to the main economic system. They will fight their own particular class struggle in their own way.

But while the absorption of immigrants has been a problem for the metropolitan economies and their working classes for a period of 25 years or so, depression in the metropolitan economies has involved a cessation of immigration. At the same time, however, as depression affects metropolitan industries, new opportunities for investment open up in the former colonial territories. If capitalism recently recruited colonial labour because native-born metropolitan workers were unwilling or unsuitable, it now begins to look to the countries of origin of those immigrants as fields for investment. Whereas until recently labour came to capital, now capital goes in search of labour. It is, however, all part of the same process in which the metropolitan working class finds itself forced into competition, if it is to work at all, with cheap labour from the colonies.

COLONIAL CLASS STRUGGLE, RACE RELATIONS AND RACISM

It might seem to some readers that this review of the problem of creating a typology of colonial social structures and relating these to the total imperial social system is somewhat removed from the study of racism and race relations. If, however, the specificity of race relations situations is defined as I have defined it, the complex relations of exploiter and exploited, of one colonial estate with another, and of colony and metropolis, are precisely the kinds of situation of severe competition, exploitation and oppression beyond that which is normal under ordinary market conditions between groups which I have said leads to racist justification. The central part of the sociology of race relations therefore has to be concerned with the description and analyses of these situations. Perhaps more generally, moreover, one might discover in the variety of these situations not merely those which are rightly called race relations situations of the more benign sort which M. G. Smith, Van den Berghe and Schermerhorn call pluralism.

REFERENCES

Alavi, Hamza (1975) 'The Colonial Mode of Production', *Socialist Register* (London).
Banarji, Jarius (1977) 'Modes of Production in a Materialist Conception of History', *Capital and Class* (London), 3.
Banton, Michael (1968) *Race Relations*. New York: Basic Books.
Bonacich, Edna (1966) 'Capitalism and Race Relations in South Africa — A Split Labour Market Analysis'. Paper presented to the ISA meeting, Uppsala, Sweden.
Bonacich, Edna (1972) 'A Theory of Ethnic Antagonism — The Split Labour Market', *American Sociological Review*, 37.
Bonacich, Edna (1976) 'Advanced Capitalism and Black/White Relations in the United States — A Split Labour Market Interpretation', *American Sociological Review*, 41 (February): 34-51.
Brenner, Robert (1977) 'The Origins of Capitalist Development — A Critique of neo-Smithian Marxism', *New Left Review* (London), 144.
Bromley, Yu V., 'Toward Typology of Ethnic Process', *British Journal of Sociology*, 3.
Castles, Stephen and Kosack, Godula (1973) *Immigrant Workers and the Class Structure*. London: Oxford University Press.
Cox, Oliver Cromwell (1970) *Caste, Race and Class*. New York: Monthly Review Press.
Dobb, Maurice (1964) *Studies in the Development of Capitalism*. London.
Doeringer, P. and Piore, M. J. (1971) *International Labour Markets and Manpower Analysis*. New York: Lexington Books.
Frank, André Gunder (1969) *Capitalism and Underdevelopment in Latin America*. New York: Monthly Review Press.
Furnivall, J. S. (1939) *Netherlands India — A Study of Plural Economy*. London: Cambridge University Press.
Genovese, Eugene (1971) *In Red and Black*. London: Allen Lane.
Genovese, Eugene and Foner, Laura (1969) *Slavery in the New World*. Englewood Cliffs, NJ: Prentice-Hall.
Johnstone, Frederick (1975) *Class, Race and Gold*. London: Routledge and Kegan Paul.
Laclau, Ernesto (1971) 'Feudalism and Capitalism in Latin America', *New Left Review* (London), 67.
Malinowski, Bronislav (1961) *The Dynamics of Culture Change*. New York: Greenwood.
Mason, Philip (1970) *Patterns of Dominance*. London: Oxford University Press.
Montagu, Ashley (1972) *Statement on Race*. London: Oxford University Press.
Myrdal, Gunnar (1969) *Challenge to Affluence*. London: Gollancz.

Peach, Ceri (1968) *West Indian Migration to Britain*. London: Oxford University Press.
Rex, John (1958) 'The Plural Society in Sociological Theory', *British Journal of Sociology*, X, 2.
Rex, John (1970a) 'The Problem of Race Relations in Sociological Theory', pp. 35-55 in *Race and Racialism*, edited by Sami Zubaida. London: Tavistock.
Rex, John (1970b) *Race Relations and Sociological Theory*. London: Weidenfeld and Nicolson.
Rex, John (1971) 'The Plural Society — The South African Case', *Race*, XII, 4. (Reprinted in Rex, 1973.)
Rex, John (1973) *Race, Colonialism and the City*. London: Routledge and Kegan Paul.
Rex, John (ed.) (forthcoming) *Apartheid and Social Research*. UNESCO.
Rex, John and Moore, Robert (1967) *Race, Community and Conflict*. London: Oxford University Press.
Rex, John and Tomlinson, Sally (1979) *Colonial Immigrants in a British City*. London: Routledge and Kegan Paul.
Schermerhorn, Richard (1964) *Comparative Ethnic Relations*. Chicago: University of Chicago Press.
Shanin, Teodor (ed.) (1972) *Peasant Society*. Harmondsworth: Penguin.
Smith, M. G. (1965) *The Plural Society in the British West Indies*. Berkeley, Calif.: University of California Press.
Smith, M. G. and Kuper, Leo (1969) *Pluralism in Africa*. Berkeley, Calif.: University of California Press.
Sweezy, Paul et al. (1959) *The Transition from Feudalism to Capitalism*. New York.
Van den Berghe, Pierre (1966) *South Africa: A Study in Conflict*. Durham, NC: Wesleyan University Press.
Van den Berghe, Pierre (1978) *Race and Racism — A Comparative Perspective*. New York: Wiley.
Wallerstein, Immanuel (1979) *The Modern World System — Capitalist Agriculture and the Origins of the World Economy*. New York: Academic Press.
Weber, Max (1961) *General Economic History*. London: Macmillan-Collier Books.
Williams, Eric (1944) *Capitalism and Slavery*. New York: Russell.
Wilson, William Julius (1977) *The Declining Significance of Race*. Chicago: University of Chicago Press.
Wolf, Eric (1966) *Peasants*. Englewood Cliffs, NJ: Prentice-Hall.
Wolpe, Harold (1970) in *Race and Racialism*, edited by Sami Zubaida. London: Tavistock.
Wolpe, Harold (1976) 'The White Working Class in South Africa', *Economy and Society* (London), 5.

7
International and Internal Migration: Towards a New Paradigm

Daniel Kubat
University of Waterloo, Canada

Hans-Joachim Hoffmann-Nowotny
University of Zurich

SIGNIFICANCE OF MIGRATION

The significance of migration as currently perceived can be measured by the extent of the data available, the literature on the subject, and the purpose to which such knowledge is being put. Data on migration are presently increasing at a very rapid pace. It is not only census agencies which tend to include progressively more questions on population mobility but also the special interest groups and the various governmental and non-governmental agencies which now collect data on migration. The latter gather data on migration either directly or indirectly by the use of panel studies, surveys, or by registration of the whereabouts of the citizens under their jurisdiction or tutelage. In this fashion one can collect information on a great number of individual moves or movers, quite often with accompanying social characteristics of movers. Thus, data on migration in any modern society are vast even though not always readily accessible and often, their translation into substantive sociological statements is quite difficult.

INTEREST IN MIGRATION

Interest in migration stems from the easy visibility of migrants, which is not only socioeconomic or cultural, but also administrative. The visibility of migrants makes the modern state aware of population shifts which are at variance with a planned optimization of resources and a preferred spatial distribution of the population. A redistribution of population may require interventionist strategies by both the civil administrative and social welfare type agencies at all levels, local, regional or international (Simmons, Diaz-Briquets and Laquian, 1977). Even in places which have a fairly effective population register system, as for example in the Netherlands, population distribution, especially in the largest cities, is very much in conflict with the wishes of the respective city administration.

To keep in step with data accumulation, ad hoc theoretical frameworks have been constructed to help the classification both of migration and of migrants. Furthermore, guidelines and orientation schemata of a theoretical nature are used to serve in interpreting data thus far collected and in guiding the acquisition of new data sets where specific objectives are to be met.

The literature on migration comes from various social science disciplines. In sociology alone there is now a steady flow of publications covering just about every aspect of migration, explaining migration as to its antecedents and assessing migration as to its impact on the social structure both of the sending and the receiving areas or countries. Traditionally, within sociology, migration has been the domain of demography.[1] This disciplinary identity, then, has to a great extent determined bibliographical listings until today. Most studies of migration today are listed in demographic or population-related publications. For instance, recent issues of the *Population Index* (Princeton) show that about 10 percent of all entries belong to migration proper.[2] Extending the classification to include population mobility and distribution doubles the proportion of entries. Were one to define demography as essentially sociology (Bogue, 1969), that is, social demography, then the literature on migration would also include, for instance, migrants' adaptation, or community studies as well as various social mobility studies and other topics directly undergirded by population distribution.

It is thus difficult to do justice to such an enormous field as the study of migration. Nonetheless, it should still be possible to point to a few prominent theories of migration and their methodologies falling within the sociology of migration. From such a necessarily eclectic stance it is possible to uncover commonalities of basic assumptions informing such theories. The basic assumptions informing their research methodologies are, to a great extent, not subfield specific.

MIGRATION AND SOCIOLOGY

It seems worthwhile at first to position the study of migration first in demography and then in sociology in order to make explicit and analytically accessible the underlying assumptions of migration theories. Within demography, during the last quarter of a century in any case, the lion's share of research and policy interest has been accorded to variations in fertility and derivative social change. Reasons for this interest may easily be found in world population growth which for some time was felt as very threatening. The interest in mortality, the oldest concern of demographers, has remained stable, fuelled as it always is by an actuarial rendering of the probability of dying and by the felicitous monitoring of a steady mortality decline.

The interaction of the two basic demographic events, fertility and mortality, should not be without effect on the resulting population balance which, being positive, is a predisposition to migration. Migration, however, appears with a considerable time lag to fertility fluctuations, long after the critical expansion of population through birth surplus has taken its course. It is perhaps for this reason that interest in migration is on the increase now, some 20 years after today's migrants were born. At that time, the population explosion was attracting most of the attention of demographers. At the present time and for the time being it appears that the two major variables of demography, namely fertility and mortality, are, as policies, under control even though, in terms of theory, they are not fully mastered.

CONCERN ABOUT MIGRATION IN THE PAST

Of course, there have been other periods in modern history when interest in migration has reached a level of systematic exploration. Migrants have pretty much peopled three continents in as many centuries as a result of the first great population surge in Europe after 1700. The open spaces on the continents of destination made migration look natural, however, as the exchange of births and deaths and its explanations were, to use a recent term, sociobiological in nature. The rapid growth of cities, on the other hand, during the last century requires a close look at migration. Not only did cities in North America grow at a tremendous rate, but cities also grew rapidly in Europe. For instance, Munich, in Bavaria, showed at the time of the 1900 census only one-third of its population as born there; Chicago in the United States at about the same time consisted heavily of foreign-born population. Even Stockholm, in the country with the best demographic data for the longest period of time and with health conditions mitigating mortality to a great extent, needed in-migrants until about 1900 to prevent a sharp population decline (Davis, 1972; Tilly, 1978).

Until Ravenstein, explanations of migration tended to be of the rape and pillage variety, fitting well into the evolutionary scheme as codified in the Darwinian demonstration of the principle of natural selection: namely, the strong bands, tribes or nations migrated as an extension of their hunting tradition, military excursions being essentially a variant of hunting. The forefathers of sociology, men like Gumplowitz, Ratzenhofer, Morgan, Westermarck or Engels, took all population movements as natural and for granted. Ravenstein, on the other hand, began to explain migration from the data distribution, removing the analysis of migration from an essentially teleological framework.

After Ravenstein, the study of migration and its explanation, both demographic and sociological, derived its underlying assumptions from the natural sciences instead of from the life sciences. The distribution of population and its movement were explained as analogous to the mechanics of inertia requiring energy to change the status quo. Thus, explanations of population distribution and movement of its particles were dictated by the goodness of fit of the statistical properties the population exhibited. One need only recall the long disputes as to the proper scientific profile of sociology in order to understand that the new science would model itself after an older and successful one, namely physics.

The sociological contributions to the study of migration which best suited the analogy to the natural sciences seem to be derived from the theories of social stability outlined by such men as Durkheim or Halbwachs and, later on, by one of the versions of functionalism best exemplified, in American sociology in any case, by the writings of Talcott Parsons. Even the ideas of Marx, once abandoned but recently again gaining currency, at least within the reach of the influence of the Frankfurt School, disregard the basic instability of social organization. This is a seeming paradox only for a school of thought which holds conflict to be immanent to any society, albeit a non-socialist one. The conflict theories, for instance those of Dahrendorf in Germany and of Coser and of the New Sociology in the United States, all have in common a certain neglect of the sociobiological forces inherent in man and profer as a basis for every social structure well-socialized persons with attributes pretty much along the notion of particles in physics. Thus, the modal explanations of migration were at first economic. This was so because the visible causality of migration seems to reside in the economic circumstances of forces which propel or draw individuals or groups to different locales. The movements themselves, inasmuch as they do not appear to be random, lend themselves easily to mathematical explanations.

THE NEW INTEREST IN MIGRATION

The interest in migration has been acquiring a new momentum, especially since the end of the 1960s. The reasons for this resurgent interest in migration are several: (1) In those areas of the world where population stationariness or a variant of a non-threatening rate of growth have been achieved, demographers, sociologists, city planners and politicians are being forced to take a hard look at the realities of population redistribution. The population shifts, both internal and international, are not always in agreement with the economic reality. (2) In those areas of the world where fertility is still threatening, it fuels population shifts primarily between the rural and the urban areas. Such shifts are a mixed blessing at best due to the social and economic as well as political problems they seem to engender. (3) Political measures of population control which are benign from a universalistic perspective encourage migration indirectly even though such migration is not economically attractive for the receiving areas. Hence, a close look at the consequences of migration is required. For instance, the various bilateral or multilateral agreements between countries with a disparate economic standing encourage migration which would otherwise have been checked by claims of national sovereignty. The case of the European Communities is very much a case in point but there are parallel situations the world over. Finally, (4) political measures of population control which are not benign, e.g. acts of aggression, may produce involuntary migration and refugee streams. Such migrations are then usually directed into areas or countries where the political climate is relaxed but aggravated by the migratory influx. The fact that certain political regimes use forced o.. migration as a political weapon is evident from the seas full of boat people not only in South East Asia but also north of Cuba, to give just two examples.

There were certainly migrations in the past which may easily fit into one or another of the above categories. More likely than not, information about them was not readily available or systematic. Today, on the other hand, the information about such population redistribution is very much better and more easily available and, moreover, the interdependence between massive population shifts and the complexity of the modern state administration is more pronounced. Thus, not only does the migration situation around the world call for humanitarian assistance but also, and quite often, it calls for national or international intervention and control. These would not be as effective had not the migration research parameters been spelled out, at least approximately.

The macrodata on migration lend themselves fairly well to straightforward interpretations expressed in generalized propositions, such as that migration reflects a demographic re-adjustment between the have and the have not areas or, that migration represents the basic human reaction to danger; in the case of flight because of political pressures, voting with one's feet is a fairly descriptive phrase for such a reaction. Nonetheless, the complex interplay of variables implicated in migration is less well understood. Thus, it is not surprising that where explanations are attempted, they are perforce problem specific or area specific or both.

The efforts to generate propositions explaining migration have thus far produced only a loose fit between the *explanandum* and the *explanans*. On the one hand, migration data were not particularly good for a long time; on the other, the natural science models were only partially useful in overcoming the fact that the assumptions of mathematics underlying the respective methodologies were not always met. The perennial problem seems to lie in the difficulty of joining the micro and macrodata. Individual decisions to migrate and the impact on collectivities or areas are still not sufficiently understood, especially since the collection of the two types of information is very difficult to coordinate. Reality is shifting faster than the data can convey.

There is no doubt, however, that the most recent work in migration has reached a commendable level of sophistication, both theoretical and methodological. Migration data, despite the fact that their mode of collection may not justify the many subsequent assumptions necessary for an advanced statistical analysis, nonetheless permit interpretation yielding very usable information on migration. The specific explanations of migration seem to be internally consistent even though they are difficult to fit into a generalized niche comprised of a set of intellectually cognate propositions. The problem is, of course, well known and is deemed unavoidable, the extant attempts at theories of migration notwithstanding (Simmons, Diaz-Briquets and Laquian, 1977, p. 8).

UNDERLYING ASSUMPTIONS OF MIGRATION EXPLANATIONS

It seems that the crux of the difficulties in bringing under one roof the divergent explanations of migration may lie in the two basic assumptions which inform most of the writing on migration. These are (1) that populations are essentially sedentary, that is sessile, and thus stimuli are needed either from inside or outside the community to bring an individual or group to migrate. This assumption is usually coupled with a specific understanding of human nature which (2) sees man as a calculating social actor. The term 'calculating' is used descriptively, not valuatively, and has its roots in the tradition of Utilitarianism, which is best expressed in the contemporary sociological theory of social exchange. In an environment of market economy where the cash nexus allows a fairly objective comparison of one's economic life chances, the described paradigm, or specifically, the two-tiered metaparadigm of a sessile and rational man makes most of the currently-held explanations of migration individually but not collectively acceptable. What this metaparadigm does not seem to accomplish, however, is to fit the divergent explanations of migration, the various ad hoc theories and models, into one matrix of cognate explanations, theories and models. This is the reason why, for instance, the often attempted marriage of micro and macroexplanations of migration has not been successfully consummated thus far. Naturally, migration is not the only area of social scientific inquiry where this has been so; explanations of fertility have met a similar fate (Matras, 1977); so have ethnic studies (Blalock, 1979).

We wish to submit that these difficulties in migration theory building may be remedied, at least partially but certainly heuristically, by inverting the underlying assumptions of the migration explanations such as to allow for subsuming the extant explanations of migration under our new metaparadigm. The methodological issues, on the other hand, will remain fairly untouched from the point of view of data manipulation. After all, the internal relationships between numbers tend to remain unaffected by the substance the numbers represent. In any case, the units of analysis will clearly become those with which sociology principally deals, namely the interrelationships between individuals and groups. This will reduce a reliance on econometric modes of analysis in favour of the analysis of structures. Ultimately, alternative modes of coding and weighing the units of analysis will have to be developed not dissimilar to other current statistical tools of sociology.

By inverting the classical migration metaparadigm we assume man to be mobile by nature, as it were; secondly, man's attributes as a calculating man are being put in question and instead an indeterminacy of human motivation is being suggested. In this fashion we are freeing the sociological theorist from the parallelism to the theory requirements of natural sciences where the component particles are subject to the laws of inertia. Instead, a dynamic stance regarding the nature of man and the nature of society allows us to introduce a philosophy of man consistent with recent work in sociobiology, for instance (Wilson, 1978), but also with the classical and extensive work of Sorokin.

Before we attempt to go into any detail about the consequences of our metaparadigm for explanations of migration, we wish to point, albeit sketchily, to a few recent extant theories and models of migration which, we believe, can be shown to profit by a subsumption under our new metaparadigm. In no case, however, do we pretend to offer a state of the art survey of current migration research. This has been done well by others.

RECENT LITERATURE ON MIGRATION

During the last decade or so a fair number of books and papers has appeared summarizing the current research on migration (internal or international) or, specifically, focussing on migration policies. The forms such literature overviews take are several: (1) evaluative essays accompanied by an extensive bibliography dealing with explanations of internal migration (Ritchey, 1976; Shaw, 1975;

Mangalam, 1968); (2) introductory essays to collections of internal migration literature (Brown and Neuberger, 1977; Kostanick, 1977; Price and Sikes, 1975; Richmond and Kubat, 1976; Simmons, Diaz-Briquets and Laquian, 1977; Torado, 1976; Zachariah and Conde, 1978); (3) survey essays on international migration (Beyer, 1969; Boehning, 1978; Petersen, 1978; Tapinos, 1974, 1976); (4) edited collections on international migration (Cornelius et al., 1976; Gould, 1974; McNeill and Adams, 1978; Pryor, 1979), including the practically limitless literature on international migration in Europe focussing primarily on the issue of guest workers (Boehning, 1972, 1979; Bernard, 1976; Beyer, 1976; Castles and Kosack, 1973; George, 1976; Harbach, 1976; Krane, 1979; Piore, 1979); finally (5) a fair number of writings dealing directly with migration policies (Gosling and Lim, 1979; Klaassen and Drewe, 1973; Kubat, 1979; Lohrman, 1976; Mehrländer, 1976; Schiller, 1975; Widgren, 1975). Not all the literature is properly speaking sociological since the disciplinary boundaries in the case of migration are blurred.

THEORIES

In addition to the above listings, which should be considered indicative but not exhaustive, there is also a substantial literature on migration which not only offers a systematic review of the methodological and theoretical issues in the sociology of migration but also contains systematic explanations of migration. Some of these publications date back some ten years or more; one cannot expect major theoretical developments to be too frequent (Albrecht, 1972; Hoffmann-Nowotny, 1970; Jackson, 1969; Jansen, 1970; Mangalam, 1968). Given the slowness with which theories develop, these theories are quite new.

Perhaps the most concise statements on migration may be found in the general overview of migrations of human population by Kingsley Davis whose writings have always been informed by penetrating sociological insights. Davis sees migratory pressures as perpetual and inherent in technological inequality (1974, p. 105). Davis also considers the advantages of immigration to be rather dubious and maintains that temporary migration translates into a permanent in-migration just about independently of the original intentions of migrants themselves. How useful such an insight is, has been borne out over and over again in the recent adjustment of immigration policies in a fair number of countries. A similar observation in the recent literature regarding the situation in North West Europe has been made, for instance by the French sociologist Alain Girard (1976) or, by the American sociologist William Petersen (1978).

A number of recent book-length reviews of migration literature have combined a new theory with a thorough review of the extant major theories of migration and have often supplied new data on which their theory is based. Into this category falls the work of Hoffmann-Nowotny (1970, 1979), for instance. His theory of migration is nestled in a sociological theory of the structural and anomic strains that a society goes through. Hoffmann-Nowotny's conception of society is an elaboration and sharpening of a theory of social change following Heintz (1968). The theory rests on the interdependence of power and prestige, the two central explanatory variables presumed to be differentially distributed in the social system. Normally, both power and prestige are evenly valued by members of the system. Strains result, however, when prestige and power accrue unequally to different groups or persons for whatever reason. In the context of migration theory, the tensions which result due to the differential accrual of power and prestige to individual actors (or groups of actors) may be resolved or at least substantially lessened by migration. In other words, when a person perceives that his prestige, i.e. his expected social status, and his actual social power in society are not commensurate, he experiences a status inconsistency; such a person may then seek an environment where the dissonances between the expected and the achieved status, power or prestige will diminish. In practical terms, this is achieved for the individual migrant by leaving the community where he has experienced frustrations. Such a person then inmigrates into a community where there are no previously stipulated status constraints defining his prestige and power rating, or where his objectively low status will function as an excuse for his insufficient prestige. In any case, and as an oversimplification: one can define this theory sociologically as a structuralist view of status imbalance, intellectually akin to Merton's deviance paradigm (Merton, 1957). In terms of psychological reductionism, the theory would come close to the theory of cognitive dissonance (Festinger, 1962) and in terms of current research interests the theory would fall into the literature on status inconsistency and role conflict (Stryker and Macke, 1978). In any case, the cognitive aspect of personal satisfaction is seen as the spring of motivation to migrate. We have to bear in mind that the differential status ascription to the various ethnic and in-migrant groups and the observable strains leading to conflict or to anomie can be identified in just about every society.

Another recent work to suggest a general explanation of migration is that of Albrecht (1972). Albrecht is able to offer not only a very comprehensive survey of the literature covering geographical mobility and its explanations, but he offers his own broadly-based theory as well. Albrecht seeks to place his theory of migration in a matrix of social change. In the first place, the age and sex composition of a population or neighbourhood and the changes through addition and subtraction of members suggest that housing and neighbourhood arrangements are inadequate and encourage moving. In other words, the major demographic changes are those during the life-cycle, namely, marriage, birth of children, children leaving home, separation of spouse or death. These are changes experienced by individuals but reflected in the composition of the community. These changes are the stimulants, the push factors of migration. On the other hand, there are counterbalance mechanisms which restrain migration, for instance the values of familism, defined essentially as traditionalism. Furthermore, social mobility aspirations foster an increased geographic mobility, resulting in an articulated need for an appropriate neighbourhood. Thus, high neighbourhood integration dissuades people from migration (Albrecht, 1972, pp. 165-70).

Albrecht treats migration as a special case of geographic mobility. This seems to be a useful approach as a technically correct definition of migration is often only a function of the reporting administrative units and of the crossing of political boundaries. Today, moves to another neighbourhood but of a different socioeconomic composition within the same political boundary may be quite drastic in terms of breaking off the old and negotiating new social ties. On the other hand, far-flung migration within a professional or religious community, as for instance a move by a scholar within his invisible college, may mitigate the considerable impact of moving.

Earlier studies of migration were able to point to the very objective differences between the place of departure, usually rural, and the place of arrival, usually urban. Under those circumstances, the differences between the two areas have been sufficiently compelling to cause a cultural shock. The issues facing the scholars of migration at that time were more explicitly those of migrants' adjustment and the host of cognate issues. In many respects, the study of migration faces issues of greater complexity today, given the interdependency of a great number of variables entering into any consideration of migration.

Richmond (1969, 1979) specifically addresses the question of migration and mobility within industrial and post-industrial societies. For Richmond, urbanism is the main characteristic of modern societies and one of the main variables explaining migration. In his emphasis, Richmond comes near to the view of Davis who saw urbanism as representing a revolutionary change in the whole pattern of social life (1955, p. 429). Once urbanization has become a modal form of human aggregation, forms of migration undergo change. A post-industrial migrant emerges whom Richmond calls a transilient.[3] A transilient is essentially today's educated, highly mobile person. The term fits into a model of migration which Richmond (1979) calls the structural change model. In this model the in-migrant population, often the foreign-born, occupies an intermediate status position in society, not the lowest, as in the case of worker migration, nor the highest, as in the case of occupation by a country or conquest. Modern immigrants are able to obtain a fair proportion of professional status positions in their new country. This may be essentially a function of present-day immigration policies, especially those in the English-speaking overseas democracies, where migration or, rather, in-migration, has become closely tied to technological occupations.[4] A post-industrial society for Richmond is one where the central allocation of power and prestige follows occupational lines. He is able to support his explanatory model of migration by recent data comparing the occupational distributions in Canada and Australia (1979).

The number of deservedly well-known theories of migration is, of course, quite large. Most of the theories have been proposed by sociologists even though this does not guarantee that the theories themselves are sociological in the technical meaning of the term (Petersen, 1978). Thus, for instance, Lee (1966) constructs his theory of migration as an intended improvement on Ravenstein (1885, 1889) and Stouffer (1940). Lee uses four interacting variables as the corner components of his explanation of migration, namely: area of origin, area of destination, the intervening obstacles, and, lastly, the attributes of migrants, the latter primarily those of psychological make-up. Even though Lee does not presume to understand precisely the factors that hold and attract or repel people (1966, p. 49), he is able to offer nineteen 'weak' hypotheses of which six refer to migration volume and intensity, six to migration streams and counterstreams and seven to the essentially psychological attributes of migrants as persons who follow their volition and act out their need to move. It would certainly not be amiss to suggest that Lee considers the characteristics of migrants as the crucial variables in the migration process inasmuch as the migrant's definition of situation is essential for any migration to take place (Lee, 1970). For Lee, 'migration is selective...and one of the paradoxes of migration [lies in the fact] that the movement of people may tend to lower the quality of population, as expressed in terms of some particular characteristics, at both origin and destination' (1966, pp. 56-7). As compared to a standard push and pull interpretation of migration, Lee puts his emphasis on the intervening obstacles which turn out to be collectively the crucible of the migrant's disposition to move.

Beshers (1967) approaches migration by concentrating almost exclusively on the decision processes which bring about migration. By focussing on individual migrants, Beshers remains at the microanalytic level, as compared to the approaches to migration suggested thus far, which would fall into the macrolevel camp. Beshers' migrant maximizes his advantages by either staying or moving, thus behaving as a true utilitarian. A sum total of such purposively rational actions, to use a Weberian term, represents a population process. Had we complete access to information, Beshers reasons, so that on balance the actual advantage of moving versus non-moving could be revealed, then we could predict for the total population by addition (1967, p. 76). In other words, sociologists could make migration predictions by knowing the value of each variable entering into the decision to move. Individual decisions to move are constrained by modes of orientation, social variables and social-psychological decision processes (1967, p. 134). Inasmuch as most persons are primarily members of families, the locale of the decision process to migrate is the family. Were we to reformulate Beshers' notions in Parsonian terms, to which he in any case comes close, the instrumental interests of the husband are counterbalanced by the expressive stance of the wife, specifically, of course, in the decision-making of a family to move.

We can see that the difficulties inherent in micro-analysis in terms of translating the result into macro-analytical statements are basically two: (1) we need a very large number of individual predictors per respondent in order to be able to fix the process of decision-making; and (2) unless we achieve a perfect interrespondent match of predictors, the model produced cannot be deemed additive. We need only to remind ourselves of the longstanding discussion in sociology dealing with the ecological fallacy, to become aware of the difficulty of forging a link between macro and microlevel data. By enlarging the number of variables, as can be demonstrated in the recent work on ethnicity (Blalock, 1979), we should be able to overcome this difficulty, at least partially.

MATHEMATICAL MODELS

Mathematical modelling of explanations of migration is dependent on the currency of mathematical models. Such approaches occur in greater measure than attempts at a theory proper. There are, very roughly speaking, two modal groups of models explaining migration: (1) those paralleling the theory of gravity and (2) those paralleling the field theory in physics. In the first group, distance is used as the major predictor variable; in the second group, the area and the distribution of its population attributes are the crucial variables.

In the United States, it was Stouffer (1940) who saw migration to be inversely proportional to the number of intervening opportunities which, to Stouffer, were reducible to distance. To Stouffer, the number of persons going a given distance was directly proportional to the number of opportunities at that distance and inversely proportional to the number of intervening opportunities. Stouffer furthermore assumed (1960) that migration is costly and that the migrant will cease moving as soon as he encounters a suitable opportunity. In other words, migration between two places is a direct function of the opportunities in the area of destination and an inverse function of the number of opportunities on the way to the receiving area and the number of other migrants competing for opportunities in the receiver area. The criticism of Stouffer's formulations is based principally on the fact that the dependent variable of migration is compounded by the independent variables of predictors of migration (Tarver and McCleod, 1973). Since Stouffer, a number of essentially econometric models of migration has been developed where distance and distance-related variables are the main predictors of migration (Greenwood, 1975; Lowry, 1966; Margolis, 1977). Ultimately, however, the notion of gravity in migration explanation equates mass and attractiveness so that the more populated cells, to use the Bosean statistics analogy, will attract more migrants than the less populated cells, the cells being human aggregates.

The recent field theory approach (Tobler, 1978) utilizes the structural qualities of available data on geographical distribution showing the area of origin for those enumerated elsewhere. Such data are usually available in the form of interregional migration tables. The tables represent tabulated answers to census questions probing for the frequency of moves, the place of last residence, the place of birth, etc. Tobler suggests that by working such tables backwards to infer motivation we may come nearer to an explanation of migration. It can be demonstrated, writes Tobler, 'that the field of relative net migration is the gradient of a potential function, and this scalar field, the "attractivity", can be calculated by integration of the vector field' (1978, p. 218). It need not be emphasized that the tables are not asymmetric due to the counterstream in migration. Furthermore, we also need not stress that what is 'attractive' is very difficult to stipulate in advance and the danger of circular reasoning remains present, as it does for a number of similar approaches to migration. The mainstay of Tobler's method, which is in itself very attractive due to its ingenuity, is based on a computer program translating migration field maps into diagrams where centroids, with their areas proportional to the magnitude of the net change, mark the depletion and accumulation regions.

Another recent approach possibly belonging to the field theory approach to migration modelling is that by Courgeau (1979). Courgeau focusses on multiple migration to the former places of residence. In other words, he studies relationships between the number of migrants and the number of migrations, a neglected area in the study of migration. Courgeau based his study on two data sets, one from France and one from the United States. The technique he uses is roughly that used in computing the Parity Progression Ratios, with which students of fertility are familiar. It means that a question as to the probability of a subsequent move is being asked after each move. Naturally, the probability tends to increase with each preceding move but like all exponential properties, moving is ultimately self-limiting and the exponential property becomes truncated quite early in the process, due to the variable of age. In some respects, Courgeau's work is similar to that of Rogers (1969), who attempted to work out a probability model for subsequent moves based on the number of previous moves.

The number of mathematical migration models in the extant literature on migration is quite impressive, but we cannot do it justice here (Margolis, 1977). Suffice it to say that because human moves appear to be stochastic in nature, the corresponding mathematical descriptions are at hand. We wish to stress, however, that a sociology of migration must seek actual explanations of migration in the social context, that is in the context of social institutions. More likely than not, such a context is also the context of social change and its facilitation (Albrecht, 1972, p. 277).

SOCIAL CHANGE, MIGRATION AND ETHNICITY

One very recent attempt to put migration into a purely sociological perspective is that of Petersen (1978). Partially drawing on the theoretical beginnings of other sociologists (Jansen, 1969, 1970; Mangalam and Schwarzweller, 1968, 1970), Petersen proposes a sociological explanation of migration. To Petersen, sociological analysis means a focus on groups and institutions and the way these combine into social structure and organization (1978, p. 557). With regard to migration, the focus must lie on individual migrants who decide, within the social constraints, whether or not to move. In other words, the potential migrant makes up his mind by criteria that he has assimilated from his social group(s) (1978, p. 557). For instance, in the case of international migration, the real intervening variable becomes the set of restrictions on physical movement. These restrictions are political and policy determination is made by respective national states or administrative units. It is quite surprising that until recently there has been very little emphasis put on the purely political influences on migration, from the point of view of cross-border controls (Kubat, 1978; Petersen, 1964). A migrant to Petersen, then, is a person who through his move enters into a different set of interaction patterns and relationships than those prevailing at his point of origin. Petersen remains fully aware of the problems of explanation which arise in the case of migration of complete networks or in the case of chain migrations, where the migrant retains the interaction patterns of his place of origin.

Petersen distinguishes further between explanations of migration arrived at by asking the migrants themselves and explanations based on analysis of the forces presumed to underlie migration. In the latter case, any imputation of rational motive is more or less irrelevant (1978, p. 559). Migrants tend to answer questions about their reasons for moving within the commonly understood rules of human behaviour and within the prevalent value system: it is rational to move to improve one's position in life.

How do collectivities of migrants become ethnic groups? Petersen's answer lies somewhere between the classical notion of assimilation and the more recent notion that discrete groups of immigrants may last indefinitely (Gans, 1962; Vecoli, 1972). Such a condition seems to require a continuous replenishment via new blood. Furthermore, the recent political independence movements attest to the ruggedness of ethnic groups as well. The relationship ethnicity has to migration is that the migrant may be able to articulate his identity after he has become migrant and once an identity is articulated, it becomes normative and therefore change-resistant (Swanson, 1971). Essentially, then, ethnic groups are migrants' social organizations and represent a re-articulation of the social ties left behind.

Whereas Petersen argues from the end product of migration, namely the ethnic group, back to the possible motivation for migration, McNeill (1978) argues from the age-sex composition as affected by fertility and mortality forward to the reasons to migrate. For McNeill, the prime mover of migration lies in the outcome of differential mortality. McNeill sees migration as bridging the two modes of human experience, namely remaining at home and defending it against the enemy and strangers, or roving far afield. Migration is dependent on the stages of life-cycle as well, thus making the roving behaviour a precondition to what becomes migration. In trying to compress the development of the civilized Eurasian society into a migration paradigm, McNeill sees migration as bimodal and reciprocal; bimodal in that low-skilled population and elites were migrating, and reciprocal in that such migrations were essentially stream and counterstream. The differential migration patterns between cities and hinterland brought population into the cities out of which a smaller number would venture further afield into the hinterland made vacant by out-migrants and by population dying off after contact with the cities. In other words, each population aggregate developed an endemic tolerance for diseases which left adults unaffected, having killed off weak children selectively. Such population became disease-experienced and essentially immune to the further ravages of death. Contact between a disease-experienced and a disease-naive population resulted in the latter suffering severe losses. This meant that the numerical impact on the urban population through in-migrants remained mild and, in the hinterland, space was created for venturesome urban dwellers.

Without going into the ingenious details of McNeill's theory of migration, suffice it to say that it is one of the few which posits a causal, that is explanatory, link between population and migration without neglecting the sociobiological bases of human cultures, on the one hand, and without invoking difficult to measure attitudinal components of migration, on the other.

In any case, both Petersen (1978) and McNeill (1978) suggest the direction a sociological explanation of migration may take, namely: to place migration squarely within the social matrix where the forms of sociation are the predictors of social coherence, on the one hand, and to ascribe a stronger role than heretofore to the biological components of the forms of human sociation, on the other.

TRANSLATING BIOLOGY INTO SOCIOLOGY WITH REGARD TO MIGRATION

We have suggested earlier that the classical assumption informing explanations of migration is grounded in the Utilitarian understanding of man as a rational being and a free agent. The aggregates of men are understood to be subject to laws analogous to those of the particles of matter in physics and therefore open to mathematical modelling. Men are primarily sessile and rational. We are suggesting, heuristically in any case, the obverse for reasons of a parsimony of explanation of migration. We expect to be able to show that our assumptions that societies are in principle constraining, are shared by most sociologists.

It appears in keeping with sociological understanding of socialization processes that human beings have to be subjected to an ongoing social pressure to conform. One of the mainstays of conformity rests in the difficulty of changing one's locale, particularly during one's economic and emotional dependence on one's family of procreation or on one's family of orientation. Social institutions, as they are understood by sociologists, are those patterned behavioural outcomes which suggest a fair regularity and repetitiveness. The regularity and repetitiveness are, naturally, grounded in the biological functions of the human body and in the emotional overlay of bodily states. The history of mankind may be an evolution into higher levels of cultural organization (Service, 1971).

It should not be forgotten, however, that sedentariness came to mankind very late in the evolutionary scheme of things and the existence of truly urban aggregates much later still. Living in large groups requires a number of adjustments on the part of individuals and regulations on the part of collectivities. Thus, a whole armamentarium of socialization mechanisms seems to be necessary to produce a socialized adult. Failures of socialization processes may have serious consequences as they affect whole cohorts of population. Our modern society shows the stark contrast between the process of individuation, on the one hand, and the need for articulated social control, on the other, perhaps more clearly than may have been the case earlier and in other societies. Given the almost perfect survivorship of each cohort, not only has the probability of deviants dying off pretty much disappeared, but also the strains on the social institutions processing the young cohorts have increased in intensity. That means that our modern society is faced with providing a sufficient number of meaningful relationships to a very wide variety of persons so that such persons remain within their respective *gemeinschaften*. *Gemeinschaften* are, naturally, localized in space and their members sessile, as it were. Whenever such relationships fail, a search for new ones may well translate into moving.

We have also suggested earlier that the state of motivation research does not encourage the view of a rational calculus as the determining force in human behaviour. This is so despite the fact that the structure of modern society seems to be based on rational planning. For some sociologists, for instance Parsons, it seems improbable that human beings would retain an irrational or at least non-rational state of mind when their own environment is rationalized or planned (Parsons, Fox and Lidz, 1973). The fact, however, that people 'survive' in a rationally-organized system does not necessarily justify the notion that their decisions are perforce rational. More likely than not, it is the well-planned system which allows for the survival of those of its members least equipped to understand it. In our view of motivation for migration, we prefer to presume a certain indeterminacy in the decision-making as a sufficient assumption when offering an explanation of migration. Furthermore, we presume that the roving disposition represents a strong explanation and the motivation indeterminacy a weak one, just as in the 'classical' explanations of migration the presumption of sessility was a strong explanation and the presumption of rationality a weak one, both combining, of course, into the basic metaparadigm of migration explanation.

We have arrived at our interpretation not without consideration of the evolutionary drift in human societies. To rely on a certain parallelism between ontogeny and philogeny in regard to human development is a tradition in the social sciences dating back to Häckel some one hundred years ago. A recent work, otherwise not related to the concern of migration but using such a parallelism, is that of Habermas (1976) who argues from the stages of development of the child to the development of the complexity in society. Habermas leans heavily on Piaget but his teleological sight is, of course, an explanation of the emergence of social classes and the demise of the 'unfair' capitalist system. We have, however, no intention of developing evolutionary taxonomies. To us, historical events are, in the Weberian sense, not salient. What is salient to us are the recurrent socialization processes as they modify social institutions. The recurrence contains, we assume, philogenetic experiences, hence our retention of the roving trait in humans.

Social institutions, on the other hand, are for us repositories of constraints on human behaviour such as to frustrate the sociobiological tendency to move about. In other words, we wish to argue that a failure to constrain population will result in migration. We are qualifying this statement by assigning the roving tendency to the young segment of the population where there is the necessary supply of energy to do so; in a modern society, nonetheless, facilities to move are such that the range of age in which migration takes place is quite broad (Tilly and Brown, 1968; Thomas, 1973).

It was traditionally assumed, and not without justification, that forces of factors-at-hand have propelled the affected population elsewhere, as in the case of difficult conditions of life, expulsions or devastation. Heuristically at least, we think we are in a better position to offer a theory of migration by viewing the individual misfortunes, for instance, to represent a loosening of the constraints to stay. Under such conditions, those who are the most difficult to control, the youthful and the healthy and the intellectually alive, are most likely to move. Let us recall that Bogue (1969) sees age as the only variable that is invariably positively associated with migration, and that Lee (1966) thinks that migrants differ from non-migrants in the amount of intelligent spunk they seem to possess. We also prefer to think about the intervening obstacles, for instance, as the continuous efforts of the processes of adult socialization where a set of obligations is usually made to override specifically individual interests.

In view of the fact that migration is selective, certainly by age where the modal age of migrants is still in early adulthood, the combination of an imperfect socialization to stay put and the sociobiological predisposition to move militates against the constraints to stay. Only an extreme functionalism in sociology and the Marxist, radical and conflict sociologies presume socialization processes to reproduce the population essentially to a status quo ante. Most moderate sociologies, on the other hand, admit to socialization as the weak link in the reproduction of social systems. Given the difficulty of it between offsprings and their parents and thus between the interests of generations (Eisenstadt, 1956), the chances of a weakening of social control from time to time are fairly great. The differences between generations are due, to say the least, to the different life chances in different phases of the respective life-cycle. In other words, the probabilities of insufficient socialization just about guarantee at least an impetus to move, given an insufficiently articulated strong inducement to stay. We now know enough about migration to presume almost no societies to be without it.

CONSTRAINTS TO STAY

What then are the primary constraint mechanisms which frustrate the wanderlust of individuals or of groups? First of all, the mechanisms encouraging staying are those of family and kinship; secondly, those of social information networks.[5] The larger the society, the larger the role of the summary control agency, the state, to intervene in migration. The demographic variables of mortality and fertility, differentially distributed as they always have been, will produce imbalances in the age and sex structure leading to population surplus or deficit, both of which encourage migration (McNeill, 1978). Or, from a strictly sociological perspective, the demographic imbalance infracts the social structures such that the weakened social bonds fail to contain individuals in their locales, letting them move. The outcome of the workings of mortality and fertility as regards family formation is such that the transfer of family obligations though progeny tends to act as a socially stabilizing force. To give a very concrete example of the latter, we refer to migration of young women from the Quebec hinterland to Montreal. These women were young and childless, either through luck or forethought. Their sex and age peers, however, who experienced an early pregnancy to be followed by additional pregnancies later on, developed a very sessile and stable social system by remaining in their accustomed rural surroundings (Veevers, 1971). In other words, the essentially accidental disbursement of a demographic fate was translated into a value system supported by peer pressures and the articulated legitimations by the Catholic Church such that staying at home and having a family has become modal not only statistically but also normatively. That there is a great correspondence between statistical and normative modalities is well known and certainly supportable by the early small group studies (Homans, 1961). In view of the fact that normative modalities are never too far from a legislative codification and in view of the fact that not all individuals are equally well socialized, some form of disruption through migration will undoubtedly occur. Saunders (1956) quite some time ago (1943) expressed serious concern as to the disruptive powers of migration which endangers the social stability of communities. Even though Saunders viewed migration as a temporary solution to population pressures, the disequillibrating forces brought about by migration far outweighed, to him, the stabilization through alleviation of the population pressures.

Viewed from our perspective, however, migration is symptomatic of the lessened force the community is exerting on its members. Even the migration processes, however, become institutionalized so that permanent damage to community stability is actually unthinkable. Human history has always been not so much a history of class struggle as a history of struggle, of constant shifts in power, of visitations by either natural or man-made disasters and pestilences. Such intrusions into normal but labile social systems end in disorienting, at least temporarily, the transmission of values to the next generation. Socialization processes are disrupted and seldom completed so that population segments refusing to become or to remain subordinate will migrate. If this form of insubordination can be defined as anomie then, for instance, the theory of migration of Hoffmann-Notwotny (1970, 1973) may be subsumed under our suggested explanation of migration, namely: migration obtains under conditions of lessened social constraints.

It is not only adversity in its various forms which weakens cohesive communities. The history of mankind is highlighted by High Cultures and their micro-versions, villages with good harvests or with good fish catches which would last long enough to allow for a substantial increase in population. In most of human history, population increases were just about always attributable to a drop in mortality due to improved conditions of life. The drops in mortality were usually temporary but insufficient to increase the population so as to strain the existing social institutions.

Only in very recent times, for instance after the Second World War in the West, was the baby boom directly attributable to an increase in fertility. In either case, viewed from a larger perspective, the size of the surviving young cohorts was such that the traditional institutions were bursting at their seams, to use an old phrase of Marx. In other words, the institutions of the status quo were unable to absorb, that is, to sufficiently socialize, the cohorts entering young adulthood. Shortcuts in handling this matter led necessarily to a weakening of social constraints resulting in migration. Thus, population growth traditionally fuelled through a decrease in mortality, on the one hand, and through an increase in fertility, on the other, tended to accelerate a strong build-up of young cohorts. The social fabric became sufficiently strained that some form of neo-localism — and here we refer to the early conditions of man — had to take place. Neo-localism, as known to anthropologists, is the simplest break-out of the tradition, a first link in the chain of events in social change (Swanson, 1971). The cognitive distance between neo-localism at founding of own family and migration belongs presumably in the matrix of social change acceptance.

It is true that from a demographic point of view the last 10,000 years or so of human history have been characterized by a slow growth of population, with occasional setbacks. It is also true that the overall rate of growth contains periods where vacillations in the rate were considerable. The acceleration of population growth is nonetheless a fairly recent phenomenon. The consequences for migration of such demographic conditions are fairly easy to suggest, namely: human settlements had to institutionalize a bleeding of their population to counteract unwelcome growth. The most natural system was that of female infanticide which created a sex imbalance. The surplus young males were then taken care of by various institutionalized competitions leading to a selective survival: war games, hunting games, and, much later, military service (Harris, 1977). Keeping in mind that the latter, when culturally accepted, tended to survive even without a sex imbalance, we can understand the similarity between migration and military service which, like hunting, was essentially a variant of the roving principle. We would like to suggest one example which is salient to the study and explanation of the cultural traditions of migration. Switzerland, or rather the various self-administrating populations living on her territory around the time when population growth began to accelerate, developed a tradition of *Reislaufen*. Starting around the time of the 17th century and continuing for some 200 years, *Reislaufen* meant that a fair proportion of young men were entering military service, mostly as mercenaries, but they were occasionally conscripted by means often foul (Hoffmann-Nowotny and Killias, 1978). An industry of recruiting around the *Reislaufen* came into existence, thus institutionalizing migration or, rather, the principle of migrating. Later on, the Swiss became a nation which supplied a fair number of emigrants overseas, even though in the cultural perception of those remaining behind, emigrants were defined as expendable. How direct, if at all, the link is between the cultural tradition of *Reislaufen* and the cultural definition of emigrants would require some study and is open to question. There is no doubt, however, that migration such as chain migration can become institutionalized. The cultural tradition of migrating can also be selective of population subgroups which are expected to migrate but which, in earlier explanations of migration, were seen as answering the push factors. In other words, we would like to rephrase our understanding of migration as follows. Firstly, there is an interaction effect between the sociobiological impulse to move when the constraints which normally hold a person to one place become weakened; secondly, migration which began as a solution to the problem of weak constraints tends to become institutionalized and thus culturally normative.

There is a set of pull factors understood to encourage inmigration. Usually, such pull factors have been interpreted to be economic. They can also be well-understood as being social in the true meaning of the word, that is as preference ties of association. In a study of welfare recipients in the United States, kinship and friendship ties were found to weigh more in the decision to move than the respective levels of welfare payments (DeJong and Ahmad, 1976). Such social ties represent a psychic income, a payoff to the migrant. Large population aggregates allow for a freer selection of social ties than smaller, primarily rural communities, hence the traditional rural to urban migration. The German medieval saying, *Stadtluft macht frei* (Albrecht, 1972, p. 116), thus has a fair amount of predictive power for migration processes. The transilients of Richmond (1969) have a large urban playfield and their migrations can be easily understood from our perspective as mechanisms allowing for an optimization of social ties, especially in view of the status increment through moving.[6] That migration tends to overcome the tyranny of space is well accepted in the migration literature (Spengler and Myers, 1977). What is not well-researched as yet is the problem of understanding migration once the essentially economic considerations are bracketed out. Thus, Spengler and Myers (1977) would presume that the migration process will slow down as major, primarily distributional and socioeconomic imbalances diminish (1977, p. 12), whereas we would suggest that migration probability is a function of social cohesion, of course inversely related. In other words, migration appears to be the most natural response to getting out of a predicament (Matras, 1977). Modernization processes, for instance, allow for out-migration from areas of previous constraints (Goldscheider, 1971).

HEURISTIC VALUE OF THE PROPOSED METAPARADIGM EXPLAINING MIGRATION

In the Introduction we suggested that the prevalent view in the study of migration is to assume inertia in the social world to parallel the notion of inertia in the world of physics (Berliner, 1977, p. 447). Our suggestion, deemed of at least heuristic value, is to reinterpret the basic position and to posit a dynamism inherent in individuals but curbed by constraints of the relevant social system. We wish to argue that our metaparadigm meets the criteria of scientific parsimony in explanations. We would like to offer a thumbnail sketch of several theories described earlier and rephrase them from the perspective of our approach: McNeill's (1978) interpretation of migration closely meets our conditions for social system disruption through demographic imbalances. Petersen's (1978) suggestion that ethnicity develops as an articulated identity from a post-migration distance suggests an imposition of constraints where such were felt inadequate at first, having brought about migration. Hoffmann-Nowotny's (1973) theory of status imbalance and anomie as favouring migration corresponds quite well to our notion that a weakening of social constraints releases the migratory dynamics inherent at least in the population most difficult to control. Albrecht's (1972) understanding of migration as resulting from a reshuffle of community ties fits our assumption of the inherent tendency to move as well. The various models treating migration as responding to numbers of participants are subsumable under our dual interpretation of social constraint: on the one hand, social constraints are inhibiting migration when imposed on the individuals within *gemeinschaften*, on the other hand, migration itself can become normative responding to a large number of migrants in streams or counterstreams.

The major problem thus far in explaining migration has lain in the joining of macro and micro-explanations, the latter being essentially questions of motivation for migration. As sociologists, without wishing to appear unduly cavalier to psychological explanations, we submit that by positing, as we do, a sociobiological dynamic to human societies — composed of individuals as they are — we can concentrate on the modalities of social constraints. It is not that we are suggesting a reduction in the number of variables influencing migration; we wish to stay with one class of variable, namely with the class of social constraints. Within that class, the number of variables defining social constraint as its infractions is bound to be respectable enough to lend itself to as complex mathematical manipulations as there are available. We do not wish to think away the extensive research on human motivation as regards migration. But we do suggest that the field of sociology can be well served by staying within its own trade, as it were, and grappling with issues involving social institutions and the interstitial relationship between them. After all, we are not too far out of the mainstream of current sociological thinking which pays very close attention to issues of social control and to issues of the differential distribution of rewards, all of which, in one way or another, encourage or discourage individuals to stay or to leave their respective *gemeinschaften*, however such be defined by their respective members.

Lest our efforts are understood to mean that social institutions function as brakes only on individual behaviour, which view would take us back to a mechanistic parallelism, we would like to emphasize that we fully recognize the reflexive character of human beings who, in a not too calculating a way, recognize their interdependence with others and migrate or not even to their own objective disadvantage. On the whole, however, in keeping with the notion of growth, progression and development, the motives for migration are to leave *gemeinschaften* which, in the eyes of migrants, are inadequate social systems and to in-migrate into *gemeinschaften* which hold a promise of benign constraints.

NOTES

1. As a cautionary note, it should be noted that demography had a different trajectory in different countries. It has found its niche in statistics and actuarial sciences or remained an independent discipline in most countries in Europe. In France, for instance, demography has enjoyed substantial governmental sponsorship as evidenced by the flourishing of the INED. In the United States and Canada, it has become nested primarily in the Departments of Sociology, in addition to its niche with the respective census bureaus. The leading American demographers have emerged from the graduate studies in the Department of Sociology at Columbia University where Franklin Giddings provided encouragement to study social statistics already early this century (Lorimer, 1958, p. 162). Later on, it was primarily Chicago where demography and sociology entered a successful marriage. In most countries of Latin America, on the other hand, demography developed patterned on the French model.

2. It should be stressed that the customary division of migration into international and internal has more an administrative than a theoretical utility. Equally, the difference between migration and moving is tenuous, at least in modern societies, and it is subject to a considerable and on-going intra-disciplinary debate.

3. The term itself does not seem to enjoy a wide currency. It should also be pointed out that a version of transilience can be found throughout history as migration of talent, since talent, such as teaching skills or, in particular, minstrel skills, tends to use up its audiences fairly rapidly. In cases when the audience does not replace itself continuously, as in schools, a frequent change of locale becomes necessary. Thus, for instance, the migratory groups of actors were frequent in medieval Europe and elsewhere. Transilience is thus not specific to a post-industrial society even though the level of urbanization allows a greater mobility now than there may have been at earlier times.

4. Even the acceptance of refugees tends ultimately to be based on occupational characteristics, in that skilled and professional manpower is accepted into highly developed countries whereas less skilled refugees tend to be absorbed into less developed countries or remain in the various refugee compounds until their ranks become considerably thinned by the unpleasant conditions of life. The example from Southeast Asia is a case in point but by no means the only one.

5. The literature on the subject is not always conclusive, primarily because the various studies in existence are neither systematic nor large enough in scale to warrant propositional statements in either direction (Ritchey, 1976; Choldin, 1973). We are here following an essentially logical argument.

6. As an example from the recent history of the United States, the high mobility of university professors during the 1960s is not explainable only as a response to the good market conditions in the field of higher education; moving was seen as status conferring. Eventually, moving was also translated into frequent absences from campus so that those professors who were absent from their campus a lot had high status. Thus, frequent mobility discouraged the formation of local ties in favour of cosmopolitanism which, in turn, encouraged migration whenever personal needs were felt to be unmet. Eventually, it was not surprising that one of the chief complaints of students in the late 1960s was the inaccessibility of professors due to their absences.

REFERENCES

Albrecht, Günter (1972) *Soziologie der geographischen Mobilität*. Stuttgart: Enke.
Berliner, J. S. (1977) 'Internal Migration: A Comparative Disciplinary View', pp. 443-61 in Brown and Neuberger, 1977.
Bernard, Ph. J. (ed.) (1976) *Les travailleurs etrangers en Europe occidentale*. The Hague: Mouton.
Beshers, James M. (1967) *Population Processes in Social Systems*. New York: The Free Press.
Beyer, Gunter (1969) 'Modern Patterns of International Migratory Movements', pp. 11-59 in Jackson, 1969.
Beyer, Gunter (1976) 'Migration from the Mediterranean Basin to Central, West and North Europe', pp. 13-19 in *Emigration from the Mediterranean Basin to Industrialized Europe*, edited by F. Angelli. Rome: University of Rome, Institute of Demography.
Blalock, H. M., Jr. (1979) 'Measurement and Conceptualization Problems: The Major Obstacles To Integrating Theory and Research, *American Sociological Review*, 44: 881-94.
Boehning, W. R. (1972) *The Migration of Workers in the United Kingdom and the European Communities*. New York: Oxford University Press.
Boehning, W. R. (1978) *Elements of a Theory of International Migration and Compensation*. Geneva: ILO.
Boehning, W. R. (1979) 'International Migration in Western Europe: Reflections on the Past Five Years', *International Labour Review*, 118: 401-14.
Bogue, Donald J. (1969) *Principles of Demography*. New York: Wiley.
Brown, Alan A. and Neuberger, E. (eds) (1977) *Internal Migration: A Comparative Perspective*. New York: Academic Press.
Castles, S. and Kosack, G. (1973) *Immigrant Workers and Class Structure in Western Europe*. London: Oxford University Press.
Choldin, H. M. (1973) 'Kinship Networks in the Migration Process', *International Migration Review*, 7: 163-75.
Cornelius, W. A., Cruz, C. I., Castano, J. and Chaney, E. M. (eds) (1976) *The Dynamics of Migration: International Migration*. Washington, DC: Smithsonian Institute.
Courgeau, Daniel (1979) *Migrants and Migrations*. Paris: INED (Selected Papers on Population, No. 3; originally published in *Population*, 1973).
Davis, Kingsley (1955) 'The Origin and Growth of Urbanization in the World', *American Journal of Sociology*, 60: 429-37.
Davis, Kingsley (1972) *World Urbanization 1950-1970*. Vol. II. Population Monograph Series No. 9, Berkeley, CA: University of California Press.
Davis, Kingsley (1974) 'The Migrations of Human Populations', *Scientific American: The Human Population*, September: 53-65.
DeJong, G. F. and Ahmad, Z. M. N. (1976) 'Motivation for Migration of Welfare Clients', pp. 266-82 in *Internal Migration*, edited by A. H. Richmond and D. Kubat. Beverly Hills, CA: Sage Publications.
Eisenstadt, S. N. (1956) *From Generation to Generation*. Glencoe, Ill.: The Free Press.
Festinger, Leon (1962) 'Cognitive Dissonance', *Scientific American*, October: 1-9.

Gans, Herbert J. (1962) *The Urban Villagers*. Glencoe, Ill.: The Free Press.
George, P. (1976) *Les migrations internationales*. Paris: Presses Universitaires.
Girard, Alain (1976) 'Postface', pp. 407-14 in Bernard, 1976.
Goldscheider, C. (1971) *Population, Modernization and Social Structure*. Boston: Little, Brown.
Gosling, L. A. P. and Lim, Y. C. (eds) (1979) *Population Redistribution: Patterns, Policies, Prospects*. New York: UNFPA.
Gould, W. T. S. (1974) 'International Migration in Tropical Africa: A Bibliographic Review', *International Migration Review*, 8: 347-65.
Greenwood, M. J. (1975) 'Research on Internal Migration in the United States: A Survey', *Journal of Economic Literature*, 12: 397-433.
Habermas, Jürgen (1976) *Zur Rekonstruktion des historischen Materialismus*. Frankfurt a.M.: Suhrkamp.
Harbach, H. (1976) *Internationale Schichtung und Arbeitsmigration*. Hamburg: Rowohlt.
Harris, Marvin (1977) *Cannibals and Kings*. New York: Random House.
Heintz, Peter (1968) *Einführung in die soziologische Theorie*. 2nd edn. Stuttgart: Enke.
Hoffmann-Nowotny, Hans-Joachim (1970) *Migration*. Stuttgart: Enke.
Hoffmann-Nowotny, Hans-Joachim (1973) *Soziologie des Fremdarbeiteproblems; eine theoretische und empirische Analyse am Beispiel der Schweiz*. Stuttgart: Enke.
Hoffmann-Nowotny, Hans-Joachim (1979) 'A Macrotheoretical Approach toward a General Explanation of Migration and Related Phenonema'. Paper before the Rockefeller Conference on International Migration, Bellagio Study and Conference Center, Lake Como, Italy, June.
Hoffmann-Nowotny, Hans-Joachim and Killias, M. (1978) 'Schweiz', pp. 169-86 in *Ausländerpolitik im Konflikt*, edited by E. Gehmacher, D. Kubat and U. Mehrländer. Bonn: Neue Gesellschaft.
Homans, George C. (1961) *Social Behavior: Its Elementary Forms*. New York: Harcourt, Brace and World.
Jackson, J. A. (ed.) (1969) *Migration: Sociological Studies*, No. 2. Cambridge, England: Cambridge University Press.
Jansen, C. J. (1969) 'Some Sociological Aspects of Migration', pp. 60-73 in Jackson, 1969.
Jansen, C. J. (1970) 'Migration: A Sociological Problem', pp. 3-35 in *Readings in Sociology of Migration*, edited by C. J. Jansen. Oxford, England: Pergamon.
Klaassen, L. H. and Drewe, P. (1973) *Migration Policies in Europe*. Farnborough, England: Saxon House.
Kostanick, Huey L. (ed.) (1977) *Population and Migration Trends in Eastern Europe*. Boulder, Colo.: Westview.
Krane, R. E. (1979) *International Labor Migration in Europe*. New York: Praeger.
Kubat, Daniel (ed.) (1978) 'Human Rights, Migration and Population Pressures'. Paper read before the 9th World Congress of Sociology, Uppsala, Sweden, August.
Kubat, Daniel (ed.) (1979) *The Politics of Migration Policies*. New York: Center for Migration Studies.
Lee, Everett S. (1966) 'A Theory of Migration', *Demography*, 1: 47-57.
Lee, Everett S. (1970) 'Migration in Relation to Education, Intellect and Social Structure', *Population Index*, 36: 436-44.

Lohrman, R. (1976) 'European Migration: Recent Developments and Future Prospects', *International Migration*, 14: 229-40.

Lorimer, Frank (1958) 'The Development of Demography', pp. 124-79 in *The Study of Population*, edited by Ph. Hauser and O. D. Duncan. Chicago: Chicago University Press.

Lowry, I. S. (1966) *Migration and the Metropolitan Growth: Two Analytical Models*. San Francisco: Chandler.

Mangalam, J. J. (1968) *Human Migration: A Guide to Migration Literature in English, 1955-62*. Lexington, Kentucky: University of Kentucky Press.

Mangalam, J. J. and Schwartzweller, H. K. (1968) 'General Theory in the Study of Migration: Current Needs and Difficulties', *International Migration Review*, 3: 3-18.

Mangalam, J. J. and Schwarzweller, H. K. (1970) 'Some Theoretical Guidelines Toward a Sociology of Migration', *International Migration Review*, 4: 5-21.

Margolis, Julius (1977) 'Internal Migration: Measurement and Models', pp. 135-44 in Brown and Neuberger, 1977.

Matras, J. (1977) *Introduction to Population*, 2nd edn. Englewood Cliffs, NJ: Prentice-Hall.

McNeill, William H. and Adams, Ruth S. (eds) (1978) *Human Migration: Patterns and Policies*. Bloomington, Ind.: Indiana University Press. Introduction: W. H. McNeill.

Mehrländer, Ursula (1976) 'Zur politischen Konzeption der Ausländerbeschäftigung', pp. 77-102 in *Wirtschaftsstruktur und Beschäftigung*, edited by H. Heidermann. Bonn: Neue Gesellschaft.

Merton, Robert K. (1957) *Social Theory and Social Structure*. Glencoe, Ill.: The Free Press.

Parsons, T., Fox, Renee C. and Lidz, Victor M. (1973) 'The Gift of Life and Its Reciprocation', pp. 1-49 in *Death in American Experience*, edited by A. Mack. New York: Schocken.

Petersen, William (1964) 'Planned Migration', pp. 301-22 in: *The Politics of Population*, edited by W. Petersen. New York: Doubleday.

Petersen, William (1978) 'International Migration', *Annual Review of Sociology*, 4: 533-75.

Piore, Michael J. (1979) *Birds of Passage*. New York: Cambridge University Press.

Price, D. O. and Sikes, M. M. (1975) *Rural-Urban Migration Research in the United States: Annotated Bibliography and Synthesis*. Washington, DC: US Government Printing Office (Department of Health, Education and Welfare publication No. (NIH) 75-565).

Pryor, R. J. (1979) *Migration and Development in South-East Asia*. New York: Oxford University Press.

Ravenstein, E. G. (1885, 1889) 'The Laws of Migration', *Journal of the Statistical Society*, XLVIII, Part II, June 1885: 167-227, and LII (June 1889): 241-301.

Richmond, Anthony H. (1969) 'Immigration in Industrial and Post-Industrial Societies', pp. 238-81 in Jackson, 1969.

Richmond, Anthony H. (1979) 'Immigrant Adaptation in a Postindustrial Society'. Paper before the Rockefeller Conference on International Migration, Bellagio Study and Conference Center, Lake Como, Italy, June.

Richmond, A. H. and Kubat, D. (eds) (1976) *Internal Migration: The New World and The Third World*. Beverly Hills, CA and London: Sage Publications.

Ritchey (1976) 'Explanation of Migration', *Annual Review of Sociology*. Palo Alto, CA: Annual Reviews, 2: 363-404.

Rogers, T. W. (1969) 'Migration Prediction on the Basis of Prior Migratory Behavior: A Methodological Note', *International Migration*, 7: 13-22.

Saunders, H. W. (1956) 'Human Migration and Social Equilibrium', pp. 219-29 in *Population Theory and Policy*, edited by J. J. Spengler and O. D. Duncan. Glencoe, Ill.: The Free Press. Reprinted, originally published 1943, *Journal of Business* (University of Iowa), 23 March: 5-15.

Schiller, G. (1975) 'Channelling Migration: A Review of Policy with a Special Reference to the Federal Republic of Germany, *International Labour Review*, 111: 335-55.

Service, Elman R. (1971) *Primitive Social Organization: An Evolutionary Perspective*. 2nd edn. New York: Random House.

Shaw, R. P. (1975) *Migration Theory and Fact: A Review and Bibliography of Current Literature*. Philadelphia: Regional Science Research Institute.

Simmons, Alan, Diaz-Briquets, S. and Laquian, A. A. (1977) *Social Change and Internal Migration*. Ottawa, Canada: IDRC.

Spengler, J. J. and Myers, G. G. (1977) 'Migration and Socio-economic Development: Today and Yesterday', pp. 11-35 in Brown and Neuberger, 1977.

Stouffer, Samuel A. (1940) 'Intervening Opportunities: A Theory Relating to Mobility and Distance', *American Sociological Review*, 5: 845-67.

Stouffer, Samuel A. (1960) 'Intervening Opportunities and Competing Migration', *Journal of Regional Science*, 2: 1-26.

Stryker, Sheldon and Macke, Anne S. (1978) 'Status Inconsistency and Role Conflict', *Annual Review of Sociology*, 4. Palo Alto, CA: Annual Reviews, 57-90.

Swanson, Guy E. (1971) *Social Change*. Glenview, Ill.: Scott, Freeman.

Tapinos, George (1974) *L'Economie des migrations internationales*. Paris: A. Colin.

Tapinos, George (1976) 'Les migrations internationales et la conjoncture presente', pp. 377-89 in *L'Emigration du basin mediterranée vers l'Europe industrialisée*, edited by F. Angelli. Rome: University of Rome, Institute of Demography.

Tarver, J. D. and McLeod, R. D. (1973) 'A Test and Modification of Zipt's Hypothesis for Predicting Interstate Migration', *Demography*, 10: 259-75.

Thomas, G. (1973) 'Regional Migration, Patterns and Poverty among the Aged in the South', *Journal of Human Resources*, 8: 73-84.

Tilly, Charles (1978) 'Migration in Modern European History', pp. 48-72 in McNeill and Adams, 1978.

Tilly, Charles and Brown, C. H. (1968) 'On Uprooting, Kinship and the Auspices of Migration', *International Journal of Comparative Sociology*, 8: 136-64.

Tobler, W. R. (1978) 'Migration Fields', pp. 215-32 in *Population Mobility and Residential Change*, edited by W. A. V. Clark and E.G. Moore. Evanston, Ill.: Northwestern University (Studies in Geography, No. 25, Department of Geography).

Torado, M. P. (1976) *Internal Migration in Developing Countries: A Review of Theory, Evidence, Methodology, and Research Priorities*. Geneva: ILO.

Vecoli, R. J. (1972) 'European Americans: From Immigrants to Ethnics', *International Migration Review*, 6: 403-34.

Veevers, Jean E. (1971) 'Childlessness and Age at First Marriage', *Social Biology*, 18: 285-91.

Widgren, J. (1975) 'Recent Trends in European Migration Policies', *International Review of Education*, 21: 275-85.
Wilson, E. O. (1978) *On Human Nature*. Cambridge, MA: Harvard.
Zachariah, K. C. and Conde, Julien (1978) *Demographic Aspects of Migration in West Africa*. Washington, DC: World Bank, Development Economics Department, Population and Human Resources Division.

8
The Sociology of Educational Systems

Margaret S. Archer
University of Warwick

The single most neglected question in the vast literature on education concerns the Educational System itself. The very concept is ill-defined and used with negligence. It has been applied to anything 'educational', from tribal initiation onwards. To cut through this jungle of inconsistencies and ambiguities I will define a State Educational System to be 'a nationwide and differentiated collection of institutions devoted to formal education, whose overall control and supervision is at least partly governmental, and whose component parts and processes are related to one another'.[1] This definition probably has its deficiencies. All I want to stress by using it is that both the political and the systemic aspects must be present *together* before education can be considered to constitute a State System. This is how the concept will be used throughout the paper.

There are two main questions about Educational Systems which have been neglected and these formed the theme of our conference.* The first concerns their *origins* — where do Educational Systems come from and why do they have different internal structures and external relations to society? The second is about their *operations* — what differences do their particular structural characteristics make to how they work and change? Theories which would answer these two questions are precisely what has been lacking in the Sociology of Education. This lack of concern about Educational Systems is probably due, as Karabel and Halsey[2] argue, to our collective preoccupation with the education policy of governments and the professional problems of educators. Throughout this century the Sociology of Education has tended to work 'upwards' from practical problems in education to sociological theory, rather than

---

*ISA Research Committee Conference on 'The Origins and Operations of Educational Systems', Paris, August 1980.

'downwards' from theoretical developments in general sociology to explain educational phenomena. Their characterization of post-war orientations is convincing, but there is another, though weaker strand in the Sociology of Education dating back to the founding fathers, which has not been irretrievably lost.[3] In this tradition those theorizing about social structure addressed education as a social institution whose workings posed problems which were of sociological interest in their own right. My main argument in this paper is that it is through mending this strand and modernizing this tradition that we will develop a Sociology of Educational Systems.

I.
TRADITIONAL AND MODERN STRANDS
IN THE SOCIOLOGY OF EDUCATION

Although education was never a major concern of Marx and Weber, unlike Durkheim, all three shared a common orientation towards it despite their differences in theoretical approach. Firstly, they unanimously treated education as a *macroscopic social institution* rather than a bunch of organizations (schools, colleges, universities), a set of collectivities (teachers, pupils, principals), or a bundle of separable properties (inputs, processes, outputs). Secondly, Marx, Weber and Durkheim placed the educational institution firmly in the wider social structure and set interesting problems about its interface with other social institutions (the economy, bureaucracy and polity respectively). Thirdly, all three saw that it was education's position in the social structure and relationship to other institutions which were the keys to the dynamics of educational change. Although only Durkheim went far in theorizing about the actual mechanics of educational development they all left no doubt that this should form an integral part of their general macroscopic theories — for Marx educational change was borne along by the dialectical interplay of infrastructure and superstructure; for Weber it was associated with the dynamics of bureaucratization, though the link with education was 'hidden at some decisive point';[4] and for Durkheim it would, and should, be tied to the polity and through it to the development of the normatively integrated organic society.

However, this fundamental orientation towards education as a macroscopic social institution, presenting large-scale problems about structure and change, was lost by the mid-20th century. In turn this meant that the radical developments taking place in the three traditions of sociological *theory*, stemming from the founding fathers, were lost on the Sociology of Education. They were neither incorporated nor worked out in the educational field. Instead 'methodological empiricism' took over the domain with its atheoretical, ahistorical and atomistic orientation. Social structure was disaggregated into a series of atomized inputs (social class, for example, ceased to refer to active groups and was translated into a static membership characteristic of individuals). Education itself was reduced to a set of equally atomized outputs (x school-leavers with y certificates). Educational processes became a black box whose contents, the definitions of instruction, knowledge and achievement, were treated as timeless 'givens' — unproblematic and immutable. Any serious concern with the Educational System was shelved. It was dealt with simply as an administrative framework whose only significance was in marking out the boundaries which the inputs and outputs crossed.

This fragmentary approach to the study of education, which was no longer treated as a macroscopic institution, was intensified by the 'new' Sociology of Education. This did delve into the black box, but its exclusive concern with educational processes, detached from social structure, makes it just as incomplete as the 'old' approach which it attacked. This time the Educational System was not merely neglected, it was often repudiated as part of the neo-phenomenological rejection of objective structures. It was argued that the contingent nature of social reality meant that 'the System' had no ontological basis external to interpersonally negotiated meanings. From this we were enjoined to abandon epistemological objectivism in favour of relativism. Equally negative in the long run were the symbolic interactionists, even though they did seek to discover networks of decontextualized meanings, unlike the ethomethodologists.[5] It was asserted in symbolic interactionism that it was only by attending to the minutiae of objectification that one could understand the facticity[6] of the Educational System which was nothing more than a collectively sustained construction of educational reality.

The question of why a particular systemic structure was objectified at one time and place, and another at different times and places was neither asked nor answered.[7] While *philosophically* interpretative sociologists condemned the study of the Educational System as an objectivist structure which shaped the (educational) situations in which people found themselves and supplied cultural symbols for their interpretation, *methodologically* they retreated from the study of macroscopic objectification, even in their own terms, and concentrated exclusively on small-scale interaction. Because of a certain symmetry between the 'old' and the 'new' Sociologies of Education (the former dealing with inputs and outputs, the latter with processes, the first explaining who achieves and what occupational rewards they get, the second explaining what achievement is and how it takes place), in short the strengths of the one being the weakness of the other, some have hoped for a synthesis between the two which would represent a more complete Sociology of Education. However, it seems to me that there are three insurmountable difficulties which stand in the way of any such synthesis.

The first one consists in a blunt but serious question about whether this synthesis is desirable. Personally, I have the greatest doubts about the utility of any hybrid which combines the atomism of methodological empiricism with the episodic character of interpretive sociology. I have no doubts at all that it would be even more *in*complete — two minuses do not make a plus in the eugenics of sociological theory. In particular the last thing that any such synthesis could produce would be a sociology of the Educational System since neither part, as it were, carries a gene relating to it.

The second difficulty is less speculative in nature. It consists in the fact that the two approaches cannot simply be amalgamated, in order to have the best of both worlds, because their theoretical premises are mutually contradictory. It is of course impossible to conceive of any meeting point between those ethnomethodologists who insist on the fundamental intransigence of indexicality and the empiricists who are eager to transform the whole social structure into a series of operational indices for statistical manipulation. However, some 'centrists' seem to think that the more moderate representatives of the two approaches could thrash out a working compromise which all would find preferable to the present hostilities. Yet the stubborn fact is that the 'old' and the 'new' Sociologies of Education stand on different sides of two if not three of the central sociological debates — Objectivism versus Subjectivism, Collectivism versus Individualism and Micro versus Macrosociology.

The third difficulty, which is related to the sides that they take in these central debates, is an insuperable difference in theoretical scope which divides them. The 'old' Sociology of Education, whether in its most atheoretical and statistical form or when blending with functionalism, dealt with the interrelations between impersonal factors or forces whose large-scale and abstract nature prevented their origins from being traced back to simpler chains of social interaction. Instead, if anything short of the societal level was examined, displacement of scope took place. The small scale was assumed to be homologous with the large scale, as illustrated by the title of Parsons' article, 'The School Class as a Social System'[8] and of Brian Jackson's book, *Streaming: An Educational System in Miniature*.[9] But the small is not a microcosm of the large, for both levels contain properties which the other does not. Large-scale systemic characteristics may have little in common with those of its component schools (a highly differentiated *system* could mean that *each school* was remarkably homogeneous). Equally the variety of day-to-day school activities may themselves be too varied to interpret them all as microcosms of the same entity.

A parallel problem is found in the 'new' Sociology of Education which has taken the classroom as its basic unit for research. In so far as their theoretical premises allow a few of these writers to entertain the challenge of understanding education at the national level, another kind of displacement of scope tends to be committed. The implicit assumption is that if sufficient sensitive ethnographies were undertaken these would, by accretion, somehow lead to an understanding of the whole. But moving from the classroom to the national level has little to do with accumulation. Some of the elements needed to explain national phenomena (e.g. legislation, resource allocation) are not found in the classroom at all, while the presence of other elements *in* the classroom (e.g. the legal authority of teachers and heads) begs for explanation at a different level, because these did not originate there but rather higher up in the educational system and further out in the wider society.

The problem of scope cannot be transcended mechanically by either of these devices — the assumption of homology or the assumption of accretion. It is a theoretical *problem* which can only be transcended by charting a methodological path leading from the smallest scale of educational interaction to the larger and seemingly impersonal operations of the System.[10] This highlights the fact that no easy or instant synthesis can be expected between the 'old' and the 'new' traditions: any possibility of synthesizing them would involve creative work of considerable theoretical sophistication. Acknowledging this, some commentators have pointed hopefully to the work of our two past Presidents.* Thus Basil Bernstein is seen by Karabel and Halsey to be the possible 'Harbinger of a New Syn-

---

* Recent Presidents of the ISA Research Committee on Sociology of Education

thesis', whilst others share a similar optimism about the contribution of Pierre Bourdieu.[11]

The importance of their work to the Sociology of Education is immense. Moreover, it seems to me indisputable that their method of theorizing about cultural transmission and cultural reproduction is superior to the approaches briefly examined above. Both accord proper theoretical importance to 'structure' as well as to 'interaction', viewing the former as shaping the contexts in which the latter takes place and conditioning the objective interests and subjective outlooks of the actors involved. Furthermore, as part of their joint Durkheimian heritage, they deserve full credit for re-establishing the analysis of education as a macroscopic social institution. This said, I hope it will not be churlish to suggest that the kind of theoretical developments that they have instituted (whether they achieve a new synthesis or not) do not unfortunately take us any closer to a Sociology of Educational Systems.

In fact I would argue that Bernstein and Bourdieu neglect the Educational *System* as such. Their theories of cultural transmission and cultural reproduction relate these processes *directly* to the stratificational principles governing societal organization, without examining the latter as *mediated* through the Educational System. In other words they ignore the interfaces between national Educational Systems and the broader social structures in which they once emerged and now operate. Since this interface (i.e. the ways in which the educational subsystem is slotted into the social system) has been shaped in different ways over time in various countries, it is not a constant which can remain underemphasized merely by presuming that it works in the same way and exerts the same influence cross-culturally. Yet Bernstein and Bourdieu tend to make precisely that assumption. This raises two questions — why do they feel justified in neglecting Educational Systems as such? Does this neglect then represent a major deficiency in both theories, especially in relation to their supposed universality?

The Permeability of Education

The main reason why both neglect the Educational System is because they make exactly the same assumption that education is a *completely permeable social institution*, eternally open to and reflective of the broader social structure. Bernstein assumes that the class structure penetrates education directly and unproblematically: 'The power relationships created outside the school penetrate the organization, distribution and evaluation of knowledge through the social context of their transmission. The definition of educability is itself at any one time an attenuated consequence of those power relationships.'[12] He therefore moves straight on to an examination of the ways in which social class regulates instruction, through the institutionalization of knowledge codes. There is no questioning of whether it does so, or if it does so exclusively.[13] The crucial boundary to Bernstein is between the *school* and *society*, since the class codes influence the transmission agencies directly: the boundary between *system* and *society* is of no significance. Like in the 'old' Sociology of Education, the System is just an administrative shell, in so far as it is anything more than the sum of component schools and colleges. The systemic boundary is unimportant for it has no gatekeepers, it does not *mediate* between society and the schools, it does not selectively filter the demands or groups or interests to which education proves responsive. Instead the System is held to operate as a fully permeable membrane which can thus be bypassed when formulating the cultural transmission thesis.

However, there is a serious discontinuity in Bernstein's work between his bold axiomatic assertions about permeability and the absence of any examination of, or evidence for, the mechanisms involved in direct 'penetration'. Exactly the same is true of Bourdieu. He starts by insisting that most pedagogic action (unlike formal communication) has a twofold arbitrariness — it is the imposition of a 'cultural arbitrary' by an arbitrary power. He then proceeds to analyze power relations between groups or classes as the universal basis upon which education, as 'symbolic violence', rests. But Bourdieu is no more specific than Bernstein about the *genetic* processes enabling power relations to be converted into symbolic control: this permeability has the same axiomatic status in his theory as in Bernstein's. Without this assumption there is no way in which either of them can hold that social domination is paralleled by educational domination, universally and unproblematically. Moreover, Bourdieu's attempt to elucidate a *general* logic of pedagogic action (embracing all forms of education) results in an even more clear-cut dismissal of differences in educational structure as unimportant variables.

Bourdieu begins by asking what an Educational System[14] *must be* in order to fulfil its essential function of cultural inculcation and its external function of social reproduction. He is concerned, therefore, with the *logical origins* of education which stem from its basic functions and not with the *social origins* of Educational Systems whose structuration was shaped by historical interaction. Bourdieu is explicit that this general logic 'is not reducible to the essentially historical search for the social conditions of the apparition of a particular E[ducational] S[ystem] or even of the educational institution in general'.[15] Almost immediately this functional induction of structure on a transhistorical and transcultural basis is given both logical and sociological priority over any attempt to understand the emergence of Educational Systems by comparative or historical analysis. 'Only when the generic conditions of the possibility of an institutionalized P[edagogic] A[ction] have been formulated is one able to give full significance to the search for the social conditions necessary for the realization of these generic conditions'.[16] Thus comparative educational history is subordinated to the role of demonstrating the working-out of the logic over time: there is no sense in which the emergent structure affects the relationship between education and society independently of this logic. Consequently, variations in the structuration of Educational Systems are reduced to the status of functional alternatives.

The Absence of Educational Politics

Both theories by their very nature raise the basic question about how a group or class gets into, and remains in, a position of educational domination. Given the insistence of both Bernstein and Bourdieu on the importance of power relations it is rather surprising to find that their answers are not in terms of a struggle for educational control and that neither author develops a politics of education *at any level whatsoever*. The term 'educational politics' is used here in its broadest sense and refers to the attempts of different social groups to influence the inputs, processes and outputs of education, whether by legislation, pressure group and union activities, experimental, traditional or sectional movements, private or collective investment, propaganda or public debate.

However, although both the dominant 'knowledge code' and 'cultural arbitrary' are held to rest on power relations, their domination in the educational domain is not the outcome of *an actual power struggle*. Thus to Bourdieu 'the P[edagogic] A[ction] which the power relations between the groups and classes making up that social formation put into the dominant position within the system of PA's is the one which most fully, though always indirectly, corresponds to the objective interests... of the dominant groups or classes'.[17] Here the unproblematic act of 'putting' is substituted for the problematic act of winning (i.e. how completely? how securely? with what concessions? despite lasting opposition? etc.). Power then operates as a passive conductor, perfect and without resistance, linking social domination to educational control. In exactly the same way, power to Bernstein is what transmits underlying social principles to school practice: it is *not* a variable in a struggle for educational control which determines *whether* there will be a close relationship and *what* form it will take. Thus whereas a politics of education would allow for the fact that the balance of educational power at any time (because of compromises or concessions and degrees of success or failure) is not necessarily in complete alignment with the balance of power in society, a correspondence theory assumes that the two are always perfectly aligned but it does not explain how. The actual processes of adaptation, adjustment and alignment which match educational practice to class structure and educational change to shifting class composition remain completely unexplained.

Instead a proper theory of educational politics within the context of the Educational System would provide, (1) a detailed specification of the *processes* producing educational change and stasis, which are structured in different ways by different Educational Systems,[18] and, (2) a theory of the *conditions* under which different social groups can influence the prevailing definition of instruction through the above processes. It will be obvious that (1) is antipathetic to the general notion of educational permeability. Instead it requires a full examination of the negotiations taking place across the boundary between System and Society. Equally obviously, (2) rejects the premise that one group or class alone — anywhere and everywhere — possesses, by virtue of its position, the conditions for imposing its definition of instruction. To have an understanding of the structure of Educational Systems, the processes of change that they condition and the politics of education which emerge, would in fact be to have a Sociology of Educational Systems. Where is this to come from? Having been so negative about its emergence from the current Sociology of Education I must clearly try to give a constructive answer to this question.

I believe that the answer in brief is 'from general sociological theory itself'. However, this does not mean that there are any ready made solutions in view. There are no theories of institutional development which can simply be borrowed from other domains and applied to Educational Systems. Neither of course is there any general theory of society into which education could simply be slotted, but this does not condemn us to inaction whilst awaiting the emergence of one. There are, it seems to me, various developments in the mainstream of sociological thought which can contribute to the generation of a Sociology of Educational Systems. Making them contribute is a *theoretical problem* in its own right, there are no short-cuts, the linkages and applications have to be thought out. I will devote the next section of this paper to an examination of three strands of modern sociological theory which seem to be of relevance to explaining the origins and operations of Educational Systems, giving particular attention to their mutual compatibility in view of earlier strictures on mindless eclecticism.

II.
THREE MODERN STRANDS IN SOCIOLOGICAL THEORY IN RELATION TO EDUCATIONAL SYSTEMS

Neo-Marxism

The neo-Marxist tradition is of equal interest in relation to questions about the origins or the operations of Educational Systems. Unfortunately, many have been over eager to conjure-up an instant Marxist Sociology of Education. Serious Marxist scholars have every right to feel ill-used by some of the educational inanities produced in their name, particularly when these commit the very errors which Marxists have painfully expunged from the time of the Third International onwards. Vulgar Marxism, 'economism', and even class conspiracy theory are having a final flowering in American sociology and history of education. If these are the overhasty products of educationalists unfamiliar with theoretical developments in European Marxism, the same is not entirely the case with 'correspondence theories', which are now enjoying an unwarranted vogue. This second short-cut pretends to 'solve' questions about the origins and operations of Educational Systems by postulating 'complementarity'[19] between the development of education and central features of capitalist development. The complex jargon in which this simple idea is expressed can conceal the fact that basically it begs the question — namely what is it which first brings about and then maintains this 'complementarity'. At rock-bottom any correspondence 'theory' is merely a verbal statement that a positive correlation coefficient has been detected: it remains logically impossible to extract causal explanations from the one as from the other. To defend this kind of 'theory' by the argument that it is not concerned with causality but with dialectical relationships only serves to dilute the meaning of dialectics by making it cover any instance of mutual influence between elements whose interconnections cannot be clearly specified.

The theories, however, which excited most attention because they provided a nearly ready-made macrosociology of education *were* well grounded in the European Marxist tradition. The work of Althusser and Poulantzas[20] avoided all the crudity of treating superstructural institutions (education of course included) as epiphenomena of the economic base and was concerned with the dynamics of social structures, not just with superficial and unexplained 'correspondences' between their parts. The second major difficulty with correspondence 'theories' is that they constantly fail to explain *fluctuations* in 'complementarity', that is if they are not completely falsified in history. French Marxism, predicated upon acceptance of the relative autonomy of social institutions, appeared to avoid this pitfall. Its main attraction was that it took this problem on board and promised to account for *variations* in relations between education and the economy across time and space, yet within a Marxist framework. This approach held that society as a whole provided the non-economic conditions for the reproduction of the mode of production; this was neither the constant, nor the exclusive, preoccupation of education which was only one of several 'ideological state apparatuses'. Ultimately, however, the stress upon relative institutional autonomy and independence, which had appeared to allow for, and had promised to explain, the differences between the Educational Systems of capitalist countries, proved to be chimerical. Instead of theorizing about the differential causal and temporal influence of institutions operating together in a system, Althusser elaborated his structural superdeterminism — a kind of deus in machina which organized the component parts of each social formation in a pattern which, in its entirety, was functional to the capitalist economy. Thus the *appearance* of institutional autonomy was in fact based 'on a certain kind of internal articulation of the whole, and thus a particular *type of dependence* on it'.[21] What had promised to be an analytical tool giving solid purchase on institutional origins and operations turned out to be as insubstantial as the metaphysics of functionalism, which it increasingly came to resemble.

This approach could still have proved useful if it had helped to explain limitations on educational variations, showing these to be bound within certain determinate parameters. However this kind of theoretical guidance to institutional analysis was precisely what French Marxism could not deliver. On the one hand, we were told that for us to start by analyzing the interrelations between education and other social institutions was quite fruitless, because the system as a whole could place and displace its components in numerous different patterns over time and in relation to changes in its external environment. Analysis of the parts therefore cannot precede examination of the whole which orchestrates relations between them. On the other hand, the way in which the whole works on the parts was said to be detectable only through its effects, that is those very relations between institutions which a Sociology of Educational Systems would seek to explain. There is a circularity involved here which defies empirical assault. If we try to examine the parts (explanadum), we are told that we need to understand the whole as it is organized by the economy 'in the last instance' (explanans), but this in turn can only be discovered through the patterning of social organization itself (back to the explanadum).

Once again the hope of finding a short-cut to a Marxist Sociology of Educational Systems proved deceptive. By now it seems we must accept the need to to go the long way round to reach this destination, that is by picking up recent refinements in the general Marxist theory of social structure and actively applying them to education. This has to be a *theoretical enterprise in its own right*, for the most useful theoretical developments have been elaborated so defensively (warding off charges of determinism, historicism, reification and so forth) that they are clearer about what Marxism is not than they are in delineating a usable model of social structure. The general developments on which we can profitably build stem from Gramsci and represent a loosening up in the conceptualization of 'base' and 'superstructure'.[22] Instead of the latter 'reflecting' the former, in a one-way relationship of domination and dependence, their dialectical interplay has been reasserted and, by corollary, a greater autonomy has been assigned to the superstructure to allow for it acting back on the base in a bilateral relationship. Simultaneously, an important amount of autonomy and independence has been accepted within the superstructure itself, thus encouraging the replacement of the radial model of spokes, in which each institution was separately linked to the economic hub, by various models of relations within the superstructure which allow for internal variations in dependence and domination. This does represent some convergence, as Sztompka has shown,[23] with General Systems Theory which also analyzes relations between parts within a given boundary in terms of their interdependence and autonomy. It seems that it was the fear of Marxism's absorption into a generic approach of this kind (i.e. losing its character by becoming a mere 'factor theory') which led French Marxists to endorse the metaphysics of 'overdetermination'. This is not a necessary conclusion. On the contrary, it seems both possible and profitable to incorporate the tenets outlined above into an approach which remains distinctively Marxist.

I wish briefly to mention two developments in Marxist sociology and historiography which succeed in this and which could contribute much to theories about the operations and origins of Educational Systems respectively. The first, whose roots probably go back to Lenin's analysis of the 'revolutionary conjuncture' in Russia (the temporal coincidence of incompatible institutional developments), has probably been stated most clearly by Lockwood.[24] He makes the notion of structural contradiction central and separates this question, which concerns systemic (dis)integration, from questions about class conflict, which concern social integration. The latter only produces far-reaching social change in conjunction with the former. Lockwood's approach says something about autonomous institutional developments in relation to the economic base which is of great interest in relation to education, but which also needs considerable elaboration. In particular an intermediary theory is needed which specifies the *conditions* under which the Educational System will be integrated with or in contradiction to the base or other institutions. This would account for why some systems are much more tightly integrated with the economy than others and would predict certain consequences (i.e. change) if gross misalignments arose at certain times and places. Another intermediary theory is required at the social integration level which details how class action makes itself felt in different structures of Educational Systems with their different machineries for decision making and different processes for introducing change. A theory with both of these elements would be specific about the what, when and where of educational stability and change, i.e. it would possess a specificity which the general model lacks.

Secondly, recent developments in Marxist historiography appear to have much more to contribute to our understanding of the origins of Educational Systems than did their predecessors. In particular they avoid the overly theoretical presentation of rigid stages of historical development or the loose and undertheoretical equation of a Marxist approach to history with one which gives central importance to social class or economic factors.[25] Marxist historiography does need to be theoretically informed (otherwise it becomes indistinguishable from labour, social or economic history):[26] historical materialism must be made to yield theories *about the weight of material factors on educational development under variable conditions.* On the other hand, the history needs to be sensitive and undogmatic, giving equal weight to the 'historical' as to the 'materialistic', in the way that Anderson has recently advocated and exemplified.[27] Further neo-Marxist contributions of this kind to a sociology of the origins and operations of Educational Systems can certainly be made, but their making is an active and demanding task of theory-building.

Neo-Functionalism

The functionalist tradition was always stronger on explaining the operations rather than the origins of social institutions. Education was held to have been promoted by, and in turn to promote, normative consensus, without much attention being given to disentangling these strands historically. A process of evolutionary adjustment was postulated rather than documented, and this skimmed over the question of whose values became institutionalized in formal education and who benefited from this process. Rather later, in the 1960s, equivalent deficiencies were recognized in the account of institutional operations. In particular the Parsonian model of social structure which posited, a priori, such a close interdependence between the parts of society that each social institution was influenced by every other and exerted a reciprocal influence back upon them, was found wanting in two major respects. As a model of social reality it was often inapplicable, as a means of investigating institutional operations it was supremely unhelpful because the notion of mutual determinism made it impossible to question which other parts of society influenced education most, when, where and under what conditions. Parsonian functionalism tried to 'solve' problems about institutional origins and operations by theoretical fiat: neo-functionalism began to break away from this by building upon Mertonian revisionism instead. Merton had always treated *specific* institutional dependencies as problematic, since he only postulated an overall 'net balance of functional consequences'.

The model of social structure advanced by Gouldner,[28] in explicit contradistinction to Parsons' model, and shared in essentials by other neo-functionalists important in the Sociology of Education (e.g. Etzioni and Eisenstadt), was intellectually superior in the following respects:
— it represented a break with the organic analogy, an abandonment of the steady-state model, of homeostatic mechanisms and of the equilibration process in general;
— it rejected mutual determinism in favour of examining the differential causal influences of the parts of a system on one another, in terms of their 'interdependence' and 'autonomy';
— it accepted the existence and importance of strains between parts of the social structure. Such tensions were logically entailed by the admission that some parts had high functional autonomy and also by the acknowledgement of coercive (nonreciprocal) interchanges between parts.

A further corollary to these points was the progressive demotion of normative consensus as the guarantor of social integration and a growing acknowledgement of value conflict.[29] Yet however welcome these shifts are in general, they do not begin to constitute an account of the origins and operations of Eudcational Systems.

To begin with, this approach remains as weak as its Parsonian predecessors on the question of institutional origins and the historical patterning of social structures. Why a particular pattern of relationships characterizes a given society at a particular time (enmeshing education in a specific way) is not discussed by Gouldner. He leaves the degree of functional reciprocity and autonomy to be established empirically, being more interested in the consequences than the causes of given structural relationships. Next, although unlike Parsons, Gouldner does wish to consider the interdependence of the system's parts as problematic not given, he remains a Parsonian in assessing the existence and degree of interdependence of any one institution from the point of view of the system as a whole, and he does so in a very mechanical way. High functional interdependence is said to exist when each institution engages in mutual exchange with all the others: high functional autonomy pertains when each part only exchanges with one other. Interdependence and autonomy are therefore defined *quantitatively* in relation to the potential number of interrelationships that the system could accommodate. This is indeed *functional autonomy*, in the systemic sense of an institution providing few services for other parts of the whole, rather than *operational autonomy* meaning that a part has a capacity for auto-determination which derives from the quality of its relations with other institutions. The latter is of course of at least equal concern to a Sociology of Educational Systems, but this holistic approach does not help us towards a practical understanding of how institutions work vis-à-vis one another. Moreover, it does not gell with considerations about the quality of relations between institutions and this leads to contradictions in Gouldner's own theory of change. Given high functional autonomy he predicted that an institution should intensify its independence and contribute to system change: given low operational autonomy (which is quite possible, Gouldner admits, if it is the subordinate partner in its one relationship) it will be unable to do either. Hence the systemic considerations (quantitative) and the institutional ones (qualitative) give rise to different expectations, unhelpful in practical research and requiring theoretical reformulation. Finally, and again part of the Parsonian influence, actors and institutions are insufficiently differentiated from one another.[30] Social and systemic integration remained confounded, thus precluding a theory of relations between them, i.e. when is a systemic strain exploited or contained by social groups, how do they do either, under what conditions and which are the salient action groups anyway?

Nevertheless, this part of Gouldner's work was important as a bridge between Parsonian functionalism and two later developments which broke from it almost entirely but which are now of considerable interest in relation to a Sociology of Educational Systems where they have only just begun to be explored. The first is General Systems Theory which has completely dropped the organic analogy and now concentrates on the sociocultural system in its own right. The most distinctive feature of social systems is 'morphogenesis', the elaboration of their own structure over time in a way which is alien to mechanical or organic systems. This in turn means that more theoretical attention is given to positive feedback chains (which amplify deviations from the existing structure, elaborating more complex forms of restructuration), than to negative feedback which is structure restoring or maintaining, as in the functionalist tradition. This type of modern Systems Theory, as outlined by Buckley,[31] seems rich in its potential applications to Educational Systems. However, these need developing theoretically, they are not found ready-made: indeed, the most useful avenues to explore seem to involve the most work, while the readiest applications represent the dead-ends. Amongst the latter I would signal three in particular. Firstly, there is a fairly sterile exercise of terminological redescription in which the translation of sociological concepts into the language of systems theory is confused with understanding the logic of social systems.[32] Secondly, there is the evergreen temptation to work with an abstract model of a system (be it mechanical, organic, cybernetic or whatever) and to accentuate only those features of the social system which fit it,[33] rather than dealing with the variagated structures which have emerged historically in real sociocultural systems. Thirdly, there are those cybernetic versions which compound the first two errors and in addition illegitimately *substitute* the subject matter of cybernetics for the substance of social life, such that communication replaces power and information takes the place of resources.

Much more profitable for a Sociology of Educational Systems is that kind of General Systems Theory which acknowledges the distinctive morphogenetic character of social structures and tries to spell out the processes and consequences of structural elaboration. The most ambitious theoretical contribution here, though it is extremely abstract, is Teune and Mlinar's, *The Developmental Logic of Social Systems.*[34] This does not pretend to have discovered some hidden principle of the workings of sociocultural systems, instead it is a logical approach which consists in defining developmental change as structural elaboration, that is as distinct from change per se, and then in asking what dynamics are necessary for developmental change to continue. In this way it deals with structuration and restructuration, specifying the aggregate properties involved and a conditional logic of structural development (or recession). Despite the purely logical form of the argument some will remain extremely cautious here to avoid reification; others like Green, Seidman and Ericson[35] will positively embrace the notion of an Educational System having a life of its own.

In any case when this General Systems Theory takes the logical form of 'if...then', there is an explicit avowal that it needs linking to a theory of social action. This is necessary to account for (1) how group interaction produced the initial structure of Social or Educational System with which the theory deals, and (2) whether social interaction will be such as to generate the 'if' or the 'if not' sequence. Only a theory of social interaction provides a full explanation of structural elaboration. Without one the abstract theorist of Social or Educational Systems has to resort to probability theory which is much inferior because it does not explain and it cannot be falsified[36] in either its predictions or its retrodictions.

It is in this context that the second breakaway from functionalism, namely Exchange Theory, comes into its own for it deals precisely with those primary interaction sequences whose consequences are emergent structures. The work of Blau[37] is particularly important in showing how elementary exchanges of a face-to-face nature themselves generate social differentiation in terms of power and resources. A number of intermediary processes then lead to the emergence of the (impersonal) institutional structure of society. In other words Blau boldly attempts to lay bare the type of interaction which both fuels and steers morphogenesis. His theory can account for the specific macro-institutional structure to develop rather than merely explaining institutionalization as a generic phenomenon. Exchange Theory therefore has a lot to contribute to the question of why different structures of Educational System originated in different countries.

Its potential for explaining the way in which Educational Systems operate in society is equally great. Blau's analysis of exchange and power transactions is capable of explaining the qualitative relations existing between parts of society (e.g. domination or subordination of one institution by another). These are seen as the direct outcome of negotiations between interest groups. Change is produced by shifts in the negotiating strengths and strategies of different social groups vis-à-vis one another. The bargaining positions of groups are themselves conditioned by alterations in the social distribution of resources (i.e. the products of earlier transactions or ones which impinge from elsewhere). In Blau's discussion of the conditions under which power relations or exchange relations characterize the interchanges between two groups[38] we have, I believe, the rudiments of a real politics of education. I have attempted to extend it to deal with negotiations between the teaching profession, the political elite and external educational interest groups, once State Systems of Education have emerged.[39] In a different way (because he does not attach the importance which I do to the boundary between Educational System and society) it seems that Bourdieu's analysis[40] of the strategic conversion of economic, social and cultural capital into one another has considerable affinity with Exchange Theory.

Given the importance of General Systems Theory and Exchange Theory to questions about the origins and operations of Educational Systems, it is extraordinarily inappropriate for so many Sociologists of Education to dismiss functionalism as a blight of the 1950s, from whose deliverance we should give collective thanks. However, this distorted (and dated) perspective on neo-functionalism is often matched by an equal distortion of Weberian sociology — the last strand to be examined.

Neo-Weberian Sociology

For the last fifteen years it has been Weber the microtheorist, preoccupied with the attribution of subjective meanings to social action, who has held the attention of sociologists of education. In other words neo-Weberian sociology has been seen to contribute most to the understanding of small-scale educational operations. Yet Weber himself devoted the majority of his work to the largest scale of events — the rise of capitalism, the relationship between world religions and rationality, the inexorable process of bureaucratization. As a macroscopic theorist, concerned with the historical dynamics of social structures and institutions, his work has a contribution to make to our understanding of the emergence of Educational Systems which has scarcely been explored.[41]

In short, contemporary sociologists of education have been guilty of dualizing Weber. Yet to minimize either his macro- or his micro-concerns is to deny the integrality of his work and the significance of his own efforts to link the two. It is a failure to recognize the problem of scope which Weber confronted and the theoretical task of transcending it which he set himself, that was to forge 'a methodological path from the "understanding" of individual behaviour to the analysis of larger interactional combinations, processes, and structures'.[42] Simply to associate Weber with the pedigree of modern interpretative sociology is to retreat from solving this problem.

Today, therefore, much attention needs to be given to his comparative and historical sociology in our specialism, for significantly these dimensions are almost entirely lacking in the 'new' Sociology of Education. This would involve a serious examination of Weber's own case-studies of the *emergence* of institutional *patterns* over time and in different places. The two aspects, emergence and patterning, are of equivalent importance: the former is relevant to the question about the origins of Educational Systems, the latter is of relevance to questions about educational operations in society.

Comparative and historical work in the Weberian tradition would tackle the origins question in a distinctive way. The historical interplay between education and other parts of the social structure would be treated as truly problematic. It would start with these structural relationships and examine their patterning in its own right. It would concern itself with discovering whether education was always related to another institution, whether it was consistently subordinate or whether there were conditions under which it could display independence. It would ask whether there were any cross-cultural generalizations that could be made about the combinations of groups, material interests and cultural switchmen whose consequence was the emergence of Educational Systems, rather than assuming that the main principles of structuration were known in advance. Yet it seems to me that there is nothing about this which is inimical to either the Marxist or the functionalist traditions.

Certainly, given their underlying belief that particular economic elements are of crucial importance in shaping the institutional order of any social formation, the Marxist selectively focusses his attention on how education was related to them over time. However, there is every difference between taking an exploratory approach which uses the comparative method to establish *degrees* of interdependence and one which assumes in advance that the same architectonic principle holds for all times and places. As far as functionalism is concerned, the Mertonian strand has always accepted the need for middle-range propositions (such as those mentioned in the previous paragraph). These link the general analytical framework to substantive reality and their theoretical role is precisely to give the abstract framework a firm purchase on empirical reality. Therefore if we consider the promising forms of neo-Marxism and neo-functionalism which were singled out earlier on, it seems that there is nothing in them which precludes a fruitful symbiosis with comparative and historical sociology in the Weberian tradition.

The comparative and historical analysis briefly outlined above would represent the kind of material which any higher-level theory must be capable of embracing, by showing how these propositions can be subsumed under more general ones. It represents a perpetual challenge to any sociological theory which claims a higher level of generality, for it constitutes a source of both refinement and refutation.

Comparative sociology, undertaken because of a central interest in a particular phenomenon like the Educational System and sifting the mass of data accordingly, actively maintains a logic of scientific discovery because it ensures that the class of potential falsifiers for larger-scale theories is filled in practice rather than merely being 'not empty' in principle. In other words comparative sociology exerts a continuous pressure towards theoretical refinement and reconstruction. Ideally one would like to see a constant working backwards and forwards from comparative sociology of education to Marxist theory, such that Marxist theoreticians are discouraged from skimming over cross-cultural variations in the origins and operations of Educational Systems with which their theory *must* grapple, but simultaneously they are encouraged to point out that certain historico-educational patternings discerned by comparative research are themselves part of broader socioeconomic regularities.

On the other hand, the patterns and connections discovered through the comparative sociology of education can point up the necessity and utility of certain kinds of theoretical development and thus invite the elaboration of general theory in certain directions. This seems to be the relationship which could fruitfully develop with the latest forms of neo-functionalism. The generic idea of 'morphogenesis' is vastly more acceptable than the earlier mechanical, organic or cybernetic analogies, but at the moment it remains an abstract notion which needs fleshing out by being put to work on just such a problem as the emergence of Educational Systems. Equally the highly abstract conceptualization of the 'developmental logic' of social systems will only avoid being a sterile academic play-thing by being made to tangle with the operations of real systems like educational ones. This should be an active two-way process in which the comparative sociology stimulates the specification of these bold conjectures about sociocultural systems and in turn this intimate involvement with theory protects the Sociology of Educational Systems against the amorphous aimlessness from which comparative education per se seems unable to escape.[43]

So far I have concentrated on neo-Weberian contributions to the historical and cross-cultural structuration of Educational Systems. Weber himself, however, was concerned to link structure and culture at both the theoretical and the empirical level. He wanted to show both the objective restrictions that social structure imposes on subjective projects entertained or realized by social groups and the opportunities for action which are rooted in the internal instability of institutional structures themselves — such action then being guided on a particular course by the ideas embraced by those involved. Thus one of Weber's main concerns, especially in his studies of world religions, was the macroscopic dynamics of belief systems as manifest in their respective historical contexts.[44] Ironically, the 'new' Sociology of Education, despite its prime concern with the cultural patterning of educational knowledge, has turned its back on Weber's contribution to this problem. It exploits only his microscopic discussions of 'meanings', whilst it neglects his large-scale work on culture. A Sociology of Educational Systems, however, would draw strongly on the latter to explain how particular selections from national culture become institutionalized as 'educational knowledge' at the systemic level.

There are two questions here: a question about the mechanics of institutionalization and a question about *which* cultural 'package' is institutionalized. I think I have already said enough about the former, for the mechanics of institutionalizing any body of ideas in education are part and parcel of the struggle for educational control — for this was (and still is) a struggle to be able to define instruction. To understand which subculture was institutionalized at the time when an Educational System first emerged we need to know who won, who lost and also how badly. Equally today the structure of the Educational System determines who is in a position to influence the contents of instruction and the particular processes through which these can be changed. In other words the nature of the contents is closely related to the nature of control. Here we reach a modicum of agreeement with the 'new' Sociology of Education, but a Sociology of Educational Systems does not rest content with vague assertions about the osmosis of class (or any other group's) culture, unsupported by even the most general account of the agencies through which this subculture is imported or the mechanisms which translate it into curricula, examinations and assessment procedures. This is where our theories of educational politics are needed to lay bare the mechanics of cultural importation into education. The second aspect of this, namely what precisely is imported, has not been touched on yet although there could be a significant neo-Weberian contribution to this problem.

Let us suppose that some given group is in a position of educational control such that they can dictate the detailed contents of instruction, what will these be? The general answer (whether its referent is ruling class ideology, the central value system, or sources of legitimation) is those cultural contents which advance that group's material interests. Here we move straight to the heart of the central debate in the sociology of knowledge about the precise relationship between interests and ideas, the general answer being almost vacuous. Even if we assume that a group in firm educational control is perfectly clear and correct about its objective interests, there is not just one set of ideas alone which can legitimate their educational domination nor only one kind of knowledge which is obviously going to serve them best by constituting the school curricula. Instead judgments are involved here and occasionally the judgmental process is quite visible — Napoleon's ponderings on his ideal lycée curriculum are fairly well documented; Catherine the Great blatantly put her etatist requirements out to tender among the philosophers. What we are weak on are the factors which guide these judgments, that is the constitutive links between knowledge and human interests. Does this mean that a Sociology of Educational Systems has to content itself with historical descriptions of the judgments which were in fact made? Is this a question on which we can make no theoretical contribution?

In practice Weber used the concept of 'elective affinity' when dealing with this problem. Yet this concept only serves to specify minimalistic constraints on the ideas adopted by a group with particular material interests — those of availability, congruence and congeniality — and thus is in need of elaboration itself. However, once the leap of elective affinity has taken place, it seems that Weber's simile about ideas then acting as switchmen does represent a kernel notion which, if worked out, could hoist the Sociology of Education out of complete empiricism in this context. The implication in his own religious studies was that Weber undertook a sensitive and detailed exploration of the cultural tract in which interest groups operated — a kind of 'cultural geography' which discovered what their subjective but collective maps of knowledge and ideas looked like. Only when these features had been well explored was it possible to discover which tracks were laid out by these 'world images', along which future action would be pushed by the dynamic of interest.

This appears to be of considerable relevance to our understanding of how educational knowledge and school curricula are derived from a much more general corpus of ideas or ideology. It points to a detailed *cartography of knowledge* which would discover, on the particular map of a given group or class, what stands next to what, which are the familiar features and which are unmarked, and how the contours are drawn between them. The products of these explorations would be a series of survey and relief maps of the cultural territories of different social groups. Although the point of this map-making is the same as Bernstein's objective in delineating cultural 'codes', the procedure would be quite different. Bernstein tried, *by intuition*, to capture directly *the basic principle* underlying each code, articulating its contents and orchestrating its respective curricula.[45] A neo-Weberian approach would not try to seize any such basic principle (having no a priori commitment to their existence) but would rather painstakingly chart the different subcultural maps of knowledge.

This, in conjunction with an analysis of educational politics, would lead towards an explanation of *which* selections from the national cultural array come to constitute educational knowledge and *how* these are subsequently translated into syllabuses, set books and examination questions. Clearly such a cartography of knowledge invites combination with comparative and historical investigations in the neo-Weberian tradition, as discussed earlier on.

CONCLUSION
LINKS BETWEEN THE ORIGINS AND OPERATIONS OF EDUCATIONAL SYSTEMS

Finally, I want to deal briefly with the relationship between the two major questions about Educational Systems — where they come from and how they work. It appears that there is an ineluctable connection between them. The System in operation today was structured yesterday; the patterns of governance and accountability now observed were shaped by past struggles for control and shape future processes of change; the educational interests which are currently defended were distributed earlier in time. In other words some of the causes of continuation are inscribed in the origins of Educational Systems, whose structure created and perpetuates vested interests in its maintenance.

I picture this development of Systems over time as a series of cycles. In each cycle the initial structure conditions educational interaction, and interaction, which is also affected by independent influences, eventually brings about a change in the structure. Thus successive cycles of structural→conditioning→interaction/structural elaboration/continue to unite 'historical' origins with current operations.

These cycles move through chronological time. In the earliest ones the influence of the structure of the Educational System as it first emerged is preponderant: in later ones this attenuates, for it is the changed structure of System, as elaborated by successive bouts of interaction, which then conditions subsequent educational interaction. How many cycles are delineated in this way depends mainly on the problem in hand. This approach explicitly allows for structural influences, but it insists that these are conditional and not deterministic. Equally explicitly it allows for the independent effects of social action on changing the systemic structure, but it denies the complete plasticity of institutional structures.

To think in terms of these morphogenetic cycles is to accord *time* a central importance when theorizing about Educational Systems. It might appear from the brief discussion so far that cycles of morphogenesis only become relevant for studies of the large scale which have considerable historical sweep. It might then be concluded that the theoretical significance of the passage of time is irrelevant to much if not most work in educational sociology which is not explicitly historical or macroscopic. Nothing, I believe, could be further from the truth. A temporal dimension is essential and implicit in the smallest scale investigation which focusses upon a single point in time. An understanding of the linkage between systemic origins and contemporary operations is necessary to a full explanation of the latter: an appreciation that these ongoing operations are already contributing to structural elaboration is essential to a full understanding of systemic change. In other words the dynamics of morphogenesis are at work at any given point in time and therefore educational operations can never be reduced to their momentary mode of existence. As Marković has succinctly argued,

> *time* in human history has quite a different meaning and different structure than it does in the history of nature. Natural events simply repeat over long periods of time... In social history it is a very different matter. Both past and future are *living in the present*. Whatever human beings do in the present is decisively influenced by the past and... the future is not something that will come later, independently of our will. There are *several possible futures* and one of them *has to be made*.[46]

Thus, on the one hand, the original structure of system, shaped in the past, affects current operations, its influence permeating downwards to mark the smallest-scale interactions. For instance, the dyadic relations between pupil and teacher are partly shaped by the Educational System in which they take place. The System *contributes* to the definition of the two roles, to the distribution of authority between them, to the allocation of positive and negative sanctions to the two positions. And this contribution *differs* with different structures of Educational System.

On the other hand, and equally importantly, current *operations* act back on the original structure of the Educational System to change it. Interaction at the microlevel is not just a kind of buzzing within confines imposed by the System or a series of games played in the interstices of structural constraints. Instead, microscopic action (stretching, bending, narrowing or reinterpreting rules, methods or procedures; transacting new resources and services; innovating new courses or programmes) contributes to the renegotiation of the System's original structure. It can do so either by altering the macroscopic characteristics of the System directly, though gradually, by the accumulation of multitudinous small shifts, or more indirectly by influencing public and political opinion to legislate changes at a later date. Eventually the original structure undergoes elaboration and the renegotiated system starts off a new cycle of interaction and change in future time.

Taking these points together we can begin to visualize the interplay between origins and operations as well as between micro and macrolevels. We can start to conceptualize the effects of (macro) origins, i.e. the structure of System shaped in the past, on present (micro) operations. These can be seen as a series of *negative feedback loops* which work to maintain the original systemic structure but which *weaken over time*. Simultaneously, the effects of current (micro) operations in modifying the (macro) characteristics of the System can be conceptualized as a series of *positive feedback loops* which amplify deviations from the original structure and *strengthen over time*. Both sets of loops are found in the present, but the causes of negative feedback lie in the past and the consequences of positive feedback lie in the future.

In this way we can escape from the sterile dualism between the 'old' and the 'new' Sociologies of Education to which we were condemned largely because the time dimension was missing and treated as having no theoretical significance; for both of those approaches were characterized by complete timelessness. In the 'new' perspective there was never any 'being', only a ceaseless 'becoming', what happens 'now' was not fundamentally constrained by what went before nor did it fundamentally constrain what came after. In the 'old' approach the present state of educational affairs was treated as a timeless 'given', whose origins were unexplored and whose operations were simply recorded as there was no looking forward to a time at which they could become other than they were. In both, therefore, the present was severed from the past and the future and it is this which should distinguish the Sociology of Educational Systems from them.

Instead the kind of Sociology of Educational Systems which I am advocating would endorse Namier's injunction to 'imagine the past and remember the future', but would go beyond it by formulating rigorous theories about these temporal sequences. In so doing I have suggested here that the Sociology of Educational Systems could profitably employ and explore the model of morphogenesis, upon which various strands in general sociological theory are now converging in their conceptualization of sociocultural systems. In Part II I discussed what a Sociology of Educational Systems could gain from these general theoretical developments, but the obverse is also the case. At the moment the notion of morphogenesis is an appealing but abstract set of assumptions, whose ontological and epistemological implications require explication and whose concrete propositions require distillation before the model is ready for practical application. By working on these issues in an attempt to generate a Sociology of Educational Systems we would simultaneously contribute to the development of sociology, for it is my firm belief that theoretical advances are produced by struggling with abstract problems in relation to substantive areas of enquiry.

NOTES

1. Margaret S. Archer, *Social Origins of Educational Systems*. London and Beverly Hills: Sage Publications, 1979, p. 54.
2. Jerome Karabel and A. H. Halsey, *Power and Ideology in Education*. New York: Oxford University Press, 1977, Introduction.
3. This is perhaps a little underplayed in Karabel and Halsey's excellent Introduction, ibid., though this is only a quibble about emphasis.
4. H. H. Gerth and C. Wright Mills (eds), *From Max Weber: Essays in Sociology*. London: Routledge and Kegan Paul, 1967, p. 243.
5. Jeff Coulter, 'Decontextualised Meanings: Current Approaches to Versthende Investigations', *Sociological Review*, 19, 3, 1971.
6. John H. Goldthorpe, 'A Revolution in Sociology?', *Sociology*, 7, 3, 1973.

7. Berger's well-known concession that 'he who has the bigger stick has the better chance of imposing his definitions' is telling in this connection. P. L. Berger and T. Luckman, *The Social Construction of Reality*. New York: Doubleday Anchor Books, 1966, p. 101.

8. In A. H. Halsey, J. Floud and C. A. Anderson (eds), *Education, Economy and Society*, London: Collier-Macmillan, 1967.

9. Brian Jackson, *Streaming: An Educational System in Miniature*. London: Routledge and Kegan Paul, 1964.

10. This discussion about the problem of scope draws heavily on Helmut R. Wagner, 'Displacement of Scope: A Problem of the Relationship between Small-Scale and Large-Scale Sociological Theories', *American Journal of Sociology*, LXIX, 6, 1964.

11. Karabel and Halsey, op. cit., p. 62.

12. Basil Bernstein, 'A Critique of the Concept of Compensatory Education', in his *Class, Codes and Control*, Vol. I. London: Routledge and Kegan Paul, 1971, p. 200.

13. Basil Bernstein, 'Introduction', *Class, Codes and Control*, Vol. 3. London: Routledge and Kegan Paul, 1975, see Diagram on p. 21.

14. The term 'educational system' is used across the spectrum from traditional informal induction carried out in the family to modern state systems of education. Pierre Bourdieu and Jean-Claude Passeron, *Reproduction*. London and Beverly Hills: Sage Publications, 1977, p. 64 (French edn. p. 81).

15. Ibid., p. 55 (French edn., p. 70).

16. Idem. (French edn., p. 71).

17. Ibid., p. 7 (French edn., pp. 21-2).

18. See Archer, op. cit., Ch. 5.

19. For example see Samuel Bowles, 'Unequal Education and the Reproduction of the Social Division of Labor', *Review of Radical Political Economics*, Vol. 3, Fall 1971. This kind of approach should be contrasted with the meticulous work of Fritz K. Ringer which throws doubt upon any such close and enduring 'complementarity': *Education and Society in Modern Europe*. Bloomington and London: Indiana University Press, 1979.

20. For a more detailed discussion of these points see Margaret S. Archer, 'The Theoretical and Comparative Analysis of Social Structure', in Salvador Giner and Margaret S. Archer (eds), *Contemporary Europe: Social Structures and Cultural Patterns*. London: Routledge and Kegan Paul, 1978.

21. Louis Althusser, 'L'Objet du Capital', in Louis Althusser, E. Balibar and R. Establet, *Lire le Capital*, Vol. 2. Paris: Maspéro, 1967, p. 47.

22. Of course the French Marxists mentioned above did themselves contribute to these refinements.

23. P. Sztompka, *System and Function: Toward a Theory of Society*. New York: Academic Press, 1974.

24. David Lockwood, 'Social Integration and System Integration', in G. K. Zollschan and H. W. Hirsch (eds), *Explorations in Social Change*. Boston: Routledge and Kegan Paul, 1964.

25. See Tom Bottomore, 'Structure and History', in Peter Blau (ed.), *Approaches to the Study of Social Structure*. London: Biddles, 1976, see esp. p. 165.

26. See E. J. Hobsbawm, 'Karl Marx's Contribution to Historiography', in R. Blackburn (ed.), *Ideology in Social Science*. London: Penguin, 1973.

27. Perry Anderson, *Considerations on Western Marxism*. London: New Left Books, 1976, pp. 109-11. See also his *Passages from Antiquity to Feudalism*. London: New Left Books, 1974, and *Lineages of the Absolutist State*. London: New Left Books, 1974.

28. A.W. Gouldner, *The Coming Crisis of Western Sociology*. London: Heinemann, 1971.

29. See A. W. Gouldner, 'Reciprocity and Autonomy in Functional Theory', in N. J. Demerath and R. A. Peterson (eds), *System, Change and Conflict*. New York: Free Press, 1967.

30. A point made by Lockwood, op. cit., p. 249, note 6.

31. Walter Buckley, *Sociology and Modern Systems Theory*. New Jersey, 1967 and Walter Buckley (ed.), *Modern Systems Research for the Behavioral Scientist*. Chicago: Prentice-Hall, 1968.

32. For the most ambitious attempt to unify the concepts used in all the social sciences by translating them into the terminology of systems theory see Alfred Kuhn, *The Logic of Social Systems*. San Francisco: Jossey-Bass, 1976.

33. An example of a work which seeks to fit the social system to an organic model would be David Easton, A *Systems Analysis of Political Life*. New York: Wiley, 1965; one which fits it to a cybernetic model would be Karl Deutsch, *The Nerves of Government*. New York: Free Press, 1963.

34. Henry Teune and Zdravko Mlinar, *The Developmental Logic of Social Systems*. London: Sage Publications, 1978.

35. T. F. Green, D. P. Ericson and R. H. Seidman, *Predicting the Behavior of the Educational System*. Syracuse: Syracuse University Press, 1980.

36. See Karl Popper, *The Logic of Scientific Discovery*. London: Hutchinson, 1959, pp. 191ff.

37. Peter Blau, *Exchange and Power in Social Life*. New York: Wiley, 1964.

38. Ibid., Ch. 5.

39. Archer, op. cit., pp. 234-84 and 393-423.

40. For example see Pierre Bourdieu and Luc Boltanski, 'Changes in Social Structure and Changes in the Demand for Education', in Giner and Archer, op. cit.

41. See Ronald King, 'Weberian Perspectives and the Study of Education', *British Journal of Sociology of Education*, 1, 1, 1980.

42. Wagner, op. cit., p. 574.

43. See the last few years of the journal *Comparative Education*, Editor Edmund King, published Oxford, England.

44. Ivan James Oliver, 'The "Old" and the "New" Hermeneutics in Sociological Theory', typescript of paper.

45. Basil Bernstein, 'Introduction', *Class, Codes and Control*, Vol. 3. London: Routledge and Kegan Paul, 1975, p. 2f.

46. M. Marković, *From Affluence to Praxis*. Michigan: Michigan University Press, 1974, pp. 10-11.

9
Trends in the Development of the Sociology of Work: In Search of Identity

Jolanta Kulpinska
University of Lodz

Marc Maurice
CNRS, Aix-en-Provence

I

It is generally acknowledged that the climax of sociologists' interest in the problems of work took place in the 1950s, while the middle of the 1970s revealed a crisis of work sociology. It reflected the crisis of sociology, strictly speaking the crisis of current concepts; the criticism then was mainly of a destructive character, while the new wave of ideas, research and publications was not yet seen. According to many sociologists the wave is on the increase at present through a great number of empirical studies in which old, classical topics are explained in a new way. Of course, to place the rise and fall in exact periods must be done with great care. Research concerning the development of science shows cycles of periods in which certain topics and trends are concentrated. The polemics with and imitation of certain publications may last for a long time, giving the impression that publication is more important for the development of the discipline than might be judged when its theoretical, informative or methodological content is taken into account.

Thus the crisis mentioned above might consist in:
  1. 'Separating' certain topics — above all the sociology of organization and of industrial relations.

The text was discussed in detail by both authors, but was written by J. Kulpinska.

2. Leaving the sociology of work for another discipline by researchers, who have made their name in that discipline. It is obvious that in the period of boom the important personalities in sociology expressed their opinions concerning work similarly to those who in the years to follow expressed their views on education, social mobility or communication.
3. The absence of coherent theories embracing the main problems or aspects belonging to that branch which accounts for the fact that it is difficult to define it, its characteristic feature being the field and the subject of interest — i.e. work.

Of course, work being a universal field of human activity interests various social and sociological disciplines; what distinguishes the sociology of work is conventional, determined by national traditions and solutions accepted in various countries.

It is not our intention in this paper to bring back various problems and topics which 'have left' the sociology of work, nor do we aim to discuss all the problems at length. We want to review the main topics, show their interdependence, and outline the character of the discipline, which in spite of the redistribution of the field of interest and the crisis offers new research projects, publications and journals. Our paper has many limitations due to lack of information. Strictly speaking, we shall deal with the sociology of work in Europe and Northern America. We have not got sufficient data concerning the sociology of work in Latin America, Asia and Africa. We do not know many American publications either, since there are so many of them and there are so many centres on that continent. Generally, we shall not attach bibliographical notes so as not make the text too long and to avoid any problems of selection. Review publications devoted to the development of the sociology of work prepared for the congress of the ISA might be very helpful in this respect.[1]

II

For any scientific discipline to develop, and for a subdiscipline in particular, it is necessary to build a research centre, to establish an association or team, to publish a journal, and to read the subject at university. It depends on the research and organizational tradition in a given country and on the existence of readers or users of the 'product' of the discipline in question.

The rise of the sociology of work in the 1950s was undoubtedly due to the economic boom of that period, industrialization and urbanization, and technological reconstruction (automation). It was under those conditions that the results of the earlier American studies of the Human Relations School could be applied to management. According to local tradition the new field of study was called the sociology of work or industrial sociology. Such were the titles of various readers, manuals or journals. In spite of the 'crisis' symptoms mentioned above, lectures, journals, research centres old and new do exist and there are even more of them now then there were in the 1950s. In various countries special attention is paid to certain problems, in such a way that the sociology of work may there be identified with that specifically-defined problem — thus in France it will be the problem initiated by Friedmann and Naville concerning the consequences of technological change; in Britain, the interdependence between technology and management; in the Scandinavian countries, research connected with living and working conditions and industrial democracy; in Yugoslavia, workers' self-management; in the Soviet Union, social planning, the scientific and technological revolution, the development of work collectives; in the United States, human relations, bureaucracy, professionalization, etc. The United States were the first to separate the problems of management and enterprise from the sociology of work in order to combine the sociology of organization and the problems of employment to form the sociology of occupations and professions. As early as the 1960s, in the very influential reader *Sociology Today*, Parsons wrote about organization while Hughes wrote a paper on professions, defining the direction of further interests in this field. This division became fixed at the end of the 1960s on the wave of a thorough criticism concerning industrial relations and the functional-structural school, when the sociology of organization was identified with managerial interests, while the sociology of work was identified with the problems of workers, the workplace and criticism of working conditions.

The above examples allow us to distinguish certain groups of problems and topics, research programmes which are more permanent and universal. They determine the organization of the discipline, its role in the university and in courses for managers. The development of the discipline with all the doubts concerning borderline topics is expressed in many journals, among which *Sociologie du Travail* is the leading one. Recently, *Sociologia del*

Lavoro in Italy and *Sociologia del Trabajo* in Spain have come into existence, while the *Sociology of Work and Occupations* in the United States and the *Humanization of Work* in Poland have been published for some years. In 1970 the research committee of the ISA named the Sociology of Work was established in Varna from the former committee common with the sociology of organization. It is worth stressing that although the division is often mentioned, many members of the Sociology of Work belong to the Committee on Sociology of Organization and vice versa. It shows the common interests of both committees.

The sociology of work has many problems which are close to other social disciplines; e.g. labour economics deals with qualifications and employment and takes into account certain aspects and methods of sociology. Marxist political economy has strong sociological elements, while Marxist sociologists look for inspiration more to economic than to psychological categories.

Sociology of work will be in close contact with labour economics and labour law with regard to the problems of solving conflicts and wages. In the Anglo-Saxon countries a new discipline developed, in other European countries industrial relations belong to labour law and/or sociology. The development of ergonomics as a separate discipline revealed the problems of working conditions and strengthened the sociologists' interests in this problem. With regard to research and practice of the quality of working life the links between the sociology of work and social policy can be mentioned, though the latter is not treated as a separate scientific discipline in all countries. And finally, we come to psychology and social psychology. Psychology shares with sociology the problems of vocational choice and training, but the contacts are closer with social psychology, especially in America. Kassem, analyzing the European contribution to the sociology of organization, showed that the Americans were deeply psychologically and individualistically oriented.[2] The problems of small groups, attitudes, adaptation and satisfaction in various versions constitute the field of contact.

The links are closer due to the questionnaire method, when individual opinions constitute the material directly accessible for analysis. European criticism of the sociology of work often stressed this psychological reductionism and the weakness of the method itself, and attempts were made to use the questionnaires in a way more adequate to the real processes which occur in the work milieu (among others we have in mind the inventory of attitudes and conflicts in industry).

We have paid so much attention to the question of how scientific disciplines come into existence mainly in order to show that work sociology has not been and is not a discipline of clearly-delineated borders and precise definition. We maintain that it is a definite field of sociological interest at the edge of which various social disciplines and various branches of sociology meet. It is, however, a vast field consisting of more than mere leftovers.

III

From what we have said so far, it follows that our discipline is deprived of one paradigm common to the whole research field. It is likely that it was impossible to find it when there was a relative theoretical consensus in sociology centred around the functional and structural as well as the Marxist schools. The importance of those two schools for the development of the sociology of work was immense.

The origin of work/industry sociology as a separate, fashionable discipline is usually connected with the research in Hawthorne and the School of Human Relations; for both the disciplines which afterwards were separated it was the common source. The great theories of the social system developed later seem to be suitable for describing an enterprise and due to this approach it was possible to separate the sociology of organization. It seems that the important and interesting concepts of the sociotechnical system, open system, the significance of the environment (sociocultural, market or political) for the organization, etc., did not change the general concept of complex organization as the system of positions and roles. The criticism of the concept of organizational equilibrium in the light of social practice turned attention to the character of conflicts and the game of interests in organizations, to the mechanisms of power functioning. These interpretations, critical towards the 'classical' functional and systemic approach, brought many new elements resulting from the relations between the enterprise, industry and society.

The input of the functional-structural and systemic schools might not be equally important for all the great topics of the sociology of work. For many of them it was necessary to look for other concepts, or they became important because of other theoretical links. In this context we would like to recall our previous remark that work sociology kept its identity in opposition to the sociology of organization treated as a concept defending the managers' power due to the equilibrium and organizational consensus.

In anti-functional criticism, in Europe in particular, Marxism plays the most important role. In the middle of the 1960s the concept of alienation (in the Marxist or modified sense) initiated research which threw new light on the problems of job satisfaction and conditions of work. This analysis gave rise to the programme of work humanization. On the other hand, the Marxist theory of working conditions changed the approach to the problem of conflicts, labour market, technology and productivity, power and class structure. We have here in mind mainly the trends in West European sociology. It applies to America to a smaller extent.

The problem is different in socialist countries, where the official ideology of social sciences and social practice is based on Marxist theory. It should thus be stressed at the very start that in both Western and Eastern groups other elements of Marxist theory were developed and referred to. In the Soviet Union it was Marxism-Leninism, in Western Europe it was the young Marx and his philosophical and economic works, interpreted by the Frankfurt, French structural and 'creative' schools. From the middle of the 1960s empirical sociology gained the status of a research discipline in the Soviet Union and other countries of Eastern Europe. (It was only in Poland and Yugoslavia that sociology as a research and didactic discipline was developed as early as the 1950s.) In various respects a kind of combination of the functional and systemic approach with Marxism took place, because the essential problems of conflicts and power are not looked upon as very important in the Soviet Union, where, on the contrary, a lot of attention is paid to the integration of working groups, which is possible in a nonantagonistic society. From the point of view of the impact of great sociological theories on research and middle-range theories the most important fact is that the Marxist approach gave rise to new, interesting interpretations. It seems to be most evident in the problems of technology and the labour force.

The third — although not homogeneous — theoretical trend is the so-called humanistic sociology. Interest in this trend grew in the 1970s; in Europe, however, the influence of these American theories is not easy to discern. It may be due to the fact that some elements so attractive in the United States have always been present here. Nevertheless, humanistic sociology, like humanistic psychology, influences the method of criticizing institutions, the analysis of attitudes towards work and satisfaction, the understanding of the work situation and professional socialization. In a certain sense it makes it possible to treat 'in a new way' the traditional topics of American sociology, the involvement of man (the individual) in the working group and organization, the place of work in man's everyday life.

IV

The next section will be devoted to a review of the main topics always found in research and didactic programmes.

Occupations, professions and skills constitutes one of the central problems in the sociology of work, although the most interesting research concerning medical occupations is frequently included in the sociology of medicine. The classical topics deal with the social division of labour as the source of differentiating occupations and jobs. It particularly concerns professions which require high qualifications and university diplomas. Particular attention is paid to the occupational situation of white-collar and industrial workers whose qualifications are determined by the content of their post more than by any diploma they may have. The number of sociological descriptions concerning various occupations is considerable, and the place of occupations in stratification and social mobility is worth mentioning since it is based on the idea of the comparability of various occupational groups and their place in the socio-occupational structure.

The focus on occupational qualifications is connected with the problem of training, on the one hand, and with the analysis of employment and the labour market, on the other. The *labour market* in life does not show functional features, but is segmentalized, i.e. divided into groups varying with respect to professional qualifications and social prospects (e.g., old people, young people beginning their work, women, etc.). It seems that in the 1970s the problems of professionalization and the labour market (more generally employment and qualifications) came to the foreground, as may be noticed in the vast American literature and interesting didactic programmes.

Another topic of central importance is the impact of *technology* on the work situation, its content and workers' behaviour. As has been said previously, this is a permanent topic of study, but the explanation may be new. It includes automation, computing, innovations, technical creativity, differences in industrial branches due to technology, etc. This seems to be the special field of interest in Europe — in France, England and the Soviet Union. B. Lutz, in characterizing the return of those problems in the German Federal Republic, stressed the new approach. In the previous period the main interest focussed on the impact of technology and technological changes on the situation of the employee and his education. In the new approach the innovation process in which technology and human work are mutually interrelated is analyzed.[3] Technology constitutes the basic variable which is to explain attitudes and behaviour, organizational structure, the way of life and the development trends of the society. It is evident in connection with the concept of the scientific and technological revolution so fervently discussed a few years ago in the socialist countries in particular.

Although the sociology of work is most frequently referred to certain segments of social life, our previous considerations show the tendency to combine the micro and macrosocial analysis — on the level of the individual, place of work, working group and organization as well as on the level of the global society.

The problem of *attitudes* towards and *behaviour* at work is similar. It is another 'great' problem always to be found in the sociology of work. Several research trends can be pointed out there:

1. Attitudes to work in connection with the motivational function of management, the improvement of personnel management and the elimination of behaviour treated as pathological and disorganizing work.

2. The satisfaction and dissatisfaction with work connected with the processes of alienation and humanization of work, the pedagogical functions of the enterprise. Here the research concerning employees' behaviour carried out in the socialist countries should be mentioned, including their interest in voluntary productive activity (work competition, innovation, participation, etc.).

3. Total investigation of employees' behaviour in which are sought indicators of the long-range processes of greater social scope. This tendency seems to be characteristic of European sociologists. Workers' consciousness differentiated with regard to type of technology and community were presented in famous works

in France, Britain, the German Federal Republic and the Soviet Union.[4]

Although the problems of the *enterprise* (organization) have been separated, the frame of reference in many research programmes of the sociology of work is focussed on the enterprise looked upon as an organization of capital and labour and/or as an integrated social group. In this context the following problems are analyzed: industrial relations, participation in management, the specific features of the enterprise in socialist countries which assume that it should carry out social welfare and educational functions.

The way of analyzing the enterprise and its social and institutional context is the most decisive factor differentiating the theoretical and methodological approaches. The criterion for differentiation would consist in treating the enterprise as a system of positions and roles either as conflicting or functional and homogeneous, or else as a cooperating group or groups of opposite interests. Another criterion would consist in treating the relations between the enterprise and its social environment and the way of distinguishing the micro-macrosocial problems with regard to work.

V

The sociology of work belongs to those research fields which developed because they could be *applied in practice*. That is why two approaches to the practical functions of this discipline very soon appeared — one took this function as a basis for selecting research problems, the other stressed only the cognitive functions. It was mostly connected with the refusal to subordinate research activities to the needs of industrial managers who might use the research results for their own benefit. A distinction should also be made between interventionist and managerial investigations and those which criticize the status quo and do not want to participate in the direct forms of exploiting the workers.

The division of researchers and sometimes of the research itself is of an ideological nature and grew in strength, particularly in Western Europe, at the end of the 1960s, reflecting the growth of social conflict. France provides an example of the division between research and its direct application, while an example of indirect application consists in including problems and sociological diagnosis in instructional programmes for managerial staff. This concerns almost all countries. It should also be noticed that in those programmes the research experiences of American psychology are applied to a greater extent than those of native sociology, the critical one in particular. We will illustrate this with French and Polish examples. Following the classification by A. Podgórecki, a diagnostic and practical (sociotechnical) tuition can be distinguished besides the cognitive and theoretical ones.[5] The sociotechnical function consists in formulating directives for activities as a result of diagnosis and evaluation (criticism) of the situation. These directives may be of a more general character aiming at changes or at a definite social policy, or else they may concern real improvements in the functioning of the system. In the experience of work sociologists various sociotechnical methods/procedures can be found. To a great extent they are connected with local (country, national) tradition.

The basic procedures are:

1. Research projects for government and trade union organizations concerning working and living conditions, preparing long-range programmes in this respect.

2. Application in employment agencies and other institutions dealing with the human factor.

3. Application in the personnel departments of enterprises.

4. Action-research activity combining research and the change of situation.

Examples of researchers' practical involvement are numerous and were studied by the sociologists themselves. As typical of the procedures mentioned above the following examples will be quoted:

1. Scandinavian experiences concerning the programme of industrial democracy, as well as those concerning working and living conditions and the so-called marginal working groups.

2. The experiences of various countries and enterprises concerning the introduction of new forms of work organization and humanization, often of an action-research nature, i.e. the researchers' participation in the introduction process.

3. The experiences of the Soviet Union and other socialist countries concerning social planning in the enterprise and the employment of sociologists in the personnel departments.

For obvious reasons various information and comments concerning Polish experiences will follow. From the early 1960s the sociologists of work in Poland propagated the idea of establishing research units in the enterprises whose aim would be to analyze the problems of the employees and to work toward the humanization of work and improvements in the quality of working life. Over 1,000 sociologists and psychologists are employed in big industrial enterprises. Their activities are focussed on the improvement of personnel departments and courses for lower management. They are also responsible for the long-range programmes of work humanization which sometimes cover many years (the plans for the social development of the employees — various names are used).

Like academic sociologists, the enterprise sociologist-practitioners (as they are called) appreciate the sociotechnical possibilities of their discipline, while they are more critical towards the real conditions of their work. These are very difficult because work is often formalized, management inflexible, the position of the service very low in the structure of the plant and the interest of managers and trade unions only occasional. Nevertheless, many positive achievements may be quoted and the experiences of industrial sociologists deserve the attention of researchers, the more so because the diagnostic studies and observations of the industrial sociologists contain important and vast data closer to the real problems of industry than even the ideal academic projects based on 'bookish' knowledge.

VI

The problems of work sociology were presented according to the following assumptions. The 1970s brought a considerable decrease in interest; finally, the sociology of organization emerged as an independent discipline. Although the list of research problems in the sociology of work is long there are no coherent or universal theories covering the whole field of the discipline. The great theories made their contribution to the origin of the theories concerning particular problems, nevertheless (like sociology as a whole) a certain discrepancy between the empirical data collected and diagnostic investigations, and the theoretical achievements and practical applications may be noticed. Thus the sociology of work is more of a research field in which the sociological approach to work is of an eclectic nature. But there is no fear that there might be a shortage of sociological problems connected with work, since this sphere of life is very important for society and the individual. If we tried to sum up the trends it might look like this: the introduction of sociology to the improvement of management (Human Relations) and technological changes constituted a great research subject in the 1950s and 1960s; after this period followed the critical approach to the capitalist enterprise and industrial society (at the end of the 1960s). The economic boom brought about hopes that life might be reconstructed according to the concepts of humanization of work and quality of working life based on rational technology and social planning. Recent years have again brought out the problem of employment in enterprises and in society as a whole, and as a result interest has focussed on group characteristics of various segments of the labour force alongside research into individual needs and psychosocial features of the employees. The sociology of work has to a greater extent become a discipline dealing with macrosocial and long-range processes with work as their centre. It seems that what is known about work in society may be considerably cumulated and used in the new situation in the framework of new concepts.

When we try to determine the place of the new discipline in the achievements of sociology two methods may be applied: those great authors belonging to the obligatory sociological reading list who expressed their views on work may be identified. Another list containing publications concerning work should be compiled and treated as important for all sociologists. The first list is easy to compile since all the 'classics' of sociology have made their contribution to this field, from Marx, Weber and Durkheim to Parsons, Merton, Goffman and Marcuse. The other list is more difficult because of the specialization and segmentalization of our current sociological interest. It is difficult to find universal and holistic works but it might be advisable to compile an international reader in which the contributions of many researchers from various countries could be taken into account.

NOTES

1. *Sociologie du travail*, 1 (1980) and 1 (1981); J. Berglind, T. Hanish and E. Haavio-Mannila (eds), *Sociology of Work in the Nordic Countries*. Oslo: Scandinavian Sociological Association, 1978.
2. M. S. Kassem, 'Introduction: European versus American Organization Theories', in *European Contributions to Organization Theory*, edited by G. Hofstede and M. S. Kassem. Assen: Van Gorcum, 1976.

3. B. Lutz, 'La renaissance de la sociologie industrielle en République Fédérale', *Sociologie du travail*, 1 (1978).
4. A. Touraine, *La conscience ouvrière*. Paris: Seuil, 1966; J. H. Goldthorpe, D. Lockwood, F. Bechgofer and J. Platt, *The Affluent Worker*. Cambridge: Cambridge University Press, 1968; H. Kern and H. Schumann, *Industriearbeit und Arbeiterbewusstsein*. Frankfurt: Europaische Verlagsanstalt, 1970; V. Rozin, A. Zdravomyslow and W. Yadov, *Celovek i iego rabota* (Man and his Work). Moscow: Mysl, 1967; L. Gordon and E. Klopov, *Celovek posle raboty* (Man after Work). Moscow: Nauka, 1976; R. Blauner, *Alienation and Freedom*. Chicago: University of Chicago Press, 1964; D. Gallie, *In Search of the New Working Class*. Cambridge: Cambridge University Press, 1978.
5. A. Podgórecki, 'Pięć funkcji socjologii', *Studia Socjologiczne*, 2 (1966).

10
Economic Crisis and Urban Austerity: Issues of Research and Policy in the 1980s

John Walton
University of California, Davis

In the short space of the last decade urban social science has undergone a revolution. What began in the late 1960s and early 1970s as a critical reaction to certain anomalies in received doctrines of urbanism, has in the last few years culminated in a true paradigm shift.

The previous paradigm rested on an amalgam of ideas summed up in the terms of social organization (disorganization) and ecological succession — the master theme of community as it emerged from the market mechanisms of social differentiation and political pluralism. In genealogy the paradigm drew heavily from European theories of social integration (e.g., Durkheim and Simmel) and reached its fullest development in the United States with the Chicago School of Urban Sociology (e.g., Wirth, Park and Burgess). By the 1970s this paradigm had reached maturity and exhaustion. In contrast to the historical processes it was fashioned to address, such as primary urbanization, immigration and community formation, or the elaboration of spatial structure, the paradigm was unequipped to deal with the new urban crisis.

Doubtless, this paradigm shift is gradual in some quarters and resisted in others. But the Kuhnian metaphor is apropos as suggested by several indicators. Beginning in the late 1960s anomalies multiplied as the urban crisis posed unanswerable questions about increasing class and racial inequalities rather than social integration, urban decay rather than ecological competition and succession, protest organization rather than anomic disorganization, and the politics of domination and accumulation rather than pluralism. The paradigm crisis was the social crisis and, characteristically, the new approach combined fertility with answers (however concise) to the now-critical questions. The new approach recruited rapidly from the ranks of younger scholars and related disciplines. A final and tell-tale sign is the fact that the basic textbooks are being rewritten from the standpoint of the new approach.

By now it seems safe to conclude that the revolution in urban social science is nearing completion, that a new period of normal science (with its own limitations) has set in, and that the most compelling task is to indicate the critical and progressive steps that must be taken next. In that connection it is necessary at the outset to characterize the new approach. Since particular labels incur the risks of reification and reaction, I prefer to call this simply the new urban social science and to characterize it in the points that follow. From these I hope to make clear that if the approach has 'structural' emphases they are not at the expense of process, if it stresses the economy it does not diminish the society and polity, if it alludes to Marx it does so in the same forward-looking manner that Weber would have. If there are to be demurs with the perspective, let them concern the analytical issues.

The new urban social science has diverse origins in theory and practice. As I have suggested, it was partly a product of the urban crisis that erupted internationally from Watts to Paris in the late 1960s. The familiar ingredients of the crisis that defied conventional interpretation and called for a new vision included social protest, declining city resources and services, the loss of jobs and industry, new responsibilities for enfeebled local governments, a changing population base and (migratory, casual) labour market, the socioeconomic polarization of the city and its surroundings (the suburbs and new cities), official efforts to pacify or suppress inner city residents, and ultimately the signs of fiscal crisis.

The urban crisis had the ironic consequence of producing a great deal of descriptively useful conventional research which, nevertheless, proved inadequate to the task of explaining these developments. Studies of riot participants and their targets, for example, produced some informative results that tended to refute theories of social disorganization and irrational alienation. Inquiries into local politics that revealed the power of business and governmental coalitions implied but never analyzed their connections to the class structure and national economy. Research that documented ecological segregation and political fragmentation stopped short of any explanation of how these transformations came about and what interests they served, once it became clear that the hidden hand of competition and equilibrium could not account for these crisis-provoking changes. The conventional approach in a deluge of empirical efficiency washed away its own quasi-theoretical foundations.

Coincident with this accumulation of anomalies about the urban crisis in the advanced societies, and particularly the United States, other approaches to urban development were maturing. Notably, research on dependent urbanism in the underdeveloped countries made rapid headway due in part to the 'advantage of backwardness' that it did not start out from the balkanized disciplinary views of urban sociology, economics, and political science. Urbanization and its consequences could be seen as cause and effect of societal transformation. Another key element was the development of assiduous empirical research in Europe that grew out of a more holistic theoretical tradition. This combination of anomaly, prescient yet theoretically uninterpreted research, and emergent holistic traditions combined to provide the foundation of the new urban social science.

As it has developed over the last decade the new urban social science embraces several characteristic premises. First, from a theoretical and historical standpoint it holds that urbanism itself requires definition and explanation rather than being taken for granted or treated simply as a phenomenon of aggregation. Urbanism and urbanization must assume the status of 'theoretical objects' in the sense of phenomena that arise (or do not) and take different forms under various modes of socioeconomic organization and political control (Castells, 1978; Harvey, 1973). Second, the approach is concerned with the interplay of relations of production, consumption, exchange and the structure of power manifest in the state. None of these can be understood separately or as analytically prior except in the sense of a logical exercise (i.e. ceteris paribus). Third, as in the case of urbanism generally, concrete urban processes (e.g., ecological patterns, community organization, economic activities, class and ethnic politics, local government) must be understood in terms of their structural bases or how they are conditioned by their connection with economic exigencies, political arrangements, and the sociocultural milieu. Fourth, the approach is fundamentally concerned with social change and conceives of this as growing out of conflicts (or contradictions) among classes and status groups. These conflicts are the basis of the political process which, increasingly, is coincident with the arena of the state. Changes in the economy are socially and politically generated as well as mediated. Political and social changes are in no sense independent of the economy. Finally, the perspective is inextricably tied to the concerns of normative theory. It is concerned not only to draw out the ideological and distributive implications of alternative positions, but is critically aware of its own premises and the dilemmas they too pose.

If the new urban social science has secured for itself a paradigmatic role more or less consistent with these premises, its work has just begun. At this juncture the challenge is to move beyond an elegant — and sometimes formalistic — critique of conventional urban sociology or economics and to demonstrate the value of the approach in research and explanation concerning the major transformations experienced by cities within the context of the national and international political economy. While this task is necessarily historical, particular importance attaches to an explanation of the dislocations presently being felt by cities as a result of the global economic crisis and attendant austerity politics that have succeeded the urban crisis of the 1970s as the fundamental problem of the urban milieu. This problem is experienced in different forms across urban settings depending on a host of circumstances including the location and resources of the national society within the global system, the local economy, population and class structure, distinctive political arrangements, and so forth. The challenges facing the new urban research consist precisely in determining the nature and significance of this local variation and relating it to the more general systemic trends. Briefly stated, this is the charge and the agenda for urban social science in the 1980s.

The historical conditions that give rise to the new urban social science and generate much of its subject matter can be described collectively, and without risk of hyperbole, in the theoretical terms of economic crisis. The word 'crisis' is employed here in the concrete sense of a periodic imbalance in the development of advanced capitalism that forces a fundamental reorganization or rationalization of the economy and social policy. Crises occur at various levels and do not necessarily signal the denouement. They may be partial, sectoral, or, as in this case, global (Harvey, 1978) and represent normal, even necessary, interludes.

The contemporary global economic crisis is, of course, historically unprecedented. In scope it rivals the 1930s, but its substance and impact are different. The crisis that began in the advanced capitalist countries in 1973 is, at bottom, a crisis of overproduction (Mandel, 1978). It comes at the close of a period of massive and fairly continuous expansion of the advanced industrial economies after the Second World War. That period witnessed the recovery of Western Europe and Japan as economic powers eventually rivalling the United States in world trade and investment — imperial competitors and occasional multinational corporate collaborators in the contest for Third World markets, themselves becoming increasingly resistant to denationalization. This core competition was responsible for the collapse of the Bretton Woods accord, the end of the dollar's convertibility to gold as an international currency, the adoption of floating exchange rates, and the general unpredictability of the current world financial system.

In the advanced capitalist societies, particularly the United States, the international crisis is reflected in reduced world trade (with the saving exception of agricultural exports), trade deficits, declining industrial production, declining rates of profit, increased idle capacity, rising unemployment, and, generally, the characteristic features of deep recession. In the United States the initial crisis of 1973 was followed by a temporary recovery as the result of accelerated consumption stimulated by an explosion of consumer credit, institutional borrowing, government borrowing and deficit spending, and steady expansion of the money supply. The result was an enormous acceleration of public and private debt that fuelled inflation while only briefly stalling stagnation. Oil price increases certainly contributed to this 'stagflation', but their timing, relative amounts, recirculation (e.g., OPEC purchases), and differential effects across national economies all rule them out as primary causes. The interlude of recovery was brief (1975-77) and by 1979 the recession had returned with a growing vengeance.

As we begin the 1980s the effects of the global crisis are plain to see. Rates of industrial production across the advanced capitalist countries continue to decline. World trade slumps further with individual countries having increasing recourse to protectionist measures (Strange, 1979). Inflation continues its upward movement to the point where countries like the United States are forced to abandon hopes of recovery through credit expansion or debt financing and turn instead to austerity measures to curb borrowing and balance the budget. The immediate impact is increasing unemployment, reduction in social expenditures, and the further depression of key industrial sectors such as housing, steel, automobiles, and so forth. Welfare state policies that sealed the pact between capital and labour in periods of expansion are progressively eliminated while the labour force spared unemployment is chastened by reductions in real income. As the crisis unfolds we may anticipate the devaluation also of fixed capital (Harvey, 1978) and generally a process of the 'recapitalization of capital' (Miller, 1978).

Proceeding from this very general characterization of the current economic crisis we may, for present purposes, indicate the links with urban issues or some of the more compelling ways in which the crisis shows up on a locality basis. At this level we are concerned to indicate the structural implications that require concrete comparative research and which provide the theoretical basis of the new research agenda.

Beginning with the obvious, there is a sense in which the global economic crisis is identical with the urban crisis as the former takes shape in the highly urban industrial advanced countries. National problems such as unemployment and austerity policies are to a large extent the problems of cities that have historically been an essential requisite for capitalist development. Yet the urban effects of crisis are far more specific and exacting. The differential effects of unemployment, for example, are borne more heavily by central city populations that include higher proportions of recent migrants, elderly, minorities, and less-skilled working class. Austerity measures that concentrate on social expenditures are apt to be pursued more vigorously in the field of social consumption (vs. social investment, cf. O'Connor, 1973), that is with respect to projects and services that benefit labour (or reduce the costs of its reproduction) such as health, housing, transportation, and social insurance. The most volatile and immediately affected private industries, especially housing, are at once the most desperate problem areas of the city.

As we pursue the fall-out of economic crisis the uniquely urban manifestations appear in greater relief. The 'urban fiscal crisis' is prototypical. If we may take the example of New York as somewhat representative of situations common to other United States and world cities, the origins of the local plight can be traced to broader structural dislocations such as overproduction, the collapse of the post-war boom, competition in export markets, the loss of industry and jobs, and shortsighted financial solutions based on expanding debt (Edel, 1977). In a closely related vein, the central cities are most prone to devaluation of fixed capital in housing and rental stock, commercial buildings, and public lands and investments that may be sold off to meet other pressing governmental obligations (cf. Harvey, 1978 for historical examples and Cleveland for contemporary ones). Once adequately devalued, the repurchase of these properties or infrastructural systems is sometimes hailed as evidence of an urban renaissance (Edel, 1977). What this optimism fails to reckon with is who has won and lost in the process. In the case of both refinancing the urban fiscal crisis and reinvesting in devaluated urban properties, the costs have been shifted heavily on to pension fund members, tax payers, home owners, and small business.

To a large extent big capital does not suffer these burdens by virtue of its mobility and possession of money capital (that, too, a product of overaccumulation). Devalued fixed capital becomes a tax advantage in reinvestment strategies that have increasingly taken capital and jobs abroad (Walton, 1981) or to more inviting domestic regions such as the 'sunbelt' of the United States (Perry and Watkins, 1977). These 'switching crises' (Harvey, 1978) are doubly disadvantageous to older urban areas since they involve both geographic and sectoral shifts. Investment not only abandons the older industrial, working-class cities, but also moves domestically into new product lines in which previous workers would have no special advantage should they migrate with capital. Typically their jobs have been exported to the Third World, the poorer European countries (Ireland, Spain, Portugal) or enclave economies (e.g., Taiwan, Hong Kong, Singapore).

Finally, it should be noted that where austerity and fiscal crisis even-handedly produce reductions in public expenditures, the burdens are still disproportionately shouldered by the urban working class. For example, while cuts in public employment may at a given moment take place across-the-board, the historical significance of public sector expansion has in some considerable part involved the absorption of workers displaced by capital-intensive industrial growth. Moreover, the various forms of collective consumption mentioned previously serve not only to augment the social wage, but provide the entire wage for many of the least privileged strata of the urban labour force (especially women and minorities since these jobs have been the most progressive in affirmative action).

Before us, then, are a number of issues that relate to the broader course of contemporary history, yet are rendered at a more tractable level of immediate concern. From these rather loosely and casually organized themes the new urban researcher could move in a variety of directions. Obviously, no such initiative is to be discouraged. Nevetheless, recent developments in urban social science have taken some important steps in specific directions, guided at once by characteristic theoretical sensitivities and by the informative contributions of earlier traditions in urban research. In short, certain foci may now be especially strategic and fruitful. In what follows I shall list and comment critically on a set of these which is offered as *one* research agenda. Numerous limitations, which I shall conveniently attribute to space, prevent detailed discussion of these points. For the moment they are presented as a vehicle to move our considerations forward.

The first general issue on this research agenda concerns the *integration of levels* within holistic analyses. It has become almost platitudinous in criticism of conventional research to insist on the recognition of 'broader structural forces' that are at the 'roots' of changes on the urban scene — to lament the spurious character of research that catches a piece of an important development, but misconstrues it for want of an adequate causal analysis. Despite the near-axiomatic status of such criticisms, there is a dearth of exemplary analyses that actually trace global processes to urban effects in systematic (as opposed to contextual) ways through all of the socially specific detours along the way and back again in the sense of what those concrete deviations may mean for the general theory. This lacuna is ironic since some of the most elegant and compelling theory is addressed precisely at 'the structural links we need to understand the urban process under capitalism' (Harvey, 1978, p. 114; see also Lojkine, 1976 and Lamarche, 1976).

Naturally, there are some instructive exceptions to this gap. As suggested previously, it has been in the study of Third World urbanization that the most elaborate research has traced the determinate and varied impact of capitalist development on urban structure (e.g., Castells, 1978; Slater, 1978; Quijano, 1968; Hardoy, 1975; Lubeck and Walton, 1979). With respect to the advanced countries some heuristic efforts include Edel's (1977) analysis of the New York fiscal crisis in the context of the global economy and Gordon's (1978) treatment of periods in United States urban development that correspond to stages in the changing modes of production and labour control. A recent piece of my own dealing with the internationalization of capital and the class structures of the advanced countries attempts to trace the effects of the export of capital and jobs to urban and regional transformations (Walton, 1981; see also Cohen, 1977).

An excellent and timely illustration of global-urban linkage is Mingione's (1978) analysis of 'capitalist crisis, neo-dualism, and marginalization.' Mingione conceives the global crisis of the advanced countries not in terms of overproduction but of a decrease in the rate of accumulation and the increase of surplus labour. Previously successful responses to this recurrent problem through the capture of new markets or technological innovation are now unlikely due to the overexploitation of the Third World (as well as competition from the socialist countries) and technological stagnation, itself partly owing to underaccumulation. These and other conditions combine to suggest an 'internal solution' whereby the large numbers of underemployed and unemployed are converted to a new kind of informal economy within the advanced countries: 'One option is for capitalism to expand these marginal sectors whose features are low wages, irregular employment and super-exploitation of labour, by diverting some of the economic activities which were previously carried out in the great industrial concerns' (1978, p. 215). The potential consequences of this change are then traced to urban and regional struggles. Although the analysis is quite brief, it is loaded with fascinating implications and research issues given the tremendous consequences of the informal economy demonstrated in work on Third World urban social organization (Portes, 1981) and the growing importance of this phenomenon in the advanced countries.

Yet these and some related efforts are very modest beginnings given the theoretical (not to mention the rhetorical) significance of the problem. Urban effects of the present economic crisis are pervasive, not only in the export of jobs and capital, fiscal crises, and the informal economy, but also in the basic domestic sectors of production, in private and collective consumption, and in a panorama of state measures designed to cope with austerity. Much remains to be done in the systematic and researchable linkage of these levels.

Second on this agenda is the broad question of *alternative responses* to the exigencies or crises in the economy and polity. Clearly, the fundamental, and frequently valid, criticism of research within the new paradigm is its penchant for lapses into functionalism, teleology, or ex post facto determinism — in retrospect a particular development is 'explained' as the necessary outcome of a particular constellation of economic and political forces. As certain writers (Marx included) are fond of saying, 'how could it be otherwise?' In a moment of candour Marx (1857) once wrote to Engels about his analysis of the asiatic mode of production, 'I might be wrong but if so I can always get out of it by using a little dialectic. I have set myself up in order to be right even in the opposite case.' Although crude functionalism (as opposed to studied formulations à la Stinchcombe, 1968) is objectionable irrespective of the particular theory it serves, it is by no means an endemic feature of the approach under consideration — as many overeager critics have charged. On the contrary, sophisticated analyses frequently indicate the alternative ways in which a given crisis, or mere conundrum, may be resolved in light of available political and economic stratagems.

Illustrations come to mind drawn from the theoretical literature alluded to previously. For example, O'Connor's (1973) schematic analysis of the fiscal crisis of the state poses for resolution in the short-to-middle run: managed recession, wage and price controls, and increased productivity in the service sector, i.e. the 'social-industrial complex'. Harvey's (1978) treatment of overaccumulation and the urban process considers the possibilities of renewed accumulation and devaluation with respect to production and consumption in the three 'circuits of capital' as well as the struggles these are apt to engender.

Historical and empirical inquiries have attempted to explain the variety of contemporary adaptations to the exigencies of urban development and what they portend for the future. Hill's (1978) analysis of capital accumulation and urbanization in the United States reasons three responses to fiscal collapse, the pariah, socialist, and state capitalist city with elements of all in evidence despite the growing dominance of the latter. In parallel analyses of the conditions that once favoured expansion toward the suburbs and the sunbelt, Markusen (1978) and Perry and Watkins (1977) indicate the circumstances under which older urban centres are likely to experience a revival. European research in this area has concentrated on the circumstances in which capital is invested in various forms of urban development, construction and housing (e.g. Ascher and Levy, 1973; Duclos, 1973; Pickvance, 1976; Preteceille, 1973).

Nevertheless, these illustrations are exceptions to the general preference for imperious explanation, and even the exceptions are too often hedged with vagueness and escape clauses. What is most needed are theoretically informed explanations that arrive at the point of enumerating a delimited set of likely alternatives and indicate the *conditions* under which one or another will ensue. This is not an appeal for mechanism — itself a double-edged sword. It is, rather, an appeal for the replacement of smug assurances with consequential and researchable hypotheses. Moreover, it is precisely at this juncture that the oft-lamented (too oft unfairly) tendency for 'economistic' explanations can be most effectively addressed — the juncture at which the more elegantly derivable economic contradictions can be located on the grid of political possibility.

This leads to the third point concerning the status of research on *political struggles and social movements*. In my view there is a proclivity in some of this work for contentious assertions about class struggle — its unexamined character and portent reflected in the habit of labelling all forms of political activity as class conflict. Following the Weberian lead, it is essential that we distinguish among political actions based on considerations of status and social honour and those based on class. Efforts to merge these in a denatured notion of social class produce analytic muddles and unwieldy schemes (e.g., Giddens, 1973) that only detract from the incisiveness that recommended the concepts in the first place. Particularly, we need to identify the springs of action in class and status and to understand better their interaction — how they combine under different circumstances or evolve one from the other in different proportions and under different historical and political conditions (e.g., Bendix, 1974).

Concretely, in political struggles devoted to employment or community services, in what measure is action prompted by inequalities related to production (the money and social wage or general conditions of work), by inequalities of sex, race, or citizenship status, and how are these interrelated? Too often the tendency is to evade this knotty issue with simple assertions to the effect that class at some point 'overrides" more ephemeral concerns of status honour or, conversely, that class issues make a contribution (never capable of explaining everything) to other actions, with that which is unexplained left to residual treatment.

When we turn to thinking through some of these issues, research that has grown out of other traditions becomes especially instructive. For example, Kornblum's (1974) superb account of blue-collar community shows the intimate interplay of industrial work and ethnic community as they affect working-class politics. In a related historical vein Yancey et al. (1976) describe the urban, industrial, and labour market conditions under which ethnicity 'emerges' as a basis of action. Illustrations could be multiplied, but the point is that we have in this issue a valuable opportunity not only to profit from previous research but to move forward theoretically.

A similar problem in the study of urban social movements has been the tendency to assume theoretically that their origins lie in particular kinds of contradictions. This assumption leads to two difficulties. The first is to infer from the existence of a movement that a given contradiction arrived at analytically was in fact salient to and a cause of the movement. The second problem is to infer from an analytic contradiction the likelihood of a movement forming in response to it. Obviously, these constitute the same error or, at least, the same failure to distinguish independently contradictions and movements and to investigate empirically their interconnection. One important result of making this distinction is that we are likely to discover that movements may originate in a wide variety of settings including ones not commonly construed as contradictory, that some contradictions are more powerful than others, and, as Piven and Cloward (1977, p. 17) learned, that in the course of their development 'the demands of protestors, at least for the periods we examine, are shaped as much by their interactions with elites as by the structural factors (or contradictions) which produced the movements.' Similarly, we are more alert to the possibility that the manner in which contradictions are resolved may provide the best explanation, not of eventual breakdown, but of the very stability and resilience of the social order (Dowd, 1978).

Much of this is by way of saying that in a curious sense too much responsibility has been placed on the shoulders of the social movement as a source of change. It has been theoretically linked to all manner of contradiction and on its career ride the fortunes of any forseeable progress. Obviously, very little progressive change is to be expected in the absence of social movements. But their origins, careers, and ultimate results need to be determined by reference to the broader institutional setting that changes in some ways independently of the movements themselves, while at the same time presenting the opportunities for their differential success. The research that stands the best chance of providing flesh to these reflections will depend on more demanding comparative methods that introduce and control for different institutional settings and movement types.

Assuming that we are clear about the diverse bases of political action in class and status considerations and the complex features of social movements, the study of class struggle may proceed unencumbered. It is encouraging to witness the eclipse of atheoretical and, therefore, irreconcilable polemics about the nature and distribution of political power that has resulted from new theoretical formulations that allow of more or less definitive solution. Articulate models informed by class analysis have proven their explanatory value by contrast to others based on pluralism or elitism in comparative case studies in the United States on urban issues such as transportation (e.g., Whitt, 1979), corporate power in cities (e.g., Friedland, 1977) and states (e.g., Hicks et al., 1978), and in imaginative work combining case-study and comparative methods in the study of environmental problems (e.g., Crenson, 1971). Starting under fewer handicaps, European research on corporate and business dominance of urban politics has produced some intriguing work including the classic book of Castells and Godard (1974) on *Monopoville* and the recent comparative study of Lojkine of local politics in Lille and Marseilles. Were it ever seriously doubted, the proposition that the interests of corporate capital predominate in urban politics is now supported by the best empirical research.

Although this is a necessary and painfully-arrived-at result, it is nevertheless a fairly base proposition. It has paved the way for current and more challenging work that focusses on the political conditions and consequences of class divisions and coalitions. One avenue of approach has been the nature of intraclass division, particularly for capital. For example, several writers (e.g., Castells, 1978; Harvey, 1976; Mingione, 1977) have analyzed the manner in which expenditures on collective consumption, housing being prototypical, tend to divide fractions of capital with those dependent on land, construction, or rentals favouring greater profit in housing while industrial capital opposes such upward pressure on wages. Under these circumstances capital 'in general' (Harvey, 1976) and the state may side with industrial capital benefiting at the same time labour. The example, obviously, serves mainly to indicate how this approach opens up the possibility for analyses of more complex and realistic situations.

Mollenkopf's (1978) analysis of the diverse pro-growth coalitions that dominated United States cities in the post-war period is a choice illustration of the fruitfulness of this approach. There he shows that while the pro-growth coalitions temporarily embraced many elements (e.g., corporate capital, local officials and boosters, middle-class workers) at the expense of the urban poor dispossessed by redevelopment and suburbanization strategies, the coalition eventually fell apart opening the opportunity for disadvantaged classes to join in a potential new alignment with local officials and the urban middle class to reinvest in the city. Environmental issues are particularly fascinating in this regard since they seem to provide opportunities for both middle and working-class coalitions in favour of environmental reform as well as capital and working-class alignments opposed to their expense (cf. Schnaiberg, 1979 and the recent work of Duclos).

Just as political struggles combine elements of class and status action, they typically cross class lines as they become more intensive. With the maturation of class analysis it is now possible to become more exacting about class-based coalitions — the conditions under which these emerge, their varied configurations across time and issues, and their fates. It is in connection with these conditions of inter and intraclass alignment and their associated social movements that the real consequences of political action are to be found. Fortunately, we are now at the point where they can be pursued on a firm theoretical footing and with some valuable empirical precedents.

The fourth area of research for our consideration concerns the *state and public services*. Analysis of the state logically follows from considerations of class since the key questions about the state — its 'functions' across time and issues — depend upon first establishing the coordinates of class and class-based political action. That is, if the main concern of various theories of the state is the extent to which it acts in certain class interests or in a relatively autonomous fashion, any assessment of that issue depends upon prior clarity about what the classes and their interests are. The same holds where we are concerned with the impact of class-based social movements on the state. These analytic directions, however, should not obscure the fact that in addition to its partial determination by class action, the state also participates historically in the very determination of class structure. These distinct 'sides of the causal chain' should be kept in mind as we focus on the more immediate problems of state functions and class interests.

During the last decade the emergence of a new urban social science has coincided with renewed interest in a theory of the state. Since developments in the latter field cannot be reviewed here (and have been summarized often, e.g., Wolfe, 1974; Girardin, 1974;

Bridges, 1974; Gold et al., 1975), let me simply assert that most of those who have considered the question subscribe to the view that the state is something more than the 'executive committee of the bourgeoisie' (no one seems to really admit to being an 'instrumentalist') — that the state possesses 'relative autonomy'. Yet the exact sense of this phrase is elusive. One can imagine several senses of relative autonomy: as a compromise, stalemate, or higher synthesis of competing class interests; as the occasion of a fluid or inchoate class situation; as the occasion of centralized executive power such as Marx (1963, p. 122) described in the *Eighteenth Brumaire* as a 'completely independent' state; or as some combination of the above wherein a distinctive set of bureaucratic interests exists independently. Which of these senses may be useful or valid is as much an empirical question as a theoretical one. For the moment all we need observe on this question is that concrete research at the urban level may give us some idea of the different kinds of autonomy and the conditions under which they arise.

Returning to our theme of economic crisis and urban austerity, the role of the state is usefully illustrated in three areas. The first is the matter of state administrative structure with particular reference to taxation and finance. In a paper on the state response to the fiscal crisis in United States cities Friedland et al. (1977) argue that different forms of state intervention (e.g., those that benefit capital and those that provide social services) are differentially vulnerable to political pressures. As Friedland (1978, p. 573) elsewhere puts it succinctly.

in the United States, social services tend to be noncentrally financed through investment-sensitive and non-progressive property taxes, while state interventions which are critical to production (defense contracting, public capital projects, tax incentives for capital investment) are centrally financed through potentially more progressive income taxes. First, this makes it extraordinarily difficult to conjoin a politics of the social wage with a politics of social capital. Second, locally financed welfare and education expansions often pit unionized working-class home-owners against unemployed and low-paid workers and surplus populations. Third, labour unions are encouraged to secure health, day care, transportation and other benefits through intra-corporate collective bargaining. Fourth, social wage expenditures tend to be financed out of more visible forms of taxation and thus highly politicized, while social capital expenditures tend to be financed through less visible taxes and thereby depoliticized.

Under conditions of economic crisis, of course, this arrangement implies that necessary austerity measures are most likely to come at the cost of social services and the social wage. But the more insightful point here is that they come through the seemingly even-handed operation of the political process by virtue of the manner in which the state is organized to serve 'all' classes. The interests of legitimacy are served at the same time the least advantaged classes bear the heaviest costs of austerity policies. In this case the autonomy of the state is a fiction constituted mainly by the apparatus that camouflages a class mechanism.

At the present moment the opportunities for research on this question are, regrettably, abundant with the appearance of service-reducing measures and the tax revolt movement. One wonders, for example, under what conditions does the fever for tax revolt get arrested by perceived and consequential reductions in services (Miller, 1979), what classes and positions get politicized around these issues, what services are more and less vulnerable, under what circumstances may the structure itself become transparent?

These questions suggest a second area illustrating the role of the state, namely the mix of crisis policies directed at production and consumption. As we have seen, policies in each sphere have important and differential urban consequences. State responses to the initial crisis of 1973 attempted to aid production through greatly expanded consumer credit which might have benefited cities save for its inflationary effects. Similarly, state policy ultimately assists the relocation of production in more profitable regional and international climes. If, as some suggest, the present economic crisis is one in which overproduction is a key problem, it would be expected that state policy will focus increasingly on the consumption sphere. For example, collective consumption may increasingly be opened up to private accumulation as O'Connor (1973) forecasts with the 'social-industrial complex' notion or, more concretely, as Harvey hypothesizes (1978, p. 129): 'Investment in working class housing or in a national health service can thus be transformed into a vehicle for accumulation via commodity production for these sectors.' In short, a vital area for new research concerns the extent to which present conditions may lead to state policies that completely transform the organization of service provision in a manner of rescuing capital.

Third, these hypothetical and real changes that portend austerity in social services have deep implications for the welfare state. At the most obvious level they suggest that the welfare state is not in the business of enhancing people's welfare, but of attempting to maintain a viable economy in a one-sided pact between capital and the more privileged (and organized) sectors of labour. Again, in research stemming from the perspective under review, this point has been made innumerable times in connection with the themes of cooptation, super-exploitation, social control, and all of the seemingly beneficient measures of the state that can be interpreted as subtly accomplishing the extraction of greater profit and conformity (e.g., Marcuse, 1978). Assuming, as is doubtless the case, that these liberal and radical criticisms of the welfare state capture some truth, the question becomes what will happen to this structure of social control with the transformation of the welfare state as we know it? If the welfare state has bought social peace at the expense of capital and the general public or, from a more extreme stance, if it has been a mechanism of repression, what will happen to the stability it has engineered once its services must be directly purchased? Although this question is formulated here in a doubly hypothetical manner, it is not without empirical precedent (e.g., in health and education) and stating it in this way may help to convert a heavily ideological debate into a tractable research problem.

The final point on this research agenda is implicit in everything that has been said so far and can be summarized briefly. In connection with its normative stance and commitment to practice, the new urban social science is deeply concerned with research on public policy. Despite this orientation in its research, there is a conspicuous lack of discussion on *progressive policy alternatives.* Virtually all policy research from a critical standpoint ends up in sweeping condemnations of the regressive or repressive character of occasionally well-intended programmes — including ones the same parties may have looked upon with general favour earlier (e.g., the notion of citizen participation). To the extent that 'constructive' ideas are offered they tend to rhapsodize on socialism in the abstract or reforms adopted in China or Cuba under entirely different circumstances — and sometimes of dubious merit.

Of course, there may be good reason for this general persuasion. But, if there is no conceivable policy that researchers can endorse short of the destruction of the capitalist system or the promotion of regressive policies that heighten contradiction as a prelude to the denouement, then this needs to be admitted and the professed practice of policy research (with its associated status) abandoned for other pursuits. Conversely, if there are policies, or even realistic preconditions for policy making, then these should be laid out in terms of the research they are based upon and lead toward.

This is simply to restate the observation that the critics of conventional urban social science and urban development have so far failed to present an attractive alternative. As Miller (1978, p. 211) says in other terms

> Currently, the recapitalization approach is aided by the absence of a politically appealing, economically attractive, short-run left strategy. Can the left in capitalist nations provide more than a critique of current policies and offer a viable programme which can cope with the immediate short-run economic problems of capitalism in ways that lead to attractive socialist conditions?

Naturally, the objectives of our deliberations go beyond the formulation of discrete policy ideas. Policy tends to reflect the level of understanding on which it rests and that is at least one reason why so much of it is so bad. Yet, a genuine understanding of our problems is certain to imply avenues for their remedy. Ideally these would be the fruits of our efforts.

REFERENCES

Ascher, François and Levy, Daniel (1973) 'Logement et Construction', *Economie et Politique* (May).

Bendix, Reinhard (1974) 'Inequality and Social Structure: A Comparison of Marx and Weber', *American Sociological Review*, 39: 2 (April): 149-61.

Bridges, Amy Beth (1974) 'Nicos Poulantzas and the Marxist Theory of the State', *Politics and Society*, 4: 2 (Winter): 161-90.

Castells, Manuel (1978) *The Urban Question: A Marxist Approach*. First published in 1973. Cambridge, Mass: MIT Press.

Castells, Manuel and Godard, F. (1974) *Monopoville: L'Entreprise, L'Etat, L'Urbain*. Paris: Mouton.

Cohen, Robert (1977) 'Urban Effects of the Internationalization of Capital and Labor'. Unpublished paper, Conservation of Human Resources Program, Columbia University.

Crenson, Matthew A. (1971) *The Un-Politics of Air Pollution: A Study of Non-Decisionmaking in Cities*. Baltimore: Johns Hopkins University Press.

Dowd, Douglas (1978) 'Continuity, Change, and Tension in Global Capitalism', in *Social Change in the Capitalist World Economy*, edited by Barbara Hockey Kaplan. Beverly Hills: Sage Publications.

Duclos, Denis (1973) *Propriété Fonciére et Processus d'Urbanisation*. Paris: CSU.

Edel, Matthew (1977) 'The New York Crisis as Economic History', in *The Fiscal Crisis of American Cities: Essays on the Political Economy of Urban America with Special Reference to New York*, edited by Roger E. Akaly and David Mermelstein. New York: Vintage Books.

Friedland, Roger (1977) 'Class Power and Social Control: The Case of the War on Poverty', *Politics and Society*, 7: 459-89.

Friedland, Roger (1978) 'Space, Society, and the State: A Critique of The Urban Question', *International Journal of Urban and Regional Research*, 2: 3 (October): 569-76.

Friedland, Roger, Piven, Frances Fox and Alford, Robert R. (1977) 'Political Conflict, Urban Structure, and the Fiscal Crisis', in *Comparative Public Policy: New Approaches and Methods*, edited by Douglas Ashford. Beverly Hills: Sage.

Giddens, Anthony (1973) *The Class Structures of the Advanced Societies*. New York: Barnes and Noble.

Girardin, Jean-Claude (1974) 'On the Marxist Theory of the State', *Politics and Society*, 4: 2 (Winter): 193-223.

Gold, David A., Lo, Clarence Y. H. and Wright, Erik Olin (1975) 'Recent Developments in Marxist Theories of the Capitalist State', Parts I and II, *Monthly Review*, 27: 5 and 6 (October and November): 29-43 and 36-51.

Gordon, David (1978) 'Capitalist Development and the History of American Cities', in *Marxism and the Metropolis: New Perspectives in Urban Political Economy*, edited by William K. Tabb and Larry Sawers. New York: Oxford.

Hardoy, Jorge (1975) *Urbanization in Latin America: Approaches and Issues*. Garden City, NY: Anchor.

Harvey, David (1973) *Social Justice and the City*. Baltimore: Johns Hopkins University Press.

Harvey, David (1976) 'Labor, Capital, and Class Struggle Around the Built Environment in Advanced Capitalist Countries', *Politics and Society*, 6: 3: 265-95.

Harvey, David (1978) 'The Urban Process Under Capitalism: A Framework for Analysis', *International Journal of Urban and Regional Research*, 2: 1 (March): 101-31.

Hicks, Alexander, Friedland, Roger and Johnson, Edwin D. (1978) 'Class Power and State Policy: The Case of Large Business Corporations, Labor Unions and Governmental Redistribution in the American States', *American Sociological Review*, 43: 3 (June): 302-15.

Hill, Richard Child (1978) 'Fiscal Collapse and Political Struggle in Decaying Central Cities in the United States', in *Marxism and the Metropolis: New Perspectives in Urban Political Economy*, edited by William K. Tabb and Larry Sawers. New York: Oxford.

Kornblum, William (1974) *Blue Collar Community*. Chicago: University of Chicago Press.

Lamarche, François (1976) 'Property Development and the Economic Foundations of the Urban Question', in *Urban Sociololgy: Critical Essays*, edited by C. G. Pickvance. New York: St. Martin's.

Lojkine, Jean (1976) 'Contribution to a Marxist Theory of Capitalist Urbanization', in *Urban Sociology: Critical Essays*, edited by C. G. Pickvance. New York: St. Martin's.

Lubeck, Paul and Walton, John (1979) 'Urban Class Conflict in Africa and Latin America: Comparative Analyses from a World Systems Perspective', *International Journal of Urban and Regional Research*, 3: 1 (March): 3-28.

Mandel, Ernest (1978) *The Second Slump: A Marxist Analysis of Recession in the Seventies*. London: NLB.

Marcuse, Peter (1978) 'Housing Policy and the Myth of the Benevolent State', *Social Policy* (January-February).

Markusen, Ann R. (1978) 'Class and Urban Social Explenditure: A Marxist Theory of Metropolitan Government', in *Marxism and the Metropolis: New Perspec-*

tives in *Urban Political Economy*, edited by William K. Tabb and Larry Sawer. New York: Oxford.
Marx, Karl (1963) *The Eighteenth Brumaire of Louis Bonaparte*. Originally published in 1852. New York: International Publishers.
Marx, Karl (1857) Letter to Engels dated 15 August. *Complete Works of Karl Marx and Friedrich Engels*. Moscow Edition.
Miller, S. M. (1978) 'The Recapitalization of Capitalism', *International Journal of Urban and Regional Research*, 2: 2 (June): 202-12.
Miller, S. M. (1979) 'Proposition 13's Meaning and Implications'. Paper presented at the Annual Meeting of the American Sociological Association, Boston.
Mingione, Enzo (1977) 'Sociological Approach to Regional and Urban Development: Some Methodological and Theoretical Issues', *Comparative Urban Research*, 4 (2, 3): 21-38.
Mingione, Enzo (1978) 'Capitalist Crisis, Neo-Dualism, and Marginalization', *International Journal of Urban and Regional Research*, 2: 2 (June): 213-21.
Moffenkopf, John (1978) 'The Postwar Politics of Urban Development', *Politics and Society*, 5: 3: 247-95.
O'Connor, James (1973) *The Fiscal Crisis of the State*. New York: St. Martin's.
Perry, David C. and Watkins, Alfred J. (1977) *The Rise of the Sunbelt Cities*. Beverly Hills: Sage Publications.
Pickvance, C. G. (1976) 'Housing: Reproduction of Capital and Production of Labour: Some Recent French Work', in *The City in Comparative Perspective: Cross-National Research and New Directions in Theory*, edited by John Walton and Louis H. Masotti. Beverly Hills: Sage Publications.
Piven, Frances Fox and Cloward, Richard (1977) *Poor People's Movements: Why They Succeed, How They Fail*. New York: Vintage Books.
Portes, Alejandro (1981) 'Unequal Exchange and the Urban Informal Sector', in *Labor, Class, and the International System*, edited by Alejandro Portes and John Walton. New York: Academic Press.
Preteceille, Edmond (1973) *La Production des Grands Ensembles*. Paris: Mouton.
Quijano, Anibal (1968) 'Dependencia, Cambio Social, y Urbanización en América Latina', *Revista Mexicana de Sociologia*, July-September.
Schnaiberg, Allan (1979) *The Environment: From Surplus to Scarcity*. New York: Oxford.
Slater, David (1978) 'Towards a Political Economy of Urbanization in Peripheral Capitalist Societies: Problems of Theory and Method with Illustrations from Latin America', *International Journal of Urban and Regional Research*, 2: 1 (March): 26-52.
Strange, Susan (1979) 'The Management of Surplus Capacity: Or How Does Theory Stand Up to Protectionism 1970's Style?', *International Organization*, 33: 3 (Summer): 303-33.
Stinchcombe, Arthur L. (1968) *Constructing Social Theories*. New York: Harcourt, Brace.
Walton, John (1981) 'The Internationalization of Capital and Class Structures in the Advanced Countries: The Case of the United States', in *Labor, Class, and the International System*, edited by Alejandro Portes and John Walton. New York: Academic Press.
Whitt, J. Allen (1979) 'Toward a Class-Dialectic Model of Power: An Empirical Assessment of Three Competing Models of Political Power', *American Sociological Review*, 44: 1 (February): 81-99.

Wolfe, Alan (1974) 'New Directions in the Marxist Theory of the State', *Politics and Society*, 4: 2 (Winter): 131-59.

Yancey, William L., Ericksen, Eugene P. and Juliani, Richard N. (1976) 'Emergent Ethnicity: A Review and Reformulation', *American Sociological Review*, 41 (3): 391-403.

11
Current Problems and Perspectives in the Sociology of Leisure

Anna Olszewska
Polish Academy of Sciences
Gilles Pronovost
Université du Québec à Trois Rivières

INTRODUCTION

One could ask oneself, and with good reason, if it is pertinent or even legitimate to speak of 'leisure', knowing the ambiguities and the doubts that surround the subject — sometimes going so far as to deny its existence. The question of an eventual definition is also hazardous, as much because of the various endeavours which are contradictory and often based on diverse disciplinary approaches, as by a type of latent suspicion which permeates sociology, protecting it from notions that might seem trivial or that could be labelled common sense. As for the sociology of leisure, the cord cuts even deeper, for the study has been accused on many occasions of being something less than 'sociological' in its approach and its concepts, or else of wasting time on epiphenomena whose fundamental explanations should be sought in a somewhat more conventional demarche, notably the sociology of work or of social classes.

Furthermore, the image that we occasionally maintain of leisure is one of a pedlar of happiness and freedom, prothesying a modern-day civilization; in reality, an ideology pared from a flamboyant dissertation full of promises for the future. Still, seldom if ever have its lauders pressed on in a sociological tradition.

The sociology of leisure is without doubt at a beginning. This genuine difficulty of establishing itself in a somewhat more classical tradition must not, however, be associated with the sociology of leisure itself, but rather with a type of historical movement, as yet still young, of provisional delineation and change in the field of investigation and of research which is that of leisure.

We should also point out that the interest extended to any phenomenon whatever becomes a problem of social science after a certain social value is accorded it. Weber taught us that the understanding of social phenomena is a byproduct of the cultural importance we attach to them.[1] Consequently, if this phenomenon that we call leisure is the object of a history of sociological research, be it faulty or not, we can infer from it that the socioeconomical and historical conditions have in a way produced new problems, new values, themselves being at the outset of an initial sociological inquiry. Was it not in this manner that sociology itself was created?

In dealing with the foundations of leisure sociology it is important to regard the conditions that allow for its growth as problems of social science, referring of course to the realm of social consciousness in which leisure manifests itself. This applies to the sociologist as much as to any other researcher. The sociology of leisure, so often concerned about recognition, has possibly neglected for too long the examination of its emergent conditions, even though this is a fundamental axiom in the sociological tradition, by virtue of which all knowledge is relative to its social and economic context.

To start with, we will approach the central aspect of the existing relation between sociological studies in leisure and their social context. Using this as our basis, we will outline the recent trends of empirical research in this domain, attempting, in conclusion, to leave an opening for other perspectives and inquiries.

I.
WHAT IS THE SOCIOLOGY OF LEISURE AND WHAT ARE THE CONDITIONS THAT PRODUCE IT?

We are starting with the aphorism that all sociological knowledge of leisure is a result of the emergent conditions of such knowledge. Some fundamental points influencing the current sociological discussion of leisure are: its internal functioning, the selective dimensions one is considering, the preferred methods of approach, the general sociohistorical context on which all such discussion is dependent, not to mention the social actors who have served as its spokesmen. Accordingly, we shall very briefly analyze three national cases, chosen solely because of our relative knowledge of them: the United States, France, and the USSR.

However, one need only recall one of the more plausible hypotheses, historically speaking, to realize without question that it was in Great Britain that modern leisure arose, occurring as a byproduct of the industrial revolution, at a time when Engels and Marx were concluding some of their most fundamental analyses of the transformation in Western societies during the 18th and 19th centuries. In this respect, the end of the 18th century and the first half of the 19th is the most tragic period of the newly-born working class: terrible working conditions, large migrations of workers to the cities, the destruction of a former, more popular culture, etc.

But even as early as the first half of the 19th century in Great Britain, the movement towards the progressive reduction of working hours had gained a certain following, as had the trade unions. The living conditions had changed to such an extent that Engels himself, in the preface to an 1892 edition of *The Condition of the Working Class in England in 1844*, had written that 'the state of things described in this book today pertains largely to the past'.[2] It was in Victorian England that the majority of clubs were founded, the industry of music halls was to appear, as did modern sports and mass consumption, all for the greater pleasure of the working classes, but constantly under the reproachful eye of the puritan ethic and the repression of the police. Actually, we view 19th century England as the long process of restructuring the British social classes, but it is also an historical movement towards differentiating the time and the space occupied by economic and social life. Thus, leisure time tends to be independent of work, places of amusement become institutionalized, the entertainment industry establishes itself, and the towns themselves tend to be sectioned off according to the new models of public life.

These few observations have been presented to illustrate the importance of the social and economic history of Great Britain, as it relates to the study of the emergent conditions of modern leisure and contemporary popular culture.

The Question of Leisure and Society in the United States

Dating from before the Civil War, the Industrial Revolution produced well-known social and economic transformations in the United States. It is often overlooked that for the early American unions the reduction of working hours was a major issue,[3] and that since the end of the 19th century the eight hour work day has constituted an important demand. The industry which had grown up around leisure, i.e. the travelling circuses, the music halls, the sports clubs, and the large urban parks that had been constructed, had such a large following that we could speak in cliché of a 'recreation movement'. At the end of the 19th century it was a question of progress and the supremacy of the American civilization — a distinctly evolutionist standpoint, inspired by Darwin.

At the turn of the 20th century the trend seemed to be accelerating. In a period of twenty years a number of legislative and social reforms were implemented; the working week was reduced almost by a third; philosophers such as John Dewey were writing about democracy and culture, and most American towns had established local public recreation services, run with the help of volunteers. The years between 1900 and 1930 constituted a period of extravagance, of economic prosperity without precedent and of grand dreams for the future. It is clearly at this point in American history that the first really well-articulated ideology of leisure can be found. It is initially defined as a fundamental need of human nature, not unlike children's play, from which it borrows its essential characteristics. It plays an important role in the development of the body (originally termed 'culture of the body' and later 'physical culture') and in the formation of the human mind, to such an extent that we now insist on the coeducation of the mind and the body. Furthermore, leisure was considered as an integral part of the American democratic ideal and the means of particiaption in the culture. In the long run, it comes back to this question of a new civilization — America on the threshold of modern times.[4] This thesis was extremely well-structured and well-received at the time and has since been institutionalized to the point that it almost constitutes an official doctrine for American professionals involved with leisure, for it appears in a number of handbooks, and is taught in more than 300 colleges and universities across the United States.

Thus the basis for American thinking on leisure at the turn of the century had its roots in the conditions that were bringing about the transformation in American society as a whole. It should be added that this discourse began to take shape towards the end of the 19th century, with the expansion in industry, the progressive rise of the unions, and the constant reduction in working hours. Whatever the causes, an ideology of leisure was taking shape within the specific social context of the era, the influence of which is still a determinant in our times. Moreover, the advocates of this ideology have long been the professionals associated with American leisure, who justify their hold on public institutions, universities, and research with a doctrine that speaks of fundamental needs, human nature, and the call to liberty.

A true sociology of leisure could not exist in this situation for two reasons: the people responsible for the research were the professionals themselves, who had interests to protect other than those of the sociological comprehension of leisure. The American sociologists, for their part, were preoccupied with other questions, such as urban sociology, delinquency, cultural minorities, the problems surrounding acculturation; leisure seldom if ever appeared as a field of interest, worthy of investigation. Thus the American sociology of leisure is a very recent occurrence, coming to light shortly after 1945 on the momentum of an investigation into mass culture.

We know that originally the conception of mass culture was very pejorative (anonymity, passivity, consumption, etc.); however, what we often overlook is that this approach has its roots in older schools of thought, coming to the surface at the turn of the century, particularly in anthropological studies (e.g., the celebrated *Middletown*). We should add that the period after the war is marked by an important economic expansion, because of the rise of the middle class (who become the majority of the active population), and the creation of great suburban towns.

At the research level, the techniques and methods of enquiry develop to a remarkable degree of sophistication, and we are witness to an ever-increasing disciplinary specialization. That which intrigues the researchers is no longer the social problems or the individual problems of poverty, which have become institutionalized with the creation of schools of social work. New preoccupations are springing up relating to the growth of the American institutions and organizations, the bureaucracy of enterprise, the new forms of social control using techniques of management or the hold of the mass media and the 'dangers' of conformity or of passivity which might result.[5]

It is not hard to prove that most of the texts which concern themselves directly or indirectly with leisure in the 1950s and 1960s, and which were not influenced by the ensemble of questions in the professional doctrine previously outlined, have been profoundly influenced by this conception of mass culture. It is also interesting to note that rather than the professionals involved with leisure it is the researchers in social science and the humanists who have revived the notion. The enquiries into mass culture and those of the professional's stand on leisure brought together two different groups of participants and spokesmen. The usual themes pertaining to the research concern mass communication, the groups of intermediaries (i.e. the studies of Lazarsfeld on the 'two-step-flow'), the theory of the dominated masses (Mills), and again this very negative perception of mass culture, represented by David Reisman and others.

It is for this reason that today, the American sociology of leisure seems to be caught between these two great historical currents. In the hope of encouraging new sociological studies which address themselves specifically to the question of leisure and, in the absence of any real history of sociological research in this area, unconsciously borrowing the definitions and normative approaches of the professional doctrine, the majority of writers serve only to reinforce the 'marginality', or in truth the exclusion of the sociology of leisure from the sociological community at large. The other choice that is left us is to call upon the inquiries into mass culture to supply information about the sociology of leisure; in this case, it is common knowledge that one would find judgmental approaches, moralizing in such a way that leisure can only appear in a light that is more and more negative, ending in dissolution.

So in conclusion, it seems that the first landmarks in sociological reflection on the subject of leisure in the United States are largely tributary of the transformations in American society; on the one hand, an accelerated industrialization and economic progress engendering a euphoric doctrine of leisure and the civilization of contentment, the stylized echo of which we can still find in current manuals;[6] on the other hand, the profound cultural changes that we have been tempted to explain in terms of mass culture, this time embracing the rather pessimistic and clearly pejorative view of the intellectuals.

Leisure and Society in France

It is not hard to conceive that the sociohistorical establishment of a sociological cognition of leisure would be very different in the case of French society. In a rather abrupt manner, one could say that it begins with a type of utopian thinking, elaborated upon in the 19th century; thinking such as that of Paul Lafargue which is in direct contradiction to the historical data of the period. In the early stages, leisure was thought of only in an inaccessibly idealistic form, a radical counterpart, without substance, to the existing socioeconomic conditions. In a general sense, leisure seems to be a slow conquest over time. Nineteenth-century France is marked by a series of political struggles and the social demands of the workers for the improvement of their living conditions and the reduction of working hours. It is difficult to conceive nowadays that it took the French labour movement over 100 years to get the working day reduced from fifteen hours to eight, to abolish child labour, and to get paid holidays. The political and social excitement reached a peak with the creation of the Popular Front in 1936 and the diverse social reforms which followed.

In this context, the question of leisure had been one of education for the masses, with the intention of making education available for everyone (a view which had Cordorcet as its apostle at the time of the French Revolution). The time gained from work was serving the movements in scholastic and technical education, or reserved for activities of a more religious nature such as prayer meetings or reading the bible. The French Revolution had served as a point of departure for a very important movement in public schooling, which had nourished the 19th and early 20th century thinkers, and brought about the establishment of the free, compulsory, and secular schools in 1880. Thus, in the early 20th century more than 100 'popular universities' were already in existence in France. As a general rule, they concerned themselves with the scholastic formation of the workers, providing them with their technical qualifications, but also with their morality, their collective individual growth, with the understanding that it was for the good of the nation as a whole.[7]

The French sociology of leisure was sustained by such historical tides from the very beginning. It should be noted from the start that, as is often the case, this leisure 'consciousness' preceded the formation of an approach that was strictly speaking sociological. So it was that one of the first social thinkers in the field of leisure was Léo Lagrange, Assistant-Secretary of State Health (Organization of Sports and Recreation) in the government of the Popular Front in 1936, for whom sports and open air were synonymous with physical fitness, leisure, relaxation and the enjoyment of life.[8] Furthermore, in the style of American sociology, French sociology borrowed from these currents of social thought, integrating the popular notions of the day and only gradually being overtaken by a view that was properly speaking sociological. Georges Friedmann, starting from a critique of the industrial process and 'machinism', seems to centre his thoughts on leisure around a philosophy of work as a fundamental activity of man, attacking the effects of technical progress, and perceiving leisure in a compensatory role. It is necessary, he goes on to say, both to revalue work, and to use leisure as a means of compensation for work that is mundane or for personal intellectual development. His views on leisure were not part of an independent theory, but pertained to a more global philosophy of work, notably that part dealing with the consequences of industrial development in the 19th century. This philosophy included norms for the intelligent use of the time that was now available, time which had been won at great cost by the working classes.[9]

But the first true sociologist of leisure that France ever knew is, without doubt, Joffre Dumazedier, whose influence has been a determining factor on an international scale. This is not the place to present the foundations of his thought in detail. It is sufficient to recall as a function of our original hypothesis that Dumazedier, a militant during the Resistance, considered public education an issue of vital concern.[10] Pressing for an autonomous sociology of leisure, and one which was independent of the sociology of labour, he became well known for his definition of the three functions of leisure (relaxation, diversion, and development) which were remarkably similar to the concept of leisure as a compensation for work presented by Friedmann and Léo Lagrange before him, and to the philosophy developed within the framework of the popular universities, before the Second World War. In a later paper on the question of cultural development he proposes four values of leisure, which he calls essential characteristics: liberation, impartiality, hedonism, and personal growth. Once again, this rationalization is engulfed in a certain militantism, in the long tradition of the French militants, and is rooted in a discourse inspired by the movement within the popular universities. Naturally, the thinking of Dumazedier is rich and complex and we do not have time to describe it here. We simply wish to point out that such thinking was only able to take root in the social movements of popular education, just as in the changes that occurred in French society itself.

In the 1960s, the sociology of leisure reached a major turning point. Put simply, one could say that it had bypassed the goals of general education — which, in the beginning, were the amelioration of the people and increasing the accessibility of 'high' culture, evolving into the idea of cultural leisure at the time of the Popular Front, and finally to that of culture alone. At least three different aspects can be noted. In the first place leisure is seen as an integral part of the culture itself, in the area of cultural dynamics and the values at play; but there is also the second concept of a multiplicity of cultures — mass culture, 'high' culture, regional culture, popular culture, etc., which leisure is both reliant on and in part a witness to; the third aspect is the image of a new militantism, which in contrast to the militancy behind popular education, meets with the aspirations of the common person, attentive to the cultural diversities and even tending to support them — in fact a spokesman. This new militancy is called sociocultural animation.

Naturally, these changes had an influence on the French sociology of leisure (as did the teachings of Dumazedier), traces of which can easily be found in today's themes: cultural power, cultural action, popular culture, urban living, mass consumption, etc. Another example of these changes can be seen in the shift in the areas under discussion. Whereas formerly it was a question of the polarity of work and leisure (Friedmann for example), or of militating against the non-recognition of the cultural values of leisure, values which foreshadowed the future (Dumazedier), it is now a question of the demands of the mass culture industry, the integrating role of cultural politics, the interest in the phenomenon of popular culture and of professionalism among the sociocultural leaders. Thus, the cultural changes in French society and the socioeconomic transformations that we have touched on, correspond to the modifications in the question of French sociology, as well as the fundamental debate with which it is at odds.

Origins of the Sociology of Leisure in the USSR

The October Revolution in Russia engendered an approach to leisure that was radically different. Since we are lacking certain historical information concerning the way in which the question of leisure was first approached, as well as the successive transformations which followed, we will limit ourselves to a brief discussion of our original hypothesis, as it pertains to the first period of analysis, 1920 to 1930. What we see is the rapid development of a tradition of research — that of the time-budget study. Essentially, the study was born in Russia during this period, but it still constitutes a favoured methodology in the East European countries for gaining insights into leisure and culture. In this respect, it is impossible to deny that it is in the USSR that one finds the oldest and strongest tradition of research on the subject, and that it is an original school of thought on the international level whose influence has been profound.

But the question remains, what were they hoping to bring to light with these studies? What were the major concerns? It would seem that the prevailing approach was above all economic and quantitative, in that it consisted of measuring the conquests of the revolution in terms of work, culture, and social well-being. Under the direction of Strumilin the research teams were tempted, as it were, to certain effects of the October Revolution, of 'reading' into the facts the rise of a triumphant communism. But this research had other objectives as well, such as planning and orienting the economy. It was a question of contributing, through the appropriate statistical information, to the momentum of the political machine in terms of natural resources, human resources, the economy and planning.[11] Moreover, the question of leisure was undeniably associated with a more global concept of culture; the classic dichotomy between working hours and free time was prevalent at this time, the latter being perceived as a long drawn out battle by the working class, not only for access to a certain degree of well-being, but also for the right to participate in cultural activities (literature, theatre).

According to the general hypothesis, one could say that the time-budget studies in the USSR took place in a very particular historical context which resulted in the studies themselves. It is the problems of 'reading' the revolutionary events, of planning, of the access to culture, which led the researchers of this period to create an original method of social science research. Once again, the existing conditions have determined the orientation of the research, the development of thought on leisure and the methodology itself.

One point that we should underline is that even with the changes in the economic and social conditions of Soviet society since the October Revolution, new problems will inevitably present themselves. In the light of this one might wonder what new questions concerning leisure (differing radically from those of the time-budget studies) will be the product of these historic transformations. We need only recall the current trend of studies into different 'ways of life' to illustrate yet again that they are not a question of chance but, inevitably, a change in the analytical perspective linked directly to important social changes which remain to be described in depth.

II.
TRENDS AND PERSPECTIVES OF EMPIRICAL RESEARCH IN THE DOMAIN OF THE SOCIOLOGY OF LEISURE IN THE 1960s AND THE 1970s

The examination of the three national cases gives an indication of an initial double conclusion: on the one hand, a tradition of research into the sociology of leisure, relatively recent, which with a few notable exceptions barely goes back much further than the 1940s; on the other hand, a strong rapport between the development of this particular sociology and the socioeconomic conditions producing it. In this perspective, what has been the sociology of leisure in the last few decades? To what problems has it addressed itself? What have been the major themes? To what important empirical studies has it given rise?

In the 1960s and the 1970s the development of sociology in the field of leisure went hand in hand with an increase in empirical research. During that period, three types of interdependent relationships were established between theoretical and empirical research:

— the authors of the better-known sociological studies used the findings of other studies to support their own theories of social change, or the statistical data of other authors to illustrate their own assertions concerning leisure;
— a number of sociologists created the comprehensive theory of the sociology of leisure by setting up their own research projects, closely associated with theoretical questions;
— finally, in order to form middle-range statements, a number of sociologists undertook some special studies, connected with specific groups or problems, that were of cognitive value. These projects were often an attempt to confirm the

middle-range statements, or to pose questions that had been ignored up to that time.

The empirical studies that have been carried out over the last twenty years in the field of leisure can be classified under a few headings:

leisure and culture
time-budget studies
leisure and sports
leisure within the local community (urban or rural)
leisure within social groups (family, classes, and by generations)

Most research undertaken in this area falls into one of these categories. This does not, of course, comprise a complete list of all the cognitive themes that are under study in the field of leisure, but because of the limits of this chapter only the principal categories will be discussed.

Leisure and Culture

In the 1960s, sociologists focussed mainly on the question of culture and the extent of people's participation in its various forms, from the point of view of the sociology of leisure. The rapid growth in the mass media — television, radio, the rising number of books, magazines and newspapers, the growing popularity of films, posed a question for sociologists: to what extent were the institutions behind mass culture and the messages they were putting out being received by people, in the period designated as leisure time? How does participation in mass culture compare with other forms of leisure? The problems of mass culture and the process of cultural expansion within different social structures have been the basis for the growth of mass culture sociology. They have crossed over into the domain of the sociology of culture, at the same time becoming the subject of certain empirical studies. New research data and statistics concerning the size and possibly the specific nature of this phenomenon have stirred the sociologists' imagination.

The piece *Loisir et culture* by Dumazedier and Ripert (1966) is the most representative of the essays which deal with the problems of leisure and culture. This comprehensive study is widely quoted thanks to the general insights it provides as well as in consideration of the detailed evaluation of a particular study carried out in a French town which is generally acknowledged to be a microstructure of this dynamically developing country. Five categories of leisure (practical, physical, artistic, intellectual, and social) have been analyzed in various ways. The field of leisure as a whole and in all its forms has been shown in diachronic and synchronic development against a background of the most important events in the country's history. The following problems are touched on: leisure as a value in relation to other values, in particular to work and family life; the interest shown in different types and forms of leisure within social groups and classes; the question of close social relations and of social distances in general, in the domain of culture. Research by the French has shown that although in the past there were differences in leisure activities among the classes, there are few today.

The use of several research techniques has allowed sociologists to obtain a clearer picture of leisure within different social groups. The popularity of the activity is determined using statistics, the relation between leisure and social standing is examined as are the reasons behind the selection of popular forms of leisure. In addition, the emotional attitudes associated with the activity can be determined. The semi-leisure activities are also a subject of consideration. In the practical analysis of leisure problems, emphasis is put on the relation to art, entertainment, 'higher' culture, and popular culture. The relationship between the more traditional forms of leisure and newer forms resulting from mass culture is equally important. Research into the cultural content of leisure has given credence to the general statement that leisure in the advanced industrial community becomes not only an instrument but also an expressive value. As such it begins to weigh significantly on other spheres of both individual and community life.

The empirical studies of the 1960s also included cultural institutions, the 'institutions' of leisure and the people employed in these institutions, as well as the organizers of leisure and cultural activities connected with associations and clubs. The analysis of the level of consciousness of cultural 'workers' involving their role, and how they see it, and their aspirations and goals connected with the cultural activity they are concerned with, is one of the studies' more interesting elements. The analysis is based on the assumption that there is a connection between a person's self-image and his activities, irrespective of the other social factors that might have a bearing on these activities.

The studies mentioned above were undertaken in France, Canada, the United States, Poland and in other countries. Some of the Canadian research is characterized by a certain historical accent. The effect of the culture and the Catholic ideology on the type of leisure activities one chooses has already been established, and observation of the current changes which are of a secular nature, is one of the more important studies in progress in the Canadian sociology of leisure.[12]

The problems concerning the degree of participation in various forms of mass culture within different social groups have determined the subject of a separate branch of sociology — the sociology of mass culture. In some countries, these problems fall in the area of cultural sociology and are handled not with the anthropological approach, but are seen in the narrow sense of the word 'culture', i.e. in the sense of a symbolic culture (the works of Klowskowska of Poland, for example). The different areas of the sociology of leisure are treated against a background along with other aspects of leisure and questions to do with free time. This approach is of great educative and scientific value in that it shows in the broadest terms the life-style of a contemporary man in terms of leisure.

Practical examinations of leisure have shown that social standing has an effect on a person's preferences. At the same time, education and vocation are the variables which have the strongest influence on these preferences. Recent American studies cast an eye on yet another determining factor, i.e. the surrounding natural environment. Extended consideration of this factor in future studies will enrich their results immensely.

The Time-Budget Studies

The time-budget studies have been carried out on the largest scale. The greatest amount of funds has been set aside for these studies and they have examined the widest cross-section of the population. Apart from the comparative studies carried out in nine countries, they have been carried into effect in many countries of East and West. The findings of the time-budget studies are of great importance to sociological research into leisure. In a way, they can be regarded as the basis for these enquiries because, along with other statistical data, they form a starting point. The comparison of different countries' findings, or diachronic comparisons bring out the strong points in time-budget studies. The dynamics involved in social processes or even their absence becomes clear. Although the areas of leisure that are examined in these studies are confined to a few categories, the comparison of leisure time with the other activities, either of a group or an individual, provides interesting results, as it gives an indication of the direction of the changes taking place.

The time-budget studies have clearly shown the relation between the level of socioeconomic growth of a community and leisure. The higher the growth, the shorter the working day and the greater the time spent at leisure. This factor remains constant, but the findings of recent studies throw additional light on it. The higher growth and shorter working day do not necessarily give a balance between leisure and work. Part of this time is spent at leisure, but the greater part is used for other activities: trips to the place of work, compulsory education, a second job, etc. The time-budget studies have been carried out up till now on three continents: Europe, North America, and South America. The use of these studies in East Asia would probably yield different results, the difference being the effect of a national tradition and culture as well as the significance of other social phenomena, or even geographical factors. For instance, in the Japanese community the consistency of the relation between the level of economic growth and the increase in leisure has yet to be proven.

At the first stage in the organization of the time-budget studies, the general consensus was that here was the essence of sociological study in leisure. The current opinion is that these examinations, of a socioeconomic character, add an important element to the sociological study of leisure, but they cannot replace the study itself, and what is more they need a broader interpretation than has been available up to now. The activity described in these studies as 'the preparation and consumption of meals', for example, should not be isolated as a mechanical function. It serves an important purpose from the sociological point of view in that it brings the family together around the table.

Leisure and Sports

Studies of an empirical nature regarding participation in sports as a form of leisure are the subject of a fascinating evaluation. In the 1950s and early 1960s, interest in sports was recognized as one of the major elements in leisure studies, which were essentially trying to discover the relation between leisure and culture. The early 1960s were dominated by studies dedicated entirely to sports as leisure. The analysis, which in the beginning concerns itself with small populations, is progressively widened by the number of questions and problems with which it is presented, as well as by the size of the population under examination. A recent international study carried out in ten countries, comparing socialization in sports, is a good example of the growing interest in this direction. The following studies were undertaken: the detailed description of people's athletic activities, including the number of participants, the frequency of this participation, and the amount of time devoted to it; the first contact with sports as an event and as a participant; the roles of different people and institutions in these contacts; the atttitude toward sports resulting from the influence of schools, clubs, or sports associations; and the attitude towards sports in the different stages of life.[13]

The effect of family sports backgrounds is an interesting question. Considering the classifications existing in the sports sciences, the sociology of leisure is, first of all, interested in sports for the masses, whereas the sociology of sports is interested in record sports. The phenomenon of mass sports has been on the increase in the last few years. Sports that were formerly reserved for the privileged (tennis, equitation, etc.) now fall within the reach of other social groups. Sports with a smaller following, such as backpacking, races of various sorts, skiing competitions, etc., have caught on with millions of people.

There are many reasons for the growing interest in sports as a form of leisure: the reduction of the length of the working day, the additional free time, the increasingly significant role of record sports as entertainment along with their effect on mass sports, and physical conditioning as an essential part of good health and long life. The increase in the aesthetic needs of people, provided for by sports as entertainment, exercise, principles of behaviour, and a fight challenge are also factors which should be mentioned. The pressures of the natural human environment, which are especially evident in agglomerations, are an element which also appears with great regularity. With this concept, mass sports is a return to nature, the landscape, and the elements of space, quiet, green forests and clear water. The different forms of sport make it possible to escape from a threatening natural environment, excessive traffic, crowds, and water, air and noise pollution. Almost all forms of tourism bring into play new expectations and the searching of man. In Anglo-Saxon countries it has attracted the greatest amount of attention; in Great Britain its role in the culture has been of immense importance, more so than in other European countries, and in North America there has been a long relationship with the beauty of nature.

It should be noted that mass sports have not yet become the subject of empirical studies, as might be expected considering their place in the leisure of a contemporary community and the cultural changes of the last few years. If the sociology of leisure has gained certain insights in many countries, in as many others there is no inkling about the people's physical leisure activities. It is important that this information be obtained from empirical studies of the sociology of leisure.

Leisure and Local Community

In this area practical research concentrated first on urban communities, the traditional focal point for the main thrust of this kind of study. No doubt this comes from the historical fact that mass leisure originated as a product of industrialized urban communities. In discussing the problems of leisure in the context of an urban community we must recall certain topics and relations that have already been mentioned. Empirical research into leisure over the last few years has been characterized by viewing a person living in a town as 'an individual in general'. It follows that leisure is seldom considered from the point of view of the community in which the 'individual in general lives'; therefore, leisure in its various forms is very rarely seen in the context of the sociological problems of the town as a community. The principle behind Lynd's work is not applied. This results, to a large extent, from the research being applied at the present moment. The dominance of quantitative analysis over qualitative testing leads to an evaluation of the individual outside the essential social structures. There are still many problems concerning the relations between leisure and the functioning of urban communities which remain unexplored.

The study of rural communities is in an entirely different position, for even though it is of great social importance, it is rarely undertaken. One cause, among other things, is the fact that the sociology of leisure came into existence in a country with no villages and nothing in the way of a traditional local community. Furthermore, for a long time there was a very small rural population. Polish and Israeli studies concerning the leisure of rural populations are among the most important recent years. Practical testing has shown that there is a strong tendency for rural populations to have free time, in spite of rustic work and work in industry.[14] In comparison with urban populations, rural populations have much shorter periods of leisure and less access to different forms of leisure. They seldom take advantage of leisure and cultural institutions.

The desire for more free time and leisure often takes the form of a conflict between generations. This trend is an essential factor in making decisions concerning the modernization of a farm or a household. For young people, the amount of free time and leisure is an important factor when deciding whether to migrate to a town or to work in industry. There are often unfavourable side effects of this phenomenon in rural communities as it causes a decline in population in villages and a lack of successors on the farms. There is also the phenomenon of the transformation of existing leisure patterns in towns into more standard patterns of leisure. In general, the problem of leisure within the rural community is a wide field of investigation that is as yet relatively untouched.

Leisure and Social Groups
(Family, Classes and Generations)

Social groups such as the family, social classes, and generations, have been to varying degrees the subject of analysis for the sociology of leisure. The problem that holds the greatest interest is that of senior citizens' leisure. Certain countries such as France and Canada have been gathering interesting statistical data over the years, which have been presented in different sociological papers. Normally, the authors of these elaborations point out the need to increase practical research in the area of senior citizens' leisure activities. This is equally true for other generations: children, youths, and adults.[15]

The family as a social group and its relationship with leisure has been to a lesser extent the target of leisure sociology studies. Some essential insights have been gained as a result of these studies, but in other branches of sociology: the sociology of the family and marriage, and the sociology of culture. However, these studies were easily adapted to the formulations and categories of the sociology of leisure. One notable exception is a publication by a group of English sociologists which presents new possibilities for empirical research.[16]

The question of leisure conceived in the light of the problems connected with social classes, which are discussed in the rudiments of sociology, has not found its way into the empirical research of the last twenty years. Previous hypotheses have maintained that being a member of a certain class is the variable determining access to leisure in its various forms and that this association loses importance when the variable which could be described as 'individual likes and dislikes' comes into play. In spite of introducing the independent variable 'professional status' into recent studies, not all the conclusions relating to leisure in respect to social classes have been presented.

CONCLUSIONS

Sociology, along with philosophy, constitutes a study with one of the longest traditions of research with respect to leisure; this statement can be substantiated by an examination of the history of the social sciences of leisure. Moreover, this tradition is already long-lived enough to have sparked internal criticisms. But the sociology of leisure is not always a true sociology. It is not difficult to show that many of the so-called 'sociological explanations', and a great number of the notions, derived more from common sense, are stamped with a conformity that results in many a value judgment. This situation generally manifests itself at two levels: in the sociological literature itself, as well as in the manuals and treatises; in the latter case it is a question of a pseudo-sociological discourse, which holds back rudimentary sociological approach and of course contents itself with these interpretations. Under these circumstances, it is not surprising that the sociology of leisure is downgraded and at a disadvantage in the field of sociology in general.

This twofold dilemma — a sociology of leisure that may not always be sociology, and a strong presence of normative judgments, may be explained in part by the relative absence of demarcation within the social phenomena of leisure. The sociology of leisure has centred on the object of study without being sufficiently detached, without observing it from a distance, like a fact; on the contrary, it is often difficult to distinguish among the sociologists of leisure, that which arises out of analysis and that which arises from militantism, that which is in the nature of an explanatory concept and that which is derived from euphoric speeches which talk about individual liberty and the promised land.

Besides the variety of fields already covered in the second half of this text, there are many areas as yet untouched. We could mention for example the study of social time, space, the history of workers' struggle for time away from work, the study of the ideologies of leisure; there are still aspects of current themes that we have only looked at: sociocultural leadership, cultural politics, popular culture, professionalism among the organizers, management problems, land management; and even public holidays, vacations, the problems of aging, continuous education, etc. Leisure constitutes a vast field of research which intersects a number of other problems, and he who is interested must also occupy himself with the phenomena of work, the social classes, the culture, the way of life, to mention just a few. From this perspective, it is obvious that one must bypass the traditional notions of 'activity' or of 'free time' and go beyond the limited interpretations of the time-budget studies. These approaches, with their restrictive historical dogmas, are incapable of putting together the sociological foundations of leisure.

It seems to us that the only road left open is a return to fundamental sociology, to a more classical tradition. But that, of course, would never suffice, for it is the questions that sociology asks about the aspects of leisure and popular culture, to which Durkheim, Marx, or Weber, to name but a few, were grasping at. This return to a fundamental sociology signifies rather an objectivity, a demarcation, clearly separating these euphoric or utopian approaches to which we have made allusion and distinctly dividing the analyses from the action. Furthermore, we feel that with a return to sociology the understanding of leisure imposes itself; in this case, we say that it is indispensable for getting in touch with the conditions producing the sociological understanding of leisure in the sociohistorical situations in which they take place; in this respect, the sociology of leisure has not really begun an auto-critique, it has not positioned itself in relation to its task, so as to see clearly its relationship to the social determinants themselves; the sociology of leisure is a social phenomenon among so many others and, in this respect, is dependent on social factors...

We must point out again that resorting to a sociology of knowledge leads directly to a sociology of the social sciences of leisure and of culture. This time it really is a question of the history of the progressive introduction of scientific rationality in a new field of interest, 'the interest of understanding'. How was this modern interest in leisure developed? What historical outline has it derived from? Does this outline resemble in any way the path taken by the sociological tradition, such as can be observed in other phenomena? What epistemological obstacles did it have to face? What social and cultural changes correspond to the emergence of the social science of leisure and what is at stake? Who is served by the sociological understanding of leisure, and to what extent has this understanding been assimilated by the institutions and professionals involved?

There are as many other questions which researchers are slow to voice, and which will not be able to be brought out until after a more critical examination of the historical and sociological foundations of the sociology of leisure has taken place. A new diagnostic, new interpretations, are imposed on the field of the sociology of leisure, not only by an approach that is more critical and fundamental, but also in taking account of the current transitions in modern society: the economic crisis and unemployment, the decline in counter-cultural movements, the technological changes, the rise of technocracy, the development of international capitalism in terms of tourism — so many questions which are strongly affecting leisure and with which it must settle.

NOTES

1. Max Weber, *Gesammelte Aufsätze* zur *Wissenschaftslehre*.
2. Friedrich Engels, *La situation de la classe laborieuse en Angleterre*. Paris: Editions Sociales, 1973, p. 386.
3. Cf. Marion Cotter Cahill, *Shorter Hours: A Study of the Movement Since the Civil War*. New York: Columbia University Press, 1938.
4. Since no comprehensive study of this question has been made, we must refer to an unpublished study, Gilles Pronovost, 'Les transformations de la problématique du loisir aux Etats Unis', 110pp , biblio., mimeo.
5. Cf. Léon Bramson, *The Political Context of Sociology*. Princeton: Princeton University Press, 1961; Nicolas Herpin, *Les sociologues américains et le siècle* ('Le sociologue'). Paris: PUF, 1973.
6. Cf., as an illustration, Richard Kraus, *Recreation and Leisure in Modern Society*. New York: Appleton-Century-Crofts, 1971.
7. Cf. Cacères (1964).
8. Cf. Raude and Prouteau (1956).
9. The main pertinent publications of Friedmann are listed in the bibliography.
10. 'Ce ne sont pas les problèmes du loisir qui sont apparus en premier lieu; ce sont les questions de *l'éducation populaire*', quoted from: J. Dumazedier: 'Loisir-éducation permanente-développement culturel', in *Education ou aliénation per-*

manente? edited by Gaston Diveau. Paris, Bordas and Montréal: Dunod, 1977, p. 107.
11. Cf. Dumazedier and Markiewicz-Lagneau (1970).
12. Cf. 'Tendances de la recherche en matière de loisir au Canada/Trends in Canadian Leisure Research', *Loisir et Société/Society and Leisure*. Québec: Presses de l'Université du Québec, II, 1, April 1979.
13. This international comparative research was conducted by the International Committee on Sport Sociology.
14. See Menahum Rosner, 'Changes in Leisure Culture in the Kibbutz', *Loisir et Société/Society and Leisure*, II, 2, November 1979, pp. 451-81.
15. See 'Vieillissement, retraite, loisir/Aging, Retirement, Leisure', *Loisir et Société/Society and Leisure*, II, 2, November 1979.
16. Rapoport and Rapoport (1975).

REFERENCES

Cacères, Benigno (1964) *Histoire de l'éducation populaire.* Paris: Seuil, 253pp; biblio.
Cheek, Neil H. and Burch, William R. (1976) *The Social Organization of Leisure in Human Society.* New York and London: Harper and Row, xx, 283pp.
Coronio, G. and Muret, J.-P. (1974) *Loisir. Du mythe aux réalités.* Paris: Centre de recherche d'urbanisme, 271pp.; biblio.
Dumazedier, Joffre (1974) *Sociologie empirique du loisir.* Paris: Seuil, 269pp.
Dumazedier, Joffre and Guinchat, Claire (1969) 'La sociologie du loisir. Tendances actuelles de la recherche et bibliographie internationale (1945-1965)', in *Current Sociology. La sociologie contemporaine.* Paris: Mouton, 1969.
Dumazedier, J. and Markiewicz-Lagneau, J. (1970) 'Société soviétique, temps libre et loisirs, 1924-1964', in *Revue francaise de sociologie*, XI, 2 (April-June): 211-29.
Dumazedier, J. and Ripert, A. (1966) *Loisir et culture.* Paris, Seuil, 398pp.; annexes; biblio.
Dumazedier, Joffre and Samuel, Nicole (1976) *Société éducative et pouvoir culturel.* Paris: Seuil, 298pp.
European Centre for Leisure and Education, *Annotated Bibliography on Leisure.* 13 titles have been published: Hungary, Poland, France, Great Britain, USSR, etc.
Friedmann, Georges (1946) *Problèmes humains du machinisme industriel.* Paris: Gallimard.
Friedmann, Georges (1967) *Où va le travail humain?* (Coll. 'Idées'). Paris: Gallimard, 3rd edn., 385pp.; appendices.
Friedmann, Georges (1971) *Le travail en miettes* (Coll. 'Idées'). Paris: Gallimard, 374pp.; appendices.
Huet, Armel, Ion, Jacques, Lefebvre, Alain, Miege, Bernard and Peron, René (1978) *Capitalisme et industries culturelles.* Grenoble: Presses Universitaires de Grenoble, 199pp.

Ion, J., Miege, G. and Roux, A.-N. (1974) *L'appareil d'action culturelle*. Paris: Ed. Universitaires.

Kando, Thomas M. (1980) *Leisure and Popular Culture in Transition* (2nd edn.). St-Louis: C. V. Mosby, 343pp.

Kaplan, Max (1975) *Leisure: Theory and Policy*. New York: John Wiley, 444pp.; index.

Kaplan, Max (0000), *Leisure: Perspectives on Education and Policy*. Washington, DC: National Education Association, 1201, 16th St., NQ Washington, DC, 20036, USA, 128pp.

Lafargue, Paul (1977) *Le droit à la paresse*. Introduction by Maurice Dommanget ('Petite collection Maspéro'). Paris: Maspéro, 153pp.

Lanfant, Marie-Françoise (1972) *Les théories du loisir* ('Le sociologue'). Paris: PUF, 254pp.

Lynd, Robert S. and Lynd, Helen Merrell (1959) *Middletown, a Study in American Culture* (Copyright, 1929). New York: Harcourt and Brace, 550pp.; appendices; index.

Lynd, Robert S. and Lynd, Helen Merrell (1965) *Middletown in Transition, a Study in Cultural Conflicts* (Copyright, 1937). New York: Harcourt, Brace and World, 604pp.; appendices; index.

Mills, Charles Wright (1956) *White Collar. The American Middle Classes*. New York: Oxford University Press, 378pp.

Parker, Stanley Robert (1976) *The Sociology of Leisure*. London: Allen and Unwin, 157pp.

Pronovost, Gilles (1978) 'La recherche en loisir et le développement culturel', pp. 355-74 in *Loisir et Société/Society and Leisure*, 1, 2. Montréal: Presses de l'Université du Québec.

Rapoport, Rhona and Rapoport, Robert N. (1975) *Leisure and the Family Life Cycle*. London, Boston: Routledge and Kegan Paul, 386pp.

Raude, Eugène and Prouteau, Gilbert (1956) *Le message de Léo Lagrange*. Paris: éd. de la Compagnie du livre, 250pp.

Riesman, David (1970) *The Lonely Crowd. A Study of Changing American Character*. New Haven: Yale University Press, 4th edn., 386pp. (traduction française, Paris: Arthaud, 1964).

Roberts, Kenneth (1979) *Contemporary Society and the Growth of Leisure*. London: Longman, 191pp.

Smith, M. A. et al. (eds) (1973) *Leisure and Society in Britain*. London: Allen Lane, 324pp.

Szalai, Alexander (ed.) (1972) *The Use of Time. Daily Activities of Urban and Suburban Populations in Twelve Countries*. The Hague, Paris: Mouton, 868pp.; biblio.

12
From Medical Sociology to the Sociology of Health: Some Changing Concerns in the Sociological Study of Sickness and Treatment

Andrew C. Twaddle
University of Missouri

This paper attempts a review of major developments in the sociological study of health, sickness and activities directed toward healing over the past decade. While prompted by an invitation from the research committee of the International Sociological Association, it provides a welcome opportunity to assess changes in the field and to try to discern needed directions of research. It will explore the thesis that there has been a shift from an intellectual stance that might best be characterized as 'medical sociology', focussing on medicine as the key health-relevant occupation and treating all other concerns as they impinge on the medical, toward one that might better be characterized as 'the sociology of health', a much broader concern with social, psychic and biological wellbeing which includes medicine as only one of several relevant foci and which takes a more critical stance relative to medical interests.

A related thesis is that sociological stances relative to health, sickness, healing roles and service organization are a complex function of developments in the state of sociology as a discipline and in the state of health and sickness care in the society. They are not reducible to ideological issues, although these are certainly relevant, nor are they a simple function of documenting 'progress', technological or otherwise. As Richard Hessler and I asserted several years ago (Twaddle and Hessler, 1977), health and sickness issues are grounded in historical and cultural issues. While there have been significant changes in the discipline over time, these seem to be more developmental than a matter of a radical break with the past. Our ability to analyze problems in health care has improved and some account of this will be attempted here.

A few caveats are in order before starting. First, this paper is the product of someone who identifies in large part with the study of sickness and the social response to sickness as a field of study. In this effort, I am in the second generation. I was not among those who founded the specialty and it is with some embarrassment that I review the early developments for an audience that includes the founders (see Sokolowska et al., 1976). Second, much of my career has been in medical schools and hospitals in which I have been continuously challenged to show how social science can be used by medical people in the solution of their problems (what Strauss, 1957, called sociology in medicine). At the same time, I have been militant in my assertion of the primacy of sociological perspectives. To me, the only justification for being in a medical setting is to further the cause of sociological knowledge (sociology of medicine). Within the medical setting, I have seen myself ideologically aligned with the interests of patients and concerned to redress the enormous and growing imbalance of power I see in the physician-patient relationship. My role in teaching medical students about patient needs can simultaneously help to create a more human care and to increase the relative power of the professional. It is one about which I have profound ambivalence which shows in most of my work, not least here. Finally, within sociology, I take a theoretically eclectic position. I am interested in theory more for the questions it raises about social order and change than for the answers it provides. I am not uncomfortable with the variety of theories we now have. I regard each of them as having value in raising questions ignored by others. I do not think we have an immediate prospect of developing a single general theory, Parsonian or Marxist, that will adequately incorporate the range of needed questions.

With this background, I purpose to examine briefly and, given the limitations of space and time, somewhat superficially, (1) the social and historical context that gave rise to medical sociology in the 1950s and 1960s; (2) the early dual focus of the field on sociology *in* and *of* medicine, (3) the social and historical context that is moving us toward a sociology of health, and (4) the parameters of a sociology of health that seem to differentiate it from medical sociology.

THE SOCIOHISTORICAL CONTEXT OF MEDICAL SOCIOLOGY

As Richard Hessler and I have argued elsewhere (Twaddle and Hessler, 1977), medical sociology arose from developments in both sociology and medicine which led to an articulation of interests in the middle of this century. The main lines of this argument were as follows.

Sociological Developments

Developments in sociology had provided a groundwork for the emergence of a specialty in medical sociology. These developments could be found with reference to subject matter, theoretical concerns, and research methods.

With reference to *subject matter*, the most important sociological tradition was demography, specifically the long-standing tradition of mortality studies and the emerging concern with morbidity. Going back into the 1600s we can trace the study of mortality from the work of Graunt in London and Petty in Dublin to modern times throughout the world. Death rates have been analyzed as indicators of the quality of life and as indicators of the health of populations as well as being components of the study of population composition and change. During this period considerable sophistication has developed with respect to measurement and international conventions have been developed with respect to definitions of key concepts. Recently, the attention of demographers has turned increasingly to morbidity, as the interpretation of causes of death with reference to medical categories became important in this century.

A large number of *theoretical developments* has also created a fertile ground for medical sociology. Two of these constituted sociological traditions and several others constituted specific theoretical studies. While also serving to define medicine as part of the subject matter of sociology, they came out of the mainstream of sociological thinking. A minimum list would have to include the following.

(1) The *organic tradition*, following from Spencer, provided some common ground conceptually with medicine by conceptualizing societies as organisms. While falling into disfavour, this tradition contributed the important concept of system, in which wholes are seen as more than the sum of their parts and changes in one part are seen as affecting each of the other parts.

(2) The *debunking tradition* (Berger, 1963) is inherent in sociology as research findings inevitably challenge the cherished beliefs of some segment of the society. As a self-conscious motif this has led to the puncturing of the myths generated by and for the most powerful and prestigious groups. Such groups as physicians and corporations have received special attention.

(3) *Durkheim's study of suicide* gave central attention to a subject that was to become of central relevance to medical specialists, particularly psychiatrists. Although there was no medical sociology at the time, Durkheim might fairly be considered the first medical sociologist.

(4) The *concept of cultural lag* developed by the Chicago School was developed with medical care as a case example (Ogburn, 1922). It was a made to order concept for such work as Sydenstricker's (1930) study of health services to the poor and Moore's (1927) study of the relationship between social change and the development of medical services.

(5) *The Lynds' study of Middletown* (1929, 1937) was one of the first major empirical studies of social class. In reporting on the pervasive influence of class on American small town life, they documented differences in health practices and the treatment of disease.

(6) By far the most influential development, however, was *Talcott Parsons's* (1951) *theoretical treatment of professions and clients*. Dissatisfied with unidimensional concepts of social change, Parsons was attracted to the fact, as he saw it, that at the same time that the businessman emerged as a dominant figure in the transition to capitalism, the professional was also becoming a dominant occupation. Further, the professions differed from business in that they took a collective stance toward the interaction with clients, while the businessman took a competitive one. This analysis, whatever its merits, centred attention on the physician as a prototype professional and the patient as a prototype client. Further, Parsons conceptualized sickness as a form of deviant behaviour, placing it as an important element in the existing sociological study of social control, analyzable in comparison with crime and the law.

This treatment by the leading theorist of the century made the establishment of medical sociology an accomplished fact.

The most important *methodological development* was the survey including Lazarsfeld's creation of the panel design, the scaling techniques of the *American Soldier*, and multivariate techniques. These techniques could be not only taken over and applied to medical concerns, they provided a basis for collaboration between sociology and medicine.

Developments in Medicine

Two main developments in medicine were of major importance to the development of medical sociology, the theoretical crisis associated with the collapse of the explanatory power of the germ theory of disease and the changes in the organization of medical services that made problematic issues that were of central concern to sociology.

The theoretical crisis involved the germ theory of disease that has dominated medical thinking for the past century. With Pasteur's synthesis of the observation of microorganisms, which had been known since the 17th century, with the ancient Greek theory of contagion, microorganisms had come to be thought of as the cause of disease and the search for chemical substances that could be introduced into the sick person, killing the microorganisms without simultaneously killing the host, became the major focus of research. Immunization and vector control became the core of epidemiological thinking, and disease became the core of the medical curriculum. Skill at performing diagnostic tests and in selecting appropriate drugs became the hallmark of the good physician. The earlier focus of medicine on the social context of disease and on the public policy questions regarding health receded to the background. In the United States the Flexner Report, which set the modern medical curriculum, was implemented by the American Medical Association with major financial support from the economic elites of the society. (It is not coincidental that the focus on disease diverted attention from social reform.) (Garfield, 1979.)

The crisis in the theory had been developing slowly for many years. It has many elements, among them the following.

(1) As noted by Dubos (1959) the germ theory is an ideology that makes an implicit claim that all disease is ultimately conquerable. Instead, he observed that germs are a necessary, but not sufficient,

cause of some diseases. They do not cause disease unless other environmental conditions are present. The narrowing of focus away from social and environmental concerns would not work and such factors still needed to be taken into account.

(2) The development of psychiatry within medicine was based on demonstrations that some physical disorders did not have a physical cause. Further, psychic factors were implicated in all disease and all disease has psychological components. Coupled with recognition of the importance of social environment for the development of the personality system (Erikson, 1959; Parsons, 1964) it became difficult to treat any illness as simply a physical problem.

(3) Social epidemiology has demonstrated that disease remains socially patterned. Based on social surveys and vital records, it has been shown that the overall success of medicine in reducing the level of disease is negligible, and possibly negative, as rates of chronic disease seem to be rising. Further, the high correlation of many causes of death with social characteristics and with each other has led some epidemiologists to abandon the concept of disease as irrelevant (Syme, 1966).

(4) Health surveys have not only contributed a technique of research to medical interests, but also they have repeatedly demonstrated the continuing relevance of social structures for the patterning of disease and the utilization of health care resources.

At the very least a multicausal mode of diseases seems to be needed. While microorganic life continues to be relevant, it is clear that a germ theory of disease is not. In the search for alternatives the social sciences seem to be a promising area.

The second area of medical development, *changes in the organization of services*, also stems from the germ theory. One result of the germ theory was to establish a medical curriculum based on two years of training in basic biological and physical sciences, two years of supervised clinical experience in a hospital, and the requirements that medical students be able to pass a rigorous examination before being allowed to practice medicine. As I have analyzed elsewhere (Twaddle and Stoeckle, ms; Twaddle and Gill, 1975; Twaddle, 1979), the development of the modern medical school contributed to a chain reaction of changes including at least the following (see Figure 1).

(1) Placing medical schools in universities and requiring a core in the basic sciences improved the level of medical knowledge at a time when population changes were resulting in an increased pro-

FIGURE 1
Trends in Medicine Affecting the Physician-Patient Relationship

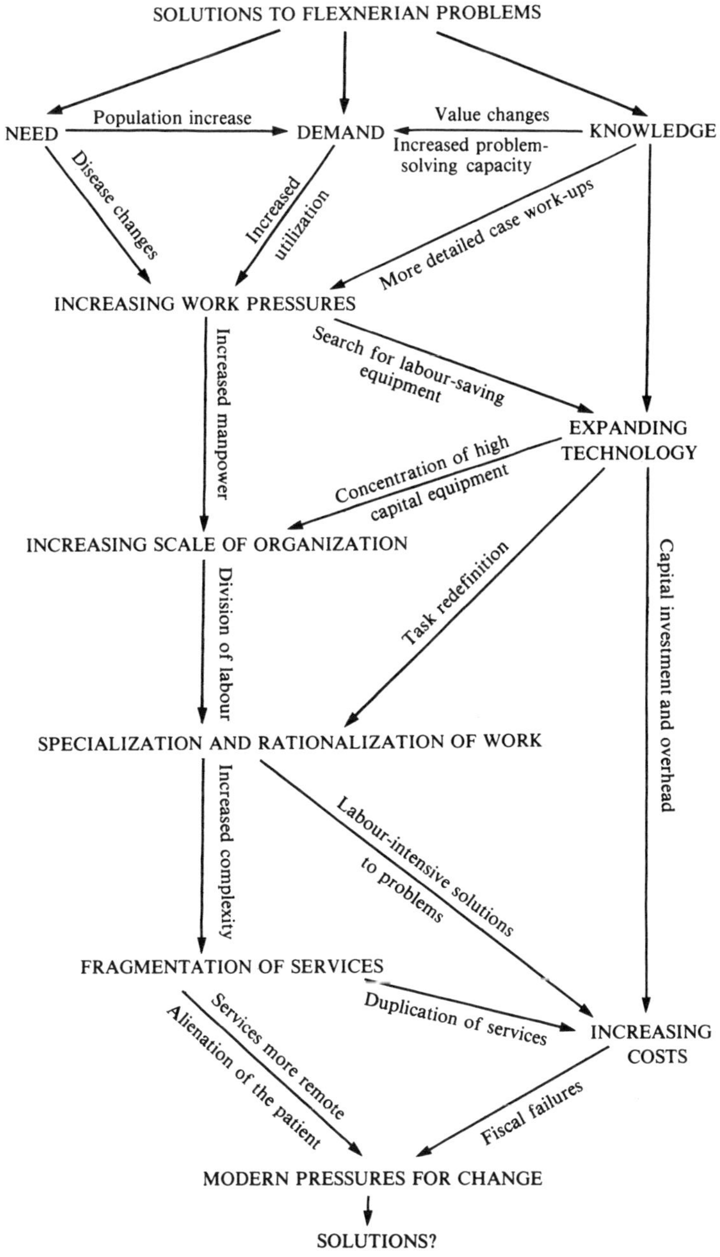

portion of aged, with an attendant increase in the prevalence of chronic disease. Combined, the greater need for medical care and the perceived increase in the effectiveness of medicine resulted in a sharp increase in the demand for medical services.

(2) As a result of improvements in knowledge, diagnosis and treatment became more intricate, requiring more effort in each case. At that same time, in countries like the United States, the number of physicians was shrinking as substandard medical schools were closed. The result was an increase in the work pressures on the medical profession. Each physician was under pressure to provide more service.

(3) Medicine responded to these pressures like any other historical system. First, it increased the scale of its organization by moving practice out of the home of the patients into the clinic and hospital. The trend toward bureaucratization was increased by the need to share expensive new technologies, developed in part in an attempt to find labour-saving means of coping with demand. Second, physicians began to specialize. In advanced countries with relatively autonomous medical professions, physicians practice small subareas of medicine. From the perspective of the patient, this constitutes fragmentation of service. The patient is often faced with the need to see several physicians to treat difficult problems. Medicine is less well coordinated and takes more sophistication on the part of the patient.

(4) The increasing reliance on high technology, the greater labour intensiveness of medicine as a result of bureaucratization and technological elaboration, the increased unit costs of specialized as compared with generally trained physicians, and the inefficiencies introduced by inappropriate consultations as patients to match symptoms with specialists, all combined to drive up medical costs.

These trends have a number of implications. For now, the important ones are that there had emerged new pressures to make the system more efficient for clients. There was a need for cost controls and better organizational forms to improve coordination, and there was a need to provide for a more humane mode of delivering service. We will take up other implications below.

Of core importance is that the central emerging issues facing medicine were those that had long been core concerns of sociology; social organization, interaction and alienation. As we have noted, the developments in sociology made the field ripe for developing a focus on medicine. In that articulation of these interests, medical sociology emerged in the 1950s and was an established specialty by 1960.

THE DUAL FOCUS OF MEDICAL SOCIOLOGY

Medical sociology developed as a specialty that took as given that an understanding of health problems and the mobilization of effective response to those problems of ill health could be found through medicine. During the period following the Second World War medicine had firmly established its credentials as an effective source of treatment of disease. Faith in science was high in Western societies, and this included medicine. Sociologists are never free of their cultures, and the attitudes of medical sociologists reflected those of their societies. Physician-centred scientific healing was 'where the action was' and that is where sociological attention was directed.

There were significant differences in the way in which this physician-centred study developed, however, that were described by Robert Strauss in 1957 as a distinction between sociology *in* medicine and sociology *of* medicine. These approaches differed in their stance toward medicine and other healing occupations, the goals for medical sociology, and in the areas that they emphasized for development. There were also some geographic differences in their development.

Sociology in Medicine

The phrase 'sociology in medicine' was used by Strauss to refer to the applied aspects of medical sociology. In extreme form it referred to sociological work that provided technical skills for the solution of medical problems or of problems in health care delivery without regard for contributions to sociological theory. The work of those primarily concerned with the prevention and treatment of disease, the allocation of resources, and similar problems fell into this category.

The basic stance of people with this orientation is to treat sociology as an adjunct of medical practice, a supporting discipline to medicine. The problems defined for investigation tend to come from the concerns of physicians. The substantive emphasis has been on understanding patients (when and how to do they come for treatment? How can they be made more cooperative? etc.), and disease (what are its social antecedents? How is it distributed in human populations? etc.). Attention has been directed toward microsystems, particularly the physician-patient dyad, sometimes treating these as a complete system of interaction.

The goals of sociology in medicine have been to improve diagnosis and treatment. This has meant getting involved in medical education and in medical settings, particularly hospitals. By teaching medical students interviewing techniques to improve history taking and the elements of social epidemiology to improve disease recognition, the hope has been to make physicians more effective diagnosticians. By teaching about patient perspectives on disease and illness and about hospital organization, it is hoped to improve therapeutic effectiveness. By studying patient behaviour, especially with reference to self-diagnosis and treatment, delay in seeking care, and compliance with treatment, the hope is to find ways to rationalize sickness behaviour and to bring it into line with physician expectations.

This approach has contributed importantly to medical education, social epidemiology, and our knowledge of utilization and compliance. It is an approach that is widespread, and examples can be found in all of the first world and much of the second. If one place were to serve as the prototype that represents an epitome of the sociology in medicine approach, however, it would be impossible to overlook the early years of the Medical Research Council's Social Science Unit in Aberdeen, Scotland, which was formed at the initiative of the Department of Obstetrics and Gynecology at the university and which has built an impressive track record in the understanding of pregnancy and its management.

Sociology of Medicine

Strauss used the phrase 'sociology of medicine' to refer to the basic research aspects of medical sociology. As with education, religion, the family, and the economy, medicine is a social institution worthy of sociological study in its own right. As with other social institutions, the study of medicine generates insights into the properties of social relationships and social organization. The goal of this approach is to learn about societies rather than to understand disease processes or otherwise contribute to medical ends.

The fundamental stance of the sociology of medicine is hence that medical practice is a social institution that can serve as an avenue for understanding society. The problems to be addressed are sociologically defined. Nevertheless, the focus has still been on the physician as the core role in responding to health needs. More attention has been given to other roles (e.g. nursing, chiropractic, social work, etc.) but mostly in the context of their relationships with medicine. Nonphysician roles are seen as adjuncts, ancillary, or supportive with reference to medicine. Moreover, attention is focussed on microsystems, dyadic and small group relationships, or complex organizations, primarily the hospital. This stance differs from that of sociology in medicine in that the world is seen externally to the perspective of the physician, while it is similar in the range of phenomena taken as a relevant.

Rather than improvements in medical practice, the goals of sociology of medicine are to improve the state of knowledge relative to social structures and processes. Such things as complex organization, the biological parameters of human behaviour, social norms and identities, status changes, roles, interaction, and deviance can be studied in medical settings. These settings make explicit some of the criteria and assumptions that are left largely implicit in other settings. For example, the evaluation of human beings on nontechnical grounds is more explicit among physicians than among schoolteachers. The unique concerns of medicine and medical settings highlight questions that are generic to the discipline. The sociology of medicine provides a way of deepening our understanding of our social situation. It has value irrespective of its contributions to medical concerns. Also, it has been argued, a strong, independent, growing social science is of more use in the long run to the healing professions.

The sociology of medicine has led to strong developments in our understanding of the role of the physician, the socialization of physicians, hopsital organization, physician-other interactions, and the social psychology of sickness and illness. While this approach is also spreading world wide it was most characteristic of the early development of medical sociology in the United States, in both the Harvard and Chicago axes.

Medical Sociology: An Appreciation

Medical sociology was well-established as a specialty in the early

1900s. In the United States, it had grown to be the largest specialty group in the American Sociological Association. In the United Kingdom it had become the largest group in the British Sociological Association. A large number of sociologists had devoted part of their research energies to the social institution of medicine.

Toward the end of the 1960s, when I entered the field, the major debate internally was between those studying sociology *in* medicine and those studying the sociology *of* medicine. Those with a more basic approach tended to regard those with an applied focus as having abandoned a sociological perspective and become technicians. Those working in medicine counterclaimed that their contributions to the parent discipline were greater because they had better access to data. David Mechanic suggested a fundamental dilemma for the field in 1968. Medical sociologists could serve medical interests, thus gaining access to valuable information while running the risk of losing their unique perspective, or they could serve basic interests of the discipline, thus retaining their perspective while making access to information more difficult. Some colleagues outside the specialty were led to conclude that the tensions were insoluble and that the field should be considered stillborn.

In fact the focus of the specialty has changed, again for reasons to be found in both the internal dynamics of the discipline and in the character of the problems encountered by the society in coping with health needs. Before looking at these developments, however, it is worth briefly reflecting on the importance of the contributions of those who created the specialty: Talcott Parsons, Raymond Illsley, Robert Merton, Renee Fox, Howard Becker, Saxon Graham, Aaron Antonovsky, Mark Field, Leonard Syme, Samuel Bloom, Julius Roth, Blanche Greer, Eliot Freidson, Magdalena Sokolowska, Hans Mauksch, William Rosengren, David Mechanic, Irving Zola and Peter New to name just a few. The literate reader in the field needs no more assurance that its stillbirth constituted a bizarre misdiagnosis. Further, the focus on medicine has led to important collaborations with some physicians who have also made important contributions to sociology. Manfried Pflanz, George Reeder and John Stoeckle come immediately to mind.

There is, then, value in medical sociology. Yet the field has changed toward what might be considered an emerging paradigm, the sociology of health. I now turn to making some account of that development.

THE SOCIOHISTORICAL CONTEXT OF THE SOCIOLOGY OF HEALTH

The theoretical crisis that contributed to the development of medical sociology has continued and deepened along several lines: the trends already described have led to significant changes in the professional-client relationship and aggravated the problem of cost. New questions have been raised about the effectiveness of medicine and its relevance for solving health problems in the society, and technological developments have led to heightened concern with ethical issues. Partly as a result, medicine has been experiencing increased competition and challenge from other healing occupations and systems. It has also suffered from the crisis of positivism which is a dominant feature of the intellectual landscape of the past decade.

Within American sociology there has been a continuing shift of emphasis, partly as a result of the political crisis of the 1960s and 1970s. There has been a general shift of theoretical focus 'upstream', to use John McKinlay's (1974) image, away from microsystemic concerns of interaction and group dynamics toward a macrosystemic focus on the character of the society. This has led to, or been accompanied by, a renewed emphasis on Marxist thinking and on taking a critical stance with reference to social institutions in general.

Developments in Medicine

The assumptions about the benefits of medicine that were characteristic of the society during the 1950s have been significantly challenged in the 1970s. In the United States, with parallel trends in virtually all European countries, we have already noted the increasing bureaucratization, specialization, technological sophistication and cost of medical services. In the 1960s these were often seen as evidence of 'progress', and certainly of benefit to sociology, as it placed core issues in medical practice within the mainstream of sociological concerns. A second set of implications received more attention in the late 1970s. These same trends, which might be argued to have improved the technical quality of medicine, had also led to deterioration in the quality of medical care.

As Eliot Freidson showed us in 1970, a core feature of medicine is that it had achieved autonomy. Physicians were able to define the content of their work, the criteria for entrance into the profession, the curriculum of study, and the quality of practice. No other group was thought to have sufficient expertise to make such judgments. Further, this autonomy was achieved at a point in history *before* competence had been established as a feature of medical practice. Autonomy was, historically, a function of power and the social definition of reality, rather than something that had been established by objective criteria.

In 1976, at the Fogarty Center Conference on the Physician-Patient Relationship organized by Eugene Gallagher, I was struck with the implicit underlying theme of alienation of patients that seemed to me to run throughout the conference papers. Beginning with that conference, and increasingly over the past several years I have linked the issue of alienation with Freidson's analysis of autonomy and with the analysis of trends in medical practice outlined above. Alienation and autonomy are linked by the central issue of resource control. The more any group gains control over an important set of resources (e.g. the means of production), the more any other group is barred from meaningful decision making (e.g. the more that group is alienated). This refers, of course, to objective alienation. The subjective form analyzed by Seeman (1959) seems to me to be a function of the objective form, but this has not been well investigated yet. The trends in the organization of medical practice seem to me to have resulted in increased professional autonomy for physicians and increased alienation of patients along at least four dimensions (see Figure 2).

(1) With reference to *clinical control*, physicians have increased their level of knowledge about the functioning of the human body and abouts ways of intervening when things go wrong. Relative to physicians, the patient is typically more ignorant and hence more dependent upon medical expertise than at earlier times. The knowledge base of medicine is not simply a justification for autonomy, it has become an essential element. Unless we elect to do away with medical experts, it seems unlikely that physician autonomy in this sector can be reduced significantly. The current emphasis of American public policy toward community health education, improving the competence of the consumer, can have some benefits in teaching interaction skills and, perhaps, with reference to health habits. As a main thrust of health policy, however, it seems at best to be of limited value and at worst a case of victim blaming (Ryan, 1971) that distracts us from more important issues.

FIGURE 2
Professional Autonomy and Client Alienation Dimensions

Professional Autonomy	*Client Alienation*
CLINICAL	
Development of specialized knowledge base and monopoly over distribution of drugs; license to practice	Isolation from medical knowledge; 'true' causes of disease not part of common sense; physician needed as intermediary to gain access to drugs; lay practice illegal
ORGANIZATIONAL	
Concentration of practice in settings controlled by physicians (e.g. clinics, offices, hospitals)	Removal of practice from settings controlled by clients (e.g. the home)
ECONOMIC	
Increasing limitation of payment schemes to a monetary fee-for-service system that gives total control over charges to medicine; insurance systems made to conform to fee-for-service	Elimination of barter and weak development of capitation and salaried practice; client must accept medical terms or do without service
CLASS	
Physician achieves the highest income of any occupational group; compared to others has the best in housing and virtually unlimited opportunities to choose and develop his/her own life-style	Patient is assumed to have a capacity to pay far beyond what actually exists; victim blaming common; treatment instructions beyond capacity of many patients

(2) Autonomy and alienation have increased with reference to the *organizations and settings* in which medical care is provided. The movement of medical services out of the home of the sick person and into the clinic and hospital was not a simple change of location that improved physician productivity or a means of increasing the technical sophistication of the service delivered. It was also from the territory of the patient to that controlled by the physician. The physician was no longer a guest of the patient, a role that partially redressed the imbalance of power inherent in disease and in knowledge differentials. On the territory of the physican, the patient faces requirements of showing proper deference. (S)he must act like a guest as well as one in need of service. The literature on territoriality suggests that this is in itself a problem of power.

(3) In the United States, physicians have gained *economic* autonomy through their ability to have the system adhere to a fee-for-service model. How long this will continue, however, is doubtful, as this model makes costs unpredictable, even on an actuarial basis. Insurance companies find themselves increasingly unable to provide coverage for high-risk populations, forcing the government to assume responsibility for the aged, the chronically disabled and other groups for whom coverage is expensive. Both the private and public insurers are increasingly interested in finding an alternative method of financing care, one which makes cost more predictable and controllable. In countries with a much more important public role in health care financing and organization, organizations of physicians still maintain a strong voice in setting fees (as in the private sector in Sweden), salaries (as in the public sector in Sweden and Denmark) or capitation allowances (as in the public sector in the United Kingdom). While varying enormously in degree, economic autonomy of physicians and corresponding alienation of patients seems to be a widespread phenomenon.

(4) The last dimension is the most difficult to describe. Because of the high rewards received by physicians in terms of income, prestige and power it is related to *social class*. Being rich and powerful, physicians are more free than any other segment of the society to choose their own *life-styles*. Both these facets influence patient-physician interaction. Not only does the patient have to cope with the disabilities and discomforts of disease, the strangeness of alien organizations, and the economic problems of sickness, but (s)he must also bridge a widening gulf of social class as well. From the patient side the physician is increasingly an awesome figure who represents people in the community who are

otherwise unapproachable. From the physician's side it is increasingly difficult to grasp, much less understand or appreciate, the circumstances of the patient, particularly the degree to which the patient is constrained by a lack of resources needed to cope with symptoms, follow treatment regimens, etc. With class-linked differences in language and culture, simple communication cannot be taken for granted. By imposing categories and explanations, the physician not only diagnoses and explains, (s)he also claims the power to dictate the nature of reality for the encounter. The childlike dependence of the patient, often attributed to the psychological aspects of sickness, seems equally a matter of surrender against overwhelming odds relative to the terms of interaction itself.

In principle, with the possible exception of clinical autonomy/alienation, these problems can be redressed. In all countries, it seems, steps aimed in that direction can be found. In the United States, and elsewhere to differing degrees, there are movements to 'rehumanize' medicine, by teaching physicians principles of human behaviour and social organization applied to the situation of the patient; consumer movements designed to help avoid physicians by self-care, use of nonmedical care, and 'holistic health' programmes to promote wellness; rationalization movements designed to constrain medical practice and its costs; and a malpractice litigation movement to 'get even' with physicians when other avenues fail. In Sweden, the medical care system is under attack in a more overtly political way from dissident medical students, politicians, and even from the medical community itself, as illustrated in P. C. Jerslid's *Babels Hus*, a novel built around two hospital admissions of Primus Svenson, one to a medical and the other to a surgical service. The nightmares of communication between staff and patient, staff and family, staff and staff and the attendant series of disasters befalling the patient are vividly shown to be just as characteristic of Stockholm as they are of Boston. While taking different forms, the issues in Sweden seem not to be different from those in the United States, with the exception that out-of-pocket cost to the patient is solved in Sweden. Accessibility, acceptability, cost and other problems of providing decent service have not *all* been solved anywhere.

One important manifestation of growing alienation of the public from medicine is found in the growth of malpractice litigation in the United States and equivalent indicators in other countries. Not only have the numbers of malpractice claims risen in recent years, but the size of settlements has also risen dramatically. A parallel development in Sweden is the rise of complaints to the medical responsibility board, which has the power to adjudicate and settle allegations of incompetent or careless practice. In both countries it seems that it is not the out-of-date or poorly-trained or incompetent physician who is the target of such actions, but the highly-trained specialist in the university teaching hospital practicing with state-of-the art technology. This is precisely where medical autonomy and patient alienation are the greatest.

A second development in medicine is a loss of innocence relative to the effectiveness and relevance of medical intervention in disease. In the early 1960s it was almost uniformly assumed that scientific medicine in principle was the solution to health problems, both individually and collectively. This assumption has been significantly challenged in the last decade.

There was a tendency in the 1950s and 1960s to attribute declines in mortality to medical intervention in the disease process. This was in spite of work by demographers and social epidemiologists that demonstrated close associations between social class, urbanization and other features of social organization with the death rate. It was also in spite of earlier work by people like Zinsser (1935) who argued in *Rats, Lice and History* that disease is a historically limited stage in the development of relationship between a microorganism and a host. In time, the organism can be accommodated without causing disease. As developed by Dubos (1959), germs are seen as a necessary, but not sufficient, condition for *some* diseases. It is only under certain environmental conditions that germs cause diseases. With this, the most fundamental theoretical foundation of medicine, the germ theory of disease, appears as an ideological posture which diverts attention from environmental concerns, that may require radical solutions, to the individual host organism, who can be treated without disruption of the social order, what Ryan (1971) later called 'blaming the victim'.

Even if medicine could claim credit for the declining death rate, there were problems. In the United States, a technologically advanced medical system would have to explain why, from the mid-1950s, the death rate ceased to decline for more than a decade. Obviously, some dynamic other than the medical was at work. Virtually every explanation other than the organization of the society has been tried by the medical community.

Further, and of major importance, McKeown (1976) in England has published arguments based on his analysis of death rates in

England and Wales over the past two centuries, that almost all of the decline in the death rate can be attributed to (1) improvements in nutrition, (2) environmental control, and (3) changes in personal habits. Somewhat less than 1% can be attributed to medical intervention into the disease process, either by prevention or therapy. Partial replication of these results in the United States by John and Sonja McKinlay (1977) have produced the same results along with the findings that, for ten of eleven causes of death which accounted for the vast majority of the decline in mortality the first effective medical intervention came after the mortality decline had occurred. The question of the relevance and effectiveness of medicine is now very much an issue.

A third development within medicine has arisen with reference to its moral claims, that it places the welfare of patients first and that in selecting practitioners an ethically-aware recruitment process ensures the safety of the public within the confines of available knowledge. Starting with the Nazi period in Germany it became apparent that in the area of human experimentation there was no reason to believe that medical recruitment or training produced any reason for public assurance. Further, as illustrated by several public cases, gross violations of informed consent were documented. And even further, Beecher reviewed several months of medical journals and concluded that ethical problems were the norm in published research (Beecher, 1970). Medicine faced a moral as well as a technical challenge. There were efforts in the profession to reassess its mission and to 'clean house'. This required a new hard look at the nature of our commitment to things medical.

Competition among Healing Groups

The restriction of medical attention to disease has provided an opportunity for other healing occupations to establish their credentials as independent and autonomous professions, as in the case of nursing, or as clear alternatives to medicine, as in the case of chiropractic.

The leaders of nursing have claimed that the care, as opposed to cure, of the patient with central attention to illness (the subjective, psychological component of poor health) and sickness (the social component) is their central focus. Medicine, according to this ideology, can be left to the diagnosis and treatment of disease, nursing can take over the care of sick people. While enjoying some limited success, particularly in influencing the consciousness of nurses, this ideology is limited in its prospects until physicians, who hold the power, come to recognize the equal importance of care and cure. Nurses who work closely with physicians, have a unique opportunity to influence medical practice by insisting upon the importance of a broadened perspective as well as to provide care on their own to the degree that the system permits.

Another strategy involving nurses and others is to identify tasks now performed by physicians that can be done equally well by others. In part, this follows a de facto shift in decision making, particularly in high-technology settings, where nurses and technicians, being the only ones on the scene at the time of crisis, have been forced to make life and death decisions. Much of what physicians do can be done equally well by others. Much experimentation has been done in transferring responsibility for technical tasks to nurses and technicians, particularly in emergency services and chronic disease management. How far this will go, and whether there will be retrenchment as more physicians enter the market in the next decade (Stoeckle and Goldstein, 1980) remains to be seen.

Nonmedical practitioners are also enjoying a new vitality. There seems to have been an increase in the popularity of chiropractic among groups that have not been the traditional users of those services. In one midwestern United States university town, for example, the number of chiropractors has increased from two to eighteen in the last decade, while the town's population grew by less than 50%. Anecdotally, a visit to a chiropractor's office in 1971 showed a waiting room sparsely populated by working-class and rural people. In 1980, the waiting rooms are filled with middle-class, business and professional people. Most spectacular has been the growth of university students among chiropractic patients.

Professionals outside medicine have taken increased interest in the cost of medical services. Particularly among the insurance agencies, public and private, that have been asked to pay for the services there has been increasing demand for cost control through rationalization of service. Steps are being taken to limit duplication of expensive services, tentatively as in the case of the Health Systems Agencies recently established in the United States, or more emphatically as in the legislated regionalization of hospital and medical specialist services in Sweden. Overproduction of specialists is a major issue in the developed countries. Only Denmark and the United Kingdom seem to have been able to regulate the production of specialists and maintain a system of care based on general practice. Interestingly, these are the only countries spending less than 6% of their Gross National Product on health services. Other countries will have to take similar steps to avoid bankrupting their systems.

The ideological shift of emphasis from disease to 'holistic health' found in many Western countries has also carried with it a shift in the kinds of practitioners that seem to be in demand. Following McKeown, mentioned above, there is reason to believe that improvements in personal habits (e.g. smoking, drinking), environmental changes (air pollution, chemical contamination of land and water resources, etc.) and nutritional improvements have more potential impact on health than medical activities. Accordingly, there have been increased demands for professionals who are expert in these areas: psychologists, nutritionists, physical educationists, environmental scientists and so forth.

Crisis of Posivitism

The past two decades have been witness to a major change in the epistemological basis of science that has started to penetrate both sociological and medical consciousness to different degrees.

One of the most fundamental assumptions we have made about the world for the past two centuries is that it is composed of matter, substance that occupies space, has mass, and can be objectively measured. This was the basis of Newtonian physics, the master paradigm of the modern age. An important development has taken place in physics, which we can associate with Einstein as much as any one person, that has seriously challenged this assumption. Quantum mechanics, with the study of subatomic matter, has come to the conclusion that when we move to units smaller than atoms matter disappears. There is nothing that has mass, takes up space, that can be measured lineally. Instead there is only energy. This is not just a shift in a disciplinary conceptual structure, but one of cultural consciousness. There is no doubt that it is the most important intellectual development of our age or that we have not even begun to understand its implications. We should be alert to two kinds of implications in the short run. First, there is a crisis in theory for all disciplines based on scientific method. Second, the claims of science in the political arena are problematic (cf. Yankelovitch and Barrett, 1970).

For sociology there has been much reappraisal of the epistemological roots of the discipline, particularly with reference to its theoretical structure and its methodological stances. During the 1940s and 1950s there was a tendency toward modelling the field on Newtonian physical science. The assumption was made that there is an externally measurable social reality and that it could be analyzed through rigorous quantitative techniques. This was an era of increasing mathematical sophistication, the development of the beginning of formal theory, and the refinement of survey analysis. By the mid-1960s we became aware of the fact that the physical science model was a construct that was being applied uncritically. Alternative paradigms not only existed but were in use. Increased attention came to bear on the assumptions of the field and the consequences of those assumptions for the subject we were investigating. More methodological caution seemed to be called for and there was a resurgence of exploratory designs to develop concepts empirically.

For medicine, the impact of these developments has yet to be felt. Physicians still assume that positivism is reality, at least with reference to disease and its treatment. In psychiatry the abandonment of Freudian theory has led implicitly to the use of methods that have a nonpositivist basis. Even here, I can identify only Alex Comfort as a physician who has explicitly noticed that the crisis of positivism exists and has implications for medicine.

The crisis, however, has implicitly affected medicine. Without the connections being made articulate, there has been a loss of public confidence in science as the way to solve problems. Partly this is a matter of public expense, as government funds are supporting research and the benefits of such support are not obvious. Partly it is the accumulating evidence that the growth of technology, that is popularly associated with science, has been seen to be ineffective in solving many problems and in some ways it has become part of the problem itself. There is a general 'back-to-basics' movement that rejects experts, particularly scientists. How far this will go remains to be seen. It is having an impact, however, even now.

Developments in Sociology

The past decade or so of sociology has seen a substantial shift in theoretical interest toward macrosystemic theories focussing on

FIGURE 3
Some Current Sociological Frameworks by Forced Domains*

FOCAL UNITS (SUBUNITS)	DEPENDENT VARIABLES (MAIN TYPES)		
	Physical properties	*Physical and symbolic*	*Symbolic properties*
Societies Communities	Ecosystem theory (Duncan) Human ecology (Park, Hawley)	Conflict theory (Marxism and derivatives)	Social systems (Parsons)
Subunits	Area subgroups, individuals	Interest groups, individuals	Institutions, norm patterns
Complex organizations Smaller groups	Organization science**		Latent-manifest functionalism (Merton, Gouldner)
Subunits	Task subgroups, specialists		Interest and reference groups, individuals
Interpersonal relations Individuals	Elementary social behaviour (Homans)	Psychoanalytic theory (Freud, Sullivan and derivatives)	Symbolic interaction (Mead, Blumer)
Subunits	Response patterns	Needs, mechanisms	Defined acts

*Domain refers to the main dependent properties whose variations a given approach seeks to explain and the units these properties characterize. The selected approaches and named representatives are in some cases arbitrary, as may varyingly be said of their placements in the Figure, which aims only to highlight overall, typical contrasts in use. Apart from Parsons and Homans, theorists named are Herbert Blumer, Otis Dudley Duncan, Sigmund Freud, Alvin W. Gouldner, Amos H. Hawley, George H Mead, Karl Marx, Robert K. Merton, Robert E. Park, and Harry Stack Sullivan.

**No single 'organization science' man quite typifies its placement in the Figure, but some work of Conrad M. Arensberg, F. J. Roethlisberger and William F. Whyte is illustrative.

Source: Taken from Martin U. Martel, 'Academentia Praecox: The Aims, Merits and Empirical Scope of Parsons' Multisystemic Language Rebellion', in H. Turk and R. Simpson, *Institutions and Exchange* (Indianapolis: Bobbs-Merrill, 1971).

social change and a shift of methodological interest toward exploratory design aimed at grounding concepts in the cognitive orientations of acting human beings. There has been a turn away from formalism in both theory and method.

Martel (1971) offered a useful classification of theory which focusses on (1) paradigms (this is not his term, but corresponds reasonably well to Kuhn's [1970] and Friedrichs's [1970] usage) which he classifies as physical (modelled on the physical sciences and viewing social events independent of human meaning), symbolic (taking meaning and meaning systems as central data), and mixed (combining aspects of physical and symbolic paradigms); and (2) focal units, or the scope of human groups or aggregates made problematic by the theory, ranging from societies to dyadic interaction (see Figure 3). Describing theoretical changes in the last decade or so, my impression is that there has been a decline of interest in the physical paradigm and an increase of interest in the mixed and symbolic paradigms. Further, there has been a shift toward larger focal units. Looking at this shift in terms of more traditional theoretical classes, there has been less interest in exchange theory, human ecology and psychoanalytic theory, probably some increased interest in symbolic interaction and phenomenology, some decline in concern with latent and manifest functionalism, increased interest in social systems theories, and a marked increase of interest in conflict theories drived from Marxism.

One way of looking at this change is to say that sociology, which especially in the United States but also importantly in Europe generally, has become less psychological. There is less concern with the individual and the understanding and prediction of individual behaviour as this can be understood by analyzing the immediate social situation of individuals. More attention has been given to understanding societies, political and economic structure, and the like.

In the process there has been some acrimony, claims that the new macrofocus, by taking attention from individuals and their concerns, leads to a dehumanized conception of sociological interests, counterclaims that focussing on the individual and the structures of small groups leads to false consciousness by psychologizing events that can only be adequately understood at the macrolevel. If Martel's classification means anything, it is that theories differ not only in their assumptions, specification of variables, and strategies for research, but also, and most importantly, in the kinds of phenomena they attempt to explain. The kind of 'either-or' thinking reflected in the claims and counterclaims noted must be replaced by a 'both-and' approach that takes the view that all of the theoretical approaches so far developed have likely succeeded in capturing some aspects of social reality. None has captured all. There is no refuge in psychological reductionism or in ignoring actors. But the ecological and the atomistic fallacies still hold.

Methodologically, attention seems to have turned toward 'softer' approaches to data collection that put more emphasis on meaning and on the 'grounding' (Glaser and Strauss, 1965) of concepts in the experience of respondents. There has been a resurgence of work using participant observation techniques and there has been more work using focussed interviews and content analysis. While there has been no decline in mathematical sophistication and the use of formal methods, this area is much less the centre of our technical armoury than was true in the 1950s and early 1960s. Less relative attention is given to survey research techniques (partly because of funding difficulties), mathematical modelling, and experimental design.

That there are disjunctures and contradictions between the theoretical and methodological trends seems obvious enough. We seem to be in a period of ferment in a field that is seeking new breakthroughs, not just in our understanding of societies and other dimensions of social life, but in the way in which those understandings are to be achieved. In this climate predictions are hazardous and none are offered here.

Of core importance is that in both medicine and sociology there have been changes that seem to mandate a closer look at larger units of analysis and that demand better understanding of the effects of social systems on individuals. There is a new appreciation of the fact that smaller units need to be understood in the context of larger ones.

Toward a Sociology of Health

The changes in the issues facing health services have forced a reappraisal of the efforts of medical sociology that have redirected effort in a direction we can call a sociology of health. This shift has resulted from a critical stance taken by sociology toward itself in recent years.

At a conference organized by the International Sociological Association in 1973 in Jablona, Poland, Bloom (1976) noted that there was an emerging international convergence of academic and applied interests as European sociology became more academic and American more applied. In the United States, Bloom noted a shift in medical sociological writings in the 1950s and 1960s.

From	To
A social-psychological frame of reference	Institutional analysis
Small-scale social relations as subjects of research	Large social systems
Role analysis in specifically limited settings	Complex organizational analysis
Basic theoretical concerns with classic social analysis of behaviour	Policy science directed toward systematic translation of basic knowledge into decision making
A perspective of human relations and communication	Power structure analysis

In 1974, at the Fourth International Conference on Social Science and Medicine, Illsley traced the development of British medical sociology. It began by collaboration with medical scientists and focussed on concerns of practitioners and evolved toward a more independent, theoretical stance in which sociological problems took central place. Writing in 1977, Gill and Twaddle saw medical sociology as coopted by medical interests along several dimensions. The common assumption of positivism between medicine and sociology kept the focus of the field unduly on disease and commitment to technological solutions to health problems, on an emphasis on Western medicine as the only relevant type, and on a belief in the benefits of medicine. The focus of the field was on physicians to the extent that alternatives were barely visible in the literature and the professional-patient relationship was seen through physicians' eyes (e.g. with 'compliance' as the central issue). Critical analysis was notably absent. Evidence that medicine has little impact on health has not received sufficient attention. The commitment to technology may debase health in the developed countries by diverting resources from more tractable problems and its export to developing countries intensifies this problem while enriching the industries of the exporters. The implications of the 'medicalization of deviance' (Zola, 1975), in which medicine is becoming the system of social control, requires critical attention that it has not received.

From these critiques and from observation of the literature in recent years there seems to be a shift of focus emerging that encompasses the paradigm models we employ, the units of analysis we use, our definition of health problems, the identification of key healing roles, identification of the main means of healing, the goals of healing activities and the organizations to be taken as central to health. Sociology is divorcing from the medical perspective and medicocentric perspective to one that takes medicine as one element associated with the health of both individuals and populations, the relevance and salience of which needs to be empirically established. This shift is from what we have called medical sociology to what we may call the sociology of health (see Figure 4).

While medical sociology was modelled on biological and sociopsychological paradigms, the sociology of health is based on social-structural and humanistic paradigms. The main change of emphasis has been from a positivist emphasis on the organism and its physiological foibles (sociology in medicine) and on the human personality, social roles and deviance (sociology of medicine) toward an emphasis on social structures in which human beings are enmeshed and the problems we all have in coping with those structures.

There has been a corresponding shift in the units of analysis from individuals and interaction (sociology in medicine) and groups and organizations (sociology of medicine) toward societies and social structures. Diseased people, physician-patient encounters and hospital organization have become less central and the economic and political organization of societies, social classes and ethnic groups have become more central to the sociological analysis of health.

Medical sociology was centrally concerned with disease, illness, and sickness (respectively the biological, psychological and social dimensions of individually focussed poor health). Disease and illness were more characteristic of sociology in medicine while illness and sickness were more characteristic of sociology of medicine. The sociology of health seems to be taking a broadened perspective on all kinds of events, structures, etc. that limit freedom of choice and/or reduce personal effectiveness. A recent Swedish report of a commission to set policy recommendations for the city of

FIGURE 4
Some Dimensions of the Shift From Medical Sociology Toward a Sociology of Health

From: MEDICAL SOCIOLOGY	To: SOCIOLOGY OF HEALTH
1. *Paradigm models* in*: Biological sciences (the organism, physical failure) of*: Psychological and social sciences (personality/ role; deviance	Social science and humanism (coping)
2. *Units of analysis* in: Individuals, interaction of: Groups, organizations	Societies, social structures
3. *Health problems* in: Disease and illness of: Illness and sickness	Limitation of freedom of choice, reduction of personal effectiveness
4. *Key healing roles* in: Physician/patient of: Physician/patient/other professionals	Politicians, nutritionists, educators, lay healers, positive health promoters, public health practitioners, physician substitutes, physicians
5. *Main means of healing* in: Medicines, surgery of: Use of chemicals, changes in activities	Exercise, nutrition, smoking, environmental control, social change
6. *Goals of healing activities* in: Cure (individual) of: Cure, care (individual)	Health, well-being, reduction of morbidity and mortality in populations
7. *Central organizations* in: Hospitals of: Ambulatory and self-care	Informal settings, legislatures, schools, etc.

*'in' and 'of' refer to the distinction between sociology in medicine and sociology of medicine.

Göteborg, for example, has concluded that alienation is the key health problem. Rather than medical care, the core of health policy should be to decentralize public administration so as to return control to local communities, and to improve the physical environment. Whereas disease, illness and sickness are important considerations in that report, medical care has very low profile (Friskvårdsdelegation, 1979).

In medical sociology, the key healing roles were located within medical institutions. For sociology in medicine, attention was given primarily to the physician and secondarily to the patient, who was seen most often as a passive recipient of services. Sociology of medicine paid some limited attention to other health occupations, mostly nursing, but primarily from the perspective of the relationships between physicians and nurses. For the sociology of health, all of the traditional healing roles seem likely to have a lower profile. Politicians, who can legislate changes with major implications for health; powerful groups in the economy who have interests that may be detrimental to or supportive of health concerns and who can most effectively influence politicians; nutritionists, physical educators, positive health promoters, many of whom are loosely organized, have knowledge and resources that can have a major impact on health as this is influenced by personal behaviour and diet; environmentalists, public health practitioners, sanitary engineers, can influence the quality of the physical environment and provide settings that increase resources for coping with stress; these are likely to have a much more important place in sociological consideration. Lay healers, physician substitutes and physicians will receive attention more proportional to their actual impact on health.

While medical sociology emphasized the use of medicines and surgery (sociology in medicine) or a broader focus on the use of chemical substances and activity changes associated with health changes (sociology of medicine) the sociology of health is moving toward a different conception of the main means of healing which focusses attention on social change, environmental control, smoking, nutrition and exercise.

Medical sociology saw the goals of healing activity as bound up with already diseased individuals. The focus was on cure of disease and illness (sociology in medicine) or cure plus the care of the sick person (sociology of medicine). The sociology of health seems to be taking a stance that sees health goals bound up with preventing people from becoming diseased in the first place. Promoting well-being and reducing mortality and mordibity in populations is the newer focus.

Finally, for our purposes here, there is a change occurring in the kinds of organizations taken to be central to the field. This shift is away from the hospital, clinic and self-care centre, which were most important to medical sociology, toward legislatures, schools, public recreational settings, and more informal settings.

This list is by no means exhaustive. The changes we are suggesting are in their early phases and to some degree I am guessing as to what will emerge.

The new issues can be identified, at least in broad outline. They revolve around health promotion and the prevention of disease and illness. The health promotion emphasis must direct attention to the social and physical environments that cause health problems. More work needs to be done to identify and decribe basic human needs (cf. Etzioni, 1968), the social structures that facilitate or frustrate the attainment of the goods, services, settings and facilities necessary for meeting those needs, and the ideologies that support those structures. One major focus will be a relatively new one for sociology, the physical environment. Another will be an old traditional one, alienation.

The preventive emphasis with respect to disease will follow from the McKeown studies. Improved personal behaviours, particularly with respect to the ingestion of chemical substances and smoking are of central importance. Improved nutrition requires attention to an area that has been almost totally neglected sociologically. The physical environment has been noted above. With respect to illness, it will require, in addition to disease prevention, attention to stress, resources needed for effective coping with stress, and alienation (cf. Antonovsky, 1979). Both will require greater attention to corporate interests, social class, and power as key variables and processes.

ON BABIES AND BATHWATER: A SUMMARY AND A CAVEAT

In this paper we have reviewed some developments in the sociological issues surrounding health, sickness and the management of disease and illness. This review has been painted in broad terms in an attempt to identify the main sweep of changes over the past two decades. It has not attempted a literature review (which was considered but rejected as beyond the scope of a short report of this nature). What we have tried to show is that the field has changed along several dimensions in a way that we might characterize as from medical sociology to the sociology of health. These changes have been:

From	To
Sociology as an adjunct of medical practice	Sociology as an autonomous discipline
A microsystem focus on individuals and interaction	A macrosystem focus on social systems and institutions
A physician-centred conception of healing	A system-centred conception of prevention
A technical support stance relative to cure of disease	A critical stance relative to health
A biopsychological stance	A sociocultural stance

These changes have been a result of interactions between changes in the health and medical care systems that have demonstrated the limitations of an individualistic approach to health problems and called into question the efficacy of current social responses to disease and illness, and changes in sociology, both theoretical and methodological, that have called for a more critical stance, both with regard to the concepts and methods employed in research and with regard to subject matter. This paper has called attention selectively to some of the historically specific aspects of these changes as they might be found in the United States and other Western industrialized societies.

If it is conceded that there has been a shift from medical sociology to the sociology of health, it remains to suggest what sort of position we should take with reference to that change. Should we take the position that there has been an evolutionary change that has resulted in an expansion, or shift, in the kinds of variables taken as central to our study; or should we take the position that we have undergone a revolution that makes earlier concepts, methods and variables obsolete? Let me illustrate using photographic imagery.

The evolutionary image is one that I associate with a macrozoom lens, one which allows for extreme close-up photographs and at the same time allows one to 'pan back', taking in a wider and wider area. With this imagery, the same things that were in the close-up photograph remain in the wide angle one and they may even retain a central place in the picture. Those items, however, are not seen in as great detail while at the same time they are seen much more in context.

The revolutionary image I associate with photographs of very different scenes which feature entirely different objects in the photographs. Looking from a wide angle or a close-up perspective suggests that entirely different things are important even apart from their centrality to the overall picture.

Some sociologists have preferred the revolutionary image. Excited by the discovery of new variables and by the importance of social contexts to the understanding of social events, there has been a tendency to reject the social-psychological perspectives and physician-nurse-patient subject matter as obsolete and irrelevant. Certain properties of social life, roles for example, have been ruled ineligible for funded study by certain American government sources. Othes are suddenly 'in', on what seems to be faddish variable-of-the-month mentality in setting social science research policy.

Others take the position that there has been no basic change. The same things need explanation. The only thing that has changed is that gradually we have developed a greater capacity to understand social contexts that illuminate our understanding of the primary problems.

I am not about to enter this division on either side, although I am inclined, if forced to a choice, to see an historical-evolutionary process rather than a revolutionary one. At the same time, it can be argued that the evolution has been rapid and comprehensive in scope, making it very difficult to see the world with the same consciousness. Our approach has changed radically. The new consciousness involves not only new variables and concepts, however, but new ways of seeing the old ones, which maintain their relevance for a complete understanding of health.

Both the internal needs of sociology to develop better understanding of social organization and the crisis in the delivery of health and medical care services in the Western world require much more development of cross-national research than we have yet seen. If we simply list the major criteria for effective systems that have been developed in the last twenty years (availability, accessibility, acceptability, affordability, relevance and flexibility) it is obvious that no nation has created a system that has solved all of the problems (see

FIGURE 5
Criteria for an Effective Health Care System (as Discussed in the US Literature)

An Effective Health Care System Is One in Which Services Are:

Available. They are provided in locations where it is possible for people to reach them. Varies by type of service according to frequency of use and speed with which it is needed

Issues: Distribution of (wo)man power

Accessible. People can avail themselves of them easily

Issues: Plant architecture; charges for service, personnel attitudes, working hours, screening procedures, referral patterns

Acceptable. They are of types that seem reasonable to people and that people want; provided under conditions that preserve the dignity and self-respect of patients and which help to solve their problems rather than worsen them

Issues: Waiting times, physical privacy, personnel attitudes, interpersonal skills, fragmentation of service, alienation

Relevant. They are of a type that meets the needs of the people they are intended to serve and that is appropriate to the kinds of health problems they have

Issues: Appropriate technology, specialization, scale of organization, professional autonomy

Affordable. They are designed so as to not bankrupt the larger systems they ostensibly support. The society can absorb the cost

Issues: Appropriate technology, specialization; fragmentation, scale of organization, professional autonomy, alternative roles, taxation policy

Flexible. The services can adapt to individual needs, local conditions and changes in the population being served

Issues: Alternative systems, administrative rigidity, process planning

Figure 5). Equally true, all nations have taken steps to address some of them and there is universally growing concern with the rest. We need good research as never before that compares national systems with reference to such criteria. We need to identify the degree to which these goals are attainable, separately and jointly, and the conditions that predict success. Tradeoffs need to be made explicit. Mark Field, Magdalena Sokolowska, Derek Gill, Vincente Navarro, John Butler and others have begun to break the trail. The work has yet to really begin.

I am very distrubed by the stance of some of my colleagues that understanding macrosystemic processes and structures is both necessary and sufficient. Equally necessary, and equally insufficient, are the microsystemic structures and processes: personalities, roles, interaction, identities, group dynamics, and the like. We need to beware of both the atomistic and the ecological fallacies. There is a critical need for maintaining a dialectal consciousness of the fact that societies are simultaneously made of structures and people. We are at a very exciting point of new departures, but we will lose the potential of the moment if we attempt either a dehumanized conception of society or a desociologized conception of humanity.

REFERENCES

Antonovsky, A. (1979) *Health, Stress and Coping*. San Francisco: Jossey-Bass.
Beecher, H. (1970) *Research and the Individual: Human Studies*. Boston: Little, Brown.
Berger, P. (1963) *Invitation to Sociology*. Garden City, NY: Doubleday.
Bloom, S. (1976) 'From Learned Profession to Policy Science: A Trend Analysis of Sociology in the Medical Education of the United States', pp. 435-37 in Sokolowska et al., 1976.
Dubos, R. (1959) *Mirage of Health*. Garden City, NY: Doubleday.
Erikson, E. (1959) 'Identity and the Life Cycle'. New York: International Universities Press, *Psychological Issues*.
Etzioni, A. (1968) 'Basic Human Needs: Alienation and Inauthenticity', *American Sociological Review*, 33: 870-85.
Freidson, E. (1970) *Profession of Medicine*. New York: Dodd-Mead.
Friedrichs, R. (1970) *A Sociology of Sociology*. New York: Aldine.
Friskvårdsdelegation (1979) *Göteborgarnas Hälsa*. Göteborg: Kommonfullmaktiges Handlingar.
Garfield, J. (1979) 'Social Stress and Medical Ideology', pp. 33-44 in *Stress and Survival*, edited by C. Garfield. St. Louis: C. V. Mosby.

Gill, D. and Twaddle, A. (1977) 'Medical Sociology: What's in a Name?', *International Social Science Journal*, 29, 3: 369-85.
Glaser, B. and Strauss, A. (1965) *The Discovery of Grounded Theory*. New York: Aldine.
Illsley, R. (1974) 'Promotion to Observer Status', *Social Science and Medicine*, 9, 2: 63-7.
Jersild, R. C. (1979) *Babels Hus*. Stockholm: Primus.
Kuhn, T. (1970) *The Structure of Scientific Revolutions*. Chicago: University of Chicago Press.
Lynd, R. and Lynd, H. (1929) *Middletown*. New York: Harcourt, Brace and World.
Lynd, R. and Lynd, H. (1937) *Middletown in Transition, a Study in Cultural Conflicts*. New York: Harcourt, Brace and World.
Martel, M. (1971) 'Academentia Praecox: The Aims, Merits and Empirical Scope of Parsons' Multisystemic Language Rebellion', in *Institutions and Exchange*, edited by Turk and Simpson. Indianapolis: Bobbs Merrill.
Mauksch, H. (1972) 'Nursing: Churning for Change', in *Handbook of Medical Sociology*, edited by Freeman, Levine and Reeder. Englewood Cliffs, NJ: Prentice-Hall.
McKeown, T. (1976) *The Role of Medicine: Dream, Mirage or Nemesis?* London: Nuffield Provincial Hospitals Trust.
McKinlay, J. (1974) 'A Case for Refocusing Upstream: The Political Economy of Illness', *Applying Behavioral Science to Cardiovascular Risk*. Washington, DC: American Heart Association. Reprinted in Jaco (1979), *Patients, Physicians and Illness*. New York: Free Press.
McKinlay, J. and McKinlay, S. (1976) 'The Questionable Contribution of Medical Measures to the Decline of Mortality in the United States in the Twentieth Century', *Milbank Memorial Fund Quarterly*, 55, 3: 405-28.
Mechanic, D. (1968) *Medical Sociology*. New York: Free Press.
Moore, H. (1927) *American Medicine and the People's Health*. New York: Appleton.
Ogburn, W. (1922) *Social Change with Respect to Culture and Original Nature*. New York: B. W. Huebsch.
Parsons, T. (1951) *The Social System*. Glencoe, Ill.: Free Press.
Parsons, T. (1964) *Social Structure and Personality*. New York: Free Press.
Ryan, W. (1971) *Blaming the Victim*. New York: Vintage.
Seeman, M. (1959) 'On the Meaning of Alienation', *American Sociological Review*, 24, 6: 783-91.
Sokolowska, M. et al. (eds) (1976) *Health, Medicine, Society*. Dordrecht: D. Reidel.
Stoeckle, J. and Goldstein, R. (1980) 'Views From the Clinic: Doctors, Jobs and Money in the USA', *Social Science and Medicine*, 14A: 80-90.
Strauss, R. (1957) 'The Nature and Status of Medical Sociology', *American Sociological Review*, 22: 200-204.
Sydenstricker, E. (1930) *Hagarstown Morbidity Studies*. Washington, DC: US Government Printing Office.
Syme, L. (1966) 'The Clinical Bias in Epidemiology'. Paper presented at the annual meeting of the American Public Health Association.
Twaddle, A. (1979) *Sickness Behavior and the Sick Role*. Boston: G. K. Hall, and Cambridge: Schenkman.
Twaddle, A. and Gill, D. (1975) 'The Concept of Alienation', *Sociological Symposium*, 23: 41-60. (This paper was mistitled through editorial error. The intend-

ed title was 'Autonomy, Alienation and the Allocation of Patients to Physicians'.)

Twaddle, A. and Hessler, R. (1977) *A Sociology of Health*. St. Louis: C. V. Mosby.

Twaddle, A. and Stoeckle, J. (ms) 'Autonomy, Alienation and the Physician-Patient Relationship'. Unpublished manuscript, University of Missouri, Columbia and Masschusetts General Hospital.

Yankelovitch, D. and Barrett, W. (1970) *Ego and Instinct*. New York: Random House.

Zinsser, H. (1935) *Rats, Lice and History*. Boston: Little, Brown.

Zola, I. (1975) 'Medicine as a System of Social Control', in *A Sociology of Medical Practice*, edited by Cox and Mead. London: Collier-Macmillan.

13
The History of Sociology and Substantive Sociological Theories

Jerzy Szacki
University of Warsaw

Let us begin by recalling some questions formulated by Joseph A. Schumpeter:

> Well, why do we study the history of any science? Current work, so one would think, will preserve whatever is still useful of the work of preceding generations. Concepts, methods, and results that are not so preserved are presumably not worth bothering about. Why then should we go back to old authors and rehearse outmoded views? Cannot the old stuff be safely left to the care of a few specialists who love it for its own sake?[1]

Similar questions have often been posed by sociologists as well. Their attitude towards the past of their own discipline could certainly be the subject matter of a separate study that would shed much light upon changes in their states of mind. That attitude was not the same in all stages of the development of sociology and in all its branches. There have been sociologists who denied the usefulness of the classics, but there have also been those, such as Randall Collins, who did not hesitate to state that '[...] in relation to major figures like Marx and Weber [and others] we are like the scholars of the Renaissance rediscovering the Greeks [...].'[2]

It may be said, however, that the sociologists have fairly often been nonchalant about the heritage of the past. Even if they referred to the founding fathers, they would not necessarily read their texts but would remain satisfied with second-hand information, as is shown by the mass of inaccuracies and nonsense written by successive generations of sociologists about their predecessors. I am not sure whether the situation has changed radically despite the visible advances in the study of the history of sociology to be discussed in this paper. An average sociologist has a rather superficial knowledge of the past of his discipline, nor does he think that such a knowledge could add any essentials to his theoretical consciousness. In that respect he certainly differs from an average philosopher, for whom the knowledge of the history of philosophy is usually an important part of his intellectual endowment.

The factors which account for that scantiness of historical interest are fairly complex. In some countries there has been a real breach in the development of sociology, which after the Second World War was being revived by a hasty adaptation of the patterns current in American empirical sociology, and not as a continuation of earlier interests. But the general causes, linked to the changes which sociology underwent in the middle of the 20th century, seem much more important. The accelerated striving for being scientific resulted in an understandable dislike of most earlier works, whose scientific status was very dubious in the light of the new standards. The belief became common that in sociology, as in the natural sciences, it suffices to read the latest works. Moreover, following advances in the division of labour and specialization the works of the classics ceased to be directly useful to an average sociologist. To do correct research in a specialized branch of sociology one does not in fact have to read the works — bulky, often abstruse, and semi-philosophical in nature — written by Marx and Spencer, Simmel and Weber, Mead and Znaniecki. To do such research it suffices to master, on the basis of a possibly recent handbook, the standard techniques and the current theories of the middle range.

It can be argued with reason that such theoretical asceticism disadvantageously affects interpretation of the results of research, and also makes it difficult to cumulate them at a higher level of generality, but this is not the concern of those who practise such asceticism. Further, in modern sociology there are also many specialists in theory construction who think that knowledge of the works of those theorists who were born long ago and did not abide by the patterns of theory construction obligatory for the last few or a dozen years is absolutely unnecessary.

There is no space to discuss here how far a knowledge of the history of a discipline is useful for that discipline itself.[3] Personally, I am inclined to share the opinion voiced on that matter by Ernest Becker, which one historian of sociology adopted as the motto of his book:

A sociology without any sense of its own history will also be a sociology without any knowledge of what its own illustrious scientists have already lived and thought through; it will be a sociology without any sense of its own achievement, a sociology of the 'utterly convinced' beliefs of each new generation of graduate students. Thus for all its methodological pretensions to 'hard' scientific standing, it will be unscientific.[4]

It is not my intention to enlarge upon and to substantiate that opinion. I merely wish to state that the controversy over the attitude toward the history of sociology is always in a sense a controversy over sociology itself. The pursuit of the history of sociology is rarely a completely disinterested undertaking from the point of view of sociological theory and opinions on the vocation of sociology. Note also in this connection that the consciousness of a crisis in sociology has usually been accompanied by some 'returns to the classics'.

The history of sociology has usually been cultivated by sociologists and it is accordingly linked to sociology rather than to history in general or to the history of science. This has had its disadvantages because as *history* it has been pursued in an amateurish manner and in isolation from a broader context. This will be discussed later. For the time being let us consider what sociologists are looking for when they undertake studies of the past of their discipline. I disregard here as a self-evident procedure the study of the opinions of those who have inspired or originated one's own research, because they are a normal element of one's theoretical work and do not constitute a pursuit of historical studies, even if they happen to result in findings that are important for a historian. It seems that interest in the past of sociology on the part of sociologists has had the following sources (which are, of course, not mutually exclusive):

(1) History has certainly been an element that helped to develop the sense of group identity; it was needed as the tradition which held together scholars who otherwise had little in common. This has been pointed out by Edward Shils — who wrote that sociology as '[...] a heterogeneous aggregate of topics' is '[...] held together [...] by a more or less common tradition — a heterogeneous one in which certain currents stand out — linked to common monuments or classical figures or works.'[5]

(2) The history of sociology has often been treated as a convenient way of showing what that discipline is. In particular, sociological theory was often expounded by making a historical or

quasi-historical review of theories. Thus the well-known and still useful book by Nicholas S. Timasheff was oriented to '[...] the historical unfolding of the thought system which is theoretical sociology.'[6] Albion W. Small wrote many years ago 'that the best way of finding out what sociology is, and what it is worth, is to approach it historically.'[7] This opinion has had its advocates to this day.

(3) The history of sociology has been resorted to in order to evaluate the actual value of earlier conceptions as seen from the point of view of one's own ideas. Here is a characteristic statement by Pitirim A. Sorokin:

> At the present moment the field of sociology is overcrowded by a multitude of various and contradictory systems. Every novice who enters the field is likely to be lost in it, and what is more important, such a novice has the greatest difficulty in discriminating between what in all these theories is valid and what is false. Therefore, one of the most urgent tasks of the contemporary sociologist is to separate what is really valid from that which is false or unproved in these theories.[8]

(4) The history of sociology has also often been resorted to as the cumulation of the knowledge already acquired. The classics have been studied in order to find in their works those elements of knowledge which are indisputably valuable. A classical example of this approach can be seen in *The Structure of Social Action* (1937), written by Talcott Parsons with the intention of finding in the sociology of the turn of the 19th century '[...] a coherent body of theoretical thinking.'[9] When it comes to later works, the same statement applies to *The Foundations of Sociological Theory* (1970) by Theodore Abel.

(5) There have been many works whose primary intention seems to have been to order things: their authors, by analyzing earlier sociological conceptions, primarily strive to single out their definite categories and types. This serves both the demonstration of the variety of sociological thinking and the revelation of its always topical dilemmas and problems, but need not necessarily result in drawing up an unequivocal balance sheet. A good example of this approach to the history of sociology may be seen in *The Nature and Types of Sociological Theory* (1960) by Don Martindale.[10]

(6) Many sociologists used to have recourse to the past of their discipline in order to find additional arguments in contemporary discussions of theoretical issues. Thus C. Wright Mills, as editor of *Images of Man* (1960) and author of *The Sociological Imagination*

(1959) wanted to show the superiority of 'the classical tradition' to the 'abstracted empiricism' of contemporary sociology and to find in its 'models' sources of inspiration for sociological reflection. A similar use has been made of the history of sociology by Anthony Giddens, who wrote in the preface to his book on Marx, Durkheim and Max Weber: 'This book is written in the belief that there is a widespread feeling among sociologists that contemporary social theory stands in need of a radical revision. Such a revision must begin from a reconsideration of the works of those writers who established the principal frames of reference of modern sociology.'[11]

(7) Finally, people used to seek in the history of sociology information about the social conditioning of sociology and its connections with ideologies and practical life. Thus, for instance, Hermann Strasser demonstrated, on a historical basis, that '[...] conceptual and explanatory models cannot escape from being affected by normative considerations.'[12] Alvin W. Gouldner made his excursion into the history of sociology in *The Coming Crisis of Western Sociology* (1970) to bring out the moral infrastructure of that discipline.[13] It is also worthwhile mentioning in this connection the interestingly conceived book by G. A. Bryant, namely his *Sociology in Action. A Critique of Selected Conceptions of the Social Role of the Sociologist* (1976).

I do not claim that this review of the uses of the history of sociology in contemporary sociology is complete. The point rather was to demonstrate, by way of examples, that sociologists' interest in the history of their own discipline is not as a rule theoretically disinterested: the underlying intentions, which can easily be discovered, are usually didactic in nature. There is, accordingly, nothing extraordinary in the fact that studies concerned with the past of sociology are not in the least always *historical* in the strict sense of the word. And some authors are quite well aware of the fact.[14] In such fields as sociology, where some 'paradigms' show astonishing vitality, the very fact that a person studies the views presented in the past does not make him a historian. If someone analyzes the works of Marx, Max Weber, or Mead, he can do so as if he studied the works of a theorist who is his contemporary. By the way, such is in general the mechanism of the social functioning of tradition. As a result of this the sphere defined thematically as the history of sociology proves to be fairly heterogeneous in practice. Even the various studies are often heterogeneous: historical in the sense of being concerned with facts from the past, they are not historical from the point of view of the underlying intention, or from the point of view of the research techniques used. A student of the past of sociology usually plays a double role, that of a theorist and that of a historian, and if he is a sociologist who defends his own theoretical or ideological standpoint, his role as a historian is pushed into the background.

A theorist is interested in the past only with regard to what is still topical and can, regardless of its original context, be presented as a systematized set of theorems. A historian is interested in that original context and is inclined to think that, as Mannheim claimed, a change in the context of a theorem inevitably changes its meaning. A theorist sees in every thinker one of his contemporaries, while a historian looks at him from a distance. This dual approach is a danger to the very sense of identity of a historian of sociology: by becoming a theorist he wins a strong position among sociologists and probably can influence their way of thinking more strongly; by engaging in the study of the past he ceases to be a sociologist and becomes one of the many representatives of intellectual history, history of ideas, or history of science, whose production need not be of any interest to sociologists. One extreme can best be illustrated by *The Structure of Social Action* by Talcott Parsons, already mentioned above, a work concerned with the past of sociology, but in no sense historical in nature. The other extreme can be illustrated, say, by *Consciousness and Society* (1958) by H. Stuart Hughes and *Evolution and Society* (1966) by J. W. Burrow, both largely concerned with the views of sociologists but lacking any ambitions except purely historical ones.[15]

The history of sociology (and probably also the history of other social sciences) seems to oscillate all the time between these two extremes. To make matters worse, it is often neither a theory nor a history, but a gallery of portraits of deceased sociologists, whose views are laboriously summarized, such a summary being completed with a few items of biographical information, a modicum of critical remarks, and some clichés on the topicality of this or that idea. Robert K. Merton made a pertinent criticism of this mode of cultivating the history of sociology when he wrote that

> [...] sociologists retain a most parochial, almost Pickwickian conception of the history of sociological theory as a collection of critical summaries of past theories spiced with short biographies of major theorists. This helps to explain why almost all sociologists see themselves as qualified to teach and to write the 'history' of sociological theory — after all, they are acquainted with the classical writings of an earlier day. But this conception of the history of theory is in fact neither history nor systematics, but a poorly thought-out hybrid.[16]

Is then nothing else left to a historian of sociology but to make a choice between the role of a theorist and that of a historian: a theorist engaged in a supratemporal dialogue with his predecessors and a historian who tries to understand his predecessors in the context of time and place? Nothing indicates that historians of sociology are inclined to accept this simplest way out of the dilemma now under consideration. The two most eminent studies in the history of sociology written in recent years seem to prove that other solutions are being looked for. I mean here *Masters of Sociological Thought* (1971) by Lewis A. Coser and *Emile Durkheim. His Life and Work: A Historical and Critical Study* (1973) by Steven Lukes.

Coser's book resembles by its scope and composition a typical 'collection of critical summaries of past theories spiced with short biographies of major theorists'; but it is nevertheless something essentially new in its content because it shows sociological ideas 'in historical and social context'. Coser starts from the assumption that '[...] a correct appraisal of a particular thought is often difficult, if not impossible, if the social context in which it took root cannot be understood'.[17] 'We have', he says, 'a great number of books that attempt to elucidate what Marx or Weber or Pareto really meant but only few and scattered efforts to use the tools of the sociologist to investigate the role of sociological theorists within the social structure in which they are variously placed.'[18] Coser's endeavour to engage in 'the social ecology of sociological ideas' does not break the link between the history of sociology and sociological theory: it does not, obviously, provide criteria of the validity of the latter, nor does it pretend to draw up a balance sheet, but it helps us comprehend it more fully. A historical analysis does not offer any indication as to what sociological theory should be; it merely shows what that theory happened to be and how it really develops. Theory is given a historical interpretation, and history becomes sociological history, and not a mere list of past ideas, with marks of a contemporary sociological wiseacre attached to them.

Lukes's book is a conscious and perhaps even more consistent attempt at linking the theoretical and the historical viewpoints. He says in his extremely instructive introduction that 'This study of Durkheim seeks to help the reader to achieve a historical understanding of his ideas and to form critical judgments about their value [...]. It is a study in intellectual history which is also intended as a contribution to sociological theory...'[19] For considerations of space I cannot engage here in any detailed analysis of that imposing work which shows the way of escape from 'a most parochial, almost Pickwickian conception of the history of sociological theory' without abandoning the search in the history of sociology for something more than just 'a sympathetic understanding' of people of past historical epochs.

One could probably point to to other monographs and short contributions whose authors adopt a similar approach to the issue. It should be borne in mind that in recent years we have witnessed a marked intensification of studies in the history of sociology, which is shown by a number of studies that strive for a synthesis, a growing number of monographs and of editions of sociological classics.[20] It may be said in general terms that in recent sociological literature the tendency to make the interest of sociologists in the past of their discipline really historical is quite clearly marked, although there still appear studies on earlier sociological theories which only apparently approach their subject matter historically.[21]

It seems that this new orientation in the history of sociology is only possible on certain conditions that not all sociologists would be inclined to accept. The first condition is to adopt the view that sociological statements are fully comprehensible only in the framework of the historical context in which they have been formulated, and outside of that context they become devoid of meaning or obscure, and that regardless of our effort to make them precise and systematized. Hence the essential issue is not so much to refer them to what we consider to be the contemporary sociological *science* as to reconstruct the historical wholes to which they belonged.[22]

The second condition is to make sociological conceptions a subject matter of sociological analysis, to formulate a thorough sociology of sociology. The point is not to compare earlier conceptions with contemporary sociology, and to decide whether they have been better or worse than the latter, but to avail oneself of the tools offered by contemporary sociology in a historical study of those conceptions. It has been correctly pointed out that the history of sociology is often less 'sociological' than is the history of other disciplines.[23] Many authors engaged in the study of the history of sociology seem to have believed in the development of pure theory and to have forgotten the sociology of knowledge, the sociology of science, the sociology of ideologies, and many other sociological subdisciplines concerned with the formation and propagation of knowledge. This is why 'the social reconstruction of sociology' remains to be written.

The task is, however, extremely intricate. Without going into details we have to consider what is probably the greatest difficulty, due to the very nature of the subject with which the history of sociology is to be concerned. It is self-evident that that subject matter is strikingly heterogeneous; in fact it is a group of different subject matters held together by the common label 'sociology' or, to put it more broadly, 'social thought'. Even if we confine our interest to 'sociological analysis' or 'sociological thought', the situation will not change radically: we are like those historians who try to write a truly 'universal' history.

A theorist who studies the history of sociology is in a much more convenient situation: he is in a position to shape it into a whole, either by bringing out of it 'a coherent body of theoretical thinking' or by forming such or other constellation of 'types' or 'paradigms'. He simply moves the blocks left by history, without being excessively concerned about how and of what they have been made and what buildings they formed at one time. A historian who would proceed in a similar manner would violate the fundamental rules that hold in his profession. Hence historians in most cases write monographs and brief contributions, without offering any vast panorama of the development of the discipline. In fact, Coser's book I have praised so much is just a collection of monographs. The same applies to the latest and most comprehensive book on the history of sociology, namely *A History of Sociological Analysis* (1979), edited by Tom Bottomore and Robert Nisbet. My own book, *History of Sociological Thought* (1979), is not a historical synthesis either.

What are the obstacles encountered in the making of such a synthesis? Certainly there is an insufficiency of partial studies that would cover the production of the various sociologists and its reception, the history of the various ideas and themes, the development of sociology in the various countries, periods and milieus, the various 'schools' and scholarly periodicals, etc. This is obvious. Research on those matters is progressing, although the studies are still too scattered. Other difficulties are much more serious.

(1) Sociology as a scientific discipline has never formed an organic whole and it is a debatable point whether it can ever become such.[24] Sociology has never been concerned with a homogeneous set of problems that would be typical of it: it has been concerned with all that which did not find a place in other social sciences, or tried unsuccessfully to absorb all those sciences, as was the case of the Durkheim school. The various sociologists

have had little in common except for calling themselves 'sociologists' and working within the framework of the same institutions. This is why we may say about the history of sociology what Christopher Dawson has said of universal history:

> There is as yet no history of humanity, since humanity is not an organized society with a common tradition or a common social consciousness. All the attempts that have hitherto been made to write a world history have been in fact attempts to interpret one tradition in terms of another, attempts to extend the intellectual hegemony of a dominant culture by subordinating to it all the events of other cultures that come within the observer's range of vision.[25]

(2) The evolution of sociology has been strongly multilinear in nature. In this connection we have to point to a number of facts. (a) It would be difficult to disagree with Raymond Aron's statement that modern sociology has two principal sources: the historico-social doctrines, on the one hand; the administrative statistics, surveys and empirical investigation, on the other.[26] As a result of this we note the practice of writing separately the history of sociological thought and the history of empirical research. This division is found, for instance, in the entry for 'Sociology' in *The International Encyclopaedia of the Social Sciences*. The history of empirical research is, by the way, a recent discipline,[27] and it is to be expected that further studies will considerably expand its spheres of interest. (b) What Gouldner has termed 'the binary fission of Marxism and academic sociology' is a well-known fact. Even though Marx's theory has been one of the principal sources of contemporary sociology, there is no doubt that the history of Marxism and the history of sociology have formed, for all the meetings and discussions, two largely separate trends in intellectual history. As a result of this we are still lacking a history of sociology that would also be a full-fledged history of the sociological conceptions in Marxist theory. (c) The differences among the paths of sociology in the various countries are striking, and a historically-minded sociology should necessarily take them into consideration. There are, accordingly, and there will be such books as *Les sociologues américains et le siècle* (1973) by Nicolas Herpin, which greatly contribute to our knowledge of the problem, but in a sense make the possibility of arriving at a comprehensive synthesis even more remote. (d) Sociology has been and is 'a multiple paradigm science' (the term that has become fashionable after the appearance of works by Thomas S. Kuhn) which means that its historian must

always bear in mind its division into 'schools'. Hence an event that is of key importance for one school may be insignificant for (and even unknown to) the remaining ones. To illustrate the significance of this problem it suffices to recall the case analyzed by Edward A. Tiryakian in 'A Problem for the Sociology of Knowledge: The Mutual Unawareness of Émile Durkheim and Max Weber'.[28]

(3) Sociology has been and still largely is a fairly open discipline, by which I mean the comparative ease with which it has absorbed ideas and discoveries arrived at in other areas (not only social sciences, by the way) and also the fact that problems vital for sociology have been and are discussed and solved outside sociology. Can we therefore imagine a history of sociology that does not wander quite far into the spheres of the history of philosophy, social anthropology, psychology and social psychology, and other disciplines as well? It suffices to open any handbook of the history of sociology to see how often its author has to take into consideration the production of scholars who could not be treated as sociologists on institutional grounds. To put it briefly, the history of sociology can only in a limited way be separated from the history of other social sciences, which accounts for the fact that the number of data it has to consider grows alarmingly and exceeds the working capacity of any single researcher.

(4) Finally, we have to pay attention to the fact that, as Parsons put it, '[...] the growth of sociology is a function not only of the sheer scientific merits of the contributions of its practitioners, but also of larger intellectual currents of the time, which have been in part "existentially" determined.'[29] The history of sociology, whatever the degree of autonomy which sociology itself can achieve, remains an integral part of intellectual history and is almost completely incomprehensible out of that context. I mean here not only the links between sociological thought and ideologies,[30] which have been comparatively most frequently studied and are of extraordinary significance. The earlier statement applies to connections between sociology and the entire culture of a given epoch and country, to its roots in social consciousness. A good example of such a look at sociology is provided by the previously mentioned book by H. Stuart Hughes, *Consciousness and Society. The Reorientation of European Social Thought 1890-1930*, or, to take a much more recent one, by Arthur B. Mitzman's *Sociology and Estrangement: Three Sociologists of Imperial Germany* (1973).

All this accounts for the fact that writing a single history of sociology appears to be an almost impossible task, the more so if the requirement of its real, and not merely apparent, historicity is to be taken seriously. It is possible to write a history of sociology in the various countries, a history of sociological 'schools', a history of the concepts and categories used in sociological analyses, a history of the institutionalization of sociology, a history of the various doctrines and theories, a history of empirical research and the techniques used in it, but not a history of sociology as such — at least a history of sociology which would comply with all the requirements we would tend to formulate in the light of the critical appraisal of most work done in that field so far. This statement is not refuted even by the appearance of S. N. Eisenstadt's study (with M. Curelaru) *The Forms of Sociology — Paradigms and Crises* (1976), imposing as to the number of the dimensions considered in it.

And yet we have to try to write such an impossible history of sociology, and that not only for university students, who need such a historical introduction to the problems of their discipline but are not likely to reach for specialized monographs and contributions: such a history of sociology has an important educational role to play when it comes to sociologists themselves. It is just because sociology is so heterogeneous a discipline that its practitioners must all the time bear in mind the large variety of opportunities it offers, opportunities which a history of sociology is in a position to bring out. Just because sociology is not yet a fully-formed discipline '[...] it might be said', following Bottomore and Nisbet, 'on one side, that no sociological theory ever properly dies but becomes "comatose", and is always capable of subsequent revival; and, on the other side, that there are no real "scientific revolutions" in which a reigning paradigm is unmistakably deposed and another becomes sovereign.'[31] A history of sociology is needed by sociologists to protect them against the parochialism of the various 'paradigms' and against the pride which successive apparent 'scientific revolutions' develop in them. Recalling to them the peculiarities of the evolution of sociology can be a very useful lesson for them. The history of sociology also provides empirical data for reflection on the philosophy and sociology of the social sciences in general.

When we consider the educational advantages of the history of sociology we have to point to one more essential question. Now every historian of ideas (and a historian of sociology is primarily, though not only, concerned with ideas) faces the dilemma of whether to treat them — to use the terms of M. Bakhtin, the eminent Russian literary historian — 'homophonically' or 'polyphonically'. From the former point of view, best embodied by Hegel's history of philosophy, the history of ideas appears to form a single stream: we have in fact always to do with one and the same philosophy, whose successive 'moments' take the form of the various philosophical systems that follow successively in time. No such system has any value of its own: they have sense only as a preparation for the one final system. From the latter point of view, the history of ideas takes the form of an unending dialogue: no system solves the puzzle of history and every one remains liable to many different continuations.

This dilemma, in a different formulation, of course, is not alien to the historians of sociology. It is linked directly to the essential question: how far a real cumulation of knowledge does take place in sociology and, possibly, what are the characteristics of that cumulation? Now two opposing tendencies can certainly be seen to prevail among the historians of sociology. Some of them tend to maintain, as does for instance William R. Catton, Jr., that '[...] the history of sociological thought includes more cumulative development than is revealed by the manner in which it is usually presented.'[32] Others, on the contrary, stress the discrepancies, conflicts, rivalry, dialogue, or 'polyphony', and show, as a result of this, a tower of Babel rather than a community of scholars who arrive at common results. Moreover, emphasis is laid not so much upon a dialogue as upon the coexistence of 'schools' and standpoints.

The problem of cumulation of results of research obtained by different sociological orientations is too intricate to be discussed in this paper. Suffice it to say that in practice every historian of sociology assumes some progress of social knowledge to take place: he does so by first drawing a demarcation line between 'social thought', on the one hand, and 'sociology' or 'sociological analysis',[33] on the other, and then making references to 'enrichment', 'extension', 'adding precision', 'peak achievements', etc. True, the criteria of such a progress are rarely formulated with adequate precision. There is also more than a silent agreement about the fact that the cumulation of social knowledge is governed by regularities different from those which govern the cumulation of results in natural science. These matters, however, require a separate discussion with the participation of others besides historians.

On the other hand, it is worthwhile mentioning that from the point of view of a historian of sociology the sphere of unity which he discovers within that discipline need not consist merely of a verified knowledge whose validity is universally accepted. It may be that from the point of view of the formation of a uniform sociological tradition the more important issue was that of the emergence of a set of questions typical of sociology, not always fully verbalized, but serving as the centres of crystallization of sociological reflection represented by various groups and theoretical trends. Such a view of sociology has been suggested by Robert A. Nisbet in his most inspiring book, *The Sociological Tradition* (1966) in which he availed himself of Lovejoy's conception of 'unit-ideas'. His book is an attempt at discovering 'the unit-ideas of sociology' (community, authority, status, the sacred, alienation) which determined the inner unity of that discipline from the early 19th century until the times of Durkheim, Max Weber, Simmel, and Tönnies. I do not claim that Nisbet's idea has been carried out in a way which does not provoke reservations, but I merely point to the possibility of looking for a foundation of the unity of sociology other than the agreement of assumptions and statements.

In short, for all the difficulties on the path towards a synthesis, the search for it is being continued. This synthesis is the utopia of the history of sociology just as in the case of any other historiography.

NOTES

1. Joseph A. Schumpeter, *History of Economic Analysis*. London: Allen and Unwin, 1954, p. 4.
2. Randall Collins, 'Reassessments of Sociological History: The Empirical Validity of the Conflict Tradition', *Theory and Society*, 1 (1974), p. 147.
3. I wrote about that in the Introduction to my *History of Sociological Thought*. Westport, Conn.: Greenwood, 1979, pp. xiii-xv.
4. Cf. Ronald Fletcher, *The Making of Sociology*. London: Nelson, 1972, Vol. I, p. vii.
5. Edward Shils, 'Tradition, Ecology, and Institution in the History of Sociology', *Daedalus*, Fall 1970, p. 760.

6. Nicholas S. Timasheff, *Sociological Theory. Its Nature and Growth*, 3rd edn. New York: Random House, 1967, p. 11.
7. Cf. note 4.
8. Pitirim A. Sorokin, *Contemporary Sociological Theories through the First Quarter of the Twentieth Century*. New York: Harper and Row, 1928, p. xvi.
9. Talcott Parsons, *The Structure of Social Action*. New York: Free Press, 1968, Vol. I, p. ix.
10. Sorokin's book mentioned above is of a similar kind; the same applies to such books as Werner Stark, *The Fundamental Forms of Social Thought*. London: RKP, 1962; Gabor Kiss, *Einführung in die soziologischen Theorien*. Opladen: Westdeutscher Verlag, 1977; George Ritzer, *Sociology. A Multiple Paradigm Science*. Boston: Allyn and Bacon, 1975; and many others.
11. Anthony Giddens, *Capitalism and Modern Social Theory*. Cambridge: University Press, 1971, p. vii.
12. Hermann Strasser, *The Normative Structure of Sociology*. London: RKP, 1976, p. vii.
13. Alvin W. Gouldner, *The Coming Crisis of Western Sociology*. New York: Avon, 1972, Ch. 4.
14. For instance, the excellent book by Gianfranco Poggi, *Images of Society. Essays on the Sociological Theories of Tocqueville, Marx and Durkheim*. Stanford: Stanford University Press, 1972, is programmatically non-historical in character.
15. Of course, the work of a historian does not preclude actualization, but it is then, as a rule, an actualization of a quite different kind, and consists rather in discovering similarities of situations, problems, and dilemmas.
16. Robert K. Merton, *On Theoretical Sociology*. New York: Free Press, 1967, p. 2.
17. Lewis A. Coser, *Masters of Sociological Thought. Ideas in Historical and Social Context*, 2nd edn. New York: Harcourt Brace Jovanovich, 1977, p. xiii.
18. Ibid., p. xiv.
19. Steven Lukes, *Émile Durkheim. His Life and Work*. Harmondsworth: Penguin Books, 1975, p. 1.
20. A fairly comprehensive bibliography of studies in the history of sociology, including the latest works, can be found in Szacki, op. cit., pp. 531-68. Much current information on contributions by historians of sociology is offered by the *Newsletter* of the ISA Research Committee on the History of Sociology, which has been appearing for five years.
21. Cf. Graham C. Kinloch, *Sociological Theory. Its Development and Major Paradigms*. New York: McGraw-Hill, 1977.
22. A similar tendency is found in a growing number of historians of science. Cf. Thomas S. Kuhn, *The Structure of Scientific Revolutions*, 2nd edn. Chicago: University of Chicago Press, 1970, p. 3.
23. Cf. Coser, op. cit., p. xiv.
24. W. G. Runciman, *Sociology in Its Place and Other Essays*. Cambridge: University Press, 1970, pp. 1-44.
25. Christopher Dawson, *The Dynamics of World History*. New York: Mentor Omega, 1962, p. 268.
26. Raymond Aron, *Les étapes de la pensée sociologique*. Paris: Gallimard, 1967, p. 16.
27. It has originated from Paul F. Lazarsfeld's 'Notes on the History of Quantification in Sociology — Trends, Sources and Problems', *Isis*, 52, 2 (1961),

pp. 277-333. Cf. Anthony Oberschall (ed.), *The Establishment of Empirical Sociology*. New York: Harper and Row, 1972.

28. Cf. Edward A. Tiryakian (ed.), *The Phenomenon of Sociology*. New York: Appleton, 1971.

29. Parsons, op. cit., p. vi.

30. Cf. Irving M. Zeitlin, *Ideology and the Development of Sociological Theory*. Englewood Cliffs, NJ: Prentice-Hall, 1968.

31. Tom Bottomore and Robert Nisbet (eds), *A History of Sociological Analysis*. London: Heinemann, 1979, p. 9. Cf. Shils, op. cit., pp. 815ff.

32. William R. Catton, Jr., 'The Development of Sociological Thought', in Robert E. L. Faris (ed.), *Handbook of Modern Sociology*. Chicago: Rand-McNally, 1964, p. 912.

33. Cf. Bottomore and Nisbet, op. cit.

Notes on Contributors

Margaret Archer is Professor of Sociology at the University of Warwick. Her first research on the development of national educational systems, carried out with Michalina Vaughan, appeared as *Social Conflict and Educational Change in England and France: 1789-1848* (Cambridge 1971). This was followed by an edited symposium entitled *Students, University and Society* (London 1972), and in 1979 by a major historical and structural comparison of educational systems in England, France, Denmark and Russia, *Social Origins of Educational Systems* (London and Beverly Hills, Sage Publications).

Tom Bottomore is Professor of Sociology at the University of Sussex, and was President of the International Sociological Association from 1974 to 1978. His publications include *Sociology* (Allen and Unwin 1971), *Sociology as Social Criticism* (Allen and Unwin 1975), *Marxist Sociology* (Macmillan 1975) *Political Sociology* (Hutchinson 1979) and *Modern Interpretations of Marx* (Basil Blackwell 1981).

Richard K. Fenn lectures in Sociology at the University of Maine. He is the author of *Toward a Theory of Secularization* (SSSR 1978) and *Liturgies and Trials* (Blackwell, forthcoming), and has contributed articles to the *Journal for the Scientific Study of Religion* and elsewhere.

Gwyn Harries-Jenkins is Deputy Director and Head of Extension Studies in the Department of Adult Education at the University of Hull. A former Regular Officer, he is Associate Chairman of the Inter University Seminar on Armed Forces and Society, and a past President of the Research Committee on Armed Forces and Society of the International Sociological Association. His previous publications include *The Army in Victorian Society*.

Ulf Himmelstrand is Professor of Sociology at the University of Uppsala, Sweden. He is President of the International Sociological Association (1978 to 1982) and former Professor of Sociology at the University of Ibadan, Nigeria. He has published widely in the fields of political sociology, mass communication and development studies, his most recent work being *Spontaneity and Planning* (Sage Publications 1981).

Hans-Joachim Hoffmann-Nowotny is Professor of Sociology and Director of the Sociological Institute of the University of Zurich. He is President of the Research Committee on Migration of the International Sociological Association. His publications include *Migration* (1970) and *Soziologie des Fremdarbeiterproblems; eine theoretische und empirische Analyse am Beispiel der Schweiz* (1973).

Daniel Kubat is Professor of Sociology at the University of Waterloo, Canada, having previously taught at a number of universities, including the Universities of Pittsburgh and Florida. He has edited several books on migration, including *The Politics of Migration Studies* (1979).

Jolanta Kulpinska works at the University of Lodz, Poland.

Harry Makler is Associate Professor of Sociology at the University of Toronto. His special interests are the sociology of development and of financial institutions, and the impact of the class structure in Latin American and Latin European nations. He has published books and articles on Portugal and Brazil, the most recent being *Contemporary Portugal: Antecedents to the Revolution* (1979).

Marc Maurice is Maître de Recherche at the Centre National de la Recherche Scientifique (CNRS). He is Secretary of the Research Committee on Sociology of Work of the International Sociological Association.

Stefan Nowak is Professor of the Methodology of the Social Sciences at the University of Warsaw and Visiting Professor at Columbia University, New York. He is also President of the Polish Sociological Association. His major publication in English is *Understanding Prediction: Essays in the Methodology of the Social and Behavioral Sciences* (1976).

Anna Olszewska is Director of the Research Programme on Leisure at the Institute of Philosophy and Sociology, Polish Academy of

Sciences. She is President of the Research Committee on the Sociology of Leisure of the International Sociological Association. Her publications include *The Family* (1964), *An Industrialized Village* (1969) and 'Leisure in Poland' in *Leisure: Emergence and Expansion* (1979). In press is a book on the sociology of leisure and on leisure in transition in Poland.

Gilles Pronovost is Chairman of the Department des Sciences du Loisir at L'Université du Québec à Trois-Rivières, Canada. He is also Executive Secretary of the Research Committee on Leisure of the International Sociological Association and Editor of *Loisir et Société/Society and Leisure*. Forthcoming publications include a study of popular culture and another on the historical aspects of leisure and leisure sciences in France, the USA and Canada.

John Rex is Director of the Research Unit on Ethnic Relations and Visiting Professor at the University of Aston, Birmingham. His publications include *Race Relations and Sociological Theory* (1970), *Race, Colonialism and the City* (1973) and *Apartheid and Social Research* (forthcoming).

Arnaud Sales is Professeur Agregé at the Université de Montreal. His publications include *La bourgeoisie industrielle au Québec* (1979) and he has also edited 'Développement national et économie mondiale', a thematic issue of *Sociologie et Société* (Vol. 11, No. 2, 1979).

David Schweitzer is Associate Professor of Sociology at the University of British Columbia, Vancouver, and has held visiting appointments at the University of California, Irvine and the Science University of Malaysia. He has also served as a consultant to the Canadian International Development Agency and the Colombo Plan in Southeast Asia. Editor of *Alienation Theory and Research*, his books on the topic include *Theories of Alienation: Critical Perspectives in Philosophy and the Social Sciences* (1976) and *Alienation: Problems of Meaning, Theory and Method* (1981).

Neil J. Smelser is University Professor of Sociology, University of California; he has served as a member of the Sociology Faculty of the University of California, Berkeley, since 1958. He is also co-Chairman of the Research Committee on Economy and Society of the International Sociological Association. His publications include *Economy and Society* (with Talcott Parsons), *Social Change in the Industrial Revolution* and *The Sociology of Economic Life*.

Magdalena Sokolowska is Professor and Head of the Department of Medical Sociology at the Polish Academy of Sciences. She is also Vice-President of the International Sociological Association and an expert with the World Health Organization. Her publications include *Sociology and Health* (1976), *Disabled People and the Rehabilitation System in Poland* (1978) and *Borderlines of Medicine* (1980).

Jerzy Szacki is Professor of Sociology at the University of Warsaw, and is a former President of the Polish Sociological Association. He is Editor of the *Polish Sociological Bulletin* and his publications include *Durkheim* (1964), *Utopias* (1968), *Tradition. A Survey of Problems* (1971) and *History of Sociological Thought* (1979).

Andrew C. Twaddle is Professor of Sociology and of Family and Community Medicine at the University of Missouri. His publications include *A Sociology of Health* (with R. Hessler, 1977) and *Sickness Behavior and the Sick Role* (1979).

John Walton is Professor at the University of California, Davis, and Vice-President of the Research Committee on the Sociology of Urban and Regional Development of the International Sociological Association. His publications include *Elites and Economic Development* (1977) and *Labor, Class and the International System* (with Alejandro Portes, 1981).